FRAMEWORKS

An Introduction to Film Studies

FRAMEWORKS
An Introduction to Film Studies

Thomas E. Valasek
Raritan Valley Community College

 Wm. C. Brown Publishers

Book Team

Editor *Stan Stoga*
Developmental Editor *Jane Lambert*
Designer *Mark Elliot Christianson*
Production Editor *Kennie Harris*
Art Editor *Carla Heathcote*
Photo Editor *Carrie Burger*
Visuals Processor *Ken Ley*

WCB

Wm. C. Brown Publishers

President *G. Franklin Lewis*
Vice President, Publisher *Thomas E. Doran*
Vice President, Operations and Production *Beverly Kolz*
National Sales Manager *Virginia S. Moffat*
Group Sales Manager *John Finn*
Executive Editor *Edgar J. Laube*
Director of Marketing *Kathy Law Laube*
Marketing Manager *Kathleen Nietzke*
Managing Editor, Production *Colleen A. Yonda*
Manager of Visuals and Design *Faye M. Schilling*
Production Editorial Manager *Julie A. Kennedy*
Production Editorial Manager *Ann Fuerste*
Publishing Services Manager *Karen J. Slaght*

WCB Group

President and Chief Executive Officer *Mark C. Falb*
Chairman of the Board *Wm. C. Brown*

Cover photos: (Background) © Emilio Lari/Sygma. (Insets, left to right) *Citizen Kane*
© 1941 RKO Radio Pictures Corporation. Courtesy of National Film Archives/Stills Library;
High Noon © 1951, United Artists Corporation. Courtesy of The Museum of Modern Art/
Film Stills Archive.

Printed in the United States of America by Wm. C. Brown Publishers,
2460 Kerper Boulevard, Dubuque, IA 52001

10   9   8   7   6   5   4   3   2   1

This book is for Zuzana.

Contents

U N I T 2

How Do Films Reveal Characters? 144

U N I T 3

How Do Films Depict Physical Reality? 236

10

The Realistic Tradition 263

11

The Expressionistic Tradition 295

U N I T 4

How Do Films Inform, Persuade, and Indoctrinate? 320

12

Film As Reportage 323

Preface

Very few of the students who enroll in the introductory film course I teach are film majors. Most of them simply enjoy movies and take the course because they want to get more out of them. *Frameworks: An Introduction to Film Studies* is a textbook for beginning film students who fit this description. Its purpose is to help such students appreciate and understand films better and to equip them to learn more about films on their own.

Most film textbooks package information about films in more or less accessible ways. But *Frameworks* sets out to *teach* both the concepts and the skills beginning students need to become more literate film viewers. The textbook draws on lessons that have been especially successful in my film classes over the years. I have adapted them in *Frameworks* to address four fundamental questions about cinema: How do films tell a story? How do films reveal characters? How do films depict physical reality? How do films inform, persuade, and indoctrinate? Each of these questions offers a different "framework" for film study, a different way to look at and analyze films.

Since many introductory film students never take another cinema course, one of my principal concerns as a film teacher is to encourage students to explore and understand films for themselves. Lessons in *Frameworks* are "interactive." Questions in the body of the text invite students to think about and respond to problems the lessons pose. Some lessons ask students to note their reactions to a film image, to compare and contrast two stills, to analyze a sequence of shots. Chapter 4 includes a simulation exercise where students decide how to edit a movie scenario. The lessons in *Frameworks* use an inductive approach that proceeds from observation to inference, from specific examples to general principles, from film practice to film theory. The lesson on close-ups in chapter 6, for example, compares and contrasts two stills from Carl Dreyer's THE PASSION OF JOAN OF ARC, then uses them to explain Jean Mitry's statement that a close-up is an *"analog* for a pure state of mind."

My approach to teaching film studies is grounded on the belief that students will understand and appreciate cinema more if they write about their film experiences. An important feature of *Frameworks*, therefore, is an extensive appendix, Writing about Films, which explains and illustrates how to take notes on films, keep a film journal, organize a shot-by-shot analysis, and write a reaction paper, an expository paper, or a research paper about a film. General Study Questions at the end of each chapter suggest writing topics that reinforce the chapter's lessons. Moreover, the lessons themselves are models of different ways to analyze and write about films. Chapter 4, for instance, includes a model shot analysis of an action sequence in RAIDERS OF THE LOST ARK; part of chapter 7 compares and contrasts independent women in KLUTE and LADY BEWARE from a feminist perspective; chapter 14 analyzes three classic propaganda films (POTEMKIN, TRIUMPH OF THE WILL, and PRELUDE TO WAR) from a historical perspective.

Frameworks: An Introduction to Film Studies works with all kinds of films: classic and current, "serious" and "popular," foreign and American, commercial and independent. My intention is to expose students to a broad range of films and to encourage them to become more tolerant and adventuresome viewers. *Frameworks* treats a few films in each chapter extensively enough so that students do not necessarily need to see the films to understand the lessons there. The illustrations in the book are integrally tied into the text; so students *use* stills, frame enlargements, or line drawings from films as they work through the lessons. At the same time, I have tried to make each lesson in *Frameworks* "generic," that is, applicable to many other films. Thus, for example, what students learn about editing techniques from the shot analysis of a chase scene in RAIDERS OF THE LOST ARK will apply to any well-made action sequence.

Frameworks is meant to be "user friendly." I have tried to write clearly and directly, to avoid academic jargon, and to explain film terminology and concepts straightforwardly. At the back of the book is an extensive Glossary of Film Terms; these terms are identified in **boldface** in the chapters. At the end of each chapter are suggestions for Further Reading and a list of Additional Films for Study. Students looking for resources to bolster a class project or simply to broaden their knowledge of film should find these lists helpful. Finally, the sample student papers in the appendix, and the comments about them, should be useful for students who want to improve their writing.

Acknowledgments

I am indebted to many people who in some way helped me complete this book. I want to thank Mary Corliss at the Museum of Modern Art, Nadia Shtendera at Anthology Film Archives, and Blanka Jestřábová at *Krathý film propagace* in Prague for their help with film stills; Stewart McDugall at the University of Michigan for the loan of film stills; Jarda Andel and Anthony Giampaolo for still photography; Gina Iachio for photo modeling; Felice McGlincy at "Permissions" for advice about permissions; Deborah Fine at Lucasfilm, Ltd., for help with the Indiana Jones storyboards; Stan Stoga at Wm. C. Brown Publishers for his support and encouragement; and Barbara Moore for word processing.

For advice and criticism on the manuscript I am grateful to the following reviewers: Richard Bayley, Andrews University; Anthony P.J. Cerniglia, Lincoln Land Community College; Gary L. Green, Youngstown State University; Mary Hyatt, Spokane Falls Community College; Douglas Pearson, University of Wisconsin-Eau Claire; David Popowski, Mankato State University; Gary Schmidt, Calvin College; Donald Staples, University of North Texas; and Gerry Veeder, University of North Texas.

I especially want to thank my students at Raritan Valley Community College and my colleagues Mark Bezanson, Angela Bodino, Mark Cozin, Brock Haussamen, Ed Minus, Kevin Reilly, Ken Ross, and Barbara Seater. Most of all I want to thank my wife, Zuzana, and our daughters, Katya and Sasha, for all their patience and support during the hundreds of hours I was "holed up in my cave" to write this book.

THOMAS E. VALASEK

To the Student

Why do we cry when E. T. dies? Why do we cheer when the cavalry charges across desert flats to rescue a besieged stagecoach? Why does our skin crawl when the monstrous white shark is about to strike? *Frameworks: An Introduction to Film Studies* is interested in questions like these because it is primarily concerned with discovering *why* we respond to films the way we do, and *what* filmmakers do to elicit these specific responses.

Frameworks is organized around four basic questions about films: How do films tell a story? How do films reveal characters? How do films depict physical reality? How do films inform, persuade, and indoctrinate? Each of these questions offers a different "framework" for film study, a different way to look at and analyze films.

How Do Films Tell a Story?

The first framework addresses the aspect of a film that usually attracts our interest first—the story. The five chapters in the first unit deal with film narrative. They explore how *mise en scène*, camera, lighting, editing, and sound contribute to cinematic storytelling, and they examine specific narrative techniques in films like HIGH NOON, RAIDERS OF THE LOST ARK, and CITIZEN KANE. The underlying premise in these chapters is that knowing how filmmakers tell a film story helps us understand it better and appreciate it more. The first five chapters also introduce terminology used to describe basic cinematic techniques, and demonstrate how to use it in analyzing movies.

How Do Films Reveal Characters?

The second framework is primarily concerned with the psychological impact films have on us and their power, via characters in the story, to foster deeper awareness of human experience. Chapter 6 examines how film acting and certain cinematic devices (close-ups, point-of-view shots, flashbacks, memory and dream sequences) allow filmmakers to delve into the human psyche and reveal a film character's inner being. Chapter 7 explores how archetypal and stereotypical characters in films like SHANE, RAMBO, and ALIENS influence our perceptions of heroes, villains, and gender models in our culture. It examines, for example, how popular movies sometimes perpetuate racial and sexual stereotypes. Chapter 8 looks at how films depict human interaction—in romantic relationships, power relationships, and family relationships—and how these depictions reflect our perceptions of relationships in real life.

How Do Films Depict Physical Reality?

The third framework delineates two distinct cinematic traditions: the realistic tradition, which tends to record physical reality much as it actually appears, and the expressionistic tradition, which tends to distort physical reality in some way in order to "express" strong feelings about it. Chapter 9 explores the beginnings of these traditions in film history and contrasts two futuristic films, Fritz Lang's METROPOLIS and George Lucas's THX: 1138, in order to distinguish cinematic realism and expressionism. Chapters 10 and 11 trace the development of the realistic and expressionistic traditions by examining some landmark films that represent them.

How Do Films Inform, Persuade, and Indoctrinate?

The last framework deals mainly with non-fiction films—films that inform or instruct rather than narrate invented stories. Chapter 12 raises questions about objectivity and subjectivity in film reporting and distinguishes between journalistic and poetic reportage. Chapters 13 and 14 deal with subtle distinctions between film as education and film as propaganda. Chapter 14 analyzes three classic propaganda films (Sergei Eisenstein's THE BATTLESHIP POTEMKIN, Leni Riefenstahl's TRIUMPH OF THE WILL, and Frank Capra's PRELUDE TO WAR) in order to demonstrate how filmmakers employ cinematic techniques to indoctrinate audiences.

Frameworks is grounded on two basic beliefs the author holds about film studies; you should know about them from the outset. The first is that it is important for film students to learn to question and explore films systematically on their own. Lessons in *Frameworks* are designed to help you develop and achieve this independence. Questions in the text invite you to respond to problems and issues the lessons raise: for example, to note your reactions to a film image, to compare and contrast two film stills, to analyze a sequences of shots. Chapter 4 includes a simulation exercise that asks how you would edit a hypothetical movie scenario. These questions are not rhetorical! If you take a few moments to think about them or to jot down your observations and reactions before reading on, you will be practicing the kinds of skills needed to become a more literate film viewer.

The second belief is that students will learn more about films by writing about their film experiences. To encourage you to write about films, *Frameworks* includes an extensive appendix that explains and illustrates how to take notes on films, keep a film journal, organize a shot-by-shot analysis, and write a reaction paper, an expository paper, or a research paper about a film. The sample student papers in this appendix, and the comments about them, offer helpful guidelines for writing about films. General Study Questions at the end of each chapter suggest topics to write about, and lessons in the chapters are themselves models of different ways to write about films. Chapter 2, for instance, includes a model shot-by-shot analysis of a sequence from HIGH NOON; part of chapter 7 compares and contrasts archetypal heroes in popular action-adventure movies like RAMBO and ALIENS; part of chapter 8 argues that romantic relationships in IT HAPPENED ONE NIGHT and FATAL ATTRACTION are reflections of cultural values.

There are also some features in *Frameworks* that you should note at the outset. At the back of the book is A Glossary of Film Terms in which technical terminology about filmmaking and film criticism is explained. These terms appear in **boldface** the first time they are introduced in a chapter.

At the end of each chapter are suggestions for further reading and a list of Additional Films for Study, which complement the lessons in the chapter. You may want to use these lists to find good material for a class project or simply to broaden your knowledge of films. The next time you can't decide what video to rent, consider one of the films listed at the end of the chapter you just read. Part of *Frameworks'* hidden agenda is to encourage you to become a more tolerant, adventure-some film viewer.

FRAMEWORKS

An Introduction to Film Studies

How Do Films Tell a Story?

What appeals to most viewers first about a film is the story. If a movie has an interesting story and tells it well, most of us are hooked immediately; if the story is flat or confusing, we may fall asleep or walk out. Film narrative, therefore, is the first aspect of cinema that *Frameworks: An Introduction to Film Studies* will address.

"How do films tell a story?" is one of the most basic questions about cinema. Attentive viewers quickly observe that a good movie story is not haphazardly presented but meticulously controlled from beginning to end. Filmmakers select and arrange images in individual shots and assemble them in an orderly way to piece together the story for the audience. Film students, therefore, learn to scrutinize individual shots and how they are edited together in order to glean as much information as possible about the story.

The exploration of film narrative in *Frameworks* begins with the most immediate things we experience in a movie: setting, costumes and makeup, and objects that figure prominently in the story. These physical elements of a movie often provide the first clues about its characters and story. The next two chapters deal with cinematography. Chapter 2 concentrates on camera positions, angles, and movements, and examines the crucial role the camera plays in film narrative. Chapter 3 examines cinematic lighting techniques, lighting effects, and visual tone.

Besides cinematography, the other essential tool of cinematic storytelling is editing, the process of connecting individual shots into scenes and sequences that make up a narrative movie. Chapter 4 examines editing techniques for maintaining continuity and providing transitions in a film story; it also looks at dynamic editing techniques that can excite the viewer's emotions.

Finally, chapter 5 explores how sound complements images in movies and how music, spoken language, and sound effects contribute to film narrative.

BEAUTY AND THE BEAST (1946), dir. Jean Cocteau.

In French *mise en scène* (pronounced *me zon sen´*) literally means "placing in scene." Originally a theatrical term, it referred to the staging of actors, scenery, and props for a theater production. After the coming of movies, *mise en scène* carried over from stage to cinema, where it refers generally to the arrangement of everything physical in a camera shot. Later chapters in *Frameworks* will deal with the arrangement of actors within the frame. This chapter will examine how filmmakers employ setting, costumes and makeup, and objects to help narrate film stories.

Setting

What are the first clues we pick up about a movie's story? Early in a film, frequently even before the opening credits are finished, most filmmakers establish a particular time and place in which the action unfolds. Some directors spell out the setting for the audience: Alfred Hitchcock in PSYCHO (1960) inserts screen titles just after the credits to indicate that the story begins in "Phoenix, Arizona" on "Friday, December the Eleventh"; George Lucas sets STAR WARS (1977) "Long ago in a galaxy far, far away. . . ."

But even if they do not indicate the time and place of the action with titles, filmmakers usually provide enough visual information at the beginning of a film so that the audience will recognize the setting. RAGTIME (1981), for example, directed by Miloš Forman, opens in a New York City movie house around the turn of the twentieth century where a piano man is providing music for a silent movie. His clothing and hairstyle, the ragtime music he plays, and the **grainy** black-and-white **newsreel** on the screen behind him all help set the scene. Forman reinforces the setting by identifying prominent contemporary figures like Harry Houdini and Stanford White in the newsreel. One screen title reads: "President Roosevelt Eats with Booker T. Washington: First Negro in White House."

Sometimes, however, the beginning of a film seems to disorient the viewer's sense of time and place. Sidney Lumet's FAIL-SAFE (1964), for instance, opens with a screen title, "New York City, 5:30 a.m." But on the screen we see a harshly lit bullring in which a pale-looking man in the bleachers watches a charging black bull. The man's face is lit in sharp contrast, one side overexposed and the other side completely in shadows; and he appears more and more terrified as the matador finishes the bull. At the end of the sequence, Lumet juxtaposes **extreme close-ups** of the dying bull and the man in the crowd.

To this point, about one minute into the film, there seems no logical connection between the bullfight and "New York City, 5:30 a.m."; but the bizarre images and lighting suggest this is a dream, an impression that is confirmed when Lumet cuts abruptly to the man in bed, startled awake from the nightmare. Then the film's title flashes on the screen, and a more recognizable 5:30 a.m. setting unfolds in the man's bedroom.

Filmmakers sometimes introduce several settings in quick succession to establish different spheres of action for a story. At the beginning of FAIL-SAFE, for example, the scene quickly shifts to three more locations besides New York City:

> "Wash., D.C., 5:30 a.m." At an elegant party a cynical political scientist holds everyone's attention with speculations about thermonuclear war.
> "Omaha, Neb., 5:30 a.m." A colonel at the control center of the Strategic Air Command is humiliated in front of his superior officer because of his alcoholic parents.
> "Anchorage, Alaska, 5:30 a.m." Jet bomber pilots shoot pool and talk shop before they go out to fly planes that carry hydrogen bombs.

The time notation in the titles makes it clear that events in these four locations are happening simultaneously and that they are somehow interconnected.

The setting of a movie scene often reveals important information about a character's personality or disposition, as for example, eerie stuffed birds mounted around a room suggest a schizophrenic's bizarre penchants in PSYCHO (1960). Setting can sometimes disclose as much about a character as action and **dialogue** can. For instance, in A MARRIED WOMAN (1964), directed by Jean-Luc Godard, the protagonist is a woman stuck between traditional and modern values. She is married but having an affair; she is pregnant but uncertain whether her husband or her lover is the father. She is an enigmatic character, caught up in her own thoughts and preoccupied with images of women in advertisements and popular magazines. She seems obsessed with lingerie and with "how to have a fashionable bust." Godard and his **cinematographer,** Raoul Coutard, photograph this character against backgrounds that highlight her preoccupations: a billboard featuring a "Triumph" bra or a placard asking, "How far can a woman go in love?" Like Berthold Brecht, who frequently introduces signs and placards into his stage productions, Godard overlays visual information about this character by surrounding her with signs, ads, and posters that reflect her motivation and concerns.

Figure 1.1
Examples of (*a*) an urban
landscape in MIDNIGHT
COWBOY and (*b*) a
small-town landscape in
THE LAST PICTURE
SHOW.

a

How Do Films Tell a Story?

b

Setting also figures significantly in narrative film when it provides a "landscape," or backdrop, for what happens in the story. Consider, for example, the difference between the urban landscape in MIDNIGHT COWBOY (1969) and the small-town landscape in THE LAST PICTURE SHOW (1971). Look closely at the two **stills** from these films in figure 1.1. What do you observe about the setting of each scene? What does the background suggest to you about the mood and atmosphere of each film? About the characters in the frame? About situations each film would be likely to develop?

The still from MIDNIGHT COWBOY suggests how claustrophobic surroundings and physical decay in city slums can spawn seedy characters and situations that are endemic to big cities like New York. The atmosphere looks cold and bleak; the characters appear isolated, alienated, and destitute. The still from THE LAST PICTURE SHOW, on

Figure 1.2
Sand provides both the setting and the central metaphor for WOMAN IN THE DUNES.

the other hand, suggests how space, light, and milieu in a small Texas oil town can foster characters and situations that appear more open, personable, and interactive. The atmosphere here looks warmer and less restraining than in the other film. Like fresh water and salt water for fish, movie landscapes often provide specialized environments that support some species but not others. Sometimes these environments even seem to *determine* the actions of the species who inhabit them.

Occasionally, the setting of a film completely overpowers the characters in the story. In Hiroshi Teshigahara's WOMAN IN THE DUNES (1964), for example, sand not only provides the physical landscape for a woman and a man forced to live in a sand pit but also becomes their reason for living (fig. 1.2). They must clear sand away from their house or be swallowed up by it; they must shovel sand for the villagers who keep them captive or go without food and water. The man wonders whether they are, in fact, "clearing sand to live or living to clear sand." It sifts its way into every part of their lives, clings to their skin and hair, coats them when they sleep or make love. In short, the sand in WOMAN IN THE DUNES serves not only as a setting for the film but as a visual **metaphor** as well.

Costumes and Makeup

As an example of how costumes and makeup help the audience understand a film story, consider the opening scene of STAR WARS (1977), directed by George Lucas. A small spaceship is being chased and fired upon by a much larger one. Suddenly the screen is teeming with characters engaged in a space-age gun battle. The action is furious, and the dialogue is sparse. Yet the audience immediately understands what is going on and knows which side to cheer for. How?

The first images of the star ships suggest the discrepancy between the two forces. When the scene cuts to an interior shot of a group of soldiers taking up defensive positions, we know they are the force under attack in the smaller ship. But how do we know whether they are "good guys" or "bad guys"? We notice that they wear light gray uniforms with loose black vests and helmets like those worn by modern-day firefighters and that they carry small handguns. In close-ups their faces are composed and determined as they brace for the boarding assault. On the other hand, when the attackers blast their way into the scene (fig. 1.3), we notice that they wear white body armor and helmets which cover their faces and that they wield heavy combat weapons. Nothing in their appearance distinguishes them individually, and we are unable to see any expression on their faces. In fact, they resemble robots more than humans. Is there any doubt about which side we will root for?

Lucas contrasts the two forces at the beginning of STAR WARS, in the simplest terms, as "good defenders" protecting themselves against "bad invaders." He plays on the audience's sympathy for the underdog by showing the defenders bravely fighting back against a much larger and better-armed invading force. Since children learn early that it is acceptable, even honorable, to fight back against a bully, Lucas manages to implant in even the youngest viewers a certainty about which side is in the right.

The robotlike storm troopers are unmistakably villainous. They all look exactly alike, with no individualized characteristics. And, most of all, we cannot see their faces. With the costumes for this scene, George Lucas has imitated the distinguished Soviet director Sergei Eisenstein, who employed helmets similarly in ALEXANDER NEVSKY

Figure 1.3

The costume of an imperial storm trooper in STAR WARS. With his face masked he looks more like a robot than a human being.

(1938) to depict Russian soldiers defending their homeland against a horde of German invaders (fig. 1.4). Eisenstein explained that among the shots of the two armies before the battle were several which juxtaposed "open, living emotional Russian faces" and "German faces hidden by the visors of iron masks" (208). Eisenstein understood the power of the human face to communicate emotional meaning immediately and nonverbally in **close-ups.** As film theorist Béla Balázs observes, "Facial expression is the most subjective manifestation of man, more subjective even than speech . . ." and is "complete and comprehensible in itself" (257). (See chapter 6 for a fuller discussion of close-ups.) To mask a character's facial expression, therefore, is to diminish his individuality and humanity. Thus, with helmets that cover the villains' faces, Eisenstein and Lucas not only distinguish them from the heroes but also suggest that they are less than human.

To reinforce our identification of the two groups of fighters at the beginning of STAR WARS, Lucas introduces two characters who epitomize evil and good in the film: Darth Vadar, archvillain of the Galactic Empire, and Princess Leia, leader of the spunky rebels. Vadar is a mountainous figure robed entirely in black. (See figure 7.2 in chapter 7.) His helmet does not simply cover his face in battle; it is a mechanical aspirator that apparently enables him to breathe. Princess Leia, on the other hand, wears a modest white dress with a cowl draped loosely over her head but leaving her face uncovered. Lucas uses black and white

a   b

Figure 1.4
Two stills from
ALEXANDER NEVSKY
illustrating how helmets
are used to contrast
(*a*) Russians and
(*b*) Germans in the film.

costumes, one of the oldest costume codes in movies and theater, to present Darth Vadar and Princess Leia as instantly recognizable representations of evil and good. (See chapter 7 for more about archetypes and stereotypes in movies.)

Costumes help the audience identify and remember characters. In STAR WARS, for instance, uniforms and helmets make it easy to distinguish the two opposing forces. This simple function of costumes should not be underestimated in scenes with many characters and lots of action—which is one reason uniforms are traditionally important in sports and in war. Sometimes even costumes that are not uniforms are used to differentiate groups of characters in movies. In Franco Zeffirelli's ROMEO AND JULIET (1968), for example, as in the modern-day version of Shakespeare's play, Wise and Robbins's WEST SIDE STORY (1961), costumes are color-coded to distinguish the feuding factions. The Capulets and the Sharks wear bright, hot colors; the Montagues and the Jets wear deeper, cooler colors.

Costumes and makeup can also indicate important character transformations in a film. Study the twelve **frame enlargements** (fig. 1.5) from the Breakfast Table Montage in CITIZEN KANE (1941) and note how Orson Welles combines costume, makeup, and set changes to depict in a few minutes how Kane's marriage to Emily Norton disintegrates over several years. Jot down your observations before reading further.

#1

#2

#3

#4

#5

#6

Figure 1.5
Twelve frame enlargements from the Breakfast Table Montage in
CITIZEN KANE, which illustrate how costumes and makeup help
depict a deteriorating marriage.

#7

#8

#9

#10

#11

#12

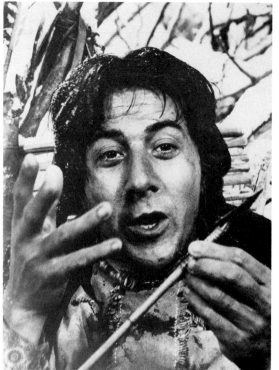

a **b**

Figure 1.6
Four stills from LITTLE BIG MAN showing how costumes and makeup help depict different phases of a film character's life.

In these twelve stills from CITIZEN KANE we see husband and wife alternately alone in the frame. Their changing appearances through the sequence indicate not only the passage of time but also their growing coldness towards each other. In shots #1 and #2 they are dressed for breakfast in evening clothes. After being out all night, they are still fresh and happy in each other's presence. Mr. Kane (Orson Welles) has not even loosened his tie; Mrs. Kane (Ruth Warrick) looks very sensual, with bared shoulders. They are young and in love. In the next four shots they wear more appropriate morning attire for a married couple at breakfast. But Mrs. Kane's straight-laced robe and hairstyle in shot #6 make her look less affectionate, and Mr. Kane's smile seems increasingly smug. In shot #7 Kane appears at breakfast in his business suit and glares across the table at his wife. Shots #9 and #10 show them openly hostile toward each other. In the last two shots, near the end of their marriage, they are still together at the breakfast table, but not communicating. Their relationship has apparently turned spiteful since Mrs. Kane is reading a morning newspaper that competes with the one her husband publishes.

c   d

      Arthur Penn's LITTLE BIG MAN (1970) is a film that
depends heavily on costumes to dramatize character transformations.
Jack Crabb (Dustin Hoffman), the sole survivor of Custer's last stand at
Little Big Horn, tells his own life story, which shifts back and forth
between the white world and the Indian world in the Old West. The phases
of Crabb's life are each characterized by a different costume (fig. 1.6 *a-d*).
As a boy, adopted by the Cheyenne, he wears a wolf's skin on his head
until he earns his name, Little Big Man, and the right to wear a warrior's
braids and paint. As a disillusioned young man in the white world, he
joins up with a swindler in the "snake oil business" and wears slick city
duds and a seedy pencil-thin mustache. Later, bent on proving his man-
hood, he becomes a gunfighter dressed from head to toe in black. When
Crabb's life hits bottom, he becomes the town drunk wallowing in mud,
and later a bearded hermit in the wilderness.

Costumes and makeup generally draw recognition for the glamor or authenticity they bring to films or for the fantastic illusions they help create, particularly in horror and science fiction movies. But costumes and makeup also contribute significantly to cinematic storytelling when they help filmmakers reveal characters immediately, as in STAR WARS and ALEXANDER NEVSKY, or when they dramatize character transformations graphically, as in CITIZEN KANE and LITTLE BIG MAN.

Objects

In movies, as on stage, an object that appears in a scene, other than painted scenery or costumes, is called a **property, or prop.** We have already seen one example of how a prop can enhance a scene: The rival newspaper Mrs. Kane reads at the end of the Breakfast Table Montage in CITIZEN KANE provides the finishing touch to Welles's depiction of their failing marriage. Sometimes seemingly insignificant objects can have a powerful effect in a scene. In Ingmar Bergman's FANNY AND ALEXANDER (1983), young Alexander is mercilessly caned by his stepfather, a stiff and fanatical bishop. As he orders Alexander to drop his trousers and bend over a table, the bishop's dour mother, who has been sewing in the room, holds Alexander's head down. In a close-up of her hand we notice that on her middle finger, pressing behind the boy's ear, she wears a metal thimble.

Objects can introduce bits of immediate information that help advance the story or delineate a character. Some of the most colorful examples of such objects are those used for **sight gags** in silent comedies. In Charles Chaplin's THE GOLD RUSH (1925), for instance, a starving prospector, played by Chaplin, prepares a boiled shoe as a gourmet feast for himself and his partner. He lifts the shoe from the pot and carves it on a platter at the table, deftly separating the sole from the top and serving up the shoelace as cooked spaghetti (fig. 1.7).

Objects are sometimes used in films for the associations they evoke. Consider this scene, for example, from Fritz Lang's M (1931): A young girl is playing alone in the street, bouncing and catching a ball. A murderer approaches her and buys her a balloon shaped like a small child, and they walk off together hand in hand. Then, out of a deserted clump of trees the balloon suddenly floats up and tangles in utility wires, and the ball rolls out of the bushes.

What is your reaction to this scene? Why does Lang feature the ball and the balloon? Why does he isolate these objects on the screen in the last shot?

Figure 1.7
An object used for a sight
gag in THE GOLD RUSH.

Most viewers, even those accustomed to blatant violence in today's movies, find this scene from M chilling. It is effective because the *suggestion* of violence leads the viewer to imagine the worst. Using simple toys associated with the child's innocence and vulnerability, Fritz Lang dramatizes a heinous murder without depicting the actual violence at all.

Another example of an object with great associative power is a small glass ball (fig. 1.8) that appears in the opening moments of CITIZEN KANE (1941) as Kane lies dying in his mansion. The shooting script describes the scene:

Figure 1.8
The glass ball containing a miniature winter scene in CITIZEN KANE, an object closely identified with Kane in the film.

Int. Kane's Bedroom—Faint Dawn—1940
A snow scene. An incredible one. Big impossible flakes of snow, a too picturesque farmhouse and a snowman.

KANE'S OLD OLD VOICE
Rosebud!

The camera pulls back, showing the whole scene to be contained in one of those glass balls which are sold in novelty stores all over the world. A hand—Kane's hand, which has been holding the ball—relaxes. The ball falls out of his hand and bounds down two carpeted steps leading to the bed, the camera following. The ball falls off the last step onto the marble floor, where it breaks . . . .
(Mankiewicz and Welles 95, 97)

Since the glass ball is introduced so dramatically, we expect it to be an important clue to Kane's identity. Why does a multimillionaire clutch this simple curiosity on his deathbed? What does it mean to him?

Welles makes us wait to find out more about the glass bibelot. Much later in the film, after Kane's second wife, Susan Alexander, has left him, Kane flies into a rage and wrecks her bedroom. He pulls down curtains and shelves, upsets furniture, and smashes everything in his path. But when Kane picks up the glass ball, he utters the word "Rosebud," slips the ball into his jacket pocket, and walks out. This is the only object Kane salvages from Susan's room, the only memento he wants to save. Why does this one object catch Kane's attention? Why does he spare it? What is its connection with "Rosebud"?

Now we find ourselves in the same predicament as Thompson, the young journalist in the film, who questions everyone close to Kane about Rosebud on the hunch that "maybe he told us all about himself on his deathbed." Unlike Thompson, however, who never does

a

b

c

d

Figure 1.9
Four stills from the puppet film THE HAND, in which objects are employed as story-telling devices.

find out the significance of Kane's dying word, we viewers discover its meaning at the end of the film and appreciate what the glass ball with the winter scene reveals about Charles Foster Kane.

        Animated films, especially those without dialogue or **narration,** often rely on objects to carry a story and sometimes employ them ingeniously as narrative devices. THE HAND (1965), a short **puppet film** without dialogue by the renowned Czech puppet-film director, Jiří Trnka, is a good example. THE HAND is a political allegory about a solitary potter in Pierrot costume who struggles against a tyrannical Hand that forces him to create replicas of hands rather than flowerpots (fig. 1.9 *a* and *b*). The Hand uses gentle persuasion at first but soon resorts to brute force. It attaches strings to the Pierrot and locks him in a bird cage where, like a marionette, he is manipulated to sculpt a monument to the

Hand (fig. 1.9c). The little man burns off the strings, however, and crashes the sculpture through the bars of the cage (fig. 1.9d). He escapes back to his room and boards up the door and window. The Hand eventually destroys the little potter but, ironically, prepares a hero's funeral for him afterwards.

Every object in THE HAND serves several purposes in the story. A potted flower, for instance, which the Pierrot nurtures and protects from the Hand, is the immediate cause of the potter's death when it falls on him from atop a wardrobe where he had placed it for safekeeping. The wardrobe itself then serves as the man's coffin. In the bird cage the Pierrot uses the candle that lit his forced labor to burn off the strings binding him to it, and then uses the monument he sculpted to crash out of the cage. Most of the objects in the film are used as **symbols** as well. The potted flower, for instance, clearly symbolizes the potter's individuality and freedom of expression.

Vittorio De Sica's THE BICYCLE THIEF (1947) is an example of a film completely built around an object. THE BICYCLE THIEF is about an unemployed worker, Ricci (Lamberto Maggiorani), living in Rome just after World War II, who is offered a job as a poster hanger, on the condition that he report for work with a bicycle. During his first day on the job, however, an organized band of thieves steals his bike. The rest of the film follows Ricci's futile attempts to get it back. Finally, in desperation, Ricci attempts to steal a bicycle himself but is caught and humiliated in front of his young son.

Ricci's bicycle is the very heart of De Sica's film. First, the bicycle itself is an important feature of the film's setting as well as an indicator of the social and economic conditions in postwar Italy. As film critic André Bazin points out, "the choice of a bicycle as the key object in the drama is characteristic both of Italian urban life and of a period when mechanical means of transportation were still rare and expensive" (50). The importance of the bicycle to Ricci personally, and to his family, is carefully established at the beginning of the film. The bike is practically a member of the family (fig. 1.10). Ricci's wife pawns the family linen to get it out of hock; his son rises before dawn to polish it before his father leaves for work; and Ricci himself protects it like he would protect an unmarried daughter.

Second, since the entire story hinges on the premise that without a bicycle Ricci has no livelihood, all the tension in the film stems from the single incident where the bike is stolen, and all the protagonist's actions are motivated by his need to get it back.

Figure 1.10

The protagonist of THE BICYCLE THIEF protecting his bicycle, the object around which the entire film turns.

Third, the bicycle is the dominant image in the film. In the film script the scene description states that when Ricci receives his bicycle out of pawn he "advances towards the bike and takes feverish hold of it." Thereafter, until it is stolen, Ricci does not let it out of his sight. When he must leave the bike in the street for a few moments, he asks some boys playing nearby to watch it. The thieves, in fact, would never have stolen the bicycle if they had not surprised Ricci while he was on a ladder hanging posters.

De Sica magnifies the bicycle image in the film in a scene where Ricci searches for his stolen property in the bicycle market. As the market opens, attendants wheel out rows of bikes and display racks of frames, tires, and parts. There are even tables piled with bells and pumps. As Ricci and his friends scour the market, looking for the stolen bike, the camera follows them along endless rows of goods. The sight is overpowering. We see that Ricci has no chance of recovering the stolen bicycle here. Similarly, near the end of the film, rows and rows of unattended bicycles parked outside a soccer stadium tempt Ricci to steal one. Ironically, he takes an old bike standing alone in a side street and is immediately apprehended.

Finally, De Sica attaches universal significance to the bicycle. What happens to Ricci in THE BICYCLE THIEF is not an incident confined only to Italy in 1946. The same misfortune could happen to anyone, should economic circumstances create an environment where "the poor must steal from each other in order to survive" (Bazin 51). The bicycle, therefore, comes to symbolize whatever stands between a worker and his livelihood, between security and desperation.

Ricci's bicycle in THE BICYCLE THIEF is an indispensable part of the story; the glass ball in CITIZEN KANE and the potted flower in THE HAND reveal deep truths about Charles Foster Kane and the little Pierrot; and carefully photographed objects enhance scenes in films like THE GOLD RUSH and FANNY AND ALEXANDER. But are such objects just clever story-telling devices and colorful details to flesh out movie scenes, or are they somehow essential to cinema?

At the most fundamental level, objects are the very stuff of movies, which unlike literature, require tangible (i.e., photographable) material for their stories. As filmmaker and theorist Michael Roemer points out, "A good film is concrete." The boiled shoe scene in THE GOLD RUSH, for example, is so memorable because Chaplin executes it moment by moment in the most exact physical detail.

> While the shoe is cooking, he pours water over it as if he were basting a bird. He carves and serves it with meticulous care, separating the uppers from the sole as though boning a fish. Then he winds the limp laces around his fork like spaghetti and sucks each nail as if it were a delicate chicken bone. Thus a totally incongruous moment is given an absolute, detailed physicality; the extraordinary is made ordinary, credible—and therefore funny.
>
> (Roemer 261)

For Roemer, situations, character relationships, and dialogue in movies become "objectified" when a filmmaker renders them "with enough immediacy and totality to call into play the perceptual processes we employ in life itself." A good film, therefore, "creates a sequence of objective situations, actual relationships between people, between people and their circumstances. Thus each moment becomes an objective correlative; that is, feeling (or meaning) rendered in actual, physical terms: objectified" (Roemer 258).

Siegfried Kracauer, a film theorist who advocates "realist cinema," argues that one of the basic properties of the film medium is that it is "uniquely equipped to record and reveal physical reality and, hence, gravitates toward it" (28). Kracauer points out that the camera's ability to single out and record objects in close-ups marks a decisive difference between cinema and theater.

> Stage imagery inevitably centers on the actor, whereas film is free to dwell on parts of his appearance and detail the objects about him. In using its freedom to bring the inanimate to the fore and make it a carrier of action, film only protests its peculiar requirement to explore all of physical existence, human and nonhuman.
>
> (45)

Kracauer notes that many films have raised inanimate objects "to the status of full-fledged actors":

> From the malicious escalators, the unruly Murphy beds, and the mad automobiles in silent comedy to the cruiser Potemkin, the oil derrick in LOUISIANA STORY and the dilapidated kitchen in UMBERTO D., a long procession of unforgettable objects has passed across the screen— objects which stand out as protagonists and all but overshadow the rest of the cast.
>
> (45)

To Kracauer's procession of unforgettable objects we can certainly add the glass ball in CITIZEN KANE and the bicycle in THE BICYCLE THIEF, as well as objects from more recent films like 2001: A SPACE ODYSSEY (1968), CLOSE ENCOUNTERS OF THE THIRD KIND (1977), and BACK TO THE FUTURE (1985).

Conclusion

For film theorists like Kracauer and Roemer, objects in films are not merely props or clever narrative devices but essential elements of cinema. Because camera close-ups can depict objects in such explicit detail, their potential for arousing emotions and communicating meaning is tremendously enhanced. The same can be said for setting, costumes, and makeup because they also help "objectify" a film's meaning in actual, physical terms. Thus, it is clear that *mise en scène* can serve several important functions in movies, depending on *how* filmmakers depict "the plastics of the image" on the screen. That will be the concern of the next two chapters, which examine camera and lighting techniques in movies.

General Study Questions

1. Study the opening scene of a film you already know. How much information about the story and the characters does the filmmaker provide there? What can you tell about the film from the setting, costumes and makeup, and props depicted in the opening scene?
2. Consider how important landscape usually is for popular movie genres, like horror and science fiction films, Westerns, murder mysteries, and war movies. Compare and contrast typical settings in two such genres. Generalize about how landscape affects the characters and action in each genre. Illustrate with examples from movies you know.
3. Develop a clear thesis statement for an essay about costumes and makeup in a specific film. Indicate in the thesis at least three important points that you would develop in the body of the paper.
4. Identify a film that contains an "unforgettable object." In how many ways does that object contribute to the film's meaning? Consider the object's value as an image, as a metaphor, as a narrative device, and, possibly, as a "protagonist" in the film.
5. What does Michael Roemer mean when he says that filmmakers "objectify" movie situations, character relationships, and dialogue when they render them "with enough immediacy and totality to call into play the perceptual processes we employ in life itself"? Illustrate with examples from films you know.

Additional Films for Study

THE GENERAL (1926), dir. Buster Keaton
VAMPYR (1931), dir. Carl Dreyer
THE MUMMY (1932), dir. Karl Freund
KING KONG (1933), dir. Merian Cooper and Ernest Schoedsack

MODERN TIMES (1936), dir. Charles Chaplin
THE MALTESE FALCON (1941), dir. John Huston
BEAUTY AND THE BEAST (1946), dir. Jean Cocteau
RED RIVER (1948), dir. Howard Hawks
SHANE (1953), dir. George Stevens
THE WILD ONE (1954), dir. Laszlo Benedek
LAST YEAR AT MARIENBAD (1961), dir. Alan Resnais
THE BIRDS (1963), dir. Alfred Hitchcock
A MAN FOR ALL SEASONS (1966), dir. Fred Zinnemann
YELLOW SUBMARINE (1968), dir. George Dunning
EASY RIDER (1969), dir. Dennis Hopper
SILENT RUNNING (1977), dir. Douglas Trumbull
ALIEN (1979), dir. Ridley Scott
LA CAGE AUX FOLLES (1979), dir. Edouard Molinaro
MANHATTAN (1979), dir. Woody Allen
MAD MAX (1980), dir. George Miller
THE GODS MUST BE CRAZY (1980), dir. Jamie Uys
TOOTSIE (1982), dir. Sidney Pollack
GHOSTBUSTERS (1984), dir. Ivan Reitman
F/X (1986), dir. Robert Mandel
WHO FRAMED ROGER RABBIT? (1988), dir. Robert Zemeckis

Further Reading

Arnheim, Rudolf. *Visual Thinking*. Berkeley: University of California Press, 1969.
Barsacq, Leon. *Caligari's Cabinets and other Grand Illusions: A History of Film Design*. New York: New American Library, 1978.
Brosnan, John. *Movie Magic: The Story of Special Effects*. New York: New American Library, 1976.
Chierichetti, David. *Hollywood Costume Design*. New York: Harmony Books, 1976.
De Sica, Vittorio. *THE BICYCLE THIEF*. Translated by Simon Hartog. New York: Simon and Schuster, 1968.
Finch, Christopher. *The Art of Walt Disney*. New York: Harry N. Abrams, 1975.
Freeburg, Victor O. *Pictorial Beauty on the Screen*. New York: Macmillan, 1923.
Gifford, Denis. *Chaplin*. Garden City, N.Y.: Doubleday, 1974.
"The Hollywood Cartoon." *Film Comment* 11 (January-February, 1975). [Special issue]
Holman, Bruce L. *Puppet Animation in the Cinema*. San Diego: A.S. Barnes, 1975.
Leese, Elizabeth. *Costume Design in the Movies*. New York: Ungar, 1978.
McCaffrey, Donald W., ed. *Focus on Chaplin*. Englewood Cliffs, N.J.: Prentice-Hall, 1971.
McConathy, Dale, and Diana Vreeland. *Hollywood Costume*. Englewood Cliffs, N.J.: Prentice-Hall, 1977.
Nilsen, Vladimir. *The Cinema as Graphic Art*. New York: Hill and Wang, 1959.
Stephenson, Ralph. *The Animated Film*. Cranbury, N.J.: A.S. Barnes, 1973.
Wood, Robin. *Arthur Penn*. New York: Frederich A. Praeger, 1969.

Works Cited

Balázs, Béla. "The Close-up." In *Film Theory and Criticism,* 3d ed., edited by Gerald Mast and Marshall Cohen, 255-64. New York: Oxford University Press, 1985.

Bazin, André. "BICYCLE THIEF." In *What is Cinema?,* Vol. II, translated by Hugh Gray, 47-60. Los Angeles: University of California Press, 1971.

Eisenstein, Sergei. *The Film Sense.* Translated and edited by Jay Leyda. New York: Harcourt, Brace and World, 1975.

Kracauer, Siegfried. *Theory of Film.* New York: Oxford University Press, 1960.

Mankiewicz, Herman J., and Orson Welles. *CITIZEN KANE: The Shooting Script.* In *The CITIZEN KANE Book.* Boston: Little, Brown and Company, 1971.

Roemer, Michael. "The Surfaces of Reality." In *Film: A Montage of Theories,* edited by Richard Dyer MacCann, 255-68. New York: E.P. Dutton, 1966.

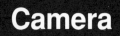

Camera

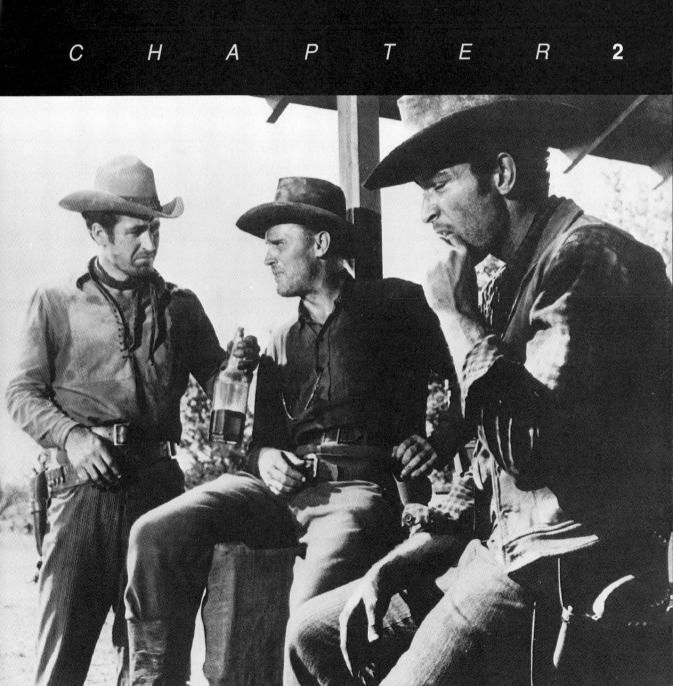

P icture this situation: A suspected murderer, suffering from amnesia, lapses into a trance late at night in the home of an elderly professor. With a straight razor in his hand, he slowly descends a staircase to the first floor where his host is working alone in the study. From below, the camera follows his silent descent and, when he stops at the bottom of the stairs, reveals the razor in his hand at close range. The audience, after following his movement from a distance, suddenly finds itself eye-level with the open razor. Alfred Hitchcock directed this scene in SPELLBOUND (1945). It is startling and memorable largely because the camera is placed so that, after following the actor uninterruptedly down the steps, it is in perfect position for a close-up of the razor in his hand when he reaches the bottom.

Camera Positions

Camera positions are commonly described in terms of the camera's apparent distance from the subject photographed: **long shots (LS), medium shots (MS), close-ups (CU).** But it is important to remember that camera distance is not the only factor that determines how near or distant the subject appears on the screen. **Lenses** are another factor. For example, using a **normal lens** for most shooting situations, the camera may be set up for a fairly long view of a scene. Yet, without changing the camera position at all, the same shot may appear as a close-up if the director switches to a longer lens. A very long lens is called a **telephoto lens** because, like a telescope, it brings an image in closer with its long **focal length.** A very short lens, on the other hand, is called a **wide-angle lens** because, with its shorter focal length, it can photograph a wider area than a normal lens. With a **zoom lens,** which has a range of focal lengths, the camera can make the subject appear closer or farther away without interrupting the shot.

A surer way to describe camera positions is according to how large the subject of a shot appears within the frame in relation to its surroundings. Using the human figure as a reference, a standard medium shot might show two characters framed together from about the knees up, focusing attention on their interaction. Such a shot is sometimes called a **two-shot,** because it features two actors. To show their entire figures in the frame, the director may call for a slightly longer shot, a **full shot.** To emphasize their surroundings more or to situate them in a larger setting, the director may draw farther back to a long shot, or even to an **extreme long shot (XLS)** to dwarf them in their surroundings. On the other hand, to call attention to character A's reaction to what B has said, the director may employ a close-up that frames only A's face, or an **extreme close-up (XCU)** that zeroes in on tears welling up in the corner of his eye.

For specific examples of how camera positions contribute to cinematic storytelling, consider the following sequence of shots from HIGH NOON (1952), directed by Fred Zinnemann with cinematographer Floyd Crosby. The Railroad Depot Sequence runs about two minutes on the screen and contains fifteen shots. There is almost no dialogue in the scene, and the only camera movements are incidental ones to follow characters when they move. Carefully chosen camera positions, therefore, tell the story. (Explanation of the purpose and format of shot-by-shot description and analysis, along with common abbreviations, can be found in the section of the appendix entitled "How to Write a Shot-by-Shot Analysis" on page 398.)

HIGH NOON: The Railroad Depot Sequence
A Shot-by-Shot Description

1. XLS. **(Establishing shot.)** A locomotive in the distance steaming toward the camera. A large expanse of prairie in the background (b/g); a water tower in the left middleground (m/g); railroad tracks in the left foreground (f/g).

2. Medium close-up (MCU). Three unshaven, rough-looking outlaws (members of the Frank Miller gang) awaiting the approaching noon train.

3. LS. Two women in a horse-drawn wagon (Mrs. Kane and Helen Ramirez) approach the Hadleyville train depot from town. The stationmaster is waiting for them.

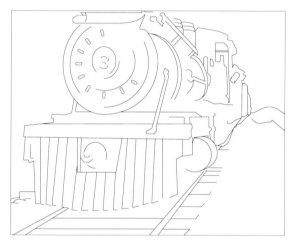

4. (Shot #1 continued.) The locomotive steams closer to the depot, slowing as it nears. The shot ends with the train passing close by the camera.

5. (Shot #3 continued.) The train pulls into the depot as the two women step down from the wagon. The stationmaster helps them with their baggage. (See figure 2.1.)

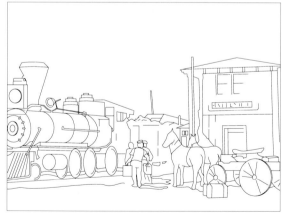

How Do Films Tell a Story?

6. MS. **High angle (H/A).** The three outlaws approach the train from the prairie side of the depot and greet a man (Frank Miller) who arrives on the train. Nearer the camera and still on the train, Miller looms over the three men standing on the ground. He is better dressed and groomed than they are. Miller steps down, and all four walk away from the camera. **Cut on action** to . . .

7. MS. (Same position but somewhat closer.) The outlaws from behind, continuing toward their end of the depot. Frank Miller removes his jacket and straps on a gun belt.

8. Medium long shot (MLS). **Reverse angle (R/A).** The depot and the standing train seen from the prairie side. The Miller gang is aligned in the left f/g, beside the depot. Miller, securing his gun holster, still has his back to the camera. In the right b/g, near the train, the two women are about to board. (See figure 2.2.)

Figure 2.1
A still from HIGH NOON illustrating shot #5 in the Railroad Depot Sequence. A long shot at about its farthest limit.

Figure 2.2
A still from HIGH NOON illustrating shot #8 in the Railroad Depot Sequence. This shot brings together the two sets of characters within the narrow space between the train and the depot.

9. MS. At the train. (*a*) The stationmaster helps Mrs. Kane step up into the train. (*b*) Miss Ramirez is next, but she pauses before boarding, looking beyond the frame toward the Miller gang.

a

b

10. CU. Frank Miller's face (the first time it is shown in the film), looking up from arranging his gun belt. He is pockmarked and hard looking and stares beyond the frame at Helen Ramirez.

11. CU. Helen Ramirez stares back at Frank Miller.

12. (Shot #10 continued.) Frank Miller staring.

13. (Shot #11 continued.) Helen Ramirez looks down and steps onto the train.

14. (Same position as shot #8.) Frank Miller and gang walk between the depot and the train (past where the women boarded), heading toward town.

15. LS. (Approximately the same position as shot #3, but closer to the depot.) The railroad depot seen from the town side. The Miller gang walks toward the camera on their way to town. Frank Miller loosens his necktie and checks his revolver. They pass close by the camera at the end of the shot. (See figure 2.3.)

 Before reading further, jot down some observations about how camera positions help tell the story in the Railroad Depot Sequence. You probably know more than you realize about camera techniques in movies. Look especially at how the camera positions complement one another in this sequence. For example, how does Zinnemann position the camera to keep Frank Miller's face hidden from us until shot #10? What does he accomplish with the series of close-ups in shots #10 through #13?

 First let us identify some of the camera positions in the Railroad Depot Sequence. Shot #1 begins as an extreme long shot of a distant locomotive steaming toward the camera. The railroad tracks in the foreground, like lines of perspective in a painting, carry the eye

Figure 2.3

A still from HIGH NOON illustrating shot #15 in the Railroad Depot Sequence. The Miller gang's movement directly toward the camera mirrors the locomotive steaming into the depot in shot #1.

deeper into the frame, beyond the water tower in the middleground, to the main subject of the shot, the locomotive, in the background. (Naturally, since the locomotive is moving toward the camera, the longer the shot continues, the closer the camera position will be relative to the locomotive.) We see a great expanse of desolate prairie, which defines the physical setting for this shot and the rest of the sequence. When a long shot is used in this way to establish a milieu at the beginning of a scene, it is called an establishing shot.

The camera position in shot #2 is closer than a standard medium shot but not yet a close-up; thus, it is medium-close. The three members of the Miller gang are grouped tightly together within the frame, a **three-shot,** and remain motionless, creating a tableau.

How Do Films Tell a Story?

Shot #5 (fig. 2.1) is a long shot at about its farthest limit. Mrs. Kane and Helen Ramirez have just arrived at the railroad depot in the wagon and are met by the stationmaster. Though they appear fairly distant on the screen, the characters are clearly identifiable, and their activity is the focal point of the shot. But we also take in a lot of the surroundings—the locomotive arriving on the left side of the frame and the Hadleyville train depot on the right—which help us understand that the ladies are approaching the depot from the side opposite the one the Miller gang occupies in shot #2.

Shots #10 through #13 are alternating close-ups of Frank Miller, who stepped off the train with his back to the camera in shot #6, and Helen Ramirez, who is about to board. Notice that the characters' faces are aligned within the frame to suggest that they are staring at each other, an editing technique known as an **eyeline match.**

Next, let us examine more closely how the camera positions in HIGH NOON's Railroad Depot Sequence help tell the story. But first we should ask why Zinnemann and Crosby bother to break up a scene that is only two minutes long into fifteen shots. Why don't they simply set up the camera to photograph the scene all at once? Why do they use so many camera positions? Film director Alfred Hitchcock explains why:

> . . . you gradually build up the psychological situation, piece by piece, using the camera to emphasize first one detail, then another. The point is to draw the audience right inside the situation—instead of leaving them to watch it from outside, from a distance. And you can do this only by breaking the action up into details and cutting from one piece to the other, so that each detail is forced in turn on the attention of the audience and reveals its psychological meaning. If you played the whole scene straight through, and simply made a photographic record of it with the camera always in one position, you would lose your power over the audience. They would watch the scene without becoming really involved in it, and you would have no means of concentrating their attention on those particular visual details which make them feel what the characters are feeling.
>
> (In MacCann 57)

How do Zinnemann and Crosby use the camera to draw the audience "right inside the situation" at the railroad depot in HIGH NOON? The sequence occurs at a climactic moment in the film, as the noon train arrives with convicted killer Frank Miller, who has returned to take revenge on the man who sent him to prison, Marshal Will Kane (Gary Cooper). But Kane must face the Miller gang alone since he has been unable to enlist any deputies. Even Kane's wife of barely an hour (Grace Kelly), a Quaker opposed to violence, is abandoning him. Ironically, she is leaving town on the same train with Kane's former mistress, Helen Ramirez. With the arrival of the noon train, therefore, the film's climactic showdown begins.

HIGH NOON's Railroad Depot Sequence juxtaposes two sets of characters: the Miller gang and the two departing women. Observe how Zinnemann brings these two groups into contact on the screen. He deals with each group separately at first, allowing each its own territory and distinct visual rhythm in the scene. The three outlaws stand motionlessly on the prairie side of the depot, staring into the distance. The women drive up to the other side of the station, from town, and move steadily toward the train. Only as the women are about to board do both groups occupy common territory and appear together in the same shot. Shot #8 (fig. 2.2) is a pivotal shot in the sequence because it shows the railroad station from a new vantage point, isolating a narrow corridor between the depot and the standing train in which the two sets of characters, separate until now, finally meet. We see them together in shot #8: the outlaws (reunited with Frank Miller) in the left foreground preparing for the gunfight and the women in the right background about to board the train.

Shot #9 shifts our attention to the women. First we watch Mrs. Kane step into the train, without recognizing or acknowledging the killers who want her husband dead. But Helen Ramirez pauses to look at Frank Miller before boarding. Then we follow the alternating close-ups of Ramirez and Miller, who were once intimate.

Though there are frequent comments in HIGH NOON about how crazy and vicious Frank Miller is, the audience does not know until this moment what he looks like. After the train arrives, Zinnemann positions the camera to withhold the villain's face from the viewer as long as possible. Miller steps off the train with his back to the camera in shot #6 and walks away from it in shot #7, and the reverse angle in shot #8 also shows him from behind. Only after Helen Ramirez looks him in the eye— a person who knows him better perhaps than anyone in town—does the camera finally reveal Frank Miller's face.

As soon as Frank Miller is revealed, the Miller gang is ready to hunt down Marshal Kane. Zinnemann emphasizes the gang's power in shot #15 (fig. 2.3), the final shot of the sequence, where they leave the depot behind and move forcefully toward town. They invade territory earlier occupied by Mrs. Kane and Helen Ramirez and stride directly toward the camera, appearing larger and more powerful as they approach it—much like the locomotive approaching the depot at the beginning of the sequence.

Zinnemann dramatizes the Miller gang's advantage in the gunfight about to begin by cutting away from the railroad depot to a close-up of Marshal Will Kane in town, ready to stand alone against the four killers. He reinforces Kane's isolation with a **crane shot,** which gradually backs up and away from Kane, revealing him from high above, a tiny heroic figure alone in the street and facing overwhelming odds.

The closer we study the Railroad Depot Sequence in HIGH NOON, the more we can appreciate how carefully Zinnemann and Crosby positioned the camera for its fifteen shots. We can observe how each shot calls the audience's attention to a particular piece of the story and leads into the next piece. Look closely, for example, at shots #8 through #14, a series that begins and ends with the camera in the same position, showing the train from the prairie side of the depot. What happens on the screen in these seven shots? How do the eye and the mind follow this segment of the narrative? Note your observations before reading further.

Shot #7 features the outlaw group from behind after Frank Miller steps off the train. When we see them again from the reverse angle in shot #8 (fig. 2.2), we are already familiar with their activity; so we quickly look deeper into the frame at the women in the background. In fact, the way the shot aligns the characters in the space between the train and the depot, the eye naturally reads the images in the frame from foreground to background, from left to right. Appropriately, then, shot #9 introduces a closer view of the ladies boarding the train. Helen Ramirez's pause to look back at Frank Miller sets up the alternating close-ups in shots #10 through #13, which allow us to witness a private exchange of glances and to imagine for ourselves what cruelties Frank Miller is capable of. When Miss Ramirez steps on the train, however, the contact between these two individuals, and between the two sets of characters in the sequence, is finished; and the tension built up between them is exhausted. It is time for the story to move forward and for other tensions to build. Zinnemann, therefore, returns to the camera position in shot #8 and shows the Miller gang heading out after Will Kane.

Camera Angles

We can tell from the Railroad Depot Sequence in HIGH NOON that *mise en scène*—the visual arrangement of people and objects within the frame—ties in very closely with camera positioning. In shot #8, for example, Zinnemann had to plan more than where to set up the camera and how to focus our attention on two sets of characters. There is more to this shot than lining up the characters so they won't block one another out. Try to imagine shot #8, for instance, without the depot building on the left side of the frame. How might we react to the shot if there were open space on the left side of the frame? We might look for last-minute help to break into the scene from that side or for Mrs. Kane to bolt back to her husband. Instead, the confined space funnels the action into that narrow corridor; confrontation between the two sets of characters is inescapable. Furthermore, without the solid border on the left, the eye would not be drawn so readily into the background. Like the railroad tracks in shot #1, the depot and the standing train in shot #8 form parallel lines in linear perspective that lead the eye toward the vanishing point in the distance.

As with paintings, visual and psychological factors affect the way we perceive film images within the frame. A lighter object attracts the eye sooner than a darker one, for example; and an object in the foreground tends to dominate one in the background. Bright colors and prominent placement in the frame also make an image stand out. And any kind of movement within a static setting immediately attracts the eye's attention.

The angle at which the camera is set for a shot also affects the way we perceive images within the frame. For instance, in shot #2 from the Railroad Depot Sequence, the three gang members are arranged in a tight portrait photographed straight on. From the way they are posed in the frame, we perceive that none is more prominent or important than the others. In shot #6, on the other hand, Frank Miller is clearly the most prominent character in the frame. The shot is lined up so that as Miller steps off the train, he is closer to the camera than the other three are and, therefore, appears larger in the frame. Since the camera is set at a **high angle**, it looks down on the men waiting on the ground, just as Frank Miller does. Consequently, we perceive the three gang members as more subservient, looking up at Miller, their leader, who stands above them. And since we can see their faces but not his, the well-dressed man with his back to the camera takes on additional mystery and authority. We recognize his power over the other three men.

An even more dramatic example of how a high-angle shot can affect the viewer psychologically is the crane shot that follows the depot sequence. As we look down on Will Kane from a **bird's-eye view**, the hopelessness of his situation is magnified. At the end of the shot when the camera reaches its highest point, he appears as a mere speck alone in the street.

The angle at which the camera photographs a shot, therefore, can affect not only what we perceive in the frame but also the way we respond to it. Associations between dominance and lofty position are deeply engrained in our culture and language. We commonly refer to powerful people as those in "high places." A dominant person is said to "lord it over" others, to have "the upper hand," or to be "top dog." On the other hand, some people "look down" on others or "put them down" because they feel superior, that is, "above" them. Filmmakers take advantage of such associations to manipulate audience reactions. With a high-angle shot, a filmmaker can create a sense of dominance or authority by tilting the camera down at the subject, making it appear small, or inferior, or overwhelmed. Conversely, using a **low-angle shot** tilted up toward the subject can create the feeling of being dominated or overwhelmed by a force that appears larger than life. These are not hard and fast rules, however. The crane shot of Will Kane in HIGH NOON proves that we can physically look down upon a character in an overpowering situation and at the same time psychologically look up to him as a model of courage and determination.

Orson Welles's CITIZEN KANE (1941), photographed by Gregg Toland, is a film that uses many high-angle and low-angle shots to dramatize character relationships. For example, the day after the abysmal singing debut of Kane's second wife, Susan Alexander, the two of them are in a hotel room scanning newspaper reviews. Susan is sitting on the floor surrounded with papers, screeching at Kane because his own newspaper, *The Inquirer*, has panned her performance. Kane loses his temper and towers menacingly over Susan. "You are to continue with your singing," he orders her. Photographed from a high camera angle, Susan appears small and vulnerable, with Kane looming over her. When he moves, Kane's shadow covers Susan's face, suggesting how completely his domineering personality obliterates her identity.

Later, when Kane and Susan are in a tent during a lavish picnic outing, Welles repeats this visual depiction of their relationship with another dramatic high-angle shot. Susan is again loudly berating her husband, complaining that he has never given her anything meaningful. Kane, furious, rises and stands threateningly above her. Susan is framed in an extreme high-angle shot, looking up toward Kane. "You don't love me," she screams at him. "You want me to love you. . . . Whatever you want—just name it and it's yours. But you gotta love me!" Kane slaps her across the face. (Welles's use of **off-screen sound** in this scene is discussed in chapter 5.)

Welles and Toland also use low-angle shots in CITIZEN KANE to reveal Kane's character cinematically. One low-angle shot, for example, depicts Kane early in his career signing a Declaration of Principles—to tell the news honestly and to champion the rights of the underprivileged. The shot features Kane prominently in the middle of the frame and enhances his stature with a low camera angle. But ironically, although Kane's hand is highlighted as he signs the document, his face falls completely into shadow, suggesting that Kane may not always adhere to these principles. (This scene is also discussed in chapter 5. See figure 5.3.)

In a later scene Welles uses low-angle shots rather unorthodoxly. Kane has just lost a gubernatorial election, though he was strongly favored to win as a reform candidate, because he was "caught in a love nest" with his mistress on the eve of the election. He is alone at night in the dark newspaper office, surrounded by "Kane for Governor" posters. His closest friend, Jed Leland, disillusioned with Kane, walks in drunk and asks to be transferred. "You don't care about anything except you," Leland accuses him. "You want love on your terms."

Having lost both election and friend in one night, Kane might well be depicted here in high-angle shots that would diminish his stature and make him appear defeated or overwhelmed. On the contrary, Welles and Toland photograph the entire scene—lasting nearly four and a half minutes—from a low-angle position at floor level (fig. 2.4). Occasionally, when Kane paces or stands near the camera, the low angle exaggerates his figure almost to distortion.

There is no rule that says a defeated man may not be depicted from a low angle, but a low camera angle in this kind of situation is very unconventional. So why do you think Welles and Toland decided to use it?

Perhaps this scene does not emphasize Kane's defeat so much as how dramatically the defeat has distorted his character. Perhaps now that the public has rejected him, Kane will abandon the reform principles he ardently espoused earlier and pursue more selfish interests. Kane concludes the scene with a toast to Leland: "A toast, Jedediah, to love on my terms. Those are the only terms anybody ever knows, his own."

As an exercise, analyze the two examples of extreme high- and low-angle shots in figures 2.5 and 2.6. The high-angle shot (fig. 2.5) is from Federico Fellini's 8½ (1963); the low-angle shot (fig. 2.6) is from Nicolas Roeg's DON'T LOOK NOW (1974). Why do you think the filmmakers chose extreme camera angles for these shots? How do you think they wanted the audience to react to the character depicted in each shot?

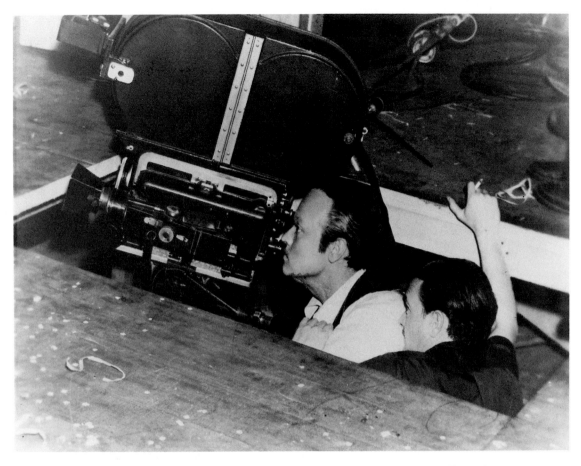

Figure 2.4
Director Orson Welles (at the camera) and cinematographer Gregg Toland preparing a low-angle shot for CITIZEN KANE.

High-angle and low-angle camera positions are fairly common in movies, and except when the angle is extreme, many viewers are barely aware that the camera is tilted at all. This is not so, however, when the camera is tilted to one side or the other—called an **oblique angle** or a **Dutch angle.** For example, in James Whale's THE BRIDE OF FRANKENSTEIN (1935), photographed by John J. Mescall, Dutch angles appear in the climactic laboratory scene where the monster's bride comes to life. Flashing gadgets and laboratory apparatus are briskly intercut with close-ups of Drs. Frankenstein and Praetorius working the controls. Whale underscores the tension in the scene and highlights the scientists' demonic intensity with oblique-angled close-ups of the two men, slanting away from each other toward the edges of the screen.

Figure 2.5
An extreme high-angle shot from 8½, directed by Federico Fellini.

Oblique camera angles are conspicuous because they are visually and psychologically unsettling. Through most of his career, the Dutch painter Piet Mondrian (1872-1944) painted abstract compositions of solid colors blocked in by strongly defined vertical and horizontal lines. In his theoretical writings about art, Mondrian discussed how vertical and horizontal lines forming right angles create repose and equilibrium in a painting and how oblique lines break that balance and repose. Mondrian's concepts also apply to film images, which are blocked in like a painting by the squared edges of the frame. Thus, when an image on the screen is oblique within the frame, the composition generally makes the viewer feel unstable or disoriented.

Dutch angles illustrate most graphically the psychological impact that camera angles can have on film audiences. But to some extent, camera angles always affect our reactions to characters and situations in films because they affect the way we perceive them. For instance, in the scenes from CITIZEN KANE where Kane stands menacingly over Susan Alexander, camera angles convey the state of their marriage more dramatically than dialogue because they allow us to *see* each character's position in the relationship.

Figure 2.6
An extreme low-angle
shot from DON'T LOOK
NOW, directed by Nicolas
Roeg.

Camera Movements

There are three kinds of camera movements: panning shots, traveling shots, and hand-held camera shots.

Panning is the movement of the camera in a stationary position when it turns on its own axis. A camera tripod or base swivels to allow the apparatus mounted on it to pivot horizontally and vertically while remaining firmly grounded in one spot. When the camera pivots horizontally, the shot, called a **pan** (derived from "panorama"), appears on screen as movement from left to right or from right to left. When the camera pivots vertically, the shot is called a **tilt** and appears as movement from top to bottom or from bottom to top. And when it combines horizontal and vertical movement, the shot is called a **diagonal.** (Sometimes "pan" is used generically to describe any turning movement of the camera.) These terms are also used as verbs. Thus, the camera pans, tilts, or diagonals whenever it turns on one of its own axes.

Most of the time, panning shots serve a very utilitarian function in movies. Like a theater spotlight that follows a performer on stage to keep her continually in a circle of light, the camera pans with an actor on a movie set to keep him continually within the frame as he moves. Generally, such panning is inconspicuous because it corresponds to the way we naturally turn our heads to follow movement.

But panning shots are sometimes more conspicuously part of the story-telling process. In an establishing shot, for example, the camera sometimes pans slowly across the set to offer the audience a panorama that displays the milieu of a scene and defines its boundaries. At other times panning allows the audience a keener awareness of space in a shot and reinforces connections between characters and their surroundings. For instance, in Sydney Pollack's JEREMIAH JOHNSON (1972), photographed by Andrew Callaghan, there is a scene where Johnson (Robert Redford) and another mountain man named Bear Claw (Will Geer) kill an elk. While they are dressing the animal, Bear Claw hears a suspicious sound off in the forest. The camera slowly pans around nearly 360 degrees to survey the surrounding wilderness where nothing is moving but wind in the trees. When the camera returns to its original position, the mountain men and their kill are gone. Only traces of blood on the snow remain.

Another way panning helps visual storytelling is illustrated in a scene from Serge Bourguignon's SUNDAYS AND CYBELE (1962), photographed by Henri Decae. In this film a remarkably close yet innocent relationship develops between a young war veteran suffering from amnesia and a twelve-year-old girl. But more narrow-minded people suspect perversion. In one scene the young man's lover, Madeleine, follows him and the girl around a park. In an extreme long shot we see the couple at the edge of a pond tossing a stone into the water. The camera then pans left to show Madeleine spying on them from behind a hedge. Shortly after, in a medium close-up, the camera frames the young man and the girl side by side in front of a tree, then pans right to reveal Madeleine watching them again from the distance.

The panning technique in these two shots from SUN-DAYS AND CYBELE is a familiar one. It is frequently used in suspenseful scenes that startle the audience by revealing a dead body or a hideous maniac after the pan. Think about why this kind of camera movement has so much potential shock value. Suppose you begin a scene with a medium shot of a child frolicking in the surf. If the camera pans to an ice cream vendor walking along the beach, the audience will react much differently than if it pans to a shark in the water. This panning technique is effective because the connection between the two images in the shot becomes apparent only after the panning movement. At the beginning of the shot only the child is on the screen; we cannot see what may be approaching along the beach or from the sea. The camera's panning then expands our view beyond the edge of the frame, revealing that the two images unexpectedly coexist within the same space.

Some panning techniques are very conspicuous and stylized. A **swish pan,** for instance—also called a **flash pan, whip pan,** or **zip pan**—is so quickly executed that the image on the screen blurs with the movement. Directors use the swish pan for very specific purposes, such as to simulate the movement of a character glancing around rapidly or to create the sensation of kinetic motion. A swish can also mask a cut between two shots, since the eye cannot detect a cut amid so much movement.

Alfred Hitchcock's **REAR WINDOW** (1954), photographed by Robert Burks, is an example of a film that depends heavily on camera panning. A photojournalist (James Stewart), laid up with a broken leg, has lots of time on his hands and little to do except observe his neighbors. From a seat by the rear window of his apartment, he scrutinizes the everyday lives of the people in the opposite building and eventually uncovers a murder. Many shots from his window pan around from apartment to apartment across the courtyard, sometimes randomly and sometimes systematically, allowing the audience to share in this spying.

In traveling shots the camera body itself, mounted on a vehicle, moves while the camera is shooting, thus covering a range of vantage points instead of only one. Originally, traveling shots were identified according to the kind of vehicle the camera was mounted on. For example, if a film crew laid down tracks for the camera to roll along during filming, the shot was called a **tracking shot.** If the camera was set up and moved on a hand dolly or a truck, these were called **dolly shots** or **trucking shots.** But today the distinctions among these terms are not strictly maintained; they are often used interchangeably, along with the more generic term, **traveling shot.** A crane shot, like the one from HIGH NOON described earlier in this chapter, is a traveling shot photographed from a **studio crane.** And an **aerial shot** is one made from a helicopter or an airplane.

Miklós Jancsó's RED PSALM (1971), with photography by János Kende, a story about the agrarian socialist movement in Hungary in the 1890s, is an example of a film that prominently features a moving camera. There are only twenty-six shots in this feature-length film, most of them with intricately choreographed camera movements that glide continuously from one group of characters to another, pass in and out of scenes, and shift the viewer's attention from one component of the story to the next.

RED PSALM's highly stylized camera movement, of course, is not typical of how films use traveling shots to tell a story. Generally, filmmakers move the camera to meet the story's needs without drawing too much attention to it. Many directors, particularly those who strive for **realism** in their films, feel that the more the audience is aware of camera movements, the less they will be dramatically involved with the story.

Chase scenes often provide good examples of effective yet unobtrusive camera movement. In STAGECOACH (1939), for example, director John Ford and cinematographer Bert Glennon use high-speed traveling shots in a climactic scene where warring Apaches chase the stagecoach across desert flats. Most of the shots are taken from a motor vehicle traveling beside the coach, photographing it from several angles, though mostly from the front and the left side. Ford also mounts cameras on the speeding stagecoach itself, one behind the driver and another on the side of the coach. At the height of the chase, when the men on the stagecoach are out of ammunition and the Apaches are poised for the kill, Ford brings the cavalry to the rescue, trucking the camera right alongside the galloping soldiers as they charge across the screen toward the Indians.

Of eighty-four shots in the chase sequence in STAGE-COACH only about one-third are actual traveling shots. But Ford maintains the sensation of movement in the sequence by including **process shots** in which the stagecoach, though actually stationary, appears to be in motion against a moving background projected behind it. Ford makes good use of the actual traveling shots, however, by clustering them at key moments in the sequence: when the Indians first move alongside the stagecoach, when the driver drops the reins, and when the cavalry comes to the rescue.

Dynamic camera movement is certainly not limited to action movies, however. Ingmar Bergman's PERSONA (1967), with cinematographer Sven Nykvist, employs very little camera movement. Most of the action in PERSONA takes place in tight quarters; and meticulous **framing,** not movement, characterizes the camera work. But in one scene the two protagonists, played by Liv Ullmann and Bibi Andersson, enact a highly emotional confrontation while walking vigorously along a beach, which is photographed in a long uninterrupted tracking shot. The scene, like other dramatic encounters between the two women in the film, could have been played without the tracking. But Bergman chose to open up this scene, to infuse more physical movement, in order to dramatize more forcefully a turning point in the relationship between the two women. The camera's persistent tracking keeps the spectator continuously in touch with the characters in this scene and captures their physical and emotional energy.

Hand-held camera movement occurs when the operator supports the camera and moves with it, rather than mounting it on a vehicle. Depending on how steady the operator is and how complicated the movements (walking, climbing stairs, maneuvering through a crowd, etc.), a hand-held camera may appear either very jumpy and conspicuous to the viewer or so smooth that it can barely be distinguished from a dolly shot. The hand-held camera offers filmmakers a relatively simple way to move the camera in rugged terrain or in restrictive settings. Quite an elaborate studio setup would be needed, for example, to follow an actor in an uninterrupted shot through several rooms of a house, along a narrow corridor, down a staircase, and out the front door into the street. (Some directors—Orson Welles in THE MAGNIFICENT AMBERSONS (1942), for instance, and Alfred Hitchcock in FRENZY (1972)—have designed studio shots nearly this complicated, but with great time and effort.) To get the same shot on location with a hand-held camera would be relatively simple.

Hand-held camera movements are usually associated with **documentary films** or television reporting—the kind of filming that is generally immediate and spontaneous. Independent filmmakers, like Alexander Hammid and Maya Deren in MESHES OF THE AFTER-

NOON (1943), also frequently prefer a hand-held camera for the freedom of movement and the opportunity for experimentation that it affords. (See chapter 11 for more discussion of MESHES OF THE AFTERNOON.) But hand-held shots, though more the exception than the rule in studio films, are sometimes very effective in conventional story films, too. Director Franco Zeffirelli and cinematographer Pasqualino de Santis, for instance, filmed most of the street fighting scenes in ROMEO AND JULIET (1968) with a hand-held camera, most notably the swordfight between Tybalt and Romeo. That scene is one of continuous, furious action as the fight spills through the streets of Verona, with onlookers circling and shoving around the combatants. The hand-held camera, mostly at medium-to-close range, enhances the immediacy and realism of the fight and situates the film viewer right in the midst of it.

A Model Shot-by-Shot Analysis: AN OCCURRENCE AT OWL CREEK BRIDGE

A good way to understand the camera's role in film narrative is to study a sequence of shots closely, observing where the camera is and what it does in each shot, and then to analyze how each shot contributes to the entire sequence; in other words, to do a **shot-by-shot analysis** of the sequence.

Robert Enrico's AN OCCURRENCE AT OWL CREEK BRIDGE (1963), photographed by Jean Bobbety, is a short narrative film, based on a story by Ambrose Bierce, about a man who is hanged and who fantasizes an elaborate escape in the instant before his death. The film is a good one to study here because it tells a story without dialogue and showcases many camera techniques. The following shot-by-shot analysis covers the first thirty shots in AN OCCURRENCE AT OWL CREEK BRIDGE, which set the scene for the hanging. The shots are first described in detail and then analyzed to illustrate how camera positions, angles, and movements all work together in telling a story cinematically.

AN OCCURRENCE AT OWL CREEK BRIDGE
A Shot-by-Shot Analysis

1. (Drum roll.) Fade in. CU. A burnt tree trunk with credits superimposed:

Cappagariff Release
MARCEL ICHAC
and
PAUL DE ROUBAIX
present

Credits fade out. Camera tilts up to CU of a poster on the tree that reads:

ORDER

Any civilian
caught interfering with
the railroad bridges,
tunnels or trains will be
SUMMARILY HANGED
The 4th of April, 1862

(Drum roll.) Diagonal up and left above the burnt tree to XLS of hills and sky in the b/g. The film title fades in:

AN OCCURRENCE
AT
OWL CREEK BRIDGE
A Film by Robert Enrico

The title fades out.

2. LS. Low angle (L/A). Leafless trees and the sky above. (Sounds of owls.) Diagonal down and right to a level XLS through trees to hills and a stream in the b/g. A bridge over the stream is visible from an extreme high angle (XH/A) in the distance below. Track right slowly, featuring the bridge. (Bugle sounds reveille, military commands, sounds of owls.)

3. XLS. Slight H/A. The bridge in the distance, but closer than shot #2, with two guards patrolling. Track right continues at the same rate as in shot #2. (Sounds of owls.)

4. LS. Extreme low angle (XL/A). A sentry posted on a high rock. Track right continues.

5. LS. H/A. The bridge with guards posted and a file of soldiers with rifles marching across to the far side where a white tent stands. Track right continues, then stops at a nearly straight-on view of the bridge as the riflemen line up to the left of the bridge. (Military commands.)

6. MS. Profile of the lieutenant in charge of the riflemen. At the top right of the frame, the sentry on the rock is visible in the distance from XL/A. The lieutenant turns his head to review his troops. Track left to reveal the file of riflemen presenting arms.

7. MLS. A sergeant with a coiled rope walks past the lieutenant and his detail toward the bridge. A cannon is visible in the upper right from L/A. The camera pans left with the sergeant, then tracks forward to follow him onto the bridge, past the guard posted at that end. The sergeant walks toward the center of the bridge where a plank laid across the railroad tracks juts over the side of the bridge. Another guard posted at the far end of the bridge stands in the b/g.

8. XLS. H/A. An officer and two guards escort the prisoner onto the bridge, following the sergeant toward the plank. The cannon and the riflemen are aligned along the lower left of the frame. The sergeant prepares to throw the rope up over the bridge timbers.

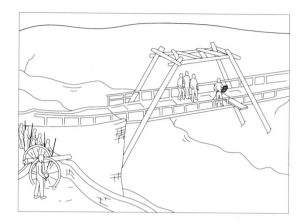

9. MCU. The prisoner in a white shirt and a dark vest and cravat stands with his head bowed. He raises his head and looks up and to the right.

10. MS. Slight L/A. The rope is thrown over the cross beams of the bridge. Diagonal down and right to MS, H/A of the sergeant handling the rope. The commanding officer with a sword on his belt stands behind the sergeant.

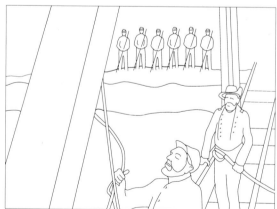

11. **MS. XL/A.** The sergeant tightens the rope over the timbers. As he prepares a noose, his head is framed within it.

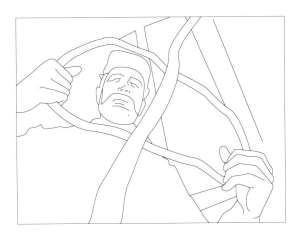

12. **LS.** The hanging party on the bridge. The officer stands on the end of the plank, while the prisoner is moved to the other end over the side of the bridge. The officer and the prisoner face each other from opposite ends of the plank.

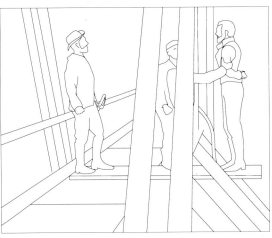

13. **MCU. Slight H/A.** One guard removes the prisoner's cravat and opens his collar; the other places the noose around his neck. The prisoner looks down toward the water below.

14. **MS. XH/A.** A point-of-view (POV) shot of the prisoner looking down at his own feet on the end of the plank and at the water farther below. Pan right, shifting his view from the left side of the plank to the right.

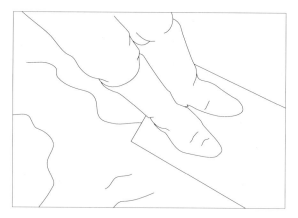

15. **XCU.** The lieutenant's hands resting on the hilt of his sword. His fingers fidget impatiently. (Sounds of birds.)

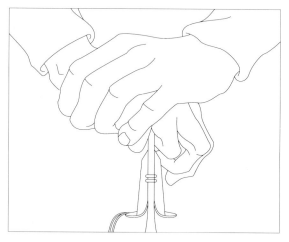

16. **MCU.** The lieutenant, apparently bored or impatient, looks off to the left, then faces front. (Continued sound of birds.)

17. MCU. The prisoner with the noose
around his neck, sweating, looks off to
the right.

18. LS. The prisoner's POV of the lieutenant and the riflemen. Track
right and pan right toward the guard at that end of the bridge with
his back to the camera.
19. CU. The prisoner turns his head from right to left.
20. LS. The prisoner's POV of the single guard on the other end of the
bridge, also with his back turned. The camera tracks forward toward
him.
21. CU. The prisoner turns his head from left to right. Swish pan up and
right to LS, L/A of the sentry on the rock.
22. MS. Slight H/A. One guard binds the prisoner's legs together at the
knees with a strip of white cloth. Tilt down to MS, H/A. The other
guard binds the prisoner's ankles.
23. LS. H/A. The hanging party on the bridge. The cannon is prominent
in the f/g. The camera tracks left past the cannon and tilts down to
LS, H/A of the riflemen.
24. (Shot #22 continued.) The guard finishes tying the prisoner's ankles
and withdraws. The prisoner's bound feet squirming on the end of
the plank stand alone in the center of the frame.
25. MLS. XH/A. The POV of a log floating in the water below. Diagonal
slightly to follow the log.
26. MCU. Slight H/A. The prisoner with his head turned to the right
watches the floating log pass behind him. He faces front and closes his
eyes as the rising sun shines on his face.
27. XLS. L/A. The sun rising behind the hills. (Sounds of birds.)
28. MCU. Slight H/A. The officer turns to look over his shoulder at the
sunrise behind him, then faces front.
29. LS. H/A. The hanging party on the bridge is ready to proceed with
the execution. Their long shadows are visible. The sergeant replaces
the commanding officer on the plank opposite the prisoner. (Sounds
of birds.)

30. MCU. H/A. The feet of the sergeant on the plank (*a*). The camera pans right to the bound feet of the prisoner at the opposite end, then tilts up and zooms in slightly to CU of the prisoner's face. He closes his eyes (*b*). (A woman's name is faintly heard at the very end of the shot.)

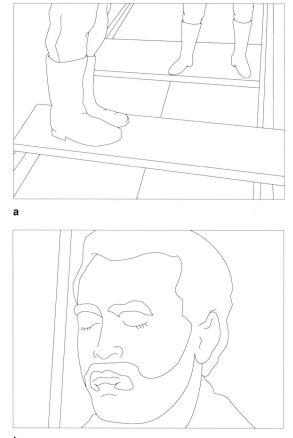

a

b

What are your impressions of the camera work in this sequence from AN OCCURRENCE AT OWL CREEK BRIDGE? Note your own observations before reading further.

First, consider how Enrico uses the camera to set the scene for AN OCCURRENCE AT OWL CREEK BRIDGE. The poster on the burnt tree in the first shot provides important information; it establishes the premise for the story and sets the time of the action. The place of action is the bridge, however; and the film's first problem is to connect the bridge with the poster. Enrico solves this problem over the next four shots by tracking the camera progressively closer to the bridge. But why does he use the tracking? Wouldn't a stationary camera in the four shots suffice? In fact, why use so many shots? Why not simply cut from the poster to the bridge? Or, better yet, connect them in the same shot, perhaps by pulling away from the poster to show it tacked right onto the bridge?

Enrico apparently intends to do more with the tracking than get us closer to the bridge. Indeed, shot #4 seems an anomaly in the opening series because it features a sentry, not the bridge. The tracking, therefore, rather than the bridge itself, actually unifies shots #2 through #5 because of its steady, relentless movement to the right, which ceases only when the camera is positioned in shot #5 to show clearly what is happening on the bridge. How does the camera's continuous tracking at the beginning of the film affect the audience? How does it help set the scene and introduce the action? Perhaps Enrico wants to make the spectator feel like he is happening upon this "occurrence" at the bridge.

Next, observe how camera angles and movements, apart from the content of shots, reinforce the apparently hopeless situation of the man about to be hanged. Low camera angles emphasize the strong positions held by soldiers—the sentry on the rock, the cannon on the high ground—while high angles stress the prisoner's desperate predicament. The slight tracking in shot #6 accentuates the soldiers' superior numbers, while the downward tilt in shot #22 drives home the prisoner's helplessness. Shot #30 recapitulates his plight by first panning across the plank from the sergeant's feet to the prisoner's, then tilting up and zooming in on his face.

At the same time, however, notice that the camera compels the viewer to identify with the prisoner's helplessness, not the soldiers' superiority. There are four **point-of-view shots** among the first thirty, all of which let us see through the condemned man's eyes. Shots from an objective vantage point dramatize his predicament as well. Shot #11 of the sergeant setting the noose, for instance, shows the rope up to the timbers from an extreme low angle as it will shortly appear to the prisoner, and further emphasizes the rope's function by framing the sergeant's face within the noose. Shots #13, #22, #24, and #30 all show at fairly close range the prisoner being prepared for hanging. Seven medium-close or close shots of the prisoner's face give the audience opportunities to build up sympathy for a human being about to die. On the other hand, the lieutenant's bored, impatient expression in shot #16, contrasted with the prisoner's anguish in the following shot, suggests the soldiers' callousness and makes the condemned man even more sympathetic.

Finally, notice how Enrico uses the camera to foreshadow the prisoner's fantasized escape, which occupies most of the rest of the film. Look closely at shots #17 through #20 in the shot description. Shots #17 and #19 are close-ups of the man turning his head left and right, which set up the point-of-view shots revealing what he sees when he looks from side to side. There is something peculiar about the camera movements in the point-of-view shots, however, which bears questioning. Both shot #18 and shot #20 track the camera toward the guards on the bridge with their backs turned. Why? The panning in shot #18 corresponds with the prisoner turning his head in shot #17. But how can we explain the tracking? The man is stationary, confined to the end of the plank; in fact, he is being bound at the knees and the ankles. Why, then, is the camera traveling from his vantage point? Are we seeing the prisoner's wishful thinking, his self-projection along possible escape routes? Is he thinking, "Only one guard to run past," ironically, just as his legs are being bound together?

Conclusion

As the beginning of AN OCCURRENCE AT OWL CREEK BRIDGE illustrates, the camera is not a passive instrument in film narrative, simply recording images that are pieced together into a story. On the contrary, the camera plays a vital, active role in the story-telling process. By carefully controlling camera positions, angles, and movements, film-makers are able to influence how the audience perceives and relates to images on the screen.

In an important essay about film esthetics Erwin Panofsky points out that the film spectator, although physically occupying a fixed seat, is esthetically "in permanent motion as his eye identifies itself with the lens of the camera, which permanently shifts in distance and direction. . . . Not only bodies move in space, but space itself does, approaching, receding, turning, dissolving and recrystallizing as it appears through the controlled locomotion and focusing of the camera. . ." (19). Thus, the motion picture camera opens up a world of narrative possibilities that the stage can never dream of and makes cinema enormously effective at stirring the emotions.

General Study Questions

1. Write a shot-by-shot description of a scene or sequence like the ones from HIGH NOON and AN OCCURRENCE AT OWL CREEK BRIDGE in this chapter, and analyze the camera techniques you observe.
2. Write a **film treatment** of an original movie scene. Include specific directions for camera positions, angles, and movements.

3. Compare and contrast camera style and technique in two films you have seen recently. Include references to specific scenes and sequences in each film.
4. Watch part of a film without sound and concentrate on camera work. Describe the camera techniques you observe and explain why the filmmaker employed them.
5. Study a scene that is partly or entirely photographed with a hand-held camera. Why did the filmmaker use a hand-held camera? How would the scene be different if the camera were not hand-held?
6. To move gradually closer to (or farther from) a subject in a continuous shot, a filmmaker may either zoom in (out) or dolly in (out). Compare and contrast how these techniques might affect the viewer. What are some advantages and disadvantages of each technique? Which technique would you say is more common today?
7. Look closely at the camera work in one of your favorite films. How have camera style and technique contributed to your enjoyment of the film?

Additional Films for Study

THE BIRTH OF A NATION (1915), dir. D.W. Griffith
THE LAST LAUGH (1924), dir. F.W. Murnau
STRIKE (1924), dir. Sergei Eisenstein
THE BLUE ANGEL (1930), dir. Josef von Sternberg
PUBLIC ENEMY (1931), dir. William Wellman
TRIUMPH OF THE WILL (1935), dir. Leni Riefenstahl
THE GRAND ILLUSION (1937), dir. Jean Renoir
GONE WITH THE WIND (1939), dir. Victor Fleming
THE MAGNIFICENT AMBERSONS (1942), dir. Orson Welles
OPEN CITY (1945), dir. Roberto Rossellini
ROPE (1948), dir. Alfred Hitchcock
THE THIRD MAN (1949), dir. Carol Reed
RASHOMON (1951), dir. Akira Kurosawa
ON THE WATERFRONT (1954), dir. Elia Kazan
REAR WINDOW (1954), dir. Alfred Hitchcock
THE MAGNIFICENT SEVEN (1960), dir. John Sturges
RED DESERT (1964), dir. Michelangelo Antonioni
JULIET OF THE SPIRITS (1965), dir. Federico Fellini
BONNIE AND CLYDE (1967), dir. Arthur Penn
MEDIUM COOL (1969), dir. Haskell Wexler
ONE FLEW OVER THE CUCKOO'S NEST (1975), dir. Miloš Forman
FANNY AND ALEXANDER (1983), dir. Ingmar Bergman
A PASSAGE TO INDIA (1984), dir. David Lean
FATAL ATTRACTION (1987), dir. Adrian Lyne
THE DEAD (1987), dir. John Huston

Further Reading

Alton, John. *Painting with Light.* New York: Macmillan, 1962.

Bacher, Lutz. *The Mobile Mise en Scène.* New York: Arno Press, 1978.

Clarke, Charles. *Professional Cinematography.* Hollywood, CA: American Society of Cinematographers, 1964.

Culhane, John. *Special Effects in the Movies: How Do They Do It?* New York: Ballantine, 1981.

Fielding, Raymond. *The Techniques of Special Effects Cinematography.* New York: Hastings House, 1965.

Halas, John, and Roger Manvell. *Design in Motion.* New York: Focal Press, 1962.

Higham, Charles, ed. *Hollywood Cameramen.* Bloomington: Indiana University Press, 1970.

Lindsay, Vachel. *The Art of Moving Pictures.* New York: Liveright, 1970.

Maltin, Leonard. *The Art of the Cinematographer.* New York: Dover, 1978.

———. *Behind the Camera: The Cinematographer's Art.* New York: New American Library, 1971.

Mascelli, Joseph. *The Five C's of Cinematography.* Hollywood, CA: Cine/Graphics, 1965.

Young, Freddie. *The World of the Motion Picture Cameraman.* New York: Hastings House, 1972.

Works Cited

Hitchcock, Alfred. "Direction." In *Film: A Montage of Theories,* edited by Richard Dyer MacCann, 53-61. New York: E.P. Dutton, 1966.

Panofsky, Erwin. "Style and Medium in the Motion Pictures." In *Film: An Anthology,* edited by Daniel Talbot, 15-32. Berkeley: University of California Press, 1972.

Lighting

Most **cinematographers** regard lighting as their most important tool, more crucial even than the camera itself. Nearly everyone realizes that a movie scene in a cozy cocktail lounge is not actually lit by shaded candles on the tables or by 100-watt bulbs in Tiffany lamps over the bar, even though a great deal of craftsmanship goes into making the scene look that way on the screen. Yet many viewers are barely conscious of the lighting as they watch such a scene. In fact, tens of thousands of watts illuminate a typical studio set. And even for outdoor scenes in broad daylight, filmmakers often augment **available light** with lamps or reflectors, diffuse and soften it with translucent **scrims**, or control it with **filters** on the camera lens.

Lighting Techniques

The main elements of film lighting are **key light**, the primary source of light in a shot, generally located to the side of the camera lens; **fill light**, located on the other side of the camera, which opposes and softens the shadows thrown by the key; and **background light**, which illuminates the background areas and adds depth. **Floodlights** and **spotlights** of various sizes and intensities produce the illumination. A **baby spot**, for example, has 500 to 1,000 watts of illuminating power; a **senior** (or **fiver**) has 5,000 watts. How a cinematographer arranges and balances such lights largely accounts for a film's visual appearance. Ultimately, film lighting determines what the viewer sees on the screen.

Styles of lighting are described in terms of key, fill, and background light. **High-key lighting** provides bright, uniform illumination that eliminates or softens shadows. **Low-key lighting**, on the other hand, provides less illumination and produces heavier shadows. **High-contrast lighting** cuts down the fill light drastically in relation to the key, producing harsher shadows and dramatic contrast between light and dark areas. More unusual lighting styles are created by manipulating foreground and background light. **Back lighting** directs light from the background toward the camera, producing an aura around objects or characters between the light source and the lens. **Limbo lighting** eliminates all background details and sets off the subject against featureless surroundings.

How does lighting affect the way the audience perceives a film image? Study the five photographs in figures 3.1-3.5, which illustrate the lighting techniques described in the previous paragraph. In each of the five shots a young woman is posed and framed the same way, with a pleasant expression on her face, looking directly at the camera lens. Her

How Do Films Tell a Story?

Figure 3.1
An example of high-key lighting.

Figure 3.2
An example of low-key lighting.

Figure 3.3
An example of high-contrast lighting.

Figure 3.4
An example of back lighting.

Figure 3.5
An example of limbo lighting.

physical appearance is the same from shot to shot; the only variable is the lighting. What differences do you observe in the woman's appearance in each of the five photographs? How do you react to the way she is lit in each shot? In what kinds of films would you expect to find each lighting technique? Write down your ideas before proceeding to the next paragraph.

The first photograph (fig. 3.1) is an example of high-key lighting. The subject's face is completely and evenly illuminated, with subtle shading on her left cheek and under her chin. Judging from the shadows on her hair and clothing, the key light is from slightly above and to the left of the camera lens. The background is evenly lit and provides some depth and physical context for the subject. The bright, smooth lighting makes the subject look friendly and forthright, perhaps even innocent and naive. We would not expect this shot to be from an especially dramatic or mysterious scene, but rather from one more relaxed and lighthearted.

The second photograph (fig. 3.2), an example of low-key lighting, shows the contours of the model's face better, creating darker shadows on her face and neck. The hint of shading on her chin and right cheek make her features look more sensual and mature. The key light still hits the subject from above and to the left of the lens, but this time the gradation of shading on the fill side of the image is greater, ranging from light gray to almost black. The background is also much darker than in the previous photo. The woman in this image shows more personality, more depth. Her gaze seems more intense, more penetrating. She appears somewhat mysterious, almost the *femme fatale.* We might expect this shot to be in a more tense and dramatic scene, perhaps in a *film noir.*

The third photograph (fig. 3.3) displays high-contrast lighting, with a very sharp demarcation between bright light and dark shadow down the middle of the model's face. There is little or no fill light here from the right side of the camera to mitigate the heavy shadows thrown by the strong key on the left. Consequently, the fill side of the woman's face remains virtually in darkness, except for faint highlights on her left cheekbone and forehead. The woman in this picture is no longer simply mysterious; she is eerie, perhaps frightening. Such stark contrast of light and dark on the human face is visually and emotionally disturbing. Is the woman in this picture a creature of violent extremes? Is she emotionally troubled? Is she schizophrenic? Questions like these, which would not occur to us with the first two photographs, seem reasonable and appropriate with the third. We might expect a shot like this in a psychological thriller.

The fourth photograph (fig. 3.4) is an example of back lighting, also sometimes called **Rembrandt lighting,** after the seventeenth-century Dutch painter, Rembrandt van Rijn, whose portraits are characterized by soft light emanating from behind the person in the picture. In this photograph, light from behind and slightly above the model illuminates her hair, producing halo-like highlights on one side of her head and deepening the shadows on the other. Back lighting makes the woman look more ethereal and romantic here than in the previous pictures by softening the outline of her image with an aura of light. It is apparent why Rembrandt lighting is a common technique, especially in Hollywood films of the 1930s and 1940s, for making movie queens appear more romantic and glamorous on the screen. We might expect lighting like this for the **ingenue** in a tale of romance.

In the last photograph (fig. 3.5), an example of limbo lighting, there is no background light at all. The model is isolated against a completely dark field. Limbo lighting eliminates any physical setting and **depth of field** from the image. In the previous photographs the background did not supply much detail, but enough for the viewer to perceive the subject within a recognizable context. Background details, moreover, provide tangible reference points for the eye to measure space around the subject. So how do we perceive the woman in the photo without spacial references and depth of field? On the one hand, it is more difficult to form a solid impression of her without spacial context and background detail. But on the other hand, we sense that this person is somehow special because she is isolated from her surroundings—like a spotlighted celebrity on a dark stage. Consequently, we may be predisposed to expect extraordinary behavior from the character in such a shot.

In figures 3.1-3.5 the balance between key and fill light or between foreground and background light varies, but the location and the arrangement of the light sources are fairly consistent for all the shots. The key light and fill light illuminate the subject in each instance from conventional positions and angles, that is, from beside the camera (at about 45-degree angles to the line of the shot) and from above the subject (at about a 45-degree angle of incline). Occasionally, however, filmmakers create highly dramatic lighting effects by directing light from unorthodox positions and angles. In the four photographs in figures 3.6-3.9, the key light hits the subject from almost directly above, below, in front, and behind. Note the lighting effects in these photos before reading further.

In movies, lighting is normally directed from a high angle because it looks more natural on the screen, softening the contours of the face and casting shadows downward where they are less obtrusive. But when lighting is from a sharp overhead angle (fig. 3.6), it conspicuously illuminates the top of the head, washes out most facial modeling, and casts heavy shadows under the nose and chin. Sometimes filmmakers use overhead lighting to suggest spirituality, as if a beam of heavenly light is

Figure 3.6
An example of lighting from above the model.

Figure 3.7
An example of lighting from below the model.

singling out the character in the shot. Conversely, when light shines upward on a face at a sharp angle (fig. 3.7), the features appear distorted, with heavy, unnatural shadows that make the face appear sinister or grotesque on film.

Lighting from directly in front of a character (fig. 3.8) flattens the contours of a face and shows it rather unflatteringly. That is why lights are normally aimed from beside the camera—to accentuate the depth and roundness of the face—and why frontal lighting is uncommon in movies. Light from directly behind a character (fig. 3.9), on the other hand, is more common and is used to create a silhouette against a bright light shining straight toward the camera. Back light, however, is not ordinarily the primary source of light in a shot, but rather an accessory to enhance and accent an image or to create the Rembrandt effect.

Lighting Effects

For cinematographers there are three important elements of film lighting: the direction, the intensity, and the diffusion of light on the shooting set. They know that by controlling these three variables they can create many different effects with the lighting techniques we have just described. For

How Do Films Tell a Story?

Figure 3.8

An example of lighting from in front of the model.

Figure 3.9

An example of lighting from behind the model.

instance, compare two examples of conspicuous back lighting (figs. 3.10 and 3.11): one from Orson Welles's CITIZEN KANE (1941) with cinematographer Gregg Toland, and the other from Tobe Hooper's POLTERGEIST (1982) with cinematographer Matthew F. Leonetti. The lighting technique is basically the same in each instance: strong back light silhouettes characters in the shot to the extent that their facial features are barely distinguishable. Yet, even without knowing the context of these two shots, we perceive that the one from POLTERGEIST is more startling and disturbing than the one from CITIZEN KANE. Why? Jot down your ideas before going on to the next paragraph.

Close observation reveals important differences in how the filmmakers employ back lighting in these two shots. There are three sources of light in the CITIZEN KANE shot—two in the background and one in the middleground—which direct light at different angles toward the edges of the frame (fig. 3.10). But there is only one source of light in the POLTERGEIST shot, which is aimed directly toward the camera lens (fig. 3.11). We feel that the back light is more forceful in the second shot, where one bright light shines straight at us, than in the first shot, where light from several sources is diffused away from the lens. Moreover, we can

Figure 3.10

An example of back lighting in CITIZEN KANE, where light is diffused toward the edges of the frame.

identify the sources of light in the CITIZEN KANE shot (a gooseneck desk lamp in the middleground and a film projection booth in the background); but we cannot easily identify the source of the unnaturally intense light in the POLTERGEIST shot.

Furthermore, the arrangement of the characters within the frame complements the back lighting in each shot and influences how we react to it. The two men in CITIZEN KANE are positioned in the middle of the frame with open space around them, helping to disperse the beams of light toward the outside of the frame. In POLTERGEIST, on the other hand, the three characters are like a wedge knifing into the light. The foreground figures fill the sides of the frame, channeling the beam of light into the center. The postures and gestures of the characters also indicate more emotional tension in this shot than in the first. The seated

Figure 3.11
An example of back lighting in POLTER-GEIST, where light is channeled straight toward the camera lens.

man in CITIZEN KANE appears at ease as the standing man addresses him. But the defensive posture of the man closest to the light in POL-TERGEIST and the tense body language of the foreground characters (clutching a rope that extends through the door into the light) communicate duress or desperation. We sense that the characters in POLTERGEIST are fighting against the light, while the characters in CITIZEN KANE are casually disregarding it.

Finally, the light is softer in the CITIZEN KANE shot because it is more diffused. The desk lamp in the middleground partially illuminates the seated man and the coffee cups on the table beside him, thereby softening his silhouette and suggesting a casual working atmosphere in the scene. Cigarette smoke in the air also helps diffuse the light. In the POLTERGEIST shot, however, there is nothing except the bodies of the characters to mitigate the harsh back light.

Figure 3.12

An example of lighting effects in JULES AND JIM.

By carefully controlling the direction, intensity, and diffusion of light in these two shots, the filmmakers are able to produce strikingly different effects with back lighting. The shot from POLTERGEIST is startling and disturbing because Tobe Hooper and Matthew Leonetti create the impression that the intense light from behind the door is very threatening.

Sometimes subtleties of light and shadow in film lighting not only create impressions but also convey important information. Consider the two examples in figures 3.12 and 3.13: from François Truffaut's JULES AND JIM (1961) with cinematographer Raoul Coutard, and from Ingmar Bergman's THE SEVENTH SEAL (1956) with cinematographer Gunnar Fischer.

Figure 3.13
An example of lighting
effects in THE SEVENTH
SEAL.

In the first shot (fig. 3.12) Truffaut sets the young woman on the right of the frame apart from the two men on the left. She is more in the foreground than they are, dressed and posed more conspicuously, and more prominently lit. How can we account for the fact that she is completely illuminated while the men are in shadows? There is strong back lighting in this scene, which casts long shadows in front of the characters, darkens the facial features of the two men, and creates an aura around the woman's head. But there is also a second important source of light in the scene, in the foreground, which selectively illuminates the woman. From the setting, we easily deduce that the light sources here are city street lamps. One lamp provides the back light; another illuminates the woman, who enters the lighted area several steps ahead of the two men.

In the shot from THE SEVENTH SEAL (fig. 3.13), on the other hand, there is a subtle anomaly in the lighting that needs explication. The two characters at the chessboard are seated on a rocky beach as the sun rises over the sea. Judging from the shadows on the knight's face and body, the light source is off screen to the left of and behind the characters. Yet the man in black on the left with his back to the sun has no shadows on his face. We also note that the white chess pieces are prominently illuminated where they should be shadowed. How can we account for these inconsistencies? Why is Bergman lighting the scene this way? Since there is no other apparent source of light in the scene, like a torch or a campfire, we infer that "unnatural" light is illuminating the character on the left and the white chess pieces. Bergman wants the lighting to look unnatural in this scene because the knight in THE SEVENTH SEAL is playing chess with Death, personified as the character in black.

Truffaut and Bergman employ special lighting effects in these shots to highlight one character in the scene. The technique is the same for both: Selective foreground light fully illuminates one character in the shot while others are in shadows cast by prominent back light.

a

b

Figure 3.14
Two examples of interior lighting in GREAT EXPECTATIONS.

But the effect of the lighting in each instance is different because the viewer recognizes that the foreground light in JULES AND JIM emanates from a natural light source (a street lamp), whereas the light in THE SEVENTH SEAL is a preternatural light.

> As an exercise, compare and contrast lighting effects in the stills (figs. 3.14 and 3.15) from GREAT EXPECTATIONS (1946), directed by David Lean and photographed by Guy Green. Which scenes most attract your attention with lighting? What reactions do you think David Lean wanted to evoke in these scenes? What differences do you note between the lighting of the interior scenes and the exterior scenes?

Visual Tone

A film's visual tone—its "look"—is the overall mood or atmosphere it projects, which is largely a matter of lighting. A scene may be made to look bright or somber, lighthearted or tense, by toning up or toning down the lighting. Cinematographer John Arnold offers this illustration:

> Consider a very simple scene: a bedroom in which a sick child lies while its mother keeps a constant vigil. If this scene be presented in sombre tones with long menacing shadows on the screen, you feel at once

 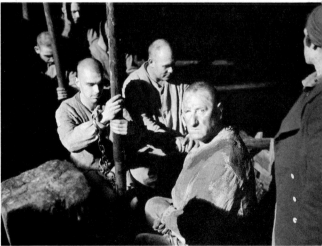

a   b

Figure 3.15
Two examples of exterior lighting in GREAT EXPECTATIONS.

that the child is gravely ill and may never recover. If, on the other hand, the room is in lighter tones, with the sunlight streaming through the windows and a cheerful sparkle evident everywhere, instinct tells you the crisis has passed, and that the child is on the road to recovery.
(171)

Consider the visual tone in the three stills in figures 3.16-3.18: from Orson Welles's CITIZEN KANE (1941) with cinematographer Gregg Toland, from Sam Peckinpah's STRAW DOGS (1971) with cinematographer John Coquillon, and from Fritz Lang's M (1931) with cinematographers Fritz Arno Wagner and Gustav Rathje. What can you observe about the lighting in each of these shots and how it helps create a distinctive visual tone? Note your observations before you read the following discussion.

The shot from CITIZEN KANE (fig. 3.16) is an example of low-key **area lighting.** The two characters are highlighted in separate pools of light. The floor lamp on the right illuminates the man lounging in the wicker chair; the table lamp partially visible on the left edge of the frame lights the woman seated at the piano. A third source of light, an overhead lamp above the canopy bed behind the woman, lights the back of the set. Furnishings in the room around these three lamps are appropriately lit; the rest of the room is in shadows. If we look closely, however, we notice that studio lamps are also used to illuminate the set. The heavy shadow of the wicker chair on the side wall, for example, cannot be cast by the floor lamp. Nor is the table lamp on the left strong enough (since it barely illuminates the woman's hair) to produce such a hard-edged shadow from across the room. The chair's shadow results from studio spotlights positioned off screen to illuminate that area of the boudoir. Nevertheless, the filmmakers create the impression here that the room is lit entirely by the three lamps we see in the shot.

This shot from CITIZEN KANE conveys intimacy. The characters are quiet and relaxed. The room is profusely decorated with furnishings that absorb and diffuse light, rather than reflect it. Soft lighting creates gentle gradations of light and shadow around the room, and pools of light on the ceiling give the room a warm, cozy glow. There is nothing harsh to detract from the scene's relaxed, romantic mood.

Harsh, on the other hand, is the very word to describe the mood conveyed in the shot from STRAW DOGS (fig. 3.17). This scene is quite tense and claustrophobic, since the man in the middle (with glasses) is backed against the wall by two armed men who have apparently invaded his bedroom. Peckinpah and Coquillon employ high-key lighting on a

Figure 3.16
An example of low-key
lighting in CITIZEN KANE.

stark set to create the harsh tone in this scene. The small table lamp beside
the window throws hard, glaring light, which is intensified as it reflects off
the coarse stone wall and the threatened man's light-colored shirt. There
is another lamp in the room, just off screen to the right, which creates the
severe, sinister shadow of the man with the shotgun. The filmmakers also
use studio lighting to illuminate this scene, but we can barely detect it in
the shot.

In the shot from M (fig. 3.18) the man cornered in the
lower right of the frame also appears threatened, but we do not sympathize with him as we do with the bespectacled man in the shot from
STRAW DOGS. He is not confronted with a knife and a shotgun but with

Lighting

Figure 3.17

An example of high-key lighting in STRAW DOGS.

a toy balloon, shaped like a small child, held by a harmless old man. So why should he be horror-stricken? The terrified expression on his face and in his hands suggests that he is a guilty man whose misdeeds have suddenly come to light. Beginning with his face, we "read" the scene along the diagonal, from the lower right foreground to the upper left background, noting first the blind man with the balloon (who divides the frame in half vertically) and then the two burly men in the background guarding the stairs. The frame is also divided horizontally: The blind man and the cornered man stand face to face in the lower half of the frame; the balloon and the two heavies on the stairs occupy the upper half. Thus *mise en scène* in this shot focuses the viewer's attention on the predicament of the guilty man trapped in the corner.

Figure 3.18

An example of high-contrast lighting in M.

This shot from M is ominous and rather mysterious, suggesting that a moment of reckoning is at hand. It is illuminated with high-contrast lighting that dramatically isolates and highlights a few salient details within the frame—faces, hands, the toy balloon—but leaves the rest of the set in heavy shadows. The most important image in the shot is the balloon. It is prominently positioned in the center of the frame and glows with an aura of light. Its reflective surface makes it more luminous than anything else in the frame. The dramatic camera and lighting techniques here clearly indicate that this balloon has some special power over the cornered man.

Each of the shots in figures 3.16, 3.17, and 3.18 illustrates a different style of lighting to achieve a distinctive visual tone: The shot from CITIZEN KANE uses low-key area lighting to create a cozy atmosphere; the shot from STRAW DOGS uses stark high-key lighting to create a threatening atmosphere; the shot from M uses evocative high-contrast lighting to create an ominous atmosphere.

Another way to describe the visual tone in these stills is to say that the CITIZEN KANE shot is **realistic,** the STRAW DOGS shot is **naturalistic,** and the M shot is **expressionistic.** These styles of lighting, and the terms used to describe them, will be covered again from a different perspective in unit 3 of *Frameworks*. (The distinctions between realistic and expressionistic lighting are discussed at length in chapter 9; naturalistic lighting is examined in chapter 10.)

Conclusion

To illustrate how lighting can affect the appearance of photographic images, Siegfried Kracauer in *Theory of Film* describes a fascinating experiment in which the German photographer Helmar Lerski shot more than one hundred close-up pictures of a young man's face, each time subtly changing the lighting with the aid of screens. "The result was amazing," says Kracauer. "None of the photographs recalled the model; and all of them differed from each other. Out of the original face there arose, evoked by the varying lights, a hundred different faces, among them those of a hero, a prophet, a peasant, a dying soldier, an old woman, a monk" (162). By subtly varying the direction, intensity, or diffusion of light, cinematic photography can also evoke a hundred different faces for a movie character. Accomplished filmmakers and cinematographers recognize this truth; accomplished film viewers learn to recognize the amazing results of it on the screen.

General Study Questions

1. Choose a film from the Additional Films for Study at the end of this chapter and analyze the lighting techniques and lighting style employed in three key scenes.
2. Select a movie scene that features special lighting effects and describe how the filmmaker controls the direction, intensity, and diffusion of light to create those effects.
3. Compare and contrast visual tone in two films directed by the same filmmaker.

4. How is lighting in a color film different from lighting in a black-and-white film? When is lighting most effective in a black-and-white film? In a color film? Cite examples from movies you know.
5. Develop a workable thesis statement for a paper that addresses this question: How does lighting help a filmmaker reveal a movie character's personality? Make a list of film scenes you might use in such a paper.
6. The three examples of visual tone in this chapter (from CITIZEN KANE, STRAW DOGS, and M) are interior scenes that are illuminated with artificial light. How differently would these scenes look and "feel" if they were (apparently) lit instead by daylight from a window or skylight? Based on your response, generalize about how audiences respond to movie scenes lit with natural lighting rather than artificial lighting.

Additional Films for Study

NOSFERATU (1922), dir. F.W. Murnau
METROPOLIS (1926), dir. Fritz Lang
IT HAPPENED ONE NIGHT (1934), dir. Frank Capra
THE GRAPES OF WRATH (1946), dir. John Ford
BEAUTY AND THE BEAST (1946), dir. Jean Cocteau
LADY FROM SHANGHAI (1948), dir. Orson Welles
SUNSET BOULEVARD (1950), dir. Billy Wilder
WILD STRAWBERRIES (1957), dir. Ingmar Bergman
THRONE OF BLOOD (1957), dir. Akira Kurosawa
THE 400 BLOWS (1959), dir. François Truffaut
SUDDENLY LAST SUMMER (1959), dir. Joseph Mankiewicz
LAWRENCE OF ARABIA (1962), dir. David Lean
WOMAN IN THE DUNES (1964), dir. Hiroshi Teshigahara
JULIET OF THE SPIRITS (1965), dir. Federico Fellini
MIDNIGHT COWBOY (1969), dir. John Schlesinger
CRIES AND WHISPERS (1972), dir. Ingmar Bergman
CHINATOWN (1974), dir. Roman Polanski
BARRY LYNDON (1975), dir. Stanley Kubrick
TAXI DRIVER (1975), dir. Martin Scorsese
BODY HEAT (1981), dir. Lawrence Kasdan
THE BOAT (1982), dir. Wolfgang Petersen
BLADE RUNNER (1982), dir. Ridley Scott
E.T. THE EXTRA-TERRESTRIAL (1982), dir. Steven Spielberg
PLATOON (1986), dir. Oliver Stone
ALIENS (1986), dir. James Cameron

Further Reading

Alton, John. *Painting with Light*. New York: Macmillan, 1962.

Fielding, Raymond. *The Technique of Special Effects Cinematography*. New York: Hastings House, 1965.

Maltin, Leonard. *The Art of the Cinematographer*. New York: Dover, 1978.

Millerson, Gerald. *Techniques of Lighting for Motion Pictures and Television*. New York: Hastings House, 1972.

Nilsen, Vladimir. *The Cinema as Graphic Art*. New York: Hill and Wang, 1959.

Works Cited

Arnold, John. Quoted in *We Make the Movies,* edited by Nancy Naumberg. London: Faber and Faber, 1938.

Kracauer, Siegfried. *Theory of Film*. New York: Oxford University Press, 1960.

Editing

I n the early 1920s Lev Kuleshov, a Russian filmmaker, conducted a classic film experiment. He photographed a close-up of an actor with a neutral expression on his face and intercut it with shots of a bowl of soup, a woman in a coffin, and a child playing with a toy bear. When audiences saw the shots edited together as a film, they praised the actor's sensitive responses to the different emotional stimuli. They saw hunger, grief, and affection on the actor's face even though it was expressionless.

The Impact of Editing

The famous "Kuleshov effect" dramatizes a filmmaker's tremendous power to suggest meaning to the viewer by juxtaposing images. In Kuleshov's film audiences saw emotions that were created not by the actor but by the filmmaker. Neither the bowl of soup alone, nor the actor's face, suggested hunger; but the combination of the two images communicated that meaning.

Theoretically, a filmmaker can connect any two images by simply splicing together two pieces of film. And sometimes directors can overwhelm viewers with a single dramatic cut that connects two startling images. For instance, in David Lean's LAWRENCE OF ARABIA (1962), edited by Anne V. Coates, there is a dazzling cut from an extinguished match to a magnificent desert sunrise. But such editing is not arbitrary. There are usually quite specific reasons why certain images can be cut together effectively and others cannot. This chapter will explore some of those reasons.

Montage, from the French word for "mounting," means to assemble film images by editing them together. Among film scholars and critics the term usually means editing that to some degree calls attention to the disjunction between shots, and sometimes the term is used to describe specific styles or techniques of editing. **American montage** or **Hollywood montage** refers to editing that condenses or summarizes many events in a few shots, as a quick succession of newspaper headlines in a vintage Hollywood gangster movie might recap a string of gangland murders. **Russian montage,** on the other hand, refers to the dynamic cutting techniques of prominent Soviet directors in the 1920s—primarily Pudovkin, Eisenstein, and Vertov—who used editing to evoke strong emotional, and even physical, reactions to images on the screen. We will examine this kind of dynamic montage later in the chapter. But first we will discuss **narrative montage**—editing that constructs a story with film images by arranging shots in carefully sequenced order.

How Do Films Tell a Story?

Narrative Montage

RAIDERS OF THE LOST ARK (1981), directed by Steven Spielberg and edited by Michael Kahn, is an excellent film to study for narrative montage. Here is one scene as an example: After many preliminary adventures, the hero of the film, Indiana Jones (Harrison Ford), unearths the Ark of the Covenant at an archaeological site in Egypt, right under the noses of Nazi soldiers and an unscrupulous archaeologist named Belloq (Paul Freeman), who want it for the Führer. The Nazis eventually take the Ark from Jones, crate it up, and transport it away by truck. A squad of soldiers travels with the Ark in the back of the truck, and an armored vehicle with a machine-gun mount follows behind it. Belloq and a Nazi officer lead the way in an open staff car. Indiana Jones sets out alone on horseback in pursuit of this armed convoy and, in one of the most action-filled scenes in the film, leaps aboard the truck and takes control of it. He fights off the soldiers who try to recapture the truck and forces the escort vehicles off the road. This scene takes about seven minutes of screen time and more than two hundred shots. It employs minimal dialogue.

To understand how narrative montage works in this scene, let's isolate one sequence and examine it closely—beginning when Jones leaps aboard the truck and ending when he forces the driver out. This sequence lasts fifty seconds and contains the following thirty-four shots. (Five of the shot descriptions are accompanied by actual Lucasfilm storyboard drawings used to plan each shot in this sequence.)

1. LS. Slight L/A. Traveling shot from in front of and to the left of the truck transporting the Ark of the Covenant. Indiana Jones gallops alongside, leaps onto the truck, and works his way forward to the running board on the passenger side.
2. MCU. Inside the truck from the driver's side, showing the driver in the f/g, a second soldier riding guard in the m/g, and Jones outside the passenger door in the b/g. Jones opens the door and pulls the guard out of the truck. Cut on action.
3. (Shot #1 continued.) The guard tumbles out of the truck to the ground.
4. MCU. H/A inside the back of the truck toward the rear. Out of the open back of the truck, one soldier sees the guard rolling on the ground and turns determinedly toward the cab.
5. (Shot #2 continued.) Jones lurches at the driver, grabs him in a headlock, punches him, and struggles for the steering wheel.
6. LS. On the ground beside the road. The staff car and the truck round a curve in the road and approach the camera at high speed. The truck swerves and bumps through the turn.

7. LS. R/A. The staff car and the truck from behind, swerving among pedestrian traffic on the road.

INDY AND DRIVER FIGHTING FOR CONTROL...

8. (Shot #5 continued.) Jones and the driver fight for control of the truck. Jones looks up at the road and grabs for the steering wheel.

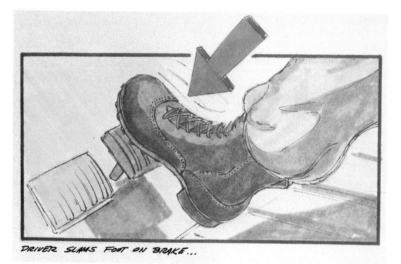

DRIVER SLAMS FOOT ON BRAKE...

9. CU. H/A. The driver slams down the truck's brake pedal.
10. MS. Slight H/A from in front of the truck's windshield. Jones and the driver, locked together in struggle, are thrown forward into the windshield.
11. MLS. L/A from the roadside. Side view of the truck braking abruptly and skidding forward. Camera pans left to follow the truck.

INT: TRUCK C.U. ARC BOX – SLIDES AWAY FROM CAM AS CREW TUMBLES EVERYWHERE... EQUIPMENT AND DEBRIS SLIDE TOWARD FRONT OF TRUCK...

12. MS. Slight H/A from outside the back of the truck. The men in the back of the truck and the crated Ark slide forward as the truck brakes.
13. MS. Slight L/A from in front of the follow car's windshield. The soldiers react to the truck's sudden braking.
14. MLS. POV through the follow car's windshield shows the truck braking suddenly in front of it.
15. MLS. From the roadside. The follow car slams into the rear of the truck.

INDY KICKS DRIVER'S FOOT OFF BRAKE... THEN...

16. CU. H/A. (Like shot #9.) Jones kicks the driver's foot off the brake pedal and steps down on the accelerator.

17. MCU. From in front of the truck's windshield. Jones and the driver are thrown back against the seat as the truck suddenly accelerates.

ARC SLIDES TO REAR OF TRUCK - STRIKES CREW-MAN WHO IS CATAPAULTED OUT...

18. MLS. From inside the back of the truck toward the rear, showing the crate in the f/g, a soldier standing behind it in the m/g, and the follow car close behind in the b/g. As the truck accelerates, the standing soldier at the back of the truck is knocked off balance.

19. MLS. L/A traveling shot beside the vehicles. The off-balance soldier flies off the back of the truck onto the hood of the follow car and crashes through the windshield.

20. MS. Traveling beside the staff car. Belloq and the Nazi officer look over their shoulders toward the truck weaving behind them.

21. CU. Inside the staff car. The Nazi officer turns his head toward the front.

22. MS. The Nazi officer's POV through the windshield of the staff car. Building construction very close to the road looms ahead on the right. The car swerves left to avoid hitting it.

23. MLS. From the roadside opposite the construction, showing high wooden scaffolding and ladders teeming with workers. Construction materials clutter the f/g. The camera pans left with the staff car, which speeds through the building site, narrowly missing a worker beside the road.

24. MCU. From in front of the truck's windshield. Jones and the driver continue struggling for the wheel. Jones looks up at the road and reacts to the obstruction he sees ahead.

25. LS. POV through the truck's windshield of the scaffolding directly ahead.

26. (Shot #24 continued.) Jones tries to keep the truck from smashing into the scaffolding.

27. LS. From the roadside opposite and ahead of the construction site. The approaching truck sideswipes the scaffolding and topples building materials and workers in the truck's path.

28. (Shot #26 continued.) One worker in a white turban and striped burnoose falls against the truck's windshield, facing Jones and the driver.

29. CU. R/A from inside the truck. POV from behind the wheel of the worker's astonished face.

30. (Shot #28 continued.) Jones and the driver stop fighting and look at each other, chuckling at the worker's comic facial expression.

31. MCU. Inside the truck from the passenger side. View from behind Jones as he prepares to sock the driver while he is off guard. Cut on action.

32. MCU. From in front of the truck's windshield. Jones punches the driver. Cut on action.

33. LS. L/A from the side of the road. The driver is knocked out of the truck and falls over a ledge beside the road.

34. CU. Inside the truck from the driver's side. Jones slams the door shut, looks back briefly over his shoulder, then turns forward and drives on.

How does a filmmaker combine thirty-four shots, averaging slightly more than one second each, into a complex visual narrative like the scene just described? What editing techniques have Spielberg and Kahn employed in this sequence to make its meaning clear and cohesive to the viewer? Before reading further, analyze this sequence for yourself. Write down your observations about the organization, logic, and flow of these thirty-four shots.

Notice that shots within this sequence from RAIDERS OF THE LOST ARK are grouped in sets. The first eight shots, for instance, establish the main action of the sequence: Jones's struggle with the driver for control of the truck. The first shot, appropriately, is from outside the truck as Jones leaps on the side of it. Shots #2, #5, and #8 depict the struggle inside the cab of the truck from the driver's side. Other outside shots are interspersed to show Jones pulling the guard out the passenger door (shot #3) and to show the truck swerving on the road as Jones and the driver fight over the wheel (shots #6 and #7).

Also notice that Spielberg and Kahn provide at least two views of every important action. In shot #2 from inside the truck, Jones pulls the guard out of the cab, but we watch the guard fly out the door from outside the truck in shot #3. Then we see him rolling on the ground from the back of the truck in shot #4.

Shot #8 provides a transition to the next phase of Jones's struggle to commandeer the truck, depicted in shots #9 through #19, in which Spielberg and Kahn provide a dash of cinematic cause and effect. When the driver slams on the brakes, he and Jones fly against the windshield; when Jones accelerates, they are thrown back against the seat. Naturally, this sudden braking and accelerating also affects the men in the back of the truck and in the armored vehicle following closely behind. After the driver hits the brakes in shot #9, we observe over the next six shots separate effects on Jones and the driver (shot #10), on the soldiers in the back of the truck (shot #12), on the men in the follow car (shots #13 and #14), and on the two vehicles themselves (shots #11 and #15). After Jones accelerates in shot #16, three shots show Jones and the driver thrown against the seat and the soldier toppled off the back of the truck. Thus, the cause-and-effect pattern is repeated twice, each time with violent events succeeding like a chain reaction from the front of the truck into the follow vehicle, concluding the second time with the soldier from the back of the truck crashing through the follow car's windshield.

Shots #20 through #30 depict another phase of the action: the near-collision with the construction scaffolding beside the road. Shots #20 and #21 provide a transition from the previous action, since Belloq and the officer in the staff car are looking back at the truck. When they turn frontward, they suddenly notice the construction site ahead. Shot #22, from the point of view of the Nazi officer, allows the audience a quick glimpse of the obstacles ahead. Shot #23, from the ground, shows the staff car speeding through the construction area, narrowly avoiding a collision.

Construction materials in the foreground of the shot and the camera's panning action emphasize the clutter in the area and suggest the hazard it poses for the truck. If the staff car barely made it through, how will the truck avoid crashing, with the two men fighting over the wheel? Appropriately, the cut back to the truck is from the outside, showing Jones's reaction through the windshield (shot #24). Then we see the scaffolding from inside the cab (shot #25). Shot #27 shows the truck sideswiping the scaffolds and the workers toppled off the ladders. Shot #28 reinforces the previous shot more specifically: *one* worker lands against the windshield. Shot #29 shows the worker from inside the cab, as Jones and the driver notice his stunned expression. We see their shared amusement, from in front of the windshield again, in shot #30.

The last four shots of the sequence show how Jones finally knocks the driver out the door and takes control of the truck. Notice that Spielberg uses two shots to depict the final blow. From inside the truck in shot #31, we see Jones cocked for the punch; but, after a **cut on action,** we watch him deliver it from outside the windshield in shot #32. We see the result of the blow from a third position, on the ground below the level of the roadway, as the driver rolls out of the truck and over the steep edge of the road. In the final shot (#34) Jones concludes the action of this sequence when he slams the door shut; then he faces forward and grits his teeth for new business ahead.

Let us summarize our observations about the editing in this sequence from RAIDERS OF THE LOST ARK. First, the sequence is subdivided into short, cohesive series of shots that systematically break down and develop the action. Spielberg and Kahn piece the film story together by combining small groups of shots into larger groups. Several series build a sequence, sequences build a scene, scenes build the movie.

Second, the sequence depicts actions from more than one vantage point: from inside and outside the truck, from objective and subjective points of view, from stationary and traveling camera positions. Some actions, like the *coup de grâce* Jones delivers in shots #31 and #32, begin from one vantage point and conclude from another.

Third, there is definite continuity in the sequence, even though the action is complex and has been photographed from many angles. Spielberg and Kahn maintain this continuity by repeating a few basic shot patterns through the sequence. For example, during the braking maneuver in shots #9 through #19, they use the cause-and-effect pattern twice to depict actions happening simultaneously in several locations. They also combine **point-of-view shots, reaction shots,** and objective shots to depict each important action in the sequence, as in shots #24 through #27 where Indiana Jones notices the building site beside the road.

Finally, the sequence provides clear transitions between actions in the sequence. The head positions and movements of Belloq and the Nazi officer in shots #20 and #21, for example, provide a visual transition that "looks back" at the action with the truck in the previous series and then "looks ahead" to the next action with the construction scaffolding. Likewise, Jones's head turn in shot #34 concludes the struggle with the driver of the truck and begins the battle with the soldiers in the back, which will be the main business of the next sequence.

Maintaining continuity of action where it is meant to be continuous and providing transitions where there are meant to be breaks in action are two major concerns of narrative montage. The next two sections of this chapter, therefore, will focus on continuity and transitions in film editing.

Continuity

Since, theoretically at least, any two images can be cut together in a movie, the film medium has tremendous potential for manipulating time and space. By simply splicing pieces of film together, a filmmaker can make different time periods and locations, characters and situations, appear together on the screen. Unlike a live stage production, a film need not interrupt the action to shift scenery or change costumes, nor dim the lights or drop the curtain to cover a scene change. In cinema, time and place can change instantaneously.

This tremendous ability to manipulate time and space raises two fundamental questions about cinematic narrative. On the one hand, if a scene is cut up into many shots, how can the filmmaker be certain that the audience will understand where time and space are meant to be continuous? And on the other hand, when a jump in time or a change of place is intended, how can the filmmaker be certain the audience will understand that such a change has indeed taken place?

These questions may seem naive and simplistic because most of the time continuity within scenes and transitions between them are determined by the setting. Directors often begin a scene with an **establishing shot,** which gives the audience an overview of the setting. As long as the visual context remains within that setting, the scene is continuous; and when it changes, the scene has changed. On the other hand, visual context alone may not always be enough to sustain a scene's continuity for the audience. Close-ups, for example, isolate details from their surroundings and sometimes make it difficult for the viewer to determine what time and space those details occupy.

There are basic editing techniques and conventions that help filmmakers maintain continuity in movies. This section of the chapter deals with some of them.

Continuity Editing: A Simulation

Imagine that you are a film editor assigned to cut the following scenario so that the audience will be able to understand the film story without any dialogue. We will assume that the scene has been photographed from enough angles and that you have enough footage to edit it any way you like. This is the scenario:

An office worker wants to leave his job a few hours early so that he can arrive home before his wife and surprise her with a special dinner for their first wedding anniversary. He is eager to bolt from the office; consequently, he concentrates poorly on his work, and time seems to drag. At exactly 3:00 p.m. he leaves work and drives off in his car. He runs several errands on the way—for wine, flowers, pastry, etc.—and arrives home about an hour later. He is relaxed and enjoying the surprise he has planned. With packages and bags of groceries in his arms, he lets himself in the front door. But inside he is stopped cold. His home has been broken into and burglarized. He notices an open window, desk drawers rifled, an empty space on the bookshelves where the tape deck used to stand. He walks down three steps into the living room, drops his packages on the couch, and begins to survey the losses. After a quick look around the home, he returns to the living room and is about to call the police.

Suddenly, the man is startled by shuffling noises outside the front door and stands frozen with the phone in his hand. He hears someone fumbling with the lock and is afraid that the burglar has returned. Then the door swings open, and his wife enters, also home early with special groceries in her arms. The end of the scene features the expressions on their faces. He is relieved to see his wife at the door, not an intruder. She is startled to find her husband home, then notices his packages on the couch, and finally takes in the burgled living room. They both react to the anniversary surprise.

Before reading on, plan how you might edit this scenario. This exercise will be more useful if you write down at least a rough outline of shots before you consider the suggestions in the following paragraphs.

Although "The Anniversary Surprise" is relatively straightforward, several basic editing problems will need to be addressed in order to maintain continuity in this scene. How would you begin to organize the cutting here? Your first observation is probably that there are four distinct segments to the scene:

1. The action in the office.
2. The errands and the drive home.
3. The man's entrance at home.
4. The woman's entrance.

Let us work separately with each segment, focusing on specific editing problems.

Expanding Time

The office segment of the scene emphasizes the character's lack of interest in his work and his feeling that time is dragging. The first editing problem, therefore, is how to convey these interior feelings without dialogue. To show him half-heartedly glancing through correspondence or shuffling files is a convenient way to depict his low enthusiasm. But can you devise a way to use these activities also to show time dragging for him? Suppose that you have a shot in which the man opens an envelope, glances at a brief message, and discards it. The shot lasts exactly as long as it normally takes a person to open and read a bit of information—let's say four seconds. So if you do not cut the shot, the action's running time on the screen will correspond exactly with the actual time it takes. But suppose you cut the shot as the man is slitting the edge of the envelope, insert a two-second close-up of an office clock displaying 2:35, and then complete the shot of him handling the message. Now you have effectively extended the action on the screen to six seconds and at the same time suggested a strong association between the character's desk work and the clock.

The easiest way to indicate the character's preoccupation with time may be to show him frequently glancing at his wristwatch. But again, by breaking up the action, you may be able to suggest that preoccupation more effectively without sacrificing economy. Suppose you insert the same shot of the clock—but this time right after a close-up of the man as he looks up from a memo and turns his head—and then cut back to him with his head still in the turned position. Now the viewer will understand that the man is looking up from his work at the clock. In other words, the

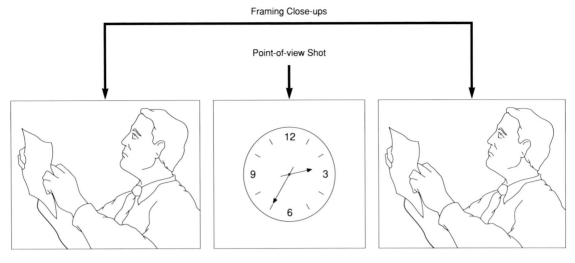

Framing Close-ups

Point-of-view Shot

Figure 4.1
Filmmakers generally enclose a point-of-view shot between two close-ups of the character whose viewpoint is depicted.

audience will accept this time check as one made by the character himself. By enclosing the shot of the clock between the close-ups of the man's face, you have created a point-of-view shot (fig. 4.1), which in this situation communicates the man's low enthusiasm for work and his preoccupation with time. And if you cut back to point-of-view shots of the clock at intervals through the sequence—each time showing that the hands have barely crept on toward 3:00—you will expand time in the scene and create a feeling of anticipation about what he will do at the top of the hour. All in all, by breaking up the action, you accomplish much more than by simply having the man repeatedly glance at his watch.

Filmmakers call a shot like the one of the clock a **cutaway** because, although it is meant to seem simultaneous with the main action, it is not explicitly connected with that action but peripheral to it. Editors find cutaways extremely useful because they can fill in between two views of an action (perhaps shot at different times or from different angles) and make them seem continuous. Basically, cutaways divert the viewer from the main action enough to cover breaks in continuity.

Condensing Time

The second segment of "The Anniversary Surprise" deals with a different time problem. Obviously, it would be both uninteresting and uneconomical to present an actual hour's worth of driving and shopping. Here, therefore, it is necessary to condense time drastically. How does an editor do that?

One technique is to cut together a few shots that highlight key moments and let viewers fill in the gaps in the action for themselves. For example, you might connect:

1. A long shot of the man unlocking his car in a parking lot near the office.
2. A close-up of the man inside the car driving along a busy thoroughfare and checking a shopping list.
3. A medium shot of the man at the checkout of a gourmet market bagging his purchases.
4. A long shot of the man walking from the car to his front door carrying grocery bags.

Since driving and shopping are commonplace activities, most viewers would not find it difficult to reconstruct from these four shots a coherent series of events from office to home.

Suppose, however, that the director wants to emphasize the husband's special care and planning for the anniversary dinner and asks you to include separate shots of him shopping for wine, flowers, and dessert. How many times can you show the character getting in and out of a car, shopping and checking out, without boring the audience? What can you do to move the action along? One technique is to cut on action—that is, to end a shot before an action or gesture is completed and cut to an action or gesture in the following shot. Cutting on action can make mundane activities like driving and shopping look more dynamic by emphasizing movement and eliminating lulls in the action.

A second technique is to show every phase of the shopping cycle in detail the first time through and trim both the number and the duration of shots as you repeat it. As the audience becomes familiar with the pattern, you will be able to depict several errands very economically with a quick series of shots that greatly abbreviate action and condense time.

Still another technique is to use **matching actions.** Instead of repeating the same series of actions, no matter how abbreviated, each time the character makes a purchase, assemble one complete cycle that cuts together a bit of action from each part of it. The result may be a series of shots like the following:

1. Exterior shot. The man leaves his car, studying a shopping list, and enters a shop that sells "Fine Wines and Spirits." As he opens the door, cut on action to—
2. Interior of a bakery shop. The man steps in the door carrying a bottle wrapped in a paper bag. He points to pastries in a large display case behind the counter. As the sales clerk slides open the glass door to the case, cut on action to—

3. Interior of a florist's shop, where another clerk is sliding open a refrigerator case containing cut flowers. The man points to a bucket of yellow roses, and the clerk selects one to show the customer. As he reaches to accept it, cut on action to—

4. The checkout area of a food market, where the man reaches into a shopping cart for fresh artichokes he just bought. After placing them on the counter beside the cashier, he bends for another item in the basket. Cut on action to—

5. A parking lot outside the market. The man bends down to place a bag of groceries into the trunk of his car beside the flowers, pastries, and wine already there. After slamming the trunk shut, he crumples his shopping list and tosses it into a nearby litter basket.

We have been assuming all along that ordinary activities like driving and shopping pose no unusual editing problems. But, carelessly edited, even commonplace actions may confuse the viewer. Suppose, for instance, that after leaving the office the man is shown in three consecutive shots driving his car from left to right across the screen. He stops for an errand and then drives off again, but this time from right to left. How do you think viewers will perceive this change of direction? Remember the chase sequence from John Ford's STAGECOACH, discussed in chapter 2. Though photographed from many camera angles, the stagecoach's movement across the screen is consistently right to left. Perhaps not many viewers consciously note this directional consistency as they watch the chase scene, but unconsciously they are aware of which way escape lies. Consequently, the audience cheers when the cavalry charges to the rescue—from left to right across the screen—directly "toward" the besieged stagecoach. The lesson here is that filmmakers risk confusing or disorienting the audience if they arbitrarily shift the direction of action across the screen.

Ordering Shots

The key to the third segment of the anniversary scenario is to dramatize the man's surprise when he enters his home and finds it burglarized. The script apparently calls for the audience to discover the break-in at the same time the character does. So it would be inappropriate, though certainly not difficult, to foreshadow it. (Since a film editor can play with time and space, you could easily show the man remembering that he had neglected to close a window, or you could even show the burglary in progress at the same time he is shopping for groceries—a technique called **parallel editing**.) One way to cut for a straight surprise is to contrast the character's mood and facial expression before and after he walks through the front door. Perhaps he is whistling cheerfully as he jaunts up the front steps jingling his keys. Then he walks in and is stopped cold in his tracks. The director will certainly have provided you with a good close-up of the man's face to be used at this point in the sequence as a reaction shot. But you will also want to include point-of-view shots of what he sees as he enters—the open window, the burgled desk, etc. By alternating between reaction shots and point-of-view shots, you can extend the dramatic moment for the audience and reveal the character's emotions more thoroughly. Since a good actor will continue to develop the initial reaction after his entrance—from surprise, to anger, to disgust—by cutting back to the reaction shot several times, you can draw more attention to subtle changes on his face. But even if his expression does not change, you will have used the Kuleshov effect to make the audience believe that it has.

For scenes like the one in the living room a director would ordinarily provide the editor with three kinds of footage:

1. A **master shot** that records the entire scene from an objective camera position.
2. Close-up reaction shots of the character's face.
3. Medium- or close-range cutaways to be used for point-of-view shots.

Depending on how you order this footage, there are several ways to depict this scene. For instance, as the character enters, would you opt for a reaction shot or a point-of-view shot first? Would you prefer to show the man's stunned facial expression first and then the cause of it? Or would you like the viewer to see the ransacked room first and then reveal the character's stunned expression? Consider the advantages and limitations of each approach.

There are basic editing problems in this third segment, however, which may leave you very few options. For example, the simple action of walking through a door is more complicated than it seems, especially in a scenario that attempts to cash in on surprise. To show a character entering a room usually takes two shots—one from outside the room and one from inside. The editor then matches the two shots and cuts them together, on action, so that the motion appears continuous on screen.

Another basic problem in the third segment of the scene is how long to sustain the point-of-view shots. An open window, a rifled desk, a gap in the bookcase are all static images. How long should an editor hold such shots? How long will it be before the viewer's attention and interest flag? An editor must decide in every situation how much time the viewer needs to absorb the information or emotion in a static shot. For our scenario you would probably damage the surprise effect by dwelling too long on the subjective shots.

Matching Shots

The final segment of the scenario, the woman's entrance, begins with the tense moment just before the man discovers who is at the door. This kind of situation is common in suspense movies, and usually calls for expanding time in the scene to create tension. Typically, we might expect a close-up of the doorknob slowly turning before the door edges open. But by itself, this shot would not suggest, as the scenario indicates, that the man is afraid that the intruder has returned. Adding a shot of him grasping a paperweight as a weapon, or another subjective shot—first the open window, then the doorknob—would reveal what he is thinking.

The main editorial challenge in the final segment of the scenario is to organize the exchange of glances between husband and wife after her entrance. The most direct approach is to alternate close-ups of the two characters' faces, like the series of close-ups in the Railroad Depot Sequence from HIGH NOON discussed in chapter 2. With an editor's eye, you can see now that those shots of Frank Miller and Helen Ramirez are very carefully matched. The two faces are not only the same size on the screen, they are also positioned within the frame to create the impression that Miller and Ramirez are actually looking at each other. Likewise, you should make sure that the camera angles match the relative positions of husband and wife in their living room. Remember that the scenario specifies that the man "walks down three steps into the living room." Thus, when the woman enters and sees her husband from the door, she is standing three steps higher than he, looking down at him. Consequently, for matching point-of-view shots, her face should be photographed from a slight low angle, and his from a slight high angle, to maintain an accurate **eyeline match** (fig. 4.2).

Continuity Editing: Conclusions

The simulated editing exercise just described demonstrates that film editing is not a rigid process. There are often many ways to cut a sequence, depending on what one wishes to emphasize. But the exercise also demonstrates that editing is not arbitrary; a film story often depends on well-established editing principles and conventions that maintain continuity.

Figure 4.2
For an eyeline match between two close-ups, the filmmaker carefully aligns the camera angles to match the relative positions of the characters in the scene.

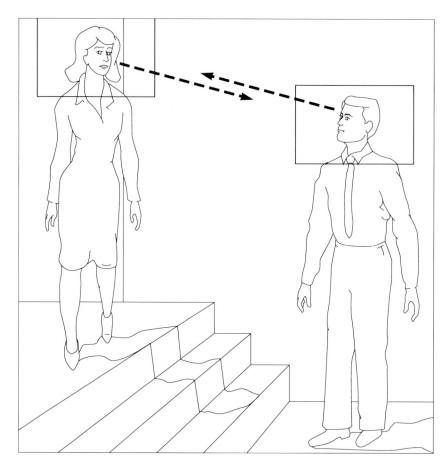

With this experience as a film editor under your belt, go back to the beginning of the chapter and study the shot-by-shot description from RAIDERS OF THE LOST ARK. Notice the specific editorial devices that help maintain continuity within and between each series of shots. Notice where the editing tries to condense and expand time, and how, even on paper, the rhythm of the shots in the sequence complements the action. Notice how much narration Spielberg and Kahn pack into fifty seconds of film. When you view this sequence again—or when you view any action sequence—train yourself to watch for the cuts, no matter how rapidly they occur, and to notice how the editing pieces together bits of action into a coherent, continuous film narrative.

Transitions

Cutting is not the only way to bridge jumps across time and space in movies. Other transitional devices include **fades,** where an image becomes gradually lighter (a **fade-in**) or darker (a **fade-out**) on the screen; **dissolves (or lap dissolves),** where one image fades out as a new one fades in so that both overlap briefly on the screen; and **wipes,** where one image displaces another by pushing, or "wiping," it off the screen. Instead of fades, silent film directors sometimes changed scenes by **irising** in or out— that is, by gradually opening or closing a mechanical diaphragm that regulates the amount of light entering the lens. Today, however, most transitions are done by cutting.

Perhaps the most conspicuous technique for effecting transitions in movies is the **shock cut,** or **smash cut,** an abrupt juxtaposition of two obviously discontinuous settings. In THE GRADUATE (1967), for example, directed by Mike Nichols and edited by Sam O'Steen, a memorable shock cut shows Benjamin (Dustin Hoffman) launching himself onto an inflated air mattress in the family swimming pool but landing atop Mrs. Robinson (Anne Bancroft) in a hotel bed. Ben's movement is matched and cut on action to appear continuous on the screen, even though there is no *physical* continuity between the two locations and events.

The cut from an extinguished match to a desert sunrise in LAWRENCE OF ARABIA, described at the beginning of this chapter, is an example of how discontinuous images can be connected by association. Like a metaphor in poetry, these two images together generate several layers of meaning. They suggest that this transition is not only from one geographical location to another but also from a life of small magnitude to one of infinitely greater magnitude. David Lean reinforces the association between the burnt match and the sun by placing the two images in the same spot on the screen.

Some directors devise transitions that are smoother and less conspicuous than shock cuts. Film and television director Richard L. Bare, for example, describes one transitional trick he likes to use:

> To bridge an actor moving from one set to another without dissolving, fading, or following him all the way—simply have him pull out his watch in a medium shot, cut to a close insert of the watch and pull the camera back to disclose that the actor is now going through the same action but in another locale and at another time. This can be successfully accomplished by the device of taking out a cigarette, or a woman starting to powder her nose. It is simply the starting of an action in a medium shot and completing it in a close shot in another setting.

(126)

Some filmmakers, however, eschew transitions and flaunt conspicuous breaks in continuity. In 1959 Jean-Luc Godard's first feature film, BREATHLESS, startled critics and viewers alike with its prominent use of **jump cuts,** which deliberately fractured spacial and temporal continuity *within* scenes. To some, it seemed that Godard and his editor, Cecile Decugis, were completely disregarding basic "rules" of editing by eliminating standard transitions and matching shots. To others, Godard was boldly rethinking conventional notions of film form and content and leading the way to a "modern" cinema, comparable to the modern novel after writers like James Joyce and Samuel Beckett. At the time, however, Godard contended that he was mainly interested in quickening the pace of the film by cutting out what he did not want and "simply putting things side by side." He commented: "I discovered in BREATHLESS that when a discussion between two people became boring and tedious, one could just as well cut between the speeches. I tried it once, and it went very well, so I did the same thing right through the film" (66-67). Curiously, the editing in BREATHLESS is not very startling today because jump cuts have become more commonplace.

Transition Editing in DON'T LOOK NOW

To understand better how transitions work in narrative film, consider the opening scene of DON'T LOOK NOW (1974), directed by Nicolas Roeg and edited by Graeme Clifford. This scene contains two noteworthy transitions that contribute significantly to the story and its emotional impact on the viewer. The scene, itself a self-contained cinematic narrative, depicts a tragic incident that serves as a prologue for the rest of the film. Two children, a boy and a girl, are playing outdoors on a country estate with spacious lawns and a pond, while their parents, Laura (Julie Christie) and John (Donald Sutherland), are relaxing inside the house. John has a premonition that something is wrong outside and races to the pond, but before he can get there his daughter, Christine, has drowned. Thus the opening scene, in a few minutes' screen time, introduces four characters engaged in separate activities inside and outside the house and weaves them together into a cohesive story.

DON'T LOOK NOW opens on the children, and the first important transition occurs when the scene shifts from outside to inside the house—a cut executed across a pair of intricately matched shots. The outside shot begins as a medium-long, high-angle view of Christine in a red raincoat crouching by the pond. The camera slowly **zooms in** to a close-up of her reflection in the water. The inside shot begins as a close-up of a fire

Figure 4.3

A close-up from the opening sequence of DON'T LOOK NOW, where meticulous editing weaves together four separate actions into a cohesive, self-contained cinematic narrative.

and then slowly **zooms out** to reveal the length of the living room. At its end point the shot shows John in the foreground viewing slides, Laura reading in the middleground, and the fireplace deep in the background. Thus, inversely matching camera action—steadily zooming in from long range to close before the cut, then zooming out again from close to long range—eases the eye across the cut by mirroring what appears before and after it.

The second important transition occurs at the end of the opening scene. By the pond John tries in vain to revive his daughter and, after stumbling and falling down with her in his arms, finally carries her back to the house (fig. 4.3). Intercut with this action we see Laura in the kitchen, unaware of the tragedy outside. The camera gradually zooms in on her and frames her in a close-up. In the final shot we see the horrible reaction on her face and hear her scream as she suddenly discovers that Christine is dead. As she screams, there is a startling shock cut to a power drill tearing into a stone wall. When the new scene unfolds, we discover that the setting has shifted to Venice, where John is supervising the restoration of an old church.

What do you think Nicolas Roeg hoped to accomplish with this jarring cut? What logic do you see in this abrupt transition? Jot down your ideas before reading further.

Specifically, this shock cut in DON'T LOOK NOW juxtaposes a close-up of Laura screaming and a medium-close, **overhead shot** of the drill boring into the church's foundation, accompanied by the piercing sound of metal ripping stone. We do not immediately know that this is a church's foundation; we just see the drill biting into stone. Since the sound of the power drill overlaps Laura's scream and continues it, the image after the cut, until the context of the shot is established, may well be a symbolic expression of Laura's excruciating emotional and physical shock at seeing her drowned daughter—as if, looking down from her point of view, that drill is tearing into her guts. Thus, the shock cut shifts the scene physically to a new setting but psychologically sustains the emotional intensity in the old setting. We might argue, therefore, that the shot of the power drill belongs as much to the first scene as it does to the second.

These two transitions in the opening scene of DON'T LOOK NOW are strikingly different in the way they affect the viewer. The first is so smoothly and gradually executed that the audience is barely conscious that the film has introduced a new location and another set of characters. The slow zooming before and after the cut eases the viewer into the transition by gradually "narrowing" the outside setting and then "expanding" the inside setting. The second transition, on the other hand, is as abrupt as a cut can be. Roeg and Clifford methodically build up the scene to an emotional climax and then joltingly cut to another time and place. The first cut is measured and methodical; the second is purely visceral. Yet, for both transitions there is a clear visual and logical connection between the juxtaposed images.

In the 1920s Soviet filmmaker and theorist V.I. Pudovkin pointed out that "editing is not merely a method of the junction of separate scenes or pieces, but is a method that controls the 'psychological guidance' of the spectator" (194). Pudovkin identified five "special editing

Figure 4.4
A still from Sergei
Eisenstein's OCTOBER
(TEN DAYS THAT
SHOOK THE WORLD),
which illustrates images in
collision. What meaning
emerges when the
dangling horse and the
open drawbridge are
juxtaposed?

methods": contrast, parallelism, symbolism, simultaneity, and leit-motif (reiteration of theme). His contemporary, Sergei Eisenstein, argued that the essence of all editing is "conflict" and that the most dynamic editing involves the "collision," rather than the "linkage," of images (fig. 4.4). (See the discussion of dynamic montage in the last section of this chapter.) But despite their different theoretical approaches to montage, both Pudovkin and Eisenstein concurred that there must be *method* in editing in order for the meaning of film scenes to be fully comprehended by the spectator. The two transitions from the opening scene of DON'T LOOK NOW are specific examples of such editing method. Ultimately, Roeg and Clifford do not employ these carefully devised cuts simply as narrative devices; they also wish to control the viewer's emotional reactions to the story.

Transition Editing: A Simulation

Having examined some examples of cinematic transitions, let us go back to the scenario of "The Anniversary Surprise" earlier in the chapter and try more simulated editing, but this time concentrating on transitions.

The simplest kind of transition for this scenario may be to use an object to connect the four segments and carry the action from the office to the living room—the husband's shopping list, for example. But how do you use a shopping list as a transitional device? Perhaps you might show the character handling the shopping list throughout the scene. Suppose, for instance, he makes up the list in the office (instead of concentrating on his work), studies it while driving the car, crosses off items as he purchases them in shops, and finally (as a gesture of anger and disgust) crushes the paper when he enters his home and flings it at the open window.

Another approach, particularly to condense time, might be to borrow Richard Bare's technique: Show the man studying the paper in his car, insert a close-up of the list, and then pull the camera back to reveal him in the market.

Still another approach might be to create associative transitions, as in DON'T LOOK NOW. For example, you might cut from a shot of the man studying the shopping list in his car to a shot of him standing before wine racks in the liquor store. He selects a bottle, turns to go, and glances again at his list. Cut to him in front of a pastry display case choosing dessert. Show him looking at the list again, and then cut to the florist shop. Et cetera. Now instead of watching him cross items off the list, the viewer "accompanies" the character from store to store as he shops. The first cut may appear abrupt, but the viewer will soon see the pattern.

This kind of associative editing might even lead you to reconstruct the entire scene. Suppose, for example, you show the character making up his shopping list in the office and, each time he writes down an item, you cut away to a shot of him purchasing it. You could incorporate all the shopping business within the office scene and then simply use the last item on the list as a transition to the living room.

Dynamic Montage

Pudovkin's and Eisenstein's comments about editing method in the preceding section explain how montage can evoke strong emotional reactions as well as narrate a film story, particularly when images are cut together rapidly or energetically. Such editing is sometimes called **dynamic montage.**

An example of dynamic editing is the famous shower sequence in Alfred Hitchcock's PSYCHO (1960), edited by George Tomasini. In this scene a young woman, played by Janet Leigh, is brutally stabbed to death in the shower by a demented character brandishing a kitchen knife. Hitchcock said it took seven days to shoot this gruesome scene and that "there were seventy camera setups for forty-five seconds of footage" (210). These setups cover the scene from many vantage points, including extreme high- and low-angle shots and eye-level shots from all sides of the shower enclosure. The violence, photographed at close range and cut on action, flashes before the viewer's eyes in shots that last only a fraction of a second: the knife stabbing at the woman, her terrified reactions, the water streaming down incessantly. The visual and emotional impact of so much brutality on the screen is overwhelming. After watching this sequence, many viewers feel that they, too, have been physically assaulted. It is understandable why some reviewers have severely criticized this scene for its blatant depiction of violence against women.

Hitchcock certainly did not need so many shots and such rapid-fire editing to show a woman murdered in the shower. He could have made the scene just as grisly with a lifelike blood-spurting dummy. In fact, Hitchcock had ordered such a dummy specially created for the scene; but he didn't use it. He used dynamic montage instead because he did not simply want to depict a bloody murder; he wanted "to achieve something of a mass emotion." Hitchcock said of PSYCHO, "It wasn't a message that stirred the audiences, nor was it a great performance or their enjoyment of the novel. They were aroused by pure film" (211).

Another example of dynamic montage is one of the most famous sequences in film history: the Odessa Steps Sequence from THE BATTLESHIP POTEMKIN (1925), directed and edited by Sergei Eisenstein. This sequence depicts events when Czarist soldiers unexpectedly attack a crowd of people waiting on the Odessa steps to welcome *The Potemkin* into the harbor. Eisenstein, a film theoretician and teacher as well as a director, wrote extensively about montage. In fact, his name is almost synonymous with the kind of editing, sometimes called Russian

a

b

Figure 4.5
Drawings of colliding images from the Odessa Steps
Sequence in POTEMKIN: (*a*) Close-ups give place to
(*b*) long shots.

Montage, used in the Odessa Steps Sequence. Eisenstein wrote that "montage is an idea that arises from the collision of independent shots—shots even opposite to one another" (*Film Form* 49). In his films he tried to create visual counterpoint (and corresponding tension) by juxtaposing "opposite" images and movements in shots of varying lengths and from varying camera positions. He described, for example, how this "collision" montage works in the Odessa Steps Sequence:

> First, there are *close-ups* of human figures rushing chaotically [fig. 4.5*a*]. Then, *long shots* of the same scene [fig. 4.5*b*]. The *chaotic movement* [fig. 4.6*a*] is next superceded by shots showing the feet of soldiers as they march *rhythmically* down the steps [fig. 4.6*b*].
>
> Tempo increases. Rhythm accelerates.
>
> And then, as the *downward* movement reaches its culmination [fig. 4.7*a*], the movement is suddenly reversed: instead of the headlong rush of the *crowd* down the steps we see the *solitary* figure of a mother carrying her dead son, *slowly* and *solemnly going up* the steps [fig. 4.7*b*].
>
> *Mass.* Headlong rush. *Downward.* And all of a sudden—
>
> A *solitary* figure. Slow and solemn. *Going up.* But only for a moment. Then again a *leap in the reverse direction. Downward* movement.
>
> Rhythm accelerates. Tempo increases.
>
> The shot of *the rushing crowd* [fig. 4.8*a*] is suddenly followed by one showing a perambulator hurtling down the steps [fig. 4.8*b*]. This is more than just different tempos. This is a *leap in the method of representation*—from the abstract to the physical. This gives one more aspect of downward movement.

a   b

Figure 4.6
(a) The chaotic rush of the mass is succeeded by (b) the rhythmic march of the soldiers.

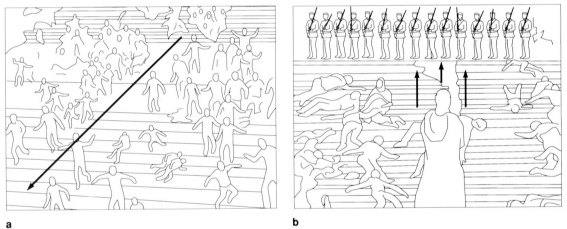

a   b

Figure 4.7
(a) Descent gives place to (b) ascent.

 Close-ups, accordingly, give place to *long shots* [fig. 4.5a and b]. The *chaotic* rush (of a mass) is succeeded by the *rhythmic* march of the soldiers [fig. 4.6a and b]. One aspect of movement (people running, falling, tumbling down the steps) gives way to another (rolling perambulator) [fig. 4.8a and b]. *Descent* gives place to *ascent* [fig. 4.7a and b]. *Many* volleys of *many* rifles give place to *one* shot from *one* of the battleship's guns [fig. 4.9a and b].

a

b

Figure 4.8
(*a*) People running down the steps gives way to (*b*) the rolling perambulator.

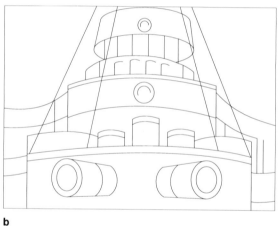

a

b

Figure 4.9
(*a*) Many volleys of many rifles give place to (*b*) one shot from one of the battleship's guns.

At each step there is a leap from one dimension to another, from one quality to another, until, finally, the change affects not one individual episode (the perambulator) but the whole of the method: the risen lions mark the point where the *narrative* turns into a *presentation through images*.

(*POTEMKIN* 14)

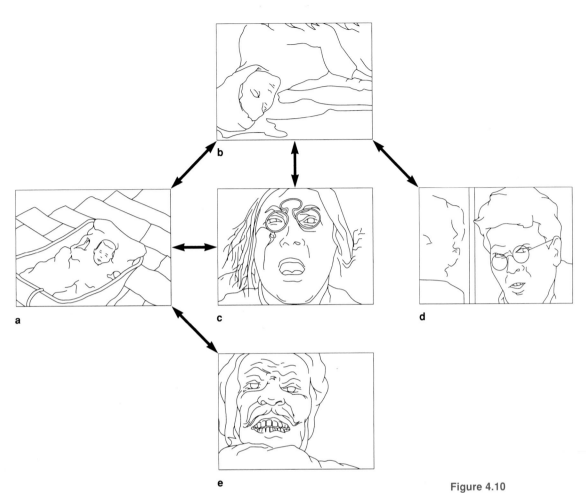

Eisenstein's italics in his analysis of the Odessa Steps Sequence highlight the various kinds of oppositions he has set up in the shots to keep emotional tension mounting in the scene. His formula here is that "the action always makes a leap into a new quality, and this new leap is usually a leap into the opposite direction" (*POTEMKIN* 15).

Consider more closely the oppositions in one segment of the Odessa Steps Sequence: the incident with the runaway baby carriage, which is the climactic horror of the scene and, as Eisenstein points out, the leap "from the abstract to the physical" in the sequence. The main visual thrust is, of course, the downward motion of the baby carriage, which moves diagonally across the screen from left to right. Eisenstein photographs the carriage from an extreme high angle (fig. 4.10*a*), sometimes showing the baby inside and sometimes only the wheels careering down the steps. He counters the carriage's movement with static shots of

Figure 4.10
Some "oppositions" Eisenstein employs in the Odessa Steps Sequence to create emotional tension: traveling shots opposed with static shots (*a* versus *b, c, d, e*); diagonal composition opposed with vertical composition (*a, b* versus *c, d, e*); high-angle shots opposed with low-angle shots (*a* versus *e*).

the baby's mother (fig. 4.10b), lying shot on the steps, and of two observers, an older woman with pince-nez (fig. 4.10c) and a student with spectacles (fig. 4.10d). The close-ups of the observers, especially the young man next to the mirror, also present strong vertical compositions that oppose the carriage's diagonal alignment. Eisenstein offsets these individualized characters with shots of the anonymous soldiers attacking the crowd. But at the end of the sequence he interjects two close-ups of a cossack who slashes downward at the camera with his saber. The camera photographs him from an extreme low angle (opposing the high angle used for the shots of the carriage), first at medium-close range and then, abruptly, very close (fig. 4.10e). This cossack is the only militiaman in the sequence whose face is clearly identifiable.

Can you summarize Eisenstein's concept of "collision" montage and explain how it works? Could you explain the Odessa Steps Sequence to someone who finds so much cutting confusing or superfluous?

Sergei Eisenstein contends that the emotional impact of a film ultimately derives from and depends on montage. "*Emotional* effect," he writes, "begins only with the reconstruction of the event in montage fragments, each of which will summon a certain association—the sum of which will be an all-embracing complex of emotional feeling" (*Film Form* 60). One important way Eisenstein increases the emotional impact of the Odessa Steps Sequence is by expanding the duration of the massacre. David Cook explains:

> Even though the rate of the cutting in this [Odessa Steps] sequence is terrifically accelerated (the average shot length is fifty-two frames, or just over two seconds, as opposed to eighty-eight frames, or nearly four seconds, for the rest of the film), it takes much longer for the massacre to occur on the screen than it would take in actuality. This is because Eisenstein wishes to suggest a *psychological* duration for the horrible event that far exceeded its precise chronological duration . . . . By drawing out, through the montage process, the time it would normally take for the militiamen and their victims to reach the bottom of the stairs, Eisenstein manages to suggest destruction of a much greater magnitude than we actually witness on the screen. . . .
>
> (168)

Conclusion

This chapter illustrates how montage can function as a narrative device in films and how it can arouse the viewer's emotions. But Sergei Eisenstein's observations about the psychological impact of montage on the spectator clearly indicate another important function of film editing: its ability to persuade or indoctrinate audiences. Chapter 14, "Film as Propaganda," will explore this aspect of montage further and will look again at the Odessa Steps Sequence as an example of cinematic propaganda.

General Study Questions

1. As an exercise, turn off the sound and watch for every cut in a movie scene. Describe the editing you see. Is the cutting conspicuous or inconspicuous, rapid or slow, smooth or jarring? Are the shots taken from many vantage points or few? Do the shots fall into patterns that repeat themselves? Afterwards, comment on what you learned about film editing from this exercise.

2. Choose a film from the list of Additional Films for Study at the end of this chapter and describe shot by shot one key sequence in it. Then analyze the editing in the sequence. How does the sequence maintain continuity of action? How does it make transitions between different locations or vantage points? What is the overall effect of the editing in the sequence?

3. Describe in detail several ways you might edit a scene in which two characters carry on a conversation. How is each editing style likely to affect the way the audience perceives the two characters and the tenor of their conversation? Afterwards, comment on what you generally take for granted about film editing in such scenes.

4. Watch for shock cuts in a film. Identify one that you find particularly bold or dramatic and analyze it. What is the actual or implied connection between the two images cut together? What makes this shock cut an effective transition?

5. Compare and contrast editing styles in two films of the same genre.

Additional Films for Study

INTOLERANCE (1916), dir. D.W. Griffith
THE LAST LAUGH (1924), dir. F.W. Murnau
OCTOBER (TEN DAYS THAT SHOOK THE WORLD) (1928), dir. Sergei
    Eisenstein and Grigori Alexandrov
THE MAN WITH A MOVIE CAMERA (1929), dir. Dziga Vertov
OUR DAILY BREAD (1934), dir. King Vidor
TRIUMPH OF THE WILL (1935), dir. Leni Riefenstahl
THE GRAND ILLUSION (1937), dir. Jean Renoir
THE GRAPES OF WRATH (1940), dir. John Ford
THE SEVEN SAMURAI (1954), dir. Akira Kurosawa
BREATHLESS (1959), dir. Jean-Luc Godard
HIROSHIMA MON AMOUR (1959), dir. Alain Resnais
NORTH BY NORTHWEST (1959), dir. Alfred Hitchcock
8½ (1963), dir. Federico Fellini
BLOW-UP (1966), dir. Michelangelo Antonioni

WALKABOUT (1971), dir. Nicolas Roeg
THE GODFATHER (1972), dir. Francis Coppola
LENNY (1974), dir. Bob Fosse
SEVEN BEAUTIES (1976), dir. Lina Wertmuller
PIXOTE (1981), dir. Hector Babenco
INDIANA JONES AND THE TEMPLE OF DOOM (1984), dir. Steven Spielberg
BACK TO THE FUTURE (1985), dir. Robert Zemeckis
WITNESS (1985), dir. Peter Weir
FATAL ATTRACTION (1987), dir. Adrian Lyne
FULL METAL JACKET (1987), dir. Stanley Kubrick

Further Reading

Bare, Richard L. *The Film Director.* New York: Collier, 1976.
Eisenstein, Sergei. *Film Form.* Translated and edited by Jay Leyda. New York: Harcourt Brace Jovanovich, 1969.
———. *The Film Sense.* Translated and edited by Jay Leyda. New York: Harcourt Brace Jovanovich, 1969.
Kuleshov, Lev. *Kuleshov on Film.* Translated and edited by Ronald Levaco. Berkeley: University of California Press, 1974.
LaValley, Albert, ed. *Focus on Hitchcock.* Englewood Cliffs, N.J.: Prentice-Hall, 1972.
Marshall, Herbert, ed. *Sergei Eisenstein's THE BATTLESHIP POTEMKIN.* New York: Avon, 1978.
Mayer, David. *Eisenstein's POTEMKIN.* New York: Grossman Publishers, 1972. [Shot-by-shot analysis]
Naremore, James. *Filmguide to PSYCHO.* Bloomington: Indiana University Press, 1973.
Reisz, Karel. *The Technique of Film Editing.* New York: Hastings House, 1968.
Rosenblum, Ralph, and Robert Karen. *When the Shooting Stops . . . The Cutting Begins.* New York: Viking, 1979.
Roud, Richard. *Godard.* Garden City, N. Y.: Doubleday, 1968.
Truffaut, François, and Helen Scott. *Hitchcock.* New York: Simon and Schuster, 1966.
Walter, Ernest. *The Technique of the Film Cutting Room.* New York: Focal Press, 1969.

Works Cited

Bare, Richard L. *The Film Director.* New York: Collier, 1976.
Cook, David A. *A History of Narrative Film.* New York: W. W. Norton, 1981.
Eisenstein, Sergei. *Film Form: Essays in Film Theory.* Translated and edited by Jay Leyda. New York: Harcourt Brace Jovanovich, 1969.
———. *POTEMKIN.* Translated by Gillon R. Aitken. New York: Simon and Schuster, 1968.
Godard, Jean-Luc. Quoted in *Godard,* by Richard Roud. Garden City, N.Y.: Doubleday, 1968.
Hitchcock, Alfred. Quoted in *Hitchcock,* by François Truffaut and Helen Scott. New York: Simon and Schuster, 1967.
Pudovkin, V.I. "Film Technique." In *Film: An Anthology,* edited by Daniel Talbot, 189-200. Berkeley: University of California Press, 1972.

Sound

M ovies were never really silent, at least not in major movie houses of the "silent era." Music was part of motion picture exhibition from the very beginning. As early as 1895, a program of one-reel films by the Lumière brothers in Paris was accompanied by a piano. From the time that movies became firmly established as dramas, around 1910, musical accompaniment was standard, sometimes scored for small orchestras, more often improvised on piano or organ. D.W. Griffith's THE BIRTH OF A NATION in 1915 was one of the first motion pictures promoted with a "full orchestral score," which Griffith composed jointly with Joseph Carl Briel. It combined original material and musical quotations from major composers like Wagner, Rossini, Liszt, Verdi, Grieg, Tchaikovsky, and Beethoven, as well as traditional American tunes like "Dixie."

Music

Some very celebrated composers wrote scores for films in the silent era. In 1907 a company in Paris known as Le Film d'Art invited Camille Saint-Saëns to compose a special score for L'ASSASSINATION DU DUC DE GUISE; it became his *Opus 128* for strings, piano, and harmonium, which consists of an Introduction and five Tableaux, all cued for film accompaniment. Noteworthy musical scores for silent films include those by Edmund Meisel for Sergei Eisenstein's THE BATTLESHIP POTEMKIN and OCTOBER; by Arthur Honegger for Abel Gance's NAPOLEON; and by Dmitri Shostakovich for THE NEW BABYLON, directed by Leonid Trauberg and Grigori Kozintsev. (Manvell 17-18)

From the earliest days of cinema, filmmakers tried to link music integrally with the mood and pace of the images on the screen. The score for THE BIRTH OF A NATION, for example, included a special Clan Call, "a strange sound produced on reed-whistles and horns, which was used as the Ku-Klux-Klan motif throughout the second part of the picture, sometimes in combination with other material such as quotations from Wagner's *Ride of the Valkyrie*, elements of "Dixie" and sound effects of galloping horses. . ." (Manvell 21). These scenes provided some of the most memorable music in the film and, in combination with Griffith's **parallel editing,** roused the spectators' emotions to a fever pitch.

In his autobiography, Louis Levy, an early film music conductor, explains that the conductor was sometimes known ingloriously as the "fitter," because he attempted to "fit music to the mood of the film."

How Do Films Tell a Story?

By the 1920s, Levy explains, "it became the custom for the same piece of music to be played for the same hero or heroine, another piece for the villain, and yet another theme for the comedian" (23).

Composers also experimented with more sophisticated techniques to combine music and film images. Edmund Meisel, for example, who wrote the music for POTEMKIN and OCTOBER,

> . . . analyzed the montage of some famous silent films in regard to rhythm, emphasis, emotional climax and mood. To each separate shot he assigned a certain musical theme. Then he directly combined the separate themes, using the rhythm, emphasis, and climaxes of the visual montage for the organization of the music. He wished to prove by this experiment that the montage of a good film is based on the same rules and develops in the same way as music . . . .
>
> (Borneman 23)

A famous example of such close correspondence between music and film images is Eisenstein's later film, ALEXANDER NEVSKY (1938), with a musical score by Sergei Prokofiev. In an essay entitled "Form and Content: Practice" Eisenstein closely analyzes a sequence from ALEXANDER NEVSKY where Russian soldiers battle German invaders on a frozen lake. He emphasizes that the strong impression created in the Battle on the Ice "does not come from the photographed shots alone, but is an *audio-visual impression* which is created by the combination of shots together with the corresponding music—which is what one experiences in the auditorium" (Eisenstein 175). Eisenstein graphs the movement of musical passages side by side with the eye's movement through corresponding shots (fig. 5.1) and concludes: "Both graphs of movement correspond absolutely, that is, we find a *complete correspondence between the movement of the music and the movement of the eye over the lines of the plastic composition. In other words, exactly the same motion lies at the base of both the musical and the plastic structures.*" (178)

On October 6, 1927, at the Winter Garden Theater in New York City, the silent era of motion pictures officially came to an end when Warner Brothers premiered a feature film with **synchronous sound**—THE JAZZ SINGER, starring Al Jolson. Adapted from a successful Broadway production, THE JAZZ SINGER is the story of a Jewish cantor's son who goes against family and religious traditions to become a music hall singer. The film featured Vitaphone sound—recordings on discs synchronized with screen images. Warner Brothers actually

Figure 5.1
Audiovisual correspondences in a sequence from ALEXANDER NEVSKY, directed by Sergei Eisenstein.

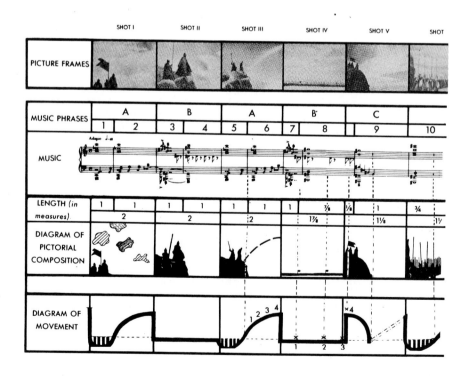

How Do Films Tell a Story?

Shot I

Shot II

Shot III

Shot IV

Shot V

Shot VI

Shot VII

Shot VIII

Shot IX

Shot X

Shot XI

Shot XII

first introduced Vitaphone about a year before THE JAZZ SINGER. But, as film historian David Cook explains, THE JAZZ SINGER is recognized as the first "talkie":

> Like previous Vitaphone productions, it [THE JAZZ SINGER] was conceived as a silent picture with synchronized orchestral score, some Jewish cantorial music, and seven popular songs performed by Jolson. It was conceived, that is, as a "singing" rather than a "talking" picture, and all dialogue was to be provided by interpolated titles (intertitles). But, during the shooting of two musical sequences, Jolson ad libbed some dialogue on the set which Warners shrewdly permitted to remain in the finished film. At one point near the beginning of the picture, Jolson speaks to his audience in the middle of a nightclub act and delivers his famous "Wait-a-minute . . . . Wait-a-minute . . . . You ain't heard nothin' yet!" Later in the film, as he sits at a piano in his mother's parlor, he has a sentimental exchange with her that lasts several minutes between verses of "Blue Skies." This was the only spoken dialogue in the film, yet its impact was sensational. Audiences had heard synchronized speech before, but only on formally contrived and easily anticipated occasions . . . . Suddenly, though, here was Jolson not only singing and dancing but speaking informally and spontaneously to other persons in the film as someone might do in reality. The effect was not so much of *hearing* Jolson speak as of *overhearing* him speak, and it thrilled audiences bored with the conventions of silent cinema and increasingly indifferent to the canned performances of the Vitaphone shorts. Thus, we say that the "talkies" were born with THE JAZZ SINGER not because it was the first feature-length film to employ synchronized dialogue but because it was the first to employ it in a realistic and seemingly undeliberate way.
>
> (240)

The **musical** is a special film **genre** that originated with Al Jolson and THE JAZZ SINGER and has been a mainstay of the movie industry ever since. Many musicals follow the traditions of staged musical comedy. Indeed, during the 1950s and 1960s many of the most popular musicals were film versions of Broadway hits: SHOWBOAT (1951), OKLAHOMA (1955), THE KING AND I (1956), SOUTH PACIFIC (1958), WEST SIDE STORY (1961), BYE-BYE BIRDIE (1963), MY FAIR LADY (1964), THE SOUND OF MUSIC (1965), and others. But many musicals in the early sound era were written *as movies* and established a distinct musical tradition for the screen. Busby Berkeley's hits of the 1930s, like 42ND STREET (1933) and the GOLD-DIGGERS series, were movie extravaganzas that dazzled audiences during the Depression. Berkeley's unusual camera angles, such as an **overhead shot** to feature kaleidoscopic dance routines, offered film audiences a perspective impossible to achieve in the legitimate theater. The Fred Astaire and Ginger Rogers musicals of the 1930s, like FLYING DOWN TO RIO (1933) and TOP HAT (1935), did not display fancy camera work; but they exuded a special energy and finesse that was much imitated in other films. Another dancer, Gene Kelly, one of Hollywood's great entertainers in the 1940s and 1950s, starred in AN AMERICAN IN PARIS (1951) and SINGIN' IN THE RAIN (1952), which are among the most exhilarating musical films ever produced.

Not all musicals follow the conventional romantic comedy format, where characters break into song or dance in implausible situations and where a full orchestra nowhere evident in the scene suddenly accompanies them. Bob Fosse's CABARET (1972), for example, realistically combines music and drama in a story about the rise of Nazism in Germany. It shifts back and forth between burlesque nightclub entertainment in the cabaret and grim political events in the streets. CABARET demonstrates that the musical, both in form and in content, is able to address serious social and political issues.

Naturally, Hollywood does not have a corner on musicals. THE UMBRELLAS OF CHERBOURG (1964), YELLOW SUBMARINE (1968), THE HARDER THEY COME (1973), Ingmar Bergman's THE MAGIC FLUTE (1975), and Carlos Saura's CARMEN (1984) are a few examples of movies from other parts of the world that reflect the tremendous range and diversity of the musical film.

The appeal of musical performances in movies is strong enough that even many nonmusical films include one or more musical interludes as a standard feature. In some films these interludes are justified by and integrated with the story line, as when Sam the piano player (Dooley Wilson) sings "As Time Goes By" in CASABLANCA (1943). In other films the interludes barely connect with the story, as when "Raindrops Keep Falling on My Head" plays behind Butch's bicycle frolic in BUTCH CASSIDY AND THE SUNDANCE KID (1969).

But apart from the musical film genre, how does music contribute to cinematic storytelling? Before reading further, jot down some ways in which music can complement and reinforce a film story. Consider both background music and music that is specifically part of the story.

Sometimes **background music** helps narrate a film by directly revealing information about the story or its characters. "The Ballad of Jeremiah Johnson," for example, presents biographical background about the protagonist of JEREMIAH JOHNSON (1972) and comments on his life as a legendary mountain man. The title song for HIGH NOON (1952) summarizes the dramatic situation of that film from the protagonist's point of view, provides essential background information, and names the villain of the story. Sometimes song lyrics indicate a character's state of mind, as Simon and Garfunkle's "The Sounds of Silence" does for Benjamin (Dustin Hoffman) in THE GRADUATE (1967) and as the Doors' "This is the End" does for Captain Willard (Martin Sheen) in APOCALYPSE NOW (1979).

Usually, however, music's contributions to film narrative are more indirect. Indigenous music often reinforces a movie's geographical or cultural setting; examples include films like GANDHI (1982), WALKABOUT (1971), and ZORBA THE GREEK (1964). **Ethnographic films** like RAMPARTS OF CLAY (1970) or A MAN CALLED HORSE (1970) even reproduce authentic songs and rituals from the cultures they depict. Similarly, music of a specific period can reinforce a film's historical setting. Marvin Hamlisch adapted Scott Joplin rags to help set THE STING (1973) in 1930s Chicago; Vangelis's electronic musical score for BLADE RUNNER (1982) complements its futuristic setting. Sometimes filmmakers use actual contemporary recordings as **source music** in movies to provide the authentic flavor of a particular time and place. Peter Bogdanovich includes 1950s country western tunes playing on transistor radios throughout THE LAST PICTURE SHOW (1971) to underscore a story that takes place in a backwater Texas oil town. George Lucas introduces contemporary pop hits in AMERICAN GRAFFITI (1973) as a continuous musical backdrop for a story about Southern California teenagers in the early 1960s.

Music also helps establish mood and atmosphere in films, a function that goes back to the earliest days of motion pictures. Musical themes often capture the essence of a movie so completely that afterwards, hearing just a few measures can recall the entire film experience. GONE WITH THE WIND (1939), THE BRIDGE ON THE RIVER KWAI (1957), LOVE STORY (1970), and CHARIOTS OF FIRE (1981) are a few examples of films with memorable musical themes. Frequently, themes from such movies become hit tunes, and their **sound tracks,** popular recordings.

Music can also intensify or accentuate an image on the screen. In Stanley Kubrick's DR. STRANGELOVE (1964), for instance, a romantic orchestral rendition of "Try a Little Tenderness" on the sound track humorously underscores an allusion to sexual copulation as a B-52 bomber is refueled in flight. In many **animated films,** particularly cartoons of the early sound period, musical scores mimic actions and gestures of film characters. For example, the first fully synchronized sound cartoon, Walt Disney's STEAMBOAT WILLIE (1928), introduced Mickey Mouse

Figure 5.2

A frame enlargement from Walt Disney's THE SKELETON DANCE, an animated film with music that "Mickey Mouses" the visual action.

as a whistling steamboat captain who transports farm animals on the river and beats, plucks, and squeezes music out of them to accompany his tune. The sounds the animals make imitate the rhythm and timbre of appropriate musical instruments. Such musical synchronization is called, fittingly, **Mickey Mousing, or Mickey Mousing the music.** Some of Disney's early Silly Symphonies remain benchmarks for synchronized music in animated film even today. In SKELETON DANCE (1929), for instance, graveyard skeletons pound on each other's bones (fig. 5.2) while xylophone melodies on the sound track perfectly match their animated antics.

      The Clan Call in Griffith's THE BIRTH OF A NATION (1915) illustrates another way music can intensify a film image. Rousing music for chase scenes and climactic shoot-outs is standard practice in action-adventure movies. John Williams is probably the best known contemporary musical composer in the world because of his sweeping symphonic scores for action blockbusters like JAWS (1975), STAR WARS (1977), SUPERMAN (1978), RAIDERS OF THE LOST ARK (1981), and their sequels. Music can also intensify film horror, as Bernard Herrmann's shrieking score for the shower murder in PSYCHO (1960) illustrates. In that famous movie scene, as Royal S. Brown points out, "Herrmann musically brought to the surface . . . the subliminal pulse of violence which, in 1960, still lay beneath the surface of American society" (648). The stylized brutalities in Stanley Kubrick's A CLOCKWORK ORANGE (1971) are set to more recognizable music, like Beethoven's *Ninth Symphony* and "Singin' in the Rain." On the other hand, film music can intensify quiet scenes, too, as in Kubrick's 2001: A SPACE ODYSSEY (1968), where strains of Richard Strauss's "The Blue Danube" accompany vehicles silently maneuvering in space.

Music sometimes establishes the rhythm of a scene, pacing or coordinating visual images much like a drummer controls the tempo of a jazz ensemble. A good example is a scene in Francis Ford Coppola's COTTON CLUB (1985), where a tap dance solo is deftly intercut with a gangland shooting. Increasingly complex rhythms of the taps build up tension for the anticipated execution, until at the climax of the scene, flurries of tap steps and machine-gun bursts explode simultaneously.

Finally, in keeping with traditions established in the silent era, film music can help introduce and identify characters. Musical themes associated with specific film characters are an important feature of many popular classics like GONE WITH THE WIND (1939), CITIZEN KANE (1941), DOCTOR ZHIVAGO (1965), and STAR WARS (1977). The distinctive James Bond theme has become the musical trademark of Agent 007 in more than a dozen films, even though each Bond movie has its own title song as well. Sometimes source music in a film reveals the essence of a character. For example, in Bob Rafelson's FIVE EASY PIECES (1970), the character of Bobby Dupea (Jack Nicholson) does not gel until late in the film when he plays a classical piano piece. Suddenly, we see Dupea in a new light. This man, who lives with a waitress and works as a roughneck in the oil fields, has had extensive musical training, which he has rejected along with his cultured, musical family.

Filmmakers from the silent era up to the present have maintained close ties between music and drama in motion pictures; consequently, music has become an integral component of narrative film. Almost any good movie can supply rich examples of how music complements and reinforces the story. We should remind ourselves that the music for most movies is prepared and "fitted" as meticulously as the cinematography and the editing.

Spoken Language

As David Cook's comments about THE JAZZ SINGER earlier in this chapter indicate, that film is significant not because it was a picture with synchronized sound but because it was a *talking* picture. The coming of sound sparked a lively debate about whether spoken dialogue would help or hurt movies. Many early sound productions were visually stagnant, as camera movement and actor mobility were sacrificed to a stationary microphone and bland dialogue. Gradually, as the novelty of sound wore off and technical advancements like the **boom microphone** restored mobility on the set, sound films became more lively; but a stubborn dependence on the spoken word hung on. How did the introduction of spoken language change motion pictures?

First of all, spoken language in movies abruptly ended the careers of silent screen actors whose voices were not charismatic enough for talkies. On the other hand, the sound era produced new performers who enriched movies with trained voices and distinctive styles of delivery. Try to imagine a silent CITIZEN KANE (1941), without the voices of Orson Welles and company, polished and refined by years of radio drama. How much would a film like THE AFRICAN QUEEN (1951) lose without the poignant exchanges between Humphrey Bogart and Katharine Hepburn? If you have ever seen a film you know **dubbed** into another language by foreign actors, you can appreciate how much individual vocal inflections and rhythms affect audiences. For this reason many viewers prefer to see foreign films **subtitled** rather than dubbed in order to hear the voices of the original actors.

Synchronized sound also made new kinds of films possible. For example, although slapstick comedy faded with the coming of sound, another kind of comedy, bristling with word play and snappy one-liners, began to flourish. The Marx Brothers, W.C. Fields, Mae West, Woody Allen, and Mel Brooks, among many others, depend extensively on the spoken word for their humor. Although a few films—like Charles Chaplin's CITY LIGHTS (1931) and MODERN TIMES (1936), in which he refused to capitulate to sound, or Mel Brooks's parody, SILENT MOVIE (1976)—harken back to the mimetic comedy of the pre-sound era, film comedy generally embraced sound and fashioned new comic styles and conventions built on verbal wit as well as on **sight gags.**

Film critic Gavin Lambert points out that "sound and dialogue give us a closer, more immediate impression of life than images alone." "An image without sound," says Lambert, "is in itself a formalization; an image with sound is a natural combination and makes a formalized style more difficult to achieve" (51). The introduction of spoken language in motion pictures, therefore, usually makes them more naturalistic. Dramatic interaction between characters is simply more true to life if they speak aloud to one another. As Cook points out with THE JAZZ SINGER, *overhearing* film characters speak brings greater intimacy and realism to the film experience.

On the other hand, film critics sometimes complain that movies talk *too* much. Walter Kerr, referring to Sidney Lumet's THE VERDICT (1982) in an article entitled "In Praise of Silence in Film," writes:

> I was looking at a motion picture, but the essential thing about any motion picture—the moving image—had no real function to perform. The actors' words told the story; the actors' words revealed character. The *picture* was left with little to do . . . . Film was most intensely *film* when the picture had to do all, or nearly all, of the work, because there was neither speech nor realistic sound to go with it.
> (42, 44)

What do you think of Walter Kerr's comments? Do movies talk too much today? In embracing the spoken word so wholeheartedly, have motion pictures sacrificed essential cinematic functions? Do Walter Kerr's observations about THE VERDICT apply to many films you have seen recently? Answer these questions for yourself before reading on about some functions of spoken language in movies.

Spoken language in films occurs in monologues, dialogues, and narration. A **monologue** is a speech by a character alone on the screen or clearly out of other characters' earshot. **Dialogue** is verbal exchange between two or more characters. **Narration** is verbal information related directly to the audience rather than indirectly through dialogue.

One major difference between spoken language in the cinema and in the theater is that in films spoken words may be presented in **lip sync** as a character speaks or as **voice-over,** heard on the sound track even though the character is not on screen or is not speaking. For example, in Laurence Olivier's film of Shakespeare's RICHARD III (1956), Olivier delivers Richard's soliloquies straight to the camera, and thus directly to each viewer. In Hitchcock's PSYCHO (1960), on the other hand, Norman Bates (Anthony Perkins), settling into a catatonic state at the end of the film, delivers his final words as an **interior monologue** while the camera shows his immobile face in a close-up.

How Do Films Tell a Story?

Most viewers associate a narrator with **documentary films** where a speaker, usually off screen, supplements visual information or provides dramatic or ironic counterpoint to the images on the screen. Alain Resnais's NIGHT AND FOG (1955), for example, about Nazi extermination camps, contrasts present-day color footage and black-and-white **archive footage** of the camps. Resnais's narrator, addressing the audience matter-of-factly about the terrible dehumanization of the camps, connects the tragedies of the past with the indifference of the present as a devastating warning about the dangers of disregarding basic human rights. The narrator's restrained, understated tone of voice contrasts dramatically with the horrible information he delivers.

More recent documentaries, however, tend to reduce the role of the narrator or eliminate it completely. Frederick Wiseman, for example, has made more than a dozen provocative documentary films about modern-day institutions like public schools (HIGH SCHOOL, 1968), hospitals (THE TITICUT FOLLIES, 1967, and HOSPITAL, 1970), police (LAW AND ORDER, 1969), and the military (BASIC TRAINING, 1971). In these films he has chosen not to use a narrator at all but to let carefully edited footage speak for itself.

Sometimes fictional films also employ a narrator to convey information directly to the audience. In Frederico Fellini's AMARCORD (1974) for example, a man who presents himself as a town historian steps forward from time to time to introduce and comment on characters, customs, and events in the story. In Ingmar Bergman's HOUR OF THE WOLF (1968), Alma (Liv Ullmann) sometimes speaks directly to the camera, as if in a television interview, to relate strange events surrounding her husband's disappearance. Some films follow the literary convention of employing a narrator who is not a character in the story. For example, in Tony Richardson's TOM JONES (1963) an off-screen narrator—modeled on the omniscient narrator in the original eighteenth-century novel by Henry Fielding—introduces characters, smooths transitions between scenes, and offers witty comments on the action.

Three important films of the 1970s—A CLOCKWORK ORANGE (1971), BADLANDS (1974), and APOCALYPSE NOW (1979)—illustrate how a film story can become more meaningful for the audience when the principal character narrates what she or he perceives. In Francis Ford Coppola's APOCALYPSE NOW, Army Captain Benjamin Willard (Martin Sheen) accepts a mission during the Vietnam War to find and "terminate" a renegade U.S. officer in the jungles of Laos. As he travels up the river in search of Colonel Kurtz (Marlon Brando), Willard's thoughts about the mission and the man he is supposed to kill are presented in voice-over narration. As we listen to Willard's words, we see that his reflections on this mission are more important than the mission itself. The real drama of the film is the personal moral dilemma Willard faces in carrying out his assignment. Will Captain Willard follow his orders and assassinate Colonel Kurtz or, like him, succumb to disillusionment and desert the military?

In BADLANDS and A CLOCKWORK ORANGE there is considerable discrepancy between the way the narrators describe events in the story and the way these events are depicted on screen. In Terrence Malick's BADLANDS, Holly Sargis (Sissy Spacek), reading from her diary, maintains a running voice-over commentary about her relationship with Kit Carruthers (Martin Sheen), a psychopathic drifter modeled after the 1950s serial murderer Charles Starkweather. Holly runs off with Kit even though he kills her father and burns down her home. Her naive observations about Kit, which sound like drivel in a movie fan magazine, contrast strikingly with the cold-blooded, remorseless killings he commits throughout the film. Her narration, in a tone that exhibits neither shock nor serious reflection, creates a layer of irony in the film which underscores Kit's psychopathic behavior and Holly's fascination with it and which helps explain how the news media can make a killer like Kit into a celebrity.

The protagonist in Stanley Kubrick's A CLOCKWORK ORANGE, Alex (Malcolm McDowell), is a psychopathic criminal who thrives on brutality and Beethoven. Alex's voice-over narration—delivered in terse, graphic street dialect—not only provides a personal account of events in the story but also reveals his sadistic tendencies and his complete disregard for other people. In one scene, for example, where Alex is looking to improve his situation in prison, we see him, apparently enthralled by religion, devoutly reading *The Bible* and turning his eyes toward heaven. Actually, Alex is fantasizing brutal, rapacious roles for himself in Bible scenes. He imagines himself, for instance, as a sadistic Roman soldier scourging Jesus on the way to Calvary.

How does spoken language contribute to film narrative? Perhaps this question seems self-obvious, like asking how air contributes to breathing. But we should remember that spoken language is not indispensable for cinematic storytelling, since many magnificent narrative films predated sound. Nor does spoken language necessarily improve a film, since inferior talkies themselves fueled arguments against synchronized sound in the 1930s. Filmmakers can employ many cinematic tools to tell a story; spoken language is an important one, but not the only one.

A dramatic story can be told entirely with spoken language, of course. In radio drama there is no visual component to the story. And in the theater, although costumes, sets, and lighting are important to the overall experience, the dialogue basically carries the story. But what can movies do with spoken language that stage and radio drama cannot? How can dialogue be used "cinematically"? Jot down some ideas before reading further.

Consider the following scene from CITIZEN KANE (1941), which takes place early in Kane's career as a newspaper publisher (fig. 5.3):

> **KANE:** There's something I've got to get into this paper besides pictures and print. I've got to make the New York "Inquirer" as important to New York as the gas in that light.
> *He turns out gas*
> **LELAND:** What're you going to do, Charlie?
> **KANE:** My Declaration of Principles. Don't smile, Jedediah.
> *Kane comes to f.g. with paper, puts it on table*
> **KANE:** I've got it all written, the declaration.
> **BERNSTEIN:** You don't wanta make any promises, Mr. Kane, you don't wanta keep.
> **KANE:** These'll be kept. I'll provide the people of this city with a daily paper that will tell all the news honestly. I will also provide them—
> *Leland comes to two in f.g.*
> **LELAND:** That's the second sentence you've started with "I."
> **KANE:** People are going to know who's responsible, and they're going to get the truth in the "Inquirer," quickly and simply and entertainingly. And no special interests are going to be allowed to interfere with that truth.
> *Leland sits down at left—Kane picking up paper*
> **KANE:** I will also provide them with a fighting and tireless champion of their rights as citizens and as human beings.
> *Kane puts paper down and signs it*
> **LELAND:** May I have that, Charlie?
> **KANE:** I'm going to print it.
> *(RKO 351-52)*

This scene is an interesting example of cinematic dialogue. It would not play as well on radio or in the theater. Study the scene again and see if you can tell why.

In the first speech, notice that Kane reinforces his intention to make *The Inquirer* "as important to New York as the gas in that light" by actually turning off the gas. The analogy between the newspaper and the gas is revealing not because Kane *states* it but because we *see* him extinguish the light. The words by themselves do not specify what

Figure 5.3
CITIZEN KANE employs
dialogue cinematically in
the scene where Kane
signs his Declaration of
Principles.

"important" means, but the action does. Kane wants *The Inquirer* to be a
"source of light" in New York and, apparently, wants the power to control
that light. This suggestion of manipulation and personal power is not
evident in the line itself nor in Kane's earnest tone of voice, but rather in
the physical action of extinguishing the gas lamp.

A few lines later, as Kane is spelling out his Declaration of
Principles, Leland interrupts him with, "That's the second sentence you've
started with 'I'," suggesting that his principles are not written in good
form. He may also be suggesting that they are too egocentric. But Kane
answers that "people are going to know who is responsible" and continues
with another promise, starting with "I" again, to make his paper the
champion of people's rights as citizens and human beings. His voice is
resolute and reverent as he speaks. Leland is inspired by Kane's promises

How Do Films Tell a Story?

and asks to keep the document. Yet the scene is almost too solemn, and Kane's principles too idealized. Will Charlie Kane be able to live up to them? Bernstein, in his colorful yet practical vernacular, voices some misgiving when he says, "You don't wanta make any promises, Mr. Kane, you don't wanta keep." Bernstein is suggesting that a time may come when Kane will not *want* to fulfill such lofty promises.

The scene directions do not indicate that as Kane steps to the table to sign his Declaration of Principles his face falls into a dark shadow and is not discernible at all, although his hand and the document are very distinctly lit. What do you think is the purpose of such unusual lighting at the climax of the scene? Why does Welles hide Kane's face in the shadows? What is he suggesting about Kane's promises to the people of New York?

Clearly, there is some irony here: Kane is signing his name to noble principles, but his face is in the dark. This disparity between what the character says in the scene and how the director photographs him awakens the viewer's suspicions. Although Kane may have the best intentions now, perhaps he will not want to keep these promises when his need for personal power makes them inconvenient. Perhaps when *Kane* is important enough to the people of New York, he will turn off his promises like the gas in the lamp.

Thus, we observe that a subtle discrepancy between the words and the images in this scene has been building up since Kane turned out the gas. The shadow that darkens Kane's face at what should be his brightest moment, as he signs the Declaration of Principles, reinforces the underlying irony in this scene. After all, Kane *created* that shadow when he turned off the gas light.

What we can learn from this scene is that spoken language in films is most cinematic when the combination of words and images produces more information about or a more complete experience of a scene than either words or images would produce alone. The scene would not be as effective on radio because the audience would not see Kane extinguish the gas lamp or step into the shadow as he signs the declaration. Nor would the scene be as effective on stage because it is too intimate for the theater. Kane's subtle gestures and facial expressions, the details of the gas lamp and the Declaration of Principles—photographed at medium-to-close range in the film—would be lost on spectators watching from the second balcony. To use spoken language cinematically, therefore, means to combine words and images in a film so that they effectively reinforce or oppose one another.

Sound Effects

Anything recorded on a film sound track that is not music or spoken language is considered a **sound effect**. Sound effects may include incidental background noise, like the wind blowing or a train passing; nonvocal sounds characters make, like footsteps or knuckle-cracking; and sounds specifically linked with the action of a scene, like gunshots or a doorbell.

Since the days of the early talkies, tremendous technical developments have taken place in sound reproduction. Sophisticated recording equipment today can pick up and magnify the minutest sounds at considerable distances, a fact dramatized in films like THE ANDERSON TAPES (1971), THE CONVERSATION (1974), and BLOW OUT (1981); and audio systems in most theaters can reproduce them in stereophonic **Dolby sound.** Sound effects are generally recorded on the shooting set, particularly for scenes shot outdoors or **on location.** But today, sound effects are often produced separately in special sound studios and later synchronized with the visual footage. For example, sound effects specialists may create the sound track for a barroom fistfight by pummeling leather dummies and smashing furniture and glass—all carefully rehearsed and timed to match the visual action. If the effects are done well and the sound track properly **mixed** and synchronized with the film footage, the audience will not recognize that the sound was recorded separately.

Sounds can serve the same narrative functions in films that images do. For instance, sound effects can help establish setting. Filmmakers often use sounds associated with particular places—like Big Ben in London or cable car bells in San Francisco—to help identify locations in films. In fact, movies sometimes popularize associations between specific sounds and places, as films about Vietnam have connected the sound of helicopters with that war. Background sound can also reinforce a film's atmosphere, as does the incessant rain in BLADE RUNNER (1982) or the trickling and drifting sand in WOMAN IN THE DUNES (1964). The prominent ticking of clocks in HIGH NOON (1953) and in CRIES AND WHISPERS (1972) both intensifies a mood and indicates a preoccupation with time (fig. 5.4). Sounds can identify characters, like the famous jungle call in the Johnny Weissmuller Tarzan movies or the computer bleeps of the little robot R2-D2 in George Lucas's STAR WARS trilogy. Sounds can facilitate transitions from one scene to another, as the jarring sound of the power drill does between the first two scenes in DON'T LOOK NOW (1973). (See chapter 4.)

Figure 5.4
The background sound of
clocks in HIGH NOON
intensifies the film's mood
and preoccupation with
time.

Some sound effects are very carefully worked into the
script. For CITIZEN KANE, director Orson Welles created a montage
technique he called the "lightning mix," which employs sound effects to
provide a **sound bridge** across several shots. For instance, Welles com-
presses Kane's snowballing political campaign into three shots, linked by
the sound of handclapping that grows in volume and magnitude across the
shots. First Kane alone applauds Susan Alexander's singing; then a modest but enthusiastic street gathering applauds a campaign speech for Kane
(fig. 5.5*a*); and finally a tumultuous crowd at an organized political rally
wildly applauds Kane himself (fig. 5.5*b*).

Sound

a

Figure 5.5
Two scenes from
CITIZEN KANE con-
nected in a "lightning
mix," where applause
serves as a sound bridge
from (a) a street-corner
speech to (b) a tumultu-
ous political rally.

The preceding paragraphs describe sound effects that enhance or reinforce images shown on the screen. Sometimes, however, the most cinematic sound effects are those that occur off screen. As early as 1929, the French film director René Clair observed: "We do not need to *hear* the sound of clapping if we can *see* the clapping hands" (42). Clair asserted that sound effects contribute the most to films in instances where sound replaces the shot: "It is the *alternative*, not the simultaneous, use of the visual subject and of the sound produced by it that creates the best effects" (43). In a conversation between two characters on screen, for example, it is often more interesting to observe the listener's face than the speaker's.

b

A striking example of **off-screen sound** complementing
action on screen occurs in CITIZEN KANE (1941) when Kane (Orson
Welles) slaps his wife, Susan Alexander (Dorothy Comingore), during an
argument. The two are in a tent at a picnic, where they can be easily
overheard by revelers outside. Instead, during a brief, tense silence after
the slap, we hear from outside the tent another woman's hysterical cries.
We never learn who that woman is or why she is screaming, but her cries
dramatically underscore the tension inside the tent. This scene could
certainly play without the off-screen sound effects, but the hysterical cries
do reinforce the raw feelings between Kane and Susan.

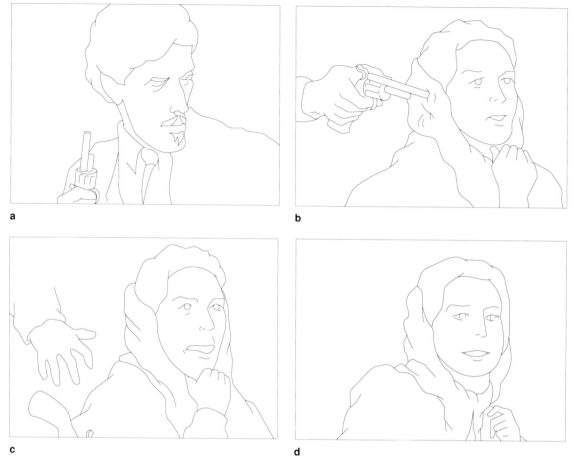

a

b

c

d

Figure 5.6
Line drawings of four frames from a shot in STAGECOACH in which off-screen sound effects complement the action on the screen. In this scene an off-screen gunshot ironically saves the woman's life.

Part of the famous chase in John Ford's STAGECOACH (1939), on the other hand, would be seriously hamstrung without the off-screen sound effects that supply essential story information to complement the visual footage. As the Apaches are about to overtake the stagecoach and the passengers have run out of ammunition, Hatfield (John Carradine), a gentleman gambler, saves one last round in his pistol to keep Mrs. Mallory (Louise Platt) out of the hands of the Indians. In a medium-close shot Ford shows Hatfield, pistol in hand, looking off screen toward Mrs. Mallory (fig. 5.6a); then the camera pans right to reveal her crouched against the side of the coach with Hatfield's cocked pistol aimed at her head (fig. 5.6b). But before he fires, a gunshot is heard off screen, and Hatfield's hand drops lifelessly (fig. 5.6c). Immediately, a bugle sounding the charge emerges faintly in the orchestral score (which accompanies the entire scene), and Mrs. Mallory's facial expression suddenly radiates hope (fig. 5.6*d*). "Can you hear it?" she exclaims. "It's a bugle. They're blowing the charge." Then, the cavalry rushes to the stagecoach's rescue, routing the Apaches. In this scene a single off-screen gunshot communicates that an Indian bullet, ironically, has saved Mrs. Mallory's life. Likewise, the faint bugle notes in the musical score explain why Mrs. Mallory's face suddenly brightens.

Roman Polanski's CHINATOWN (1974) offers a striking example of how sound effects can foreshadow a dramatic moment in a film. Private investigator J.J. Gittes (Jack Nicholson) is trying to sort out circumstances surrounding a mysterious drowning in Southern California in the 1930s. His client is Evelyn Mulwray (Faye Dunaway), wife of the deceased and daughter of an extremely prosperous Los Angeles businessman, Noah Cross (John Huston). Midway through the film, Gittes questions Mulwray in her car after she has returned from a late-night rendezvous with a young girl. The woman is withholding information, and Gittes wants to know why. Clearly very agitated during this conversation, Mulwray at one point leans forward and accidentally sounds the car horn with her forehead, startling herself.

This seemingly inconsequential business with the car horn figures significantly in the climactic final moments of the film, which also take place at night. To escape an ugly confrontation with her father, Evelyn Mulwray shoots him in the arm (fig. 5.7) and drives off in her convertible with the young girl. The police, who are on hand, fire warning shots; but one of them takes aim and shoots at the car. In an **extreme long shot** Polanski shows the convertible stopped down the street, while on the sound track we hear the steady blast of the automobile horn and, a moment later, hysterical screams.

In the long shot we cannot see either of the two people in the convertible; yet we immediately understand what has happened and, indeed, can picture it in detail. We are certain that Evelyn Mulwray has been shot and that the child is screaming. Why are we so sure? Why doesn't it occur to us that the girl in the passenger seat has been shot and that Mulwray is screaming? The automobile horn is the key. The earlier scene with Gittes and Mulwray in the car established a connection between the car horn and the woman's head falling forward against the steering wheel. We do not consciously take note of it at that time, but the unexpected blurt of the car horn in the quiet night provides a small shock to reinforce the association between the head and the horn. In the final scene, therefore, the car horn triggers that earlier association and the unpleasant feeling

Figure 5.7
A still from a climactic scene in CHINATOWN in which off-screen sound has dramatic impact.

linked with it. In fact, since the camera angle in the earlier scene photographed Mulwray from the passenger side of the front seat, we picture her head hitting the steering wheel in the later scene from that same point of view, thus visualizing the horror of the shooting through the child's eyes. The prolonged blast of the car horn reveals in an instant what has happened in the car, even though we cannot see it. The young girl's screams only confirm what we already know: that Evelyn Mulwray is fatally shot and slumped against the steering wheel.

Sometimes the interaction of sound effects with visual images can serve several narrative functions at once. In ALL THAT JAZZ (1979), directed by Bob Fosse, there is a scene in which the protagonist, a Broadway director-choreographer named Joe Gideon (Roy Scheider), assembles the cast of his upcoming musical for a first reading of the play. The actors and actresses are seated around a table with their scripts. Gideon settles everyone with some low-key banter and asks for an easy, straightforward reading. But as the first lines are read, the cast breaks into uproarious laughter (clearly an overreaction to a weak joke), which gradually **fades out** until we cannot hear their voices at all. Instead, the sound track magnifies Gideon's nervous fidgeting as he listens to the play, drumming his fingers on the table, lighting a cigarette, snapping a pencil behind his back—sounds that would ordinarily be inconspicuous or lost behind the reading. Gideon's restless noises fill the sound track until, as the final lines of the play are read, the actors' voices **fade in** again.

What narrative functions do the sound effects serve in this scene? Why does Fosse shut out the actors' voices and magnify background noises?

One function of the sound effects in this scene is to help condense time. Since we do not hear the lines of the play, dialogue is not a factor here, as it usually is, in determining the length or the continuity of the scene. Eliminating the voices from the sound track, coupled with adept editing, telescopes time and creates a convenient ellipsis during the play reading. Thus, although the voices fade out for only about one and a half minutes on screen, the viewer understands that the cast has read through the entire script.

Second, the sound effects make it clear that the lines of the script are unimportant; Joe Gideon's reactions to the reading are what count. The usual hierarchy of sound—where spoken words carry more weight than background noises—is reversed in this scene.

Third, eliminating the voices helps Fosse single out Joe Gideon from the rest of the characters in the scene and dramatize his movements and gestures rather than their words and laughter. Gideon is not laughing. His nervous behavior, isolated and magnified on the sound track, suggests a more realistic appraisal of the play's humor. Also, foreshortening time in the scene conveys his intense concentration and sense of timelessness during the reading. In short, the sound effects help Fosse present the script reading from Joe Gideon's perspective; they present *subjective* hearing, much like point-of-view shots present subjective vision.

Conclusion

Sound effects, spoken language, and music in films often affect us subliminally. In the most dramatic scenes we are sometimes least aware of the sound track. This chapter has tried to call attention to some narrative functions of sound in movies and to illustrate how filmmakers employ sound cinematically. In good films, sound does more than reiterate what images depict; in the best films, sound is an indispensable part of the cinematic experience.

General Study Questions

1. Make notes about background music in recent films you have seen. What kind of films (or scenes) employ a lot of background music? What kind do not? Try to anticipate when music will occur in a film. Write a workable thesis statement about background music in today's movies based upon your observations.

2. Compare and contrast background music in films from different decades. How do Hollywood films of the 1930s or 1940s employ music? Is music used much differently in movies of the 1950s or 1960s? How does background music in today's films compare with any of these decades?

3. Film critic Gavin Lambert argues that silent and sound approaches to filmmaking are antithetical. The emphasis of the silent approach, he says, is on concentration, essence, poetry; the emphasis of the sound approach is on narrative, incident, the diffusions of life (49). Explain what this statement means, illustrating with examples from silent and sound films you have seen.

4. As an experiment, turn off the sound during a scene where two characters interact at length. How much can you understand about the scene from the images alone? Are there visible signals about what transpires between them? Watch again with sound, and observe to what extent audio and visual components of the scene complement each other. Describe what you learned from the experiment.

5. Concentrate on sound effects in a scene with lots of action—a chase scene, a fight, a shoot-out, etc. Keep track of the different background noises in the scene and how they are used. Watch the scene again without sound. How much do sound effects contribute to the impact of the scene? Discuss what you learned about sound effects from the exercise.
6. Select a movie from the Additional Films for Study at the end of this chapter and analyze how its sound complements and reinforces the story.

Additional Films for Study

ALL QUIET ON THE WESTERN FRONT (1930), dir. Lewis Milestone
THE RED SHOES (1948), dir. Michael Powell and Emeric Pressburger
ON THE WATERFRONT (1954), dir. Elia Kazan
BLACK ORPHEUS (1959), dir. Marcel Camus
PSYCHO (1960), dir. Alfred Hitchcock
WEST SIDE STORY (1961), dir. Robert Wise and Jerome Robbins
FISTFUL OF DOLLARS (1964), dir. Sergio Leone
THE UMBRELLAS OF CHERBOURG (1964), dir. Jacques Demy
2001: A SPACE ODYSSEY (1968), dir. Stanley Kubrick
THE ANDERSON TAPES (1971), dir. Sidney Lumet
A CLOCKWORK ORANGE (1971), dir. Stanley Kubrick
PLAY MISTY FOR ME (1971), dir. Clint Eastwood
THE CONVERSATION (1974), dir. Francis Ford Coppola
JAWS (1975), dir. Steven Spielberg
ANNIE HALL (1977), dir. Woody Allen
STAR WARS (1977), dir. George Lucas
THE TIN DRUM (1979), dir. Volker Schlöndorff
ALIEN (1979), dir. Ridley Scott
BLOOD WEDDING (1981), dir. Carlos Saura
BLOW OUT (1981), dir. Brian DePalma
DIVA (1982), dir. Jean-Jacques Beineix
AMADEUS (1984), dir. Miloš Forman
RADIO DAYS (1987), dir. Woody Allen
DIRTY DANCING (1987), dir. Emile Ardolino
MOONSTRUCK (1987), dir. Norman Jewison

Further Reading

Bazelon, Irwin. *Knowing the Score: Notes on Film Music.* New York: Van Nostrand Reinhold, 1972.
Cameron, Evan W., ed. *Sound and the Cinema: The Coming of Sound to American Film.* Pleasantville, N.Y.: Redgrave, 1979.
Casper, Joseph A. *Vincente Minnelli and the Film Musical.* London: Thomas Yoseloff, 1977.

Evans, Mark. *Soundtrack: The Music of the Movies.* New York: Hopkinson and Blake, 1975.

"Film Music." *Cinema Journal* 17 (Spring 1978). [Special issue]

Geduld, Harry M. *The Birth of the Talkies: From Edison to Jolson.* Bloomington: Indiana University Press, 1975.

Hagen, Earl. *Scoring for Films.* New York: Wehman, 1972.

Limbacher, James L. *Film Music from Violins to Video.* Metuchen, N.J.: Scarecrow Press, 1974.

McMarthy, Clifford. *Film Composers in America.* New York: Da Capo, 1972.

McVay, Douglas. *The Musical Film.* Cranbury, N.J.: A.S. Barnes, 1967.

Mordden, Ethan. *The Hollywood Musical.* New York: St. Martin's Press, 1982.

Prendergast, Roy M. *Film Music: A Neglected Art.* New York: W.W. Norton, 1977.

Sterne, Lee E. *The Movie Musical.* New York: Pyramid, 1974.

Taylor, John Russell, and Arthur Jackson. *The Hollywood Musical.* New York: McGraw-Hill, 1971.

Thomas, Tony. *Music for the Movies.* San Diego: A.S. Barnes, 1973.

Thrasher, Frederic. *Okay for Sound.* New York: Duell, Sloan & Pierce, 1964.

Walker, Alexander. *The Shattered Silents: How the Talkies Came to Stay.* New York: William Morrow, 1979.

Weis, Elizabeth, and John Belton, eds. *Film Sound: Theory and Practice.* New York: Columbia University Press, 1985.

Wysotsky, Michael Z. *Wide-Screen Cinerama and Stereophonic Sound.* New York: Hastings House, 1971.

Works Cited

Borneman, Ernest. Quoted in *The Technique of Film Music,* by Roger Manvell and John Huntley. New York: Hastings House, 1969.

Brown, Royal S. "Herrmann, Hitchcock, and the Music of the Irrational." In *Film Theory and Criticism,* 3d ed, edited by Gerald Mast and Marshall Cohen, 618-49. New York: Oxford University Press, 1985.

Clair, René. "The Art of Sound." In *Film: A Montage of Theories,* edited by Richard Dyer MacCann, 38-44. New York: E.P. Dutton, 1966.

Cook, David A. *A History of Narrative Film.* New York: W.W. Norton, 1981.

Eisenstein, Sergei. "Form and Content: Practice." In *The Film Sense,* translated and edited by Jay Leyda, 157-216. New York: Harcourt, Brace & World, 1975.

Kerr, Walter. "In Praise of Silence in Films." *The New York Times Magazine.* 30 Sept. 1984: 42, 44.

Lambert, Gavin. "Sight and Sound." In *Film: A Montage of Theories,* edited by Richard Dyer MacCann, 45-52. New York: E.P. Dutton, 1966.

Levy, Louis. Quoted in *The Technique of Film Music,* by Roger Manvell and John Huntley. New York: Hastings House, 1969.

Manvell, Roger, and John Huntley. *The Technique of Film Music.* New York: Hastings House, 1969.

RKO Cutting Continuity of the Orson Welles Production CITIZEN KANE. In *The CITIZEN KANE Book.* Boston: Little, Brown, 1971.

How Do Films
Reveal Characters?

When we go to the movies, most of us expect to encounter characters on the screen who will move or entertain us—characters we can identify with, look up to, fantasize about. We know exactly what to expect from some characters; other characters are full of surprises. Some film characters fade with the closing credits; others stay with us for a lifetime. Why? What makes some characters more memorable than others? How do filmmakers bring characters to life on the screen? How do film characters reflect the way we see ourselves and the society we live in?

It is no simple matter to create memorable characters on the screen. Good acting is important, of course, but filmmakers also use various cinematic techniques and devices to develop characters. Close-up shots bring us close enough to observe a character's subtlest facial expression, and point-of-view shots allow us to see through a character's eyes. With flashbacks, the filmmaker can show a character's past, and with dream sequences, even his or her unconscious thoughts and feelings. Chapter 6, "Character Exposition," examines these cinematic devices and how they reveal characters in movies.

Chapters 7 and 8 offer models for analyzing film characters within a social-historical framework. Chapter 7, "Archetypes and Stereotypes," delves into intrinsic characteristics of heroes, villains, and gender models in movies. What does a pop hero like Rambo, for instance, reveal about American attitudes and values in the 1980s? What messages does RAMBO convey about what is heroic and villainous, manly and womanly?

Chapter 8 zeroes in on character relationships—romantic relationships, power relationships, family relationships—and what they reflect about American society. For example, how is the romantic relationship Frank Capra depicts in IT HAPPENED ONE NIGHT (1934) different from the one Adrian Lyne depicts in FATAL ATTRACTION (1987)? What do these differences tell us about American attitudes toward sex, marriage, and family? Chapter 8 explores how character relationships in such films reveal changes in our social institutions.

TOOTSIE (1982), dir. Sidney Pollack.

Think of an interesting character you have encountered recently in a story or a novel and imagine that you are going to make a film about her or him. How do you develop a character from words on a page into a vital person on the screen? How do you reproduce your image of the character's energy and personality for an audience? How do you communicate the character's inner being? Chapter 6 explores such questions about character development and exposition in movies, focusing on film acting and on the cinematic techniques of **close-ups, point-of-view shots,** and **flashbacks,** memories, and dreams.

Film Acting

If we were to count all the biographies and autobiographies of movie stars and the reams of gossip about their personal and professional lives that fill pulp magazines and tabloids, we would find that more is written about film actors than about any other single aspect of moviemaking. Most movies attract audiences because of the stars who play in them, not because of the screenwriters, cinematographers, or directors who help create them—even though each of these people contributes to a movie's success at least as much as the actors do. But since actors and actresses work in front of the camera and appear bigger than life on the screen, they become public idols. On the other hand, we should not undervalue the contribution of good acting to a movie because characters cannot exist on the screen without actors and actresses to play them. Characters, no matter how brilliantly conceived in the script, do not become real for an audience until actors bring them to life.

Acting for the camera differs from acting on the stage in several important ways. A stage play is a continuous performance in which all dramatic and technical elements of the production must fall into place at the right moment each time the show goes on. The players in a scene are on stage together, continually in character and responding to one another as they play their roles. A play may be performed many times and is complete and unique each time. A movie, on the other hand, though it appears as a continuous performance on the screen, is photographed one shot at a time over an extended period, and usually not in chronological order. Two shots in the same scene may actually have been photographed weeks apart. Film directors have the option of repeating a shot again and again until they get a satisfactory **take.** Film actors work in short spurts, starting their performances on the "Action!" cue and stopping on "Cut!" Many times an actor must play a scene to the camera lens instead

How Do Films Reveal Characters?

of to another person. Close-up shots and sophisticated sound recording equipment allow the audience intimate access to the film actor, revealing subtle facial and vocal nuances impossible to discern in the theater.

The first film actors and actresses came to the fledgling movie business from the stage at a time when burlesque and melodrama were the dominant forms of popular entertainment. They generally had to overact their roles in order to reach audiences in playhouses that were often acoustically inadequate and poorly lit. They depended heavily on pantomime, broad gestures, and exaggerated facial expressions. Many were simply not ready for the intimacy of a movie camera and a shooting set. Some early filmmakers recognized that conventional stage acting was not suitable for the new medium. D.W. Griffith, for instance, generally avoided casting theater actors for his films and boasted that for THE BIRTH OF A NATION (1915), "there was not a stage star in my company." Griffith believed that, in addition to a photogenic face, a film star needed a special quality, which he called "soul":

> By that I mean people of great personalities, true emotions, and the ability to depict them before the camera. Stage emotions will not do; some of the greatest of actors appear stilted and "stalky" in front of the camera. . . . When a really good actor stands before the camera, he puts his soul into it—he isn't wondering what the people "down front" are thinking of him. He or she knows there is no audience in front, but a grim, cold-blooded, truth-in-detail-telling camera lens which will register every quiver of the facial muscles, every gleam of the eye, every expression of the face, every gesture, just as it is given.
> (50)

Rather than borrow actors from the stage, therefore, Griffith created movie stars. For THE BIRTH OF A NATION he cast the roles "by type," rehearsed extensively for the camera before shooting, and strove for subtle, realistic performances—practices that became standard procedure for most directors after Griffith.

The movie camera completely changes the relationship between performer and audience that exists in the theater. A movie audience may occasionally participate in the film experience, as in cult movies like THE ROCKY HORROR PICTURE SHOW (1975), or they may respond to an actor's invitation to participate, as in YANKEE DOODLE DANDY (1942) when James Cagney asks the audience to sing along with "Over There"; but there can never be any real interaction between movie actors and the audience because there is no physical connection between them (Naremore 29).

On the other hand, the movie camera is able to create psychological realism that is not present in the theater. The camera can greatly reduce the physical distance between the actors and the audience. (See the discussion of close-ups in the following section of this chapter.) Moreover, the camera is not confined to a fixed spot. It can record a scene from many positions or angles and can even assume the point of view of one or more characters in the scene. (See the discussion of point-of-view shots later in this chapter.) Finally, the camera can reveal both conscious and unconscious workings of a character's mind by depicting memories and dreams. (See the last sections of this chapter on flashbacks, memories, and dreams.)

Styles of film acting developed along with the technology of moviemaking. Screen acting changed drastically, for example, once motion pictures became "talkies"; and many stars of the silent era never survived the transition to sound. It is important, therefore, to judge acting performances within a historical context and not dismiss them out of hand because they look too unnatural or old-fashioned. For example, film viewers who are not familiar with silent movies sometimes criticize the movements and mannerisms of silent movie actors, which may look jerky and stilted today. But one explanation for that jerkiness is that in the early movies **film stock** was cranked through the camera by hand, rather than by a motor; consequently, it was sometimes difficult to maintain precise, constant film speed. For comedies, in fact, directors often instructed camera operators to **undercrank**—that is, to run film through the camera more slowly than normal so that the action took up fewer frames. Then, when projected at normal speed, the action appeared zanily speeded up on the screen. **Fast motion** was commonplace in silent **slapstick comedies,** like Mack Sennett's Keystone Kops movies, where the action on the screen ran at breakneck speed to heighten comic tension for wild chases and stunts. (Conversely, to **overcrank** the camera produces action that takes up more frames, which appears on the screen in **slow motion** when projected at normal speed.)

Acting styles in movies reflect the manners of the time and place they were made. But good acting is more than behaving naturally before the camera—that is, imitating the manners of the times. Alexander Knox, a stage and screen actor from the 1930s through the 1960s, argues that true acting is "behaving plus interpretation," a rare and somewhat mystical combination found in the greatest artists: "The ability to be just like the man next door is a necessary part of an actor's equipment, but it does not make a Chaplin" (65). The best film actors, from Chaplin's time

How Do Films Reveal Characters?

to the present, have understood that the deepest character revelation occurs when an actor, without insecurity or self-consciousness, creates a personality on the screen who is at once uniquely individual and universally human.

One way to discover how film actors bring "behaving plus interpretation" before the movie camera is to observe how one actor or actress plays several major roles. Some vintage movie stars, like John Wayne or Marlene Dietrich, were repeatedly **typecast** for certain kinds of roles; but others, like Laurence Olivier or Bette Davis, played dozens of different kinds of characters during their film careers. With some of today's most versatile screen performers, like Dustin Hoffman or Robert De Niro, Faye Dunaway or Meryl Streep, the audience is never quite sure from one movie to the next what kind of character they will play.

Study the characters created by some of your favorite movie actors and actresses. What do they do to bring out the personalities and identities of the characters they portray? How do they reveal a character's inner self?

Close-ups

Anyone who looks carefully at a family photo album appreciates how expressive and revealing the human face can be. "Facial expression is the most subjective manifestation of man," observes film theorist Béla Balázs (188). But close-up shots in films can sometimes reveal a character even more intimately than a photograph. In Ingmar Bergman's PERSONA (1967), for example, a stage actress named Elizabeth Vogler (Liv Ullmann), who has suffered an emotional breakdown and has chosen to live in silence, watches the sun set from her hospital bed. Bergman and his cinematographer Sven Nykvist photograph her face in a close-up as she watches. In a very long take—more than a minute—the camera locks in on Elizabeth, who looks straight back into the lens without moving or blinking, until darkness engulfs her. Even when we can barely see her face, and her eyes not at all, the camera keeps rolling; but we *feel* her gaze. Finally, the last of the sunlight having faded, Elizabeth turns her head aside so that her face is dimly silhouetted in profile.

This shot of Elizabeth features no dialogue, no action, not even much expression on her face—only quiet chamber music playing on the radio beside her bed. So we listen to the music and vicariously experience the sunset, while maintaining unbroken eye contact with her. The close-up creates a feeling of great intimacy, an emotional bonding, between this character on the screen and ourselves. We are alone with Elizabeth Vogler, imagining what goes through her troubled mind as night falls, wondering what lurks behind her silence.

Almost immediately, Bergman follows up with another close-up that reveals a different emotion in Elizabeth as she watches television news footage of a Buddhist monk in Vietnam setting himself on fire. The horror of the scene overpowers Elizabeth. She backs into a corner away from the television and covers her mouth in shock, yet she continues to watch. The camera stalks her into the corner, from progressively closer positions, until it frames her face in an **extreme close-up.**

With these two close-ups Bergman not only suggests the range and intensity of Elizabeth's emotions but makes the audience feel them as well. In this section of the chapter we will explore how directors like Bergman use close-ups to reveal the inner being of film characters and why these close-ups have such a powerful impact on the viewer.

Two important factors determine how effectively close-ups reveal a character's inner being: the expressiveness of the actor or actress and the ability of the filmmaker to capture that expressiveness on film. Consider, for example, two stills (fig. 6.1) from Carl Dreyer's THE PASSION OF JOAN OF ARC (1928), a classic silent film that uses close-ups extensively. What can you observe about Joan's emotional state just from these close-ups of her face? What can you observe about how Dreyer uses camera and lighting to reveal her feelings? Write down your observations before reading further.

The first shot (fig. 6.1a) is uplifting. Joan (Renée Falconetti) holds her head erect, her face and eyes raised. She is faintly smiling. Her hand, with a heavy ring on the third finger, is secure and relaxed at her throat. She is looking out of the frame, and whatever she sees there raises her spirits. The low camera angle reinforces the uplifting pose and enhances her stature. The **key light** from above left highlights her upturned face, adds luster to her eyes, and features her hand against the shadows under her chin. Secondary **back lighting** from the right softens the shadows on her face and gives her a noticeable aura. Joan's strong, vertical pose, squared off and solidly grounded in the right half of the frame, projects stability and confidence, and leaves open space around her that extends beyond the frame on the left.

The second shot of Joan of Arc (fig. 6.1b), downcast and demeaned, contrasts with the first in almost every way. Her hair is cropped, and there are tears on her cheeks. Her eyes and face are turned down; her mouth is sad. Dark clothing and harsh lighting combine to

How Do Films Reveal Characters?

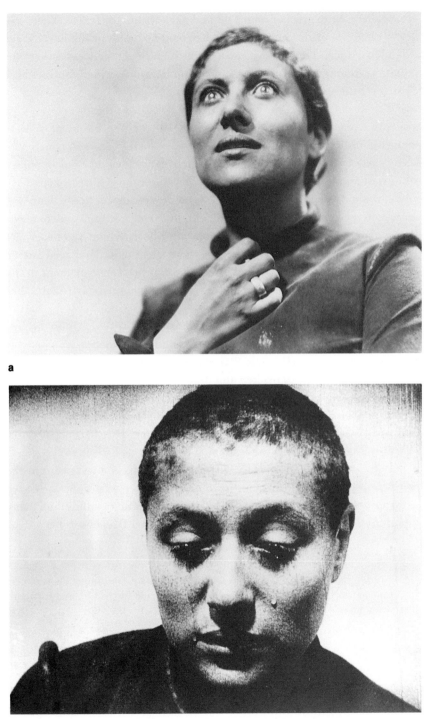

a

b

Figure 6.1
Two close-ups from THE
PASSION OF JOAN OF
ARC demonstrate the
expressiveness of the
human face. These
starkly contrasting images
reveal Joan's emotions at
critical moments during
her ordeal.

create sharp contrasts between light and dark within the frame. There are heavy shadows around her eyes, at her temples, and on the lower right side of her face. The camera, at a slight high angle, reinforces her humiliation. Joan's gaze is directed down into the frame, which confines her, closing off the space around her on every side.

Within the context of Dreyer's film, these two close-ups are quite powerful shots that lay bare Joan of Arc's soul at critical moments in her ordeal. The first occurs in a highly charged courtroom scene early in the film. The judges, French clergy loyal to English nobles who want Joan dead, have devised a trick question to entrap her: "Are you in the state of grace?" Whether she answers yes or no, they will use the answer to incriminate her. Joan is afraid, uncertain, with no one to trust. But as she turns her eyes to heaven, her face fills with light and peace. "If I am," she answers, "may God keep me there. If I am not, may God put me there." Thus, the first close-up reveals Joan at her finest moment in the film when, entrusting herself to God, she momentarily frustrates her inquisitors and triumphs over them.

The second close-up, however, reveals Joan at her bleakest moment. After much brutal questioning and increasingly serious threats of torture, Joan signs a recantation and is sentenced to life in prison. Back in her cell, broken and despairing, she must endure another humiliation. The court has ordered her head shaved. In a deeply moving scene Joan's hair is cut off snip by snip and falls to the floor around her, and with it falls the last of her dignity and spirit. The second close-up captures Joan in her darkest despair.

THE PASSION OF JOAN OF ARC is a testament to the emotional impact close-ups can have on the viewer when an expressive actor or actress and a responsive filmmaker combine talents. In an essay about his film style, "Thoughts on My Craft," Carl Dreyer wrote:

> Nothing in the world can be compared to the human face. It is a land one can never tire of exploring. There is no greater experience in a studio than to witness the expression of a sensitive face under the mysterious power of inspiration. To see it animated from the inside, and turning into poetry.
>
> (317)

Dreyer shot THE PASSION OF JOAN OF ARC almost entirely in close-up and stripped away from the film whatever might compete with or distract from the power of Renée Falconetti's face. The film is silent; the background is stark; the decor and the costumes are plain. Dreyer immersed his cast and crew in Joan of Arc's ordeal. For psychological effect he shot scenes in chronological order (very unusual and generally unprofitable in the motion picture business) and allowed neither wigs nor makeup. He had Falconetti's hair cut off on camera and reportedly drove her relentlessly, often under physical and psychological duress, to elicit the intensity he wanted in the role.

The close-up shot offers filmmakers an advantage that still photographers do not enjoy because motion pictures are not limited to a frozen moment in time. Motion pictures are able to show a dramatic moment building and receding, to set it more specifically in context, and thus to reveal a character more comprehensively. Moreover, the movie camera itself need not be static. In THE PASSION OF JOAN OF ARC, for example, the viewer sometimes senses that the camera—so persistently focused on Joan's face—is not merely *recording* her actions but somehow *determining* them. One Dreyer scholar, David Bordwell, observes that typically in THE PASSION OF JOAN OF ARC "the frame will be almost empty and the characters will move *into* it, as if the camera knew in advance where each action would end. Such deterministic framing traps the characters, creating an enclosed, claustrophobic effect" (31–2).

One can speak of "deterministic framing" and "claustrophobic effect" in a film partly because the frame itself, by definition, encloses and contains the image. The second close-up of Joan of Arc, for example, approximates how we might literally see her in a prison cell, confined on every side. Downcast and introspective, she appears trapped not only within the frame's rectangle but within herself as well. On the other hand, in the first close-up, the frame is inconspicuous. With her head and eyes raised, gazing up and out of the frame, Joan's spirit is reaching for the infinite. Why are we so aware of the frame and its confinement in one case and not in the other? What makes one close-up claustrophobic and the other expansive? The discussion that follows will be more productive if you think about these questions before reading on.

To address these questions we need to examine how space *within* the frame can suggest space *beyond* the frame. Consider how the composition of still #1 (fig. 6.1*a*) would be different, for example, if it were a typical senior yearbook picture, cropped on the left so that the subject's face is centered in the frame. Why does Dreyer frame Joan's face off center? Why does he leave so much space on the left side?

Since there is no indication in the shot about what lies outside the frame to the left, the eye assumes that the inside space extends beyond its edge. By leaving more space on the left side of the frame, therefore, Dreyer suggests an unrestrained openness and, in effect, eliminates the frame's left-hand border. Naturally, Joan's posture and facial expression contribute to the expansiveness we feel in this shot. We would not be drawn into the space beyond the frame if Joan's eyes were downcast, as in still #2 (fig. 6.1*b*), or staring directly into the camera lens, as in the close-up of Elizabeth Vogler watching the sun set in PERSONA.

But another reason one of these shots feels so claustrophobic and the other so expansive lies in the very nature of the close-up. Although it can reveal its subject in painstaking, intimate detail, the close-up can also remove that subject completely from its surroundings, thus making it abstract. The French film critic Jean Mitry explains that the close-up

> . . . gives a tactile, sensuous impression of things. But in isolating things, it makes them a kind of symbol: the object becomes the living representation of the concept which it figures forth, an *analog* for a pure state of mind. One can then say that the close-up is even more abstract on the intellectual plane than it is sensuous on the perceptual plane. Nothing is more concrete than what the close-up shows, but nothing is more abstract than what it suggests.
>
> (In Bordwell 25)

Thus, in the two stills from Dreyer's THE PASSION OF JOAN OF ARC, Renée Falconetti's face, sensuous and excruciatingly human in its detail, is at the same time an abstract representation of pure states of mind—uplifting spirituality or desperate confinement—that Joan of Arc experiences during her ordeal.

There is no guarantee that intimate character revelation will take place if a filmmaker uses lots of close-ups, for close-ups alone cannot make a film character interesting or deep. Television soap operas, for instance, shot almost entirely in close-up, turn out mostly banal, unidimensional "talking heads." But the close-up is certainly one of the greatest cinematic resources for revealing deep human experience.

Béla Balázs observes that modern theater no longer uses the spoken soliloquy because the public will not tolerate such an "unnatural" convention. On the other hand, with close-ups, film creates what Balázs calls the "silent soliloquy," in which a human face can speak with the subtlest shades of meaning without appearing unnatural.

> In this silent monologue the solitary human soul can find a tongue more candid and uninhibited than in any spoken soliloquy, for it speaks instinctively, subconsciously . . . . In the isolated close-up of the film we can see to the bottom of a soul by means of such tiny movements of facial muscles which even the most observant partner would never perceive.
>
> (190–91)

The candid and uninhibited silent soliloquy Renée Falconetti delivers in Carl Dreyer's THE PASSION OF JOAN OF ARC can serve as a benchmark against which to measure how deeply close-ups in other films plumb their characters' souls.

Point-of-view Shots

In one scene from THE GRADUATE (1967), directed by Mike Nichols and photographed by Robert Surtees, the protagonist, Benjamin (Dustin Hoffman), tries out scuba diving gear in the family swimming pool. On the screen we see exactly what Ben sees from behind the diving mask as he waddles into the pool and bobs around in the water, and on the **sound track** we hear him breathing with the aqualung.

This scene is an example of **subjective camera**, a cinematic technique in which the camera lens becomes a film character's "eyes," depicting what that character sees from his position in the scene. Such a shot is called a point-of-view shot (POV) or a **first-person shot.**

Point-of-view shots are not often designed as elaborately as this one in THE GRADUATE, where camera position, camera movement, and sound track work together to create Benjamin's view from inside the scuba gear. Usually, the filmmaker simply situates the camera where the character would be in the scene and shoots from that angle. But how do we recognize where point-of-view shots begin and end? How can we tell when the camera is subjective?

The most common way filmmakers identify a point-of-view shot is by enclosing it between close-ups of the character whose viewpoint is depicted. A close-up of the character's face (often showing focused attention) usually introduces the subjective shot; a cut back to the character's face (perhaps showing a reaction) usually closes it. Thus, the close-ups isolate the point-of-view shot like brackets isolate information in written text or in a mathematical equation. Even obvious point-of-view shots—like those that are **masked** to look like a view through binoculars or a telescope—generally use framing close-ups before and after to identify the subjective camera.

Point-of-view shots allow the audience to share a film character's perception of the world. But sometimes the subjective camera can reveal even more than what a character sees. For example, in THE LAST LAUGH (1924), F.W. Murnau's classic silent film about an aging hotel doorman who is demoted to a washroom attendant (fig. 6.2), Murnau and cinematographer Karl Freund use point-of-view shots in a scene

Figure 6.2
The hotel doorman in
THE LAST LAUGH
(*a*) standing proudly in his
splendid uniform and
(*b*) dejected after being
demoted to washroom
attendant.

a

How Do Films Reveal Characters?

b

where the doorman gets falling-down drunk. For this scene Freund strapped a lightweight camera to himself and stumbled around the room. But, as film historian David Cook points out, in the finished film the camera reveals the doorman's point of view on two levels:

> . . . in addition to assuming the position of the doorman's *physical eye*, the camera assumes the position of his *mind's eye* as well. During the same drunken scene, he feels acutely humiliated at the loss of his job and his prestigious uniform, and he imagines himself to be the object of ridicule and scorn. . . . At the height of his despair in this sequence, we see on the screen not the doorman (as with an objective camera), nor what he sees, but a visual embodiment of what he *feels*—a long lap-dissolved montage of malicious laughing faces in close-up. (124)

Point-of-view shots in a film can sometimes reveal inner character in a way that is most shocking, even horrifying. REPULSION (1965), for example, directed by Roman Polanski and photographed by Gilbert Taylor, uses subjective camera techniques to take the viewer inside the mind of a mentally disturbed person.

REPULSION is about a beautiful young woman, Carol Ledoux (Catherine Deneuve), who over a period of a few days lapses into complete schizophrenia (fig. 6.3). Alone in a sweltering apartment throughout most of the film, Carol experiences increasingly horrifying hallucinations, which we sometimes see from her point of view. In the beginning the hallucinations are fleeting: A crack appears in the kitchen wall; a man is reflected momentarily in a wardrobe mirror. But soon they become far more elaborate and threatening: Hands grab at Carol's body through the walls; she is raped by a sweaty workman.

Along with the hallucinations, horrible events actually do take place. When Colin, a young man who wants to date Carol, stops by to see her, Carol reluctantly lets him into the apartment and then bludgeons him to death with a heavy candlestick. She dumps his body in a bathtub full of water. Later, the landlord comes to collect the late rent and finds the apartment in disarray and Carol in a flimsy nightgown. When he makes clumsy advances, Carol slashes him with a straight razor, then overturns the couch on his body.

In REPULSION Polanski presents many distorted images from Carol's point of view to reveal her mental deterioration and to force us, as it were, inside her diseased mind. Sometimes there is a rational explanation for the distortion: when Carol sees her face reflected in a polished teakettle, for instance, or when she sees Colin through the peephole in the front door. But in other point-of-view shots, we cannot rationally explain the distortion. After Carol kills the two men, for instance, the bathroom and the living room appear cavernous to her, with grotesque angles and proportions. The furnishings are distant, out of reach; the light and atmosphere are menacing. To produce these startling images Polanski had duplicate sets constructed to match the normal living room and bathroom, but in much larger dimensions and with bizarre angles, and then enhanced the effect by shooting with a **wide-angle lens**. We recognize that the distorted view of these rooms reflects Carol's dreadful perception of them.

In this film Polanski wants the audience to experience firsthand the rapid deterioration of a woman cut off from other people and overwhelmed by a sickness that no one suspects in her. He wants us to feel as Carol does—trapped in the apartment and desperate against

recurring imaginary sexual attacks. Polanski wants us to see with our own eyes the horribly distorted world Carol sees; hence, he constructs duplicate sets and uses special lenses to reproduce Carol's disturbed inner vision. Polanski's point-of-view shots in REPULSION illustrate how filmmakers can use the camera to explore a film character's most private, terrifying inner experiences.

Flashbacks

A **flashback** is a shot, sequence, or scene interjected into a film story's present time to depict events that took place earlier. Sometimes an entire film story is told in flashback. For example, in Arthur Penn's LITTLE BIG MAN (1970), the protagonist, Jack Crabb (Dustin Hoffman), narrates his adventures in the Old West to a young historian. Crabb, as a wrinkled old man, appears with the historian at the beginning and end of the film—the movie's present time. During the rest of the film, which is a lengthy flashback, Crabb appears as he was when his adventures took place, except for periodic appearances as the old man commenting on his past life.

A flashback is a narrative device that helps a filmmaker move freely back and forth in time while telling a story. But it is also a valuable cinematic tool for revealing character when it depicts past events from the perspective of the person who is telling or remembering them. We learn a lot about Jack Crabb, for instance, from the way he tells his story. Crabb is a white man who as a boy was adopted by the Cheyenne. He lived among Indians as an equal, and he lived among whites and fought Indians. (See figure 1.6.) During the film, Crabb, in **voice-over narration,** states his opinions, feelings, and prejudices about both Indians and whites. He comments on famous people and events in the Old West (like General George Custer and the battle of Little Big Horn) as well as on private experiences (like discovering sex and making his first enemy). Thus, in the flashback we not only see Crabb's past, we learn what he thinks and feels about it as well.

But we must also take Crabb's story with a grain of salt because it is, after all, his subjective view of the past. Jack Crabb is a privileged storyteller. There is no one left from the Indian wars to verify or disprove his claim that he is the sole white survivor of the battle of Little Big Horn. Perhaps every word is God's truth; perhaps, in the tradition of the Old West, he is pulling the greenhorn historian's leg. So in the flashback, Crabb spins a yarn that hangs somewhere between history and tall tale.

How Do Films Reveal Characters?

Figure 6.4
A lap dissolve that leads
into the Breakfast Table
Montage in CITIZEN
KANE, one of five
flashbacks in the film that
reconstruct Kane's life
through other characters'
recollections.

Filmmakers sometimes exploit the narrator's point of view in a flashback to reveal more about another character. In Orson Welles's CITIZEN KANE (1941), for instance, Kane's life is recreated in flashbacks narrated by people who knew him (fig. 6.4). Each narrator tells about his or her relationship with Kane, and the accounts are pieced together like a jigsaw puzzle into a composite picture of Charles Foster Kane. Naturally, how these narrators feel about Kane colors what they say about him, so their biases are as revealing as the information they offer.

Akira Kurosawa makes the biases of characters narrating flashbacks the central feature of RASHOMON (1950), in which a young man and his wife are attacked in the forest by a bandit. In front of a magistrate, the three principals involved in the assault, and a woodcutter who witnessed it, each recount the incident. However, the story told in each of the four flashbacks is drastically different, as each narrator relates the events from his or her own self-serving point of view.

Some flashbacks depict what a character is thinking or remembering about past events. Throughout Tony Richardson's THE LONELINESS OF THE LONG DISTANCE RUNNER (1962), the protagonist, Colin Smith (Tom Courtenay), daydreams about circumstances leading up to his confinement in a reform school—events that are shown in fairly lengthy flashbacks after his incarceration. Although these flashbacks are not set off as conspicuously as those in LITTLE BIG MAN or CITIZEN KANE, Richardson makes it clear to the viewer that Colin is mulling over these scenes from the past, which are triggered by specific incidents or situations at the reform school. In one scene, for example, Colin is showering after a soccer scrimmage in which he scored a key goal, and the director of the reformatory visits the locker room to compliment his good play. As the director walks away from Colin, but still within earshot, he says to a young psychologist colleague, "It's not hard to imagine what kind of home life that lad had." A medium-close shot of Colin in the shower shows that the comment registers on him; then there is a **shock cut** to a scene of Colin with his family—obviously a flashback that reveals Colin's private reflections on his home life. Thus, in films like THE LONELINESS OF THE LONG DISTANCE RUNNER, memory flashbacks provide insights about a character's inner being.

Memories

Filmmakers generally present memories as flashbacks that straightforwardly reenact past experiences. A character either recalls these memories consciously (like Jack Crabb in LITTLE BIG MAN) or has them triggered unconsciously by specific situations in the story (like Colin Smith in THE LONELINESS OF THE LONG DISTANCE RUNNER). However, in Ingmar Bergman's WILD STRAWBERRIES (1957), the protagonist's memories are more like visions or reveries that take control of him.

WILD STRAWBERRIES is the story of an old recluse, Professor Isak Borg (Victor Sjöström), who journeys by car to the university in Lund to receive a distinguished academic honor, accompanied by his daughter-in-law and later, by three hitchhikers. Along the way incidents trigger memories and dreams that carry the professor on another, interior journey.

The professor's special day begins with a dream in which he sees himself dead. To clear himself of the dream's horror, Borg sits up in bed and mutters "words of reality" against the dream: "My name is Isak Borg. I am still alive . . . . I really feel quite well." Nevertheless, the bizarre unreality of the dream continues to hover around Borg throughout the day.

The professor's memories are first stimulated when he stops at a deserted country house where he spent his first twenty summers. Alone beside a familiar wild strawberry patch, Borg reminisces about his youth and suddenly finds himself, as if in a mirage, back in the past. Narrating his own story in voice-over, Borg describes the experience:

> I don't know how it happened, but the day's clear reality flowed into dreamlike images. I don't even know if it was a dream, or memories which arose with the force of real events. I do not know how it began either, but I think it was when I heard the playing of a piano.
>
> Astonished, I turned my head and looked at the house, a short distance up the hill. It had been transformed in a strange way. The façade, which only a few moments ago was so blind and shut, was now alive and the sun glittered on the open windows. . . . The old summerhouse seemed to be bursting with life. You could hear the music of the piano (it was something by Waldteufel), happy voices echoing through the open windows, laughter, footsteps, the cries of children, the squeaking of the pump. Someone started to sing up there on the second floor. It was a strong, almost Italian *bel-canto* tenor. In spite of all this, not a human being was in sight. For a few moments the scene still had a feeling of unreality, like a mirage which could instantly evaporate and be lost in silence.
>
> (Bergman 38–39)

Turning away from the house, Borg suddenly notices his cousin Sara (Bibi Andersson), with whom he was once in love, kneeling and picking strawberries. She looks quite real to him. "Mental image or dream or whatever this was, she looked just as I remembered her: a girl in a yellow summer dress, freckled and tanned and glowing with light-hearted young womanhood" (Bergman 39). But nothing has changed about Borg; he is still an old man dressed in dark, stodgy clothes. Borg tries to speak to Sara but soon realizes that he cannot converse with his memories, so decides to be quiet and enjoy this "new old world" he has been given the opportunity to visit. Immediately, however, Isak's older brother enters as a young gallant and flirts with Sara (fig. 6.5*a*). A gong sounds and calls the family together for breakfast; Isak follows indoors and eavesdrops (fig. 6.5*b*) while Sara tearfully confides to her older sister that she finds Isak stuffy and morally superior.

Figure 6.5

(*a*) A scene from the old professor's reverie in WILD STRAWBERRIES where he sees his brother flirting with his sweetheart. (*b*) The professor overhears comments made about himself in the past.

a

b

How Do Films Reveal Characters?

Figure 6.6
A young woman named
Sara becomes a living
connection between the
professor's past and
present lives in WILD
STRAWBERRIES.

The professor is awakened from his reverie by a young
woman—also named Sara and also played by Bibi Andersson—who re-
quests a ride for herself and two male companions. Thus, the young, light-
hearted hitchhiker—identical in name and appearance to his beloved
cousin Sara, and pursued by two rivals—becomes for Professor Borg a
living connection between the past and the present and a strong stimulus
for further self-exploration on the way to Lund (fig. 6.6).

How are the memory flashbacks in WILD STRAWBER-
RIES different from those in LITTLE BIG MAN and THE LONELINESS
OF THE LONG DISTANCE RUNNER?

In contrast with the memories of Jack Crabb and Colin
Smith, Professor Borg's memories of the family summerhouse are not a
straightforward reenactment of events recalled from the past. Although
he is entirely caught up in this reverie, Borg appears as in the present, an
old man, an observer whose presence no one in the reverie recognizes.
Someone mentions, in fact, that young Isak is missing from breakfast
because he is out fishing with his father and cannot hear the gong. Thus
the professor's vision permits him to witness comments about himself that
he would not have heard in the past. By the end of the film, insights about
himself gained from such reveries during the journey change the aloof
professor into a more compassionate man.

As film theorist Siegfried Kracauer points out, one crucial difference between Professor Borg's memories and ordinary flashbacks is that the "distance" between past time and present time is eliminated:

> From an observer the dreamer [old Borg] turns into a participant who resumes contact with at least one of those pale figures [Sara in the present time]. No longer a secluded province, the past thus takes on life in a literal sense and, as it develops, makes the old man himself undergo a change.
>
> (235)

Thus Bergman's depiction of Professor Borg's reveries in WILD STRAWBERRIES falls somewhere between conventional flashbacks, in which clear distinctions between past and present time are maintained, and full-blown dreams, in which there are no time distinctions at all.

Dreams

An example of how filmmakers traditionally employ a dream sequence to reveal a character's subconscious appears in F.W. Murnau's THE LAST LAUGH (1924), discussed earlier in this chapter. When the manager of a fashionable hotel notices an aging doorman (Emil Jannings) struggling with a heavy trunk, he demotes him to washroom attendant, a crushing humiliation for the doorman, who must exchange his lavishly decorated uniform for a simple frock and trudge down to the washroom in the basement (fig. 6.2). The night after his demotion, the doorman dreams of himself at his old job. In the dream a group of pale, weak gentlemen are overwhelmed by an enormous steamer trunk, which the doorman removes from the roof of a touring car and carries with one arm through oversized rotating doors into the crowded lobby. In an exhibition of power and finesse, the doorman tosses the trunk high into the air and catches it again with one arm. The astounded ladies and gentlemen in the hotel rise to their feet and applaud him.

On his way to work in the morning, the doorman apparently remembers nothing about the demotion. Not until he sees the hotel entrance and a new doorman in his place does the terrible truth come back to him.

Murnau uses the doorman's dream to show how he has repressed the humiliating demotion. The pale gentlemen in the dream, dressed in proper afternoon attire like the hotel manager, suggest how much the doorman wants to prove his superiority. By succeeding with one arm where they fail, the doorman reasserts his capability and his self-esteem. The applause of the elegant hotel guests further indicates how much the doorman craves admiration and recognition for his work.

Although the doorman's dream rather transparently reveals these needs, it also hints at the painful truth he has tried to block out. Karl Freund's **high-contrast lighting** of the dream setting—very stark and harsh—establishes a visual tone that is inconsistent with the doorman's supposed moment of glory. As he approaches the car, the doorman casts a grotesque shadow, which reinforces the nightmarish atmosphere. And the oversized revolving doors, turning mechanically like a gigantic reaper on edge, look very intimidating. Murnau's depiction of the dream, therefore, subtly suggests that the old man's wishful dreaming is covering up a harsher truth underneath.

THE LAST LAUGH employs a dream as a window straight into a character's subconscious, but Alfred Hitchcock's SPELLBOUND goes a step further and actually psychoanalyzes a character's dream as part of the story.

Produced in 1945, when psychotherapy was still relatively unknown to the general public, SPELLBOUND is a mystery thriller that showcases psychoanalytical dream interpretation. The protagonist is an amnesiac (Gregory Peck) impersonating a psychiatrist at a mental hospital. Except for a cigarette case inscribed with the initials "J.B.," he has no clue about his identity or his past. When the real psychiatrist is reported missing, J.B. becomes a murder suspect and flees, pursued by Dr. Constance Peterson (Ingrid Bergman), who is in love with him and wants to cure his amnesia. Dr. Peterson and her former professor, Dr. Brulov (Michael Chekhov), psychoanalyze J.B.'s dream, discover his identity, and ultimately solve the murder.

To impress on J.B. the importance of psychoanalysis, Brulov lectures him (and the audience) about dreams: "Dreams tell you what you are trying to hide, but they tell it to you all mixed up, like the pieces of a puzzle that don't fit. The problem of the analyst is to examine this puzzle and put the pieces in the right place." Properly admonished, J.B. narrates his dream, which Hitchcock depicts as he speaks. Designed by the surrealistic painter Salvador Dalí, the dream sequence is visually the most striking segment of the film. It features bizarre landscapes and symbols that replicate dream imagery and convey the great emotional turmoil J.B.'s conscious mind is repressing. By working with the dream, Dr. Peterson uncovers a repressed childhood trauma blocking the patient's memory, which Hitchcock reveals in a flashback from J.B.'s point of view: Sliding down a stone banister, J.B. accidently knocks his brother onto a spiked fence, impaling him. As soon as he recalls this horror, J.B.'s amnesia passes. Further interpretation of J.B.'s dream leads Peterson to discover who murdered the missing psychiatrist. Thus, the dream is the key to unlocking the double mystery SPELLBOUND poses: Who is J.B.? And who is the murderer?

Although the second mystery is the more dramatic one in the film, the first is more important for developing J.B.'s character. Since he is an amnesiac, J.B. is literally "not himself" throughout most of the film; and Hitchcock does not give the audience any privileged information about him. We must await the outcome of Brulov and Peterson's psychoanalysis to discover J.B.'s identity, which is supplied by a dream sequence lasting about two minutes and by a flashback of the repressed childhood trauma lasting only a few seconds. Hitchcock essentially creates J.B.'s character in those few minutes of screen time. When the deeply buried truths in J.B.'s unconscious are uncovered, his identity is revealed.

What can we learn from THE LAST LAUGH and SPELLBOUND about how filmmakers use dream sequences to reveal inner character? How can these films help us gauge the effectiveness of dream sequences in other movies?

Characterization in both THE LAST LAUGH and SPELLBOUND depends heavily on dreams that establish the protagonists' subconscious needs and motivation. These dreams provide the puzzle pieces that, when fitted together, reveal a whole character. One key difference between the two dreams is that we need expert interpretation from other characters to fit J.B.'s pieces together. In both cases, however, the dream sequences are not just cinematic pyrotechnics to dazzle the audience; they are rich sources of information about the characters. Murnau and Hitchcock do not only recreate dreams for the viewer; they recreate, from the emotional perspective of the character's unconscious mind, the traumatic experiences that produced those dreams. In doing so, they adhere to one of the basic tenets of dream analysis posited in Sigmund Freud's *The Interpretation of Dreams*:

> Whatever strange results they [dreams] may achieve, they can never in fact get free from the real world; and their most sublime as well as their most ridiculous structures must always borrow their basic material either from what has passed before our eyes in the world of the senses or from what has already found a place somewhere in the course of our waking thoughts—in other words from what we have already experienced either externally or internally.
>
> (F.W. Hildebrandt, in Freud 44)

At their best, dream sequences in films artfully depict tangible connections between a character's dream reality and waking reality, between the unconscious self and the outside world. In the hands of an accomplished filmmaker, dream sequences can explore some of the most intricate mysteries of human experience. (See also the discussion of Federico Fellini's 8½ in chapter 11.)

Conclusion

Chapter 6 has examined film acting and certain cinematic devices that can reveal film characters' inner experiences, even their deepest unconscious thoughts and feelings. But effective character revelation in films is not just a question of technique; the character must also have some substance to reveal. Chapter 7 examines how cinema, like literature and other arts, can tap into myths and beliefs deeply imbedded in our psyches in order to create characters that are archetypes or stereotypes of human behavior. The chapter focuses on heroes, villains, and gender models popularized in recent Hollywood movies.

General Study Questions

1. Who are your favorite film actors and actresses? What appeals to you about their acting styles?
2. Compare and contrast two roles played by the same actor or actress. What differences do you observe in the actor's voice and diction, facial expressions, body movements, and rhythm and pacing?
3. Compare and contrast the acting styles in two films of the same genre but from different time periods. What differences do you notice in the acting? What might account for these differences?
4. Some important films, like Vittorio De Sica's BICYCLE THIEF, have featured nonprofessional actors in prominent roles. What are the advantages and disadvantages of using nonprofessional actors? In what kinds of films might nonprofessionals be particularly effective?
5. Explain what film critic Jean Mitry means when he says that "nothing is more concrete than what the close-up shows, but nothing is more abstract than what it suggests." Apply this statement to a film scene that uses close-ups prominently.
6. In most close-up shots actors and actresses do not look squarely at the camera. Why not? How does the audience usually react when a film character in close-up (like Elizabeth Vogler in Ingmar Bergman's PERSONA) looks directly into the lens?

7. In the shot-by-shot descriptions in chapter 2 there are four close-ups of individual characters out of fifteen shots in the Railroad Depot Sequence from HIGH NOON and ten close-ups and medium close-ups of individuals out of thirty shots in the opening sequence from AN OCCURRENCE AT OWL CREEK BRIDGE. How would these sequences be different if they had a significantly lower (or higher) ratio of close-ups to long and medium shots?

8. Do you think a film can be faulted for employing too few or too many close-ups? Explain with examples from films you know.

9. Suppose you are a filmmaker who wants to make an entire film from a character's subjective viewpoint. What problems would you face in a film without objective shots? How might you address these problems?

10. Isolate a movie scene that employs point-of-view shots. How does the filmmaker indicate where the subjective shots begin and end? Describe the shots that precede and follow the POV shots. How different would the scene be without POV shots?

11. Using the discussion of Roman Polanski's REPULSION as a model, discuss how POV shots can reveal a character's mental state. How can a POV shot reveal more than what a character sees?

12. Compare and contrast two films that employ flashbacks prominently. How are the flashbacks used to tell the story? How are they used to reveal character?

13. Write a shot-by-shot description of a dream sequence in a film and analyze what it reveals about the character who is dreaming. Observe how the dream images are interrelated. Look for specific cinematic and thematic connections between dream reality and waking reality in the film.

Additional Films for Study

THE CABINET OF DR. CALIGARI (1919), dir. Robert Wiene
THE GOLD RUSH (1925), dir. Charles Chaplin
THE BLUE ANGEL (1930), dir. Josef von Sternberg
SCARFACE (1932), dir. Howard Hawks
LE CORBEAU (1943), dir. Henri-Georges Clouzot
SUNSET BOULEVARD (1950), dir. Billy Wilder
IKIRU (1952), dir. Akira Kurosawa
REBEL WITHOUT A CAUSE (1955), dir. Nicholas Ray
MOBY DICK (1956), dir. John Huston
ASHES AND DIAMONDS (1958), dir. Andrzej Wajda
THE VIRGIN SPRING (1959), dir. Ingmar Bergman
SHOOT THE PIANO PLAYER (1960), dir. François Truffaut

How Do Films Reveal Characters?

DAVID AND LISA (1963), dir. Frank Perry
ZORBA THE GREEK (1964), dir. Michael Cacoyannis
DARLING (1965), dir. John Schlesinger
THE PAWNBROKER (1965), dir. Sidney Lumet
CLOSELY WATCHED TRAINS (1966), dir. Jiří Menzel
THE KING OF HEARTS (1967), dir. Philippe de Broca
SEVEN BEAUTIES (1976), dir. Lina Wertmuller
SOPHIE'S CHOICE (1982), dir. Alan J. Pakula
GANDHI (1982), dir. Richard Attenborough
OUT OF AFRICA (1985), dir. Sidney Pollack
CHILDREN OF A LESSER GOD (1986), dir. Randa Haines
MANON OF THE SPRING (1987), dir. Claude Berri
THE DEAD (1987), dir. John Huston

Further Reading

Bergman, Ingmar. *WILD STRAWBERRIES*. Translated by Lars Malmström and David Kushner. New York: Simon and Schuster, 1960.

Björkman, Stig, Thorsten Manns, and Jonas Sima. *Bergman on Bergman*. Translated by Paul Britten Austin. New York: Touchstone, 1973.

Bordwell, David. *Filmguide to LA PASSION DE JEANNE D'ARC*. Bloomington: Indiana University Press, 1973.

Bowser, Eileen. *The Films of Carl Dreyer*. New York: Museum of Modern Art, 1964.

Butler, Ivan. *The Cinema of Roman Polanski*. Cranbury, N.J.: A.S. Barnes, 1970.

Dmytryk, Edward, and Jean Porter. *On Screen Acting*. London: Focal Press, 1984.

Griffith, Richard. *The Movie Stars*. Garden City, N.Y.: Doubleday, 1970.

Hurt, James, ed. *Focus on Film and Theatre*. Englewood Cliffs, N.J.: Prentice-Hall, 1975.

Kaminsky, Stuart, and Joseph F. Hill, eds. *Ingmar Bergman: Essays in Criticism*. New York: Oxford University Press, 1975.

Milne, Tom. *The Cinema of Carl Dreyer*. Cranbury, N.J.: A.S. Barnes, 1971.

Munk, Erika, ed. *Stanislavsky in America*. New York: Hill and Wang, 1966.

Nicoll, Allardyce. *Film and Theatre*. New York: Crowell, 1936.

Pate, Michael. *The Film Actor: Acting for Motion Pictures and Television*. New York: A.S. Barnes, 1970.

Pudovkin, V.I. *Film Technique and Film Acting*. London: Vision, 1958.

Richie, Donald. *Focus on RASHOMON*. Englewood Cliffs, N.J.: Prentice-Hall, 1972.

Schickel, Richard. *The Stars*. New York: Dial Press, 1962.

Shipman, David. *The Great Movie Stars: Vol. I, The Golden Years*. New York: Bonanza, 1970.

———. *The Great Movie Stars: Vol. II, The International Years*. New York: St. Martin's Press, 1972.

Steene, Birgitta. *Ingmar Bergman*. New York: Twayne, 1968.

Walker, Alexander. *Stardom, The Hollywood Phenomenon*. London: Penguin, 1974.

Works Cited

Balázs, Béla. "The Close-up." In *Film Theory and Criticism,* edited by Gerald Mast and Marshall Cohen, 185–87. New York: Oxford University Press, 1974.

Bergman, Ingmar. *WILD STRAWBERRIES.* Translated by Lars Malmström and David Kushner. New York: Simon and Schuster, 1960.

Bordwell, David. *Filmguide to LA PASSION DE JEANNE D'ARC.* Bloomington: Indiana University Press, 1973.

Cook, David A. *A History of Narrative Film.* New York: W.W. Norton, 1981.

Dreyer, Carl. "Thoughts on My Craft." In *Film: A Montage of Theories,* edited by Richard Dyer MacCann, 312–17. New York: E. P. Dutton, 1966.

Freud, Sigmund. *The Interpretation of Dreams.* Translated by James Strachey. New York: Avon, 1965.

Griffith, D.W. "What I Demand of Movie Stars." In *Focus on D.W. Griffith,* edited by Harry M. Geduld, 50–54. Englewood Cliffs, N.J.: Prentice-Hall, 1971.

Knox, Alexander. "Acting and Behaving." In *Film: A Montage of Theories,* edited by Richard Dyer MacCann, 62–72. New York: E.P. Dutton, 1966.

Kracauer, Siegfried. *Theory of Film.* New York: Oxford University Press, 1960.

Naremore, James. *Acting in the Cinema.* Berkeley: University of California Press, 1988.

What does Luke Skywalker, the youthful protagonist of George Lucas's futuristic STAR WARS trilogy, have in common with Gilgamesh, a legendary Sumerian king who may have lived more than four thousand years ago? What does RAMBO have in common with dozens of Hollywood Westerns that dramatize the taming of the American West? How do action-adventure movies like STAR WARS and RAMBO suggest appropriate behavior for men and women in our society? Chapter 7 explores questions like these. It focuses on familiar heroes, villains, and gender models in popular American movies—characters that are archetypes or stereotypes of human behavior, reflecting widely held attitudes about what is heroic and villainous, manly and womanly in American society. (An **archetype** is a universal representation of human behavior; a **stereotype** is a standardized representation of a group of diverse individuals.)

Heroes

In his classic study of myth, *The Hero With a Thousand Faces*, mythologist Joseph Campbell describes a pattern of heroic adventure common to legends, folklore, and epic literature all over the world. The adventure begins, says Campbell, when "an individual is drawn into a relationship with forces that are not rightly understood" and answers "the call to adventure" (*Hero* 51). The hero sets out on a journey to an unknown place—a distant land, a dark forest, a mountaintop, a kingdom underground or underwater—and encounters strange, polymorphous beings. Some of these beings pose great dangers or temptations, while others offer magical gifts or advice that help overcome obstacles and defeat enemies. Having crossed the threshold into the unknown, the hero must accomplish difficult tasks or survive many ordeals in order to complete the perilous journey and experience glory or illumination at the end. In the final stage of the adventure, the hero returns to the ordinary world and applies the new knowledge or power gained from the journey to a problem or hardship people face there.

This pattern of heroic adventure is universal, Campbell explains, because it is based on myth—the store of images and symbols deeply imbedded in the human psyche and inherited and shared by all people. These mythic images and symbols cannot be invented or permanently suppressed; rather, they are "spontaneous productions of the psyche" that manifest themselves in dreams, in religion, and in human creativity.

Stories of the mythic hero are found in the earliest writings of human civilization, such as *The Epic of Gilgamesh*, a Sumerian tale about King Gilgamesh of Uruk that dates back about four thousand years. Gilgamesh sets out on a great journey to learn the secret of everlasting life from Utnapishtim the Faraway, whom the gods allowed to survive the Great Flood that deluged the world and wiped out humankind. To find him, Gilgamesh must cross a great ocean to "the garden of the sun" beyond the sunrise and surmount many obstacles and hardships. Utnapishtim reveals where Gilgamesh can find a prickly underwater plant that "restores his lost youth to a man." Gilgamesh ties heavy stones to his feet and retrieves the marvelous plant. He says: "I will take it to Uruk of the strong walls; there I will give it to the old men to eat. Its name shall be 'The Old Men Are Young Again'; and at last I shall eat it myself and have back all my lost youth" (*Gilgamesh* 116). But before he can return to his city, a serpent rises out of the water and snatches the plant away. So Gilgamesh returns empty-handed to Uruk; but he rules justly thereafter, without abusing his power as he had done before the journey.

Archetypal Characters in STAR WARS

Like literature and folklore, films can also tap into the great storehouse of mythic images and symbols and create archetypal heroes who journey into unknown realms and undergo ordeals in order to benefit humankind. One such film is George Lucas's STAR WARS (1977).

In developing the story for STAR WARS, Lucas consulted Joseph Campbell's works on the hero; Campbell in turn commented on the film in his last book, *The Power of Myth*. Not surprisingly, therefore, the character of Luke Skywalker (Mark Hamill) in STAR WARS closely fits Campbell's description of the mythological hero. Skywalker, under the tutelage of an old mystic warrior, Ben Kenobi (Alec Guinness), joins a band of rebels fighting against the evil Galactic Empire, symbolized by a black-clad villain named Darth Vadar. In the course of his training with Ben Kenobi, Luke learns about the Force, an energy field created by all living things, and how to use its power to combat the evil that Vadar epitomizes. At the climax of the story Skywalker taps his newly developed power to destroy a seemingly invulnerable "death star" that threatens to vaporize a planet where the rebels are based. Skywalker succeeds in the attack because he heeds Ben Kenobi's advice to turn off his ship's computer and trust his feelings instead.

Do you see in STAR WARS elements of the mythical quest Joseph Campbell describes? Do you recognize mythical characters and situations in the story? Jot down some ideas before continuing.

George Lucas uses standard mythological figures and themes, according to Campbell, to tell the STAR WARS story. One scene, for example, where Luke Skywalker and his friends are trapped in a garbage compactor with the walls closing in, is analogous to a mythological situation Campbell identifies as "down in the belly of the whale," after the biblical tale of Jonah. "The story of Jonah in the whale," says Campbell, "is an example of a mythic theme that is practically universal, of the hero going into a fish's belly and ultimately coming out again, transformed" (*Power* 146). In *The Hero With a Thousand Faces* Campbell cites similar stories found in the folklore of Eskimos, Zulus, and Polynesians, in classical Greek mythology, and even in the fairy tale of Red Ridinghood, who is swallowed by the wolf. Campbell explains the significance of the whale's belly, in psychological terms, as a descent into the unconscious: "Metaphorically, water is the unconscious, and the creature in the water is the life or energy of the unconscious, which has overwhelmed the conscious personality and must be disempowered, overcome and controlled" (*Power* 146).

Joseph Campbell also sees a mythological dimension in STAR WARS' villain, Darth Vadar, whose monstrous mask symbolizes the machine that threatens to crush humanity. "Darth Vadar has not developed his own humanity," says Campbell. "He's a robot. He's a bureaucrat, living not in terms of himself but in terms of an imposed system. . . . When the mask of Darth Vadar is removed, you see an unformed man, one who has not developed as a human individual" (*Power* 144). The antidote to such inhumanity is to hold on to one's ideals, as Luke Skywalker does, and reject the system's impersonal claims upon the individual.

STAR WARS' mythic message is that technology is not going to save us. "Our computers, our tools, our machines are not enough," says Campbell. "We have to rely on our intuition, our true being" (*Power* xiv). For humanity to maintain predominance over machines, people must be willing to turn off the computer and trust their feelings, like Luke Skywalker, the archetypal model of such behavior in STAR WARS.

Profile of the Western Hero
SHANE

One of the most familiar archetypal heroes in American films appears in classic Westerns, like George Stevens's SHANE (1953). Robert Warshow, in an important essay about Westerns, says that in SHANE "the legend of the West is virtually reduced to its essentials and then fixed in the dreamy clarity of a fairy tale" (150). Shane (Alan Ladd) rides out of the Wyoming hills to help a colony of homesteaders defend themselves against a cattle rancher named Ryker (Emile Meyer) who wants to drive them out of the valley. A strong bond develops between Shane and Joe Starrett (Van Heflin), the leader of the homesteaders, as they stand up together against Ryker's harassment. Joe's wife Marian (Jean Arthur) is strongly attracted to Shane, and little Joey Starrett (Brandon de Wilde) idolizes him. Ryker raises the stakes in the struggle by hiring a ruthless professional killer named Wilson (Jack Palance). After a fistfight in which Shane beats Starrett unconscious to prevent him from going up against Wilson in a gunfight, the hero rides into town to face the killer alone. In the saloon Shane outdraws Wilson and shoots him, along with Ryker and his brother, while Joey looks on in awe. At the end of the film, with peace secured in the valley, Shane rides back into the hills alone.

Warshow argues that Shane is a hero of mythic proportions:

> The hero [of SHANE] (Alan Ladd) is hardly a man at all, but something like the Spirit of the West, beautiful in fringed buckskins. He emerges mysteriously from the plains, breathing sweetness and a melancholy which is no longer simply the Westerner's natural response to experience but has taken on spirituality; and when he has accomplished his mission, meeting and destroying in the black figure of Jack Palance a Spirit of Evil just as metaphysical as his own embodiment of virtue, he fades away again into the more distant West, a man whose "day is over," leaving behind the wondering little boy who might have imagined the whole story.
>
> (150)

What are some characteristics of the typical Western hero? Judging from Westerns you have seen over the years, what traits would you say are at the core of his character?

The archetypal Western hero has several important characteristics. The most obvious is a deadly proficiency with guns. It is apparent from the opening scene that Shane is a man who lives by the gun. And although he tries to put aside the gunfighter's life while he stays with the Starretts, he is soon called back into action. Shane first buckles on his gun belt again to teach little Joey, who is obsessed with guns, how to shoot (fig. 7.1). But the real demonstration of Shane's gunmanship is the showdown with Wilson, where Shane finally proves what we have known (with Joey) all along: that no black-clad, cold-blooded desperado is a match for Shane in a gunfight. Violence is not really the point of a Western, Robert Warshow observes, but rather "a certain image of a man, a style, which expresses itself most clearly in violence" (161). Shane is the epitome of that image.

Figure 7.1
Shane, the classic
Western hero, demon-
strates for Joey his
proficiency with a gun.

How Do Films Reveal Characters?

A second important trait of the Western hero is that he is an "outsider" who does not belong within society because his values and life-style are essentially antisocial. No matter how attractive the homesteader community may look to Shane, he cannot be part of it. The hero's isolation from "insiders," like Joe Starrett's family, is evident in a scene where Shane stands outside the window in the rain talking with Marian inside the cabin. Her soft manner and the gentle strains of "Beautiful Dreamer" in the background indicate that Marian is attracted to Shane, but that her ties to home and family are stronger. After Shane goes off to bunk in the barn, Marian closes the window and cautions Joey (and herself) not to get too attached to Shane. "He'll be moving along one day," she tells her son, "and you'll be upset if you get to liking him too much." This scene demonstrates why the Westerner must remain an outsider: His mere presence within society threatens its stability, just as Shane's presence in the Starrett home threatens that family's stability. For the good of the values he defends, Shane must ride on when his work is done.

However, Shane does make a great effort to fit in with and be accepted by the homesteaders. Not only does he take off his gun, he also exchanges his buckskins for "sodbuster" working clothes. He even backs down from a fistfight in the saloon with one of Ryker's hired hands. But Shane cannot change who he is; he cannot transform himself into a homesteader by changing his garb. When he next returns to town, Shane does not back down. In fact, he draws Joe Starrett into the fight, and together they whip the whole lot of Ryker's cowboys.

Shane cannot refuse the call to adventure, instinctively understanding that to do so would mean his disintegration. Therefore, he sheds the guise of the homesteader and dons his buckskins and gun belt again to face Wilson in the climactic gunfight. Afterwards, the hero says good-bye to Joey and rides off into the hills. Shane understands that he is set apart from society because he lives by the gun. In his last speech Shane likens himself to the biblical Cain, who was marked and condemned to wander over the earth for killing his brother Abel: "Joey, there's no living with a killing," Shane tells the boy. "There's no going back for me. Right or wrong, it's a brand. A brand sticks. There's no going back."

A third important quality of the archetypal Western hero is altruism. Why does Shane risk his life against the Ryker bunch for the homesteader community? When Ryker offers to hire Shane at double the wages Starrett pays, the hero flatly turns him down. Perplexed at a man who is not after personal gain, Ryker asks Shane, "What are you looking for?" The question may be taken as both practical and philosophical.

"Nothing!" Shane snaps back. As Shane leaves the Starrett farm to fight Wilson, Marian asks, "Are you doing this just for me?" Shane replies, "For you, and Joe, and little Joey." But this answer only scratches the surface. Shane is fighting for "civilization," which the Starretts and the other homesteaders are establishing in the lawless frontier, even though he knows there is no place in it for him. At bottom, Shane defends the side of justice and order because it is simply the right thing to do; his reward is to know that in doing the right thing he is defending his own honor.

THE ROAD WARRIOR

The archetypal Western hero frequently appears in different guise in other kinds of action-adventure films. In THE ROAD WARRIOR (1981), for example, director George Miller and screenwriters Terry Hayes and Brian Hannant transpose Shane's story to a futuristic setting in which outlaws in souped-up cars and motorcycles battle a colony of "settlers" for gasoline. The film's hero, Mad Max (Mel Gibson), rides a black V-8 Interceptor instead of a horse and wears a sawed-off shotgun instead of a six-shooter (fig. 7.2); but he is essentially another Shane—a seasoned warrior, an outsider, and (in the end) an altruist who uses his violent skills to help civilized society win out over lawless anarchy. In the beginning Max is more cynical and self-serving than Shane, but eventually he takes on the outlaw gang almost single-handedly, while the besieged settlers escape to a better land. At the end of the battle Max, like Shane, fades back into the wilderness alone.

George Miller and the screenwriters for THE ROAD WARRIOR wanted to create a heroic character who would transcend historical and cultural boundaries. "We came to the realization that if you go back and look at film history," says Miller, "you'll see that the samurai and the western and even MAD MAX are the same film. They just have different dressing" (in Broeske 281). Like Shane, Max is doomed to wander, always serving a greater order, even though he himself will not be a leader of that new order. No wonder, therefore, that a review of THE ROAD WARRIOR in *Newsweek* called the film "SHANE in black leather."

RAMBO: FIRST BLOOD PART II

An extreme example of the Western hero appears in one of the 1980s' most popular and most controversial action-adventure films—RAMBO: FIRST BLOOD PART II (1985), directed by George Cosmatos. John Rambo (Sylvester Stallone) is a Vietnam veteran who is recruited by his former commanding officer to investigate reports that American prisoners of war are still imprisoned in Vietnam. Rambo's field contact for the mission, a

How Do Films Reveal Characters?

Figure 7.2
Mad Max, the Western
hero in black leather, from
THE ROAD WARRIOR.

young Vietnamese woman named Co Bao (Julia Nickson), helps him locate the POWs and free one of them. At the rendezvous point, however, the rescue helicopter abandons Rambo, on orders from a corrupt government bureaucrat named Murdock (Charles Napier) who is running the operation, and Rambo and the POW are captured. A sadistic Russian officer tortures Rambo and coerces him into making radio contact with his superiors. But instead of delivering a pat propaganda statement, Rambo swears revenge on Murdock for selling out the mission. With Co Bao's help, Rambo blasts his way out of the prison camp and, after she is killed, returns alone to rescue all the POWs (fig. 7.3). In an extended battle that takes up the last quarter of the film, Rambo single-handedly

Archetypes and Stereotypes

Figure 7.3

Rambo, the Western hero exaggerated to grotesque proportions.

dispatches the Vietnamese and Russian enemy and flies the POWs to safety. Rambo then confronts Murdock; but instead of killing him, he machine-guns a bank of computers in his headquarters, the symbol of a corrupt political system that protects its own image more than human lives.

Rambo is an extreme example of the Western hero because his heroic qualities are exaggerated to grotesque proportions. Shane kills three men in a gun battle lasting less than one minute. But in RAMBO, according to one national publication, forty-four killings take place, one every 2.1 minutes on average. Shane tells Joey that some gunfighters carry two guns, "but one is all you need if you know how to use it." Rambo, on the other hand, employs an array of weapons—from a combat knife and a longbow to a .50-caliber machine gun and an attack helicopter.

Rambo is a more taciturn and cynical outsider than Shane. In this story there is no innocent, idolizing character like Joey to soften Rambo's cynicism. And Rambo's budding affection for Co Bao is snuffed out early, exacerbating his bitterness and isolation. In RAMBO there is also no admirable insider community, no higher order for the hero to serve. Murdock is slime in Rambo's eyes, and the rampant corruption he represents is polluting the American values Rambo would gladly die for. The POWs Rambo saves are, like their rescuer, victims of that corrupt system; they are fellow outsiders. Without an insider like Joe Starrett as a reference point, Rambo's heroic qualities lack perspective. He is more a killing machine than a flesh-and-blood hero.

Rambo's altruism is also highly exaggerated. What Shane is fighting for, and against, is defined very concretely; he knows his enemy and what must be done to defeat him. But Rambo is fighting for values that are more abstract, against an enemy who is ultimately faceless. At the end of the film, when Rambo's former commander asks him what he wants, Rambo hammers home the film's unabashedly patriotic message: "I want our country to love us as much as we love it!"

Film reviewers roundly attacked RAMBO, criticizing its excessive violence, its blatant machismo, its racist stereotyping (more on this later in the chapter), its reactionary political ideology, and its attempt to rewrite the history of the Vietnam War. Nevertheless, the film was one of the most commercially successful films of the 1980s and inspired a line of toys, clothing, posters, and other pop culture gimmicks featuring Rambo. This "Rambomania" clearly reflected strong patriotic sentiments in the United States ten years after American fighting in Vietnam ended. But the critical outcry also indicates that many Americans were disturbed about glorifying a hero like Rambo.

The Female Adventure Hero in ALIENS

The profile of the adventure hero is markedly different in ALIENS (1986), a futuristic action film in which the protagonist is a woman. ALIENS, directed by James Cameron (who coauthored the screenplay for RAMBO: FIRST BLOOD PART II), stars Sigourney Weaver in a reprise of the role she played earlier in Ridley Scott's ALIEN (1979).

In ALIENS, Ripley (Sigourney Weaver), the only survivor of a horrible encounter years earlier with deadly alien creatures in space (depicted in ALIEN), accompanies a landing party of Marines to the same planet, where a colony of families from Earth is endangered. The Marines discover that the creatures have wiped out the entire colony, except for one little girl named Newt (Carrie Henn), who survived by barricading herself in ventilation ducts. It is soon apparent that the heavily armed Marines are unable to destroy the vicious creatures, so Ripley takes charge of the mission.

But the aliens are not the only threat to the party's survival. Burke (Paul Reiser), a slippery civilian representative of the powerful company backing the mission, intends to smuggle the alien creatures back to Earth for profit. When Ripley threatens to expose his plan, Burke locks her and Newt in a laboratory with the creatures, but they are rescued by Hicks (Michael Biehn), a level-headed warrior who becomes Ripley's trusted ally.

Later, the aliens capture Newt, and Ripley goes alone into the alien queen's den (down into the mythological "belly of the whale") to save the child (fig. 7.4). Ripley rescues Newt and, with help from Hicks and an android named Bishop (Lance Henriksen), escapes the planet before it is destroyed in a nuclear explosion. The escape is a false climax, however, because the alien queen has concealed herself aboard their ship and, just when all appears secure, attacks again. In the film's final showdown, Ripley straps herself into a "loader" robot and battles the creature to the death. ALIENS ends with Ripley, Newt, and Hicks, the only survivors of the expedition, settling into peaceful space hibernation for their return to Earth.

Ripley is a more human, less ethereal, hero than Shane; and she is fundamentally transformed by the heroic experience in a way that he is not. Like Shane, Ripley is a loner at the beginning of the story, but she does not end up alone. Having been drawn into battle to protect Newt, she commits herself completely to the orphaned child. And at the end of the story she bonds together as a family with her co-survivors, Newt and Hicks. Shane is a compassionate man, but he remains an outsider. He cannot stay on with the Starretts without shattering that family's stability; he cannot become a parent to Joey. Shane fades into the sunset at the end of the story, presumably to answer another call to adventure. But Ripley is not isolated in a cycle of violence; at the end of the story she exits in the company of loved ones, presumably to set down roots in mainstream society back on Earth.

Thus, although the archetypal pattern of heroic adventure Joseph Campbell describes is common to many films, the heroes of these films can convey very different heroic ideals. Shane, Rambo, and Ripley all answer a call to adventure and face perilous ordeals; and in the end, they all triumph and help humanity. Yet, as models of heroic behavior, they are strikingly different and reflect radically different social values.

Figure 7.4
Ripley, more human and
less ethereal than Shane,
goes into the mythological
"belly of the whale" to
rescue Newt in ALIENS.

Villains

Just as movies have archetypal heroes, they also have archetypal villains. The monstrous creature Ripley destroys in ALIENS, for example, is a contemporary version of the mythical dragon slain by medieval knights like St. George. The creature's reptilian physical appearance corresponds to familiar images of dragons in paintings and illustrated children's books; and, like the mythical dragons, it terrorizes a large community of people—in this case, potentially the entire human race. Thus, in destroying the alien queen, Ripley, like the mythical dragon slayer, frees the community from the threat of extinction and provides an opportunity for renewal.

Joseph Campbell argues that mythical dragon slaying really signifies the slaying of monsters inside ourselves. "The ultimate dragon is within you," he says. "It is your ego clamping you down" (*Power* 149). This observation is especially apropos for ALIENS since, in an early stage of development, the alien creatures incubate within human hosts and gruesomely tear their way out.

It is noteworthy that the dragon Ripley slays is the queen mother, who lays the eggs from which the creatures first emerge. She is protecting her own inhuman offspring from extinction just as fiercely as Ripley is protecting Newt. Thus the battle between them "becomes an archetypal confrontation between the noble and dark sides of the same emotion" (Mancini 69). In slaying the dragon-queen, Ripley releases maternal feelings within herself that were repressed or dormant before she met Newt; she frees herself from a life of isolation (à la Shane and Rambo) by fully committing herself to the child. The mythical dragon slayer, says Joseph Campbell, takes on some of the slain dragon's power and reassociates himself directly with the powers of nature, that is, with the powers of life. By destroying the dragon in ALIENS, Ripley reconciles conflicting impulses toward nurturing and self-sufficiency within herself and embraces a new life and new relationships with Newt and Hicks.

Darth Vadar in STAR WARS (fig. 7.5) is an archetypal villain who represents the dark side of human nature. Dressed entirely in black and wearing a monster mask, he is without a shred of identifiable humanity. Like Wilson, the sadistic gunfighter in SHANE, Vadar is the embodiment of pure evil. Yet, one of the surprises in the story is that in the second part of the STAR WARS trilogy, THE EMPIRE STRIKES BACK (1980), Vadar is revealed as Luke Skywalker's father, a former Jedi knight who has given in to the "dark side of the Force." Therefore, Luke's relationship with Vadar in the STAR WARS films calls to mind

Figure 7.5
The villainous Darth
Vadar in STAR WARS, an
embodiment of pure evil.

one of the most basic human myths: Sigmund Freud's celebrated Oedipus complex (named after the title character of Sophocles' *Oedipus the King*, in which Oedipus slays his father and marries his mother). Thus, psychologically, Luke's struggle with Darth Vadar is the ancient struggle of a son to confront the feeling that his father is a monster and an enemy, and to resolve sexual rivalry between them.

Archetypes and Stereotypes

But movie villains today are more often stereotypes than archetypes. In ALIENS, for example, the human villain is Burke, a stereotype of an unscrupulous corporate executive like those depicted in many Hollywood movies of the 1970s and 1980s (CHINA SYNDROME, WALL STREET, BATTERIES NOT INCLUDED, to name a few), who sells out people for profit and is destroyed, physically or financially, by monstrous greed and ambition. Fittingly, Burke is killed by the deadly aliens he tries to smuggle back to earth.

Why is this stereotype of the amoral business executive so popular in recent movies? What is it about this type of character that fascinates contemporary audiences? Questions like these are certain to spark lively debate. But even meatier questions lie underneath: How do such character stereotypes affect the way we perceive villainy in ourselves and others? How do these stereotypes shape our attitudes about what is moral and immoral?

Racial Stereotyping in Hollywood Westerns

To understand better how character stereotyping in films affects us, picture the following familiar Hollywood scenario. The author exaggerates in order to dramatize the effects of stereotyping in the scene:

> White canvas-covered wagons roll forward in a column. White men, on their horses, ride easily up and down the lines of wagons. Their arms hang loosely near their guns. The walls of the buttes rise high on either side. Cakey streaks of yellow, rusty red, dried brown enclose the sun's heat boiling up on all sides. The dust settles on their nostrils, they gag and look apprehensively towards the heights, hostile and distant. Who's there? Sullenly, they ride on.
>
> Beyond the buttes, the wagon train moves centrally into the flatlands, like a spear pointed at the sunset. The wagons circle. Fires are built; guards set. From within this warm and secure circle, at the center of the plains, the white-men (-cameras) stare out. There, in the enveloping darkness, on the peripheries of human existence, at dawn or dusk, hooting and screeching, from nowhere, like maggots, swarming, naked, painted, burning and killing, for no reason, like animals, they would come. The men touch their gun handles and circle the wagons. From this strategically central position, with good cover, and better machines, today or tomorrow, or the morning after, they will simply mow them down. Wipe them out. Nothing human is involved. It's a matter of self-defense, no more. Extermination can be the only answer.
>
> (Engelhardt 2)

Before reading further, describe your reactions to this scenario. What is the author's purpose here? What is he pointing out about stereotyped characters in Hollywood Westerns?

This scenario, excerpted from a pamphlet by Tom Engelhardt entitled *Racism in the Media*, is one variation on a standard scene in Westerns. The encircled wagon train may also be a besieged fort or colony of settlers; but the constant factor is that the audience experiences the scene from *within* the circle, from the point of view of certified "human" characters who are defending themselves against "nonhuman" savages, "unknown besiegers with inexplicable customs, irrational desires, and an incomprehensible language" (Engelhardt 3). The circle becomes the focal point of the viewer's consciousness. The viewer is essentially forced behind the sights of a repeating rifle, says Engelhardt, from which position he receives a picture history of Western colonialism. "Who ever heard of a movie in which the Indians wake up one morning to find that, at the periphery of their existences, in their own country, there are new and aggressive beings ready to make war on them, incomprehensible, unwilling to share, out to murder and kill, etc." (Engelhardt 3). In Hollywood Westerns the Indians are the invaders who break in upon the circle of white settlers. Little wonder, therefore, that the viewer feels no sympathy for them as they drop each time a white man pulls the trigger. "Within this cinematic structure," Engelhardt points out, "such sympathy simply ceases to exist" (3).

Racial Stereotyping in RAMBO: FIRST BLOOD PART II

The wagon train scenario is a prototype of negative racial stereotyping that exists in other kinds of Hollywood movies as well. For example, Hollywood war movies since the 1940s have commonly vilified the Japanese, Koreans, and Vietnamese with dehumanizing stereotypes like those of the Indians in Westerns. In this respect, RAMBO: FIRST BLOOD PART II (1985) is part of a tradition of American war films that depict Asians as nonhuman.

One characteristic of third-world characters in Hollywood films is their invisibility. "In most movies about the third world," Engelhardt observes, "the non-whites provide nothing more than a backdrop for all-white drama—an element of exotic and unifying dread against which to play out the tensions and problems of the white world" (7). In RAMBO, for instance, there are no significant Vietnamese characters except for the English-speaking Co Bao (played by a non-Asian actress), who is quickly eliminated after she helps Rambo escape from the POW camp. The Vietnamese soldiers in the movie are little more than moving targets for the white super-warrior to knock over. That *dozens* of them can neither contain nor overcome Rambo certifies their inferiority. This ineptitude is best dramatized in a scene where Rambo engages the Vietnamese camp commandant in a Western-style shoot-out. Rambo stands on a rock in full view of the commandant, calmly knocking an explosive arrow into place while the Vietnamese futilely fires shot after shot at him from another rock across the river. When the commandant exhausts his ammunition and tries to flee, Rambo lets fly an arrow that blows the Vietnamese to pieces. (This scene usually draws loud cheers from the audience.) Thus Rambo obliterates the only notable Vietnamese soldier in the film.

The irony is that the Vietnamese are not even the principal villains in RAMBO. The real villains' roles are filled by two white men: a sadistic Soviet colonel and a spineless American bureaucrat. The deference that the Vietnamese soldiers show the Soviet "advisor" when he arrives by helicopter clearly indicates who is the ultimate authority in the POW camp. The Russian immediately takes charge of Rambo, but he fails to break the prisoner with torture or to recapture him after he escapes. The final coup of Rambo's escape with the POWs is to outsmart the Russian officer and blow his high-tech attack helicopter out of the sky. Then Rambo returns to base to settle the score with Murdock, the principal villain of the film.

The Russian colonel and Murdock are essential characters in RAMBO because the film's blatant patriotism will not reach full resonance without a formidable enemy for the hero to overpower. The Russian colonel is a tougher, cagier soldier than the Vietnamese commandant and, like Rambo, has mastered the sophisticated technology of modern warfare. He is a far more visible enemy than the commandant because he speaks (in English) and interacts directly with the hero. But against Rambo, he too is outmatched and finally obliterated. Murdock is the most visible and most formidable enemy in the film because his power, and his treachery, are the greatest. He is a high American government official who is guilty of selling out not only Rambo and the American POWs in Vietnam but also the most basic American principles and values. And yet Rambo allows this man to live!

Clearly, more than just racial stereotyping is at work in RAMBO. Murdock and the Russian colonel are stereotypes employed to sell a vehement political point of view. They are essentially propaganda devices to drive home messages about who America's enemies are and what should be done about them. RAMBO pits a macho superhero against stereotyped villains, and supplies relentless action and spectacular pyrotechnics. The result is an entertaining, high-intensity history lesson about Vietnam, comparable to the lesson Hollywood Westerns present about the "pacification" of the American West. (For more about film propaganda, see chapter 14.)

It is apparent that stereotypes in films can be a powerful vehicle for shaping how we perceive races and classes of people and how we form opinions about issues and events. Stereotypes often work on us subconsciously, creating impressions that sometimes even override conscious beliefs and values. To open his essay on racism in the media, Tom Engelhardt quotes the following anecdote from *Our Brother's Keeper: The Indian in White America*:

> I was visiting an Indian school and a movie was being shown in the auditorium about the cavalry and the Indians. The cavalry was, of course, outnumbered and holding an impossible position where the Indians had chased them into the rocks. The Indians, attempting to sneak up on the cavalry, were being killed, one every shot. When it finally appeared that the Indians were going to overrun the army position, the ubiquitous cavalry appeared on the far horizon with their bugle blowing, and charged to save the beleaguered few. The whole auditorium full of Indian students cheered.
>
> (In Engelhardt 2)

The cheers of these Indian students illustrate how subtle and penetrating racial stereotypes in films can be. At first glance perhaps we fail to recognize the racism in RAMBO and other films that denigrate third-world peoples, but we can become more attuned to it by scrutinizing the stereotypes such films promote. Perhaps we should recall this anecdote about the Indian students whenever we find ourselves cheering at scenes like the one where Rambo blows away the Vietnamese commandant.

Gender Models

Stereotyping characters in movies can perpetuate sexist attitudes just as insidiously as racist attitudes. Consider, for example, how women are depicted in SHANE and ALIENS. How would you compare and contrast Marian and Ripley as gender models? What personality characteristics does each of these women exhibit? What values does each represent?

Marian Starrett in SHANE serves the menfolk pie and coffee, tries (in vain) to keep her son from immersing himself in the male cult of guns and violence, and attends to her husband's cuts and bruises after fistfights. She is physically attracted to Shane but overrides the attraction and bids the hero farewell with a chaste handshake. Marian's function is to provide her man moral support and a secure home life while he fights to establish their homestead in the valley.

In ALIENS, on the other hand, Ripley is a full-fledged heroine, at the epicenter of the action in the film. She takes command of a dangerous mission that crack professional soldiers cannot control, ventures alone into the alien queen's den to rescue a child, and finally, destroys the monstrous creature single-handedly.

These two characters convey strikingly different images of women: on the one hand a dependent woman, protected by men, who completely identifies herself as a wife and mother; on the other hand, an assertive, independent woman who engages a dangerous enemy to protect others. How women are depicted in films like SHANE and ALIENS and what these depictions reveal about societal values are at the heart of **feminist film criticism,** which emerged in the 1960s and 1970s along with the Women's Liberation Movement.

Gender Stereotyping

One of the biggest issues feminist critics address is the stereotyping of women in movies: as wife/mother, bitch, whore, girl Friday, frigid career woman, etc. Sexual stereotyping, like racial stereotyping, presents an oversimplified, standardized image rather than a particularized, individualized character. Marian Starrett in SHANE, for example, is a transparent stereotype of a conventional 1950s housewife. Unlike her husband, Marian is not lifted, even briefly, out of mundane reality into the mythic fairy tale surrounding Shane; she remains the devoted wife/mother throughout the film.

Most observers agree that sexual stereotyping of women is much less blatant today than in the 1950s. Dozens of movies in the 1970s and 1980s—JULIA, NORMA RAE, THE AUTOBIOGRAPHY OF MISS JANE PITTMAN, TERMS OF ENDEARMENT, OUT OF AFRICA, among many others—show individualized women in strong, influential roles, affecting important changes and achieving significant goals. Yet feminist critics are greatly concerned that new damaging stereotypes of women may be replacing old ones. For example, consider the depiction of professional women in some popular movies of the 1980s. Films like BABY BOOM (1988) and MR. MOM (1984) show women with quite successful business careers, but their success only dramatizes how much they would rather devote themselves to the role of wife/mother. A more unsavory image of professional women appears in films like FATAL ATTRACTION (1988) and HOUSE OF GAMES (1988), where independent women are depicted as emotionally disturbed or immoral individuals who commit violence against men. In FATAL ATTRACTION, ironically, a wife/mother is forced to use violence to defend her husband and child from the attacks of a career woman. (For more extensive discussion of FATAL ATTRAC-TION, see chapter 8.) In such films the negative image of liberated women actually reinforces the wife/mother stereotype and the old values it represents. Film critics and historians have pointed out that Hollywood produced more favorable images of autonomous women in the 1940s when actresses like Katharine Hepburn, Bette Davis, and Joan Crawford frequently played energetic career women who competed with men without being overwhelmed or demoralized by them.

Joan Mellen, an influential feminist film critic, suggests in *Women and Their Sexuality in the New Film* (1975) that a much deeper issue than negative stereotyping of women is at work in films like BABY BOOM and FATAL ATTRACTION. Mellen writes:

> Despite the vociferousness of the Women's Liberation Movement and its campaign to awaken in the media, particularly in advertising and television, a sense of the sexual identity and dignity of the independent woman, the contemporary cinema persists in spitefully portraying the sexuality of its women as infantile and dependent. Hollywood has long delighted in exposing the new woman as sexually confused, self-destructive when it comes to the possibility of fulfilling her deepest desires, and masochistically at home in relationships where she can preserve "control" by renouncing feeling.
> (53)

KLUTE

One of the films Mellen cites as a depiction of a sexually confused, self-destructive independent woman is KLUTE (1971), a mystery thriller directed by Alan J. Pakula and starring Jane Fonda as a high-class New York prostitute, a role for which Fonda received an Academy Award.

In KLUTE, call girl Bree Daniels (Jane Fonda) is threatened by a man who may be the missing friend of small-town detective John Klute (Donald Sutherland). Hoping for a lead in his search, Klute questions Daniels, follows her, and taps her telephone conversations. But the harasser eludes him and vandalizes Bree's apartment. Klute begins to suspect Peter Cable (Charles Cioffi), a business executive who hired Klute, so he lays a trap for him. The ruse works, but almost costs Bree her life when Cable, who has already murdered three people to cover his tracks, follows

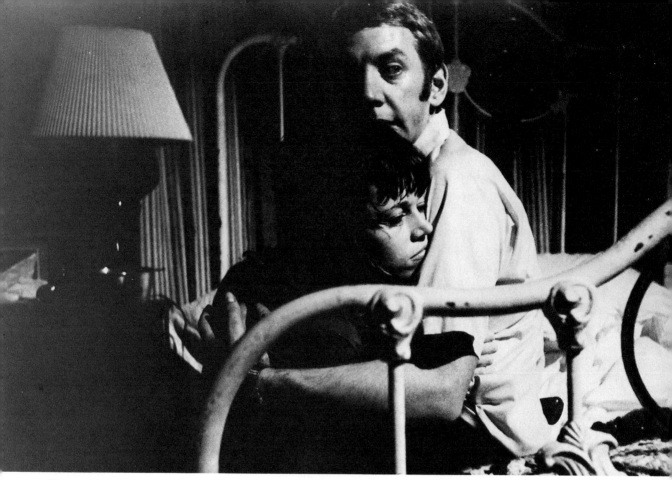

a

Figure 7.6

Contrasting images of
independent women who
are subjected to sexual
threats in films: (*a*) In
KLUTE Bree Daniels is a
deeply flawed, dependent
creature who cannot
survive without a man's
protection. (*b*) In LADY
BEWARE Katya Yarno is
imaginative and forceful,
and does not rely on a
man to fight her battles.

Bree and attacks her in a deserted garment factory. Klute arrives just in
time to rescue Bree, and Cable, seeing that he is exposed, throws himself
through a window to his death.

Despite the title, KLUTE is really about Bree Daniels,
who is the most interesting and complex character in the film. Bree is not
happy with her life; she wants to break away from prostitution but
cannot. In conversations with her psychoanalyst, Bree talks about why
she is a call girl. "It's an act," she says. "You don't have to feel anything;
you don't have to care about anybody." At bottom, Bree turns tricks
because she enjoys manipulating men, which makes her feel she has some
degree of control over her life. When she becomes attracted to Klute, she
feels she is losing control and wants "to go back to the comfort of being
numb." At the end of the film, however, Bree leaves New York to begin a
new life with Klute.

b

KLUTE was in many ways a landmark film for the 1970s. It depicted a prostitute sympathetically, paving the way for more serious treatment of sexually liberated women in films, and it addressed the issue of sexual harassment straightforwardly and realistically. Nevertheless, Joan Mellen argues that KLUTE's depiction of Bree Daniels is a patronizing and hostile portrayal which reinforces old stereotypes that independent women are deeply flawed, dependent creatures who cannot survive without a man's protection (fig. 7.6a).

Bree Daniels, says Mellen, is presented as an emotionally stunted individual who can neither free herself from being used by men nor accept a loving relationship with a man. "An expert in the mechanics of sex, Bree attains the illusion of dominating her clients by giving them what they want without allowing her own feelings to surface" (Mellen 53). But the fact that one of her clients terrorizes Bree shows the absurdity of her desire to make "the sex she sells have nothing to do with her self" (Mellen 54).

The psychiatric therapy Bree receives in the film is ineffectual, partly because her analyst does not penetrate the barriers Bree has erected and partly because the analyst cannot be reached when Bree is most in need. So Klute is Bree's rescuer. He arrives in the nick of time to save her first from the killer and then from emotional emptiness in New York City. Mellen challenges this conclusion as paternalistic and utterly unrealistic, a product of the Hollywood dream machine:

> That the very real sexuality of Bree is shown responsive only to such a [strong silent] type is satisfying as fantasy since it disturbs none of our myths, and in fact strengthens them. But it is illogical in terms of the radical changes in Bree's psychology that it effects. Bree's realism as a woman dedicated to protecting herself against false consciousness is undercut by her . . . falling for the Gary Cooper figure [John Klute] who one day knocks mysteriously at her door.
>
> (55)

LADY BEWARE

In *Women and Their Sexuality in the New Film*, Joan Mellen writes about movies of the 1960s and early 1970s. One indication that feminist criticism has raised sensibilities about the depiction of women in movies is that by the 1980s some films about women had been made that satisfied most of Mellen's objections to KLUTE. For example, LADY BEWARE (1988), directed by Karen Arthur, is a mystery thriller with a story line very similar to KLUTE, but with a female protagonist very different from Bree Daniels.

LADY BEWARE is about Katya Yarno (Diane Lane), a window dresser for a Pittsburgh department store, who has fresh but somewhat bizarre ideas about how to display the store's merchandise. Katya's windows attract an obsessive psychopath named Jack Price (Michael Woods), who believes that Katya can only be satisfied sexually by a man, like himself, with imagination to match her own. He follows her, steals her mail, and harasses her with increasingly obscene telephone calls. He invades her loft apartment while she is out and ritualistically reenacts her evening bath, a routine he knows from peeping in her window.

Jack's harassment gradually erodes Katya's peace of mind and creativity. It affects her comfortable rapport with co-workers at the department store and derails a developing relationship with a journalist named Mac (Cotter Smith). At first, Mac underestimates the seriousness of the sexual harassment, but he becomes more supportive when he gets a taste of it himself one night in Katya's loft. They are in bed together when Katya notices the intruder concealed in the shadows, his boots and the glint of a knife visible behind her clothes rack. Mac and Katya go to the police together.

After Jack violates Katya's living space, she installs bars on the windows, new locks on the door, and an answering machine on the telephone. Yet Jack manages to break in again. Katya is at the snapping point. She takes a leave of absence from work and barricades herself inside her apartment, refusing to answer any phone messages, even from friends. She unwraps a bolt of white fabric around a central area of the loft, like a cocoon, in which to hide. But finally, Katya refuses to be defeated. She takes a hard look at herself in the mirror and spits at her reflected image. She decides to confront her tormentor. She tears down the cocoon and, when Jack telephones, arranges a rendezvous with him on a deserted bridge. Katya curses Jack to his face (fig. 7.6b) and vows to fight him with the very thing he finds so attractive, her imagination.

Now Katya becomes the stalker. She discovers where Jack works and lives; she studies his routines. Finally, she devises a window display to lure him into the department store at night, where she traps him for the police.

From the descriptions of KLUTE and LADY BEWARE, how would you compare and contrast the two protagonists as gender models for independent women? What impressions of them do you form from the two stills shown in figure 7.6? Write down some observations before reading on.

LADY BEWARE offers a decidedly more favorable image of an independent woman subjected to sexual threats than does KLUTE. Both Bree and Katya are intelligent, imaginative, dynamic, but Katya is more emotionally secure and responsible for herself. Until she falls victim to Jack's perverse attention, Katya is happy with her life. She loves her work, which not only pays the bills but also provides opportunities for creative self-expression and meaningful friendships; and she enjoys a mature, loving relationship with Mac. Most importantly, Katya deals with the sexual harassment differently than Bree. She does not crumble, and she does not rely on a man to fight her battle. She confronts her attacker face-to-face and finally defeats him by drawing on her own courage and resourcefulness.

The Influence of Feminist Film Criticism

Joan Mellen lamented that movies of the 1960s and 1970s, even those written or directed by women, "failed to offer images of women possessing resiliency, forcefulness, imagination or talent" (28). LADY BEWARE, however, presents a woman of the 1980s who exhibits *all* these characteristics.

But LADY BEWARE is a relatively small, independently produced picture. Perhaps it is a fluke. Do mainstream Hollywood movies of the 1980s offer more favorable images of women than those of the 1970s? We have already noted that many feminists are offended by damaging stereotypes of women in 1980s movies like BABY BOOM and FATAL ATTRACTION. On the other hand, some popular mainstream movies of the 1980s do depict resilient, forceful, imaginative, talented women. ALIENS, for example, features such a woman as the protagonist of an action-adventure story, a genre long dominated by male heroes. MOONSTRUCK (1988), a romantic comedy, focuses on a self-assured successful woman who, even within an ethnic Italian community where women have traditionally been less independent, takes charge of her business and personal life without sacrificing strong family ties. In PEGGY SUE GOT MARRIED (1987), a fantasy romance, a woman goes back in time and reexamines how 1960s values and attitudes affected relationships with her parents, her husband, and her friends in the 1980s.

Feminist criticism arose in the 1960s and 1970s because of great concern "that 'women as women' are not represented in the cinema, that they do not have a voice, that the female point of view is not heard" (Gledhill 817). Feminist critics may debate to what extent films like ALIENS, MOONSTRUCK, and PEGGY SUE GOT MARRIED redress these complaints; but the images of women in these films indicate that some mainstream Hollywood movies in the 1980s have at least recognized feminist grievances.

Conclusion

Chapter 7 has tried to probe beneath the surface of characters we commonly find in contemporary American movies, to question what these characters reveal about our values and beliefs, to analyze how they help determine what we admire and despise in ourselves and people around us. The chapter focuses on archetypes and stereotypes, models of human behavior that we absorb from movies, consciously and unconsciously, as we become absorbed in their stories. The chapter also suggests ways that discriminating, responsive audiences can influence the models of behavior movies present. Feminist critics, for example, have demonstrated that negative stereotypes of women in films can be effectively challenged. Chapter 7 stresses, ultimately, the importance of questioning our own assumptions about, and reactions to, heroes, villains, and gender models in the movies we watch.

General Study Questions

1. What other archetypal characters besides the Western hero can you identify in films? Is Charlie Chaplin's "little tramp," for instance, an archetype? What qualities of that character would be important in deciding this?
2. Several popular films of the late 1960s, such as BONNIE AND CLYDE and BUTCH CASSIDY AND THE SUNDANCE KID, depict outlaws as "heroes." How would you explain this characterization to someone who thinks of a hero as someone like Shane, who *defends* justice and order? What values do characters like Butch and Sundance represent?
3. During the 1980s, several important films, like PLATOON and FULL METAL JACKET, depicted American involvement in the Vietnam War. Who are the heroes and villains in these pictures? How do they compare with the heroes and villains in RAMBO? What do these films reveal about American perspectives on the Vietnam War twenty years afterwards?
4. Why is the unscrupulous business executive such a satisfying villain in films like WALL STREET and BATTERIES NOT INCLUDED? What attracts and repels us about the stereotype?
5. Compare and contrast villains of crime/mystery films from different periods. How have these villains changed over time? How do these changes reflect changes in society?
6. To what extent is gender stereotyping prevalent in films today? Support your answer with examples from recent movies you have seen.

Additional Films for Study

THE CROWD (1928), dir. King Vidor
THE BLUE ANGEL (1930), dir. Josef von Sternberg
GRAND HOTEL (1932), dir. Edmund Goulding
GENTLEMEN'S AGREEMENT (1948), dir. Elia Kazan
THE RED SHOES (1948), dir. Michael Powell and Emeric Pressburger
ALL ABOUT EVE (1950), dir. Joseph L. Mankiewicz
HIGH NOON (1952), dir. Fred Zinnemann

BAD DAY AT BLACK ROCK (1954), dir. John Sturges
THE SEVENTH SEAL (1956), dir. Ingmar Bergman
DESIRE UNDER THE ELMS (1958), dir. Delbert Mann
BILLY BUDD (1962), dir. Peter Ustinov
LOLITA (1962), dir. Stanley Kubrick
TO KILL A MOCKINGBIRD (1962), dir. Robert Mulligan
LOVE STORY (1970), dir. Arthur Hiller
STRAW DOGS (1971), dir. Sam Peckinpah
SOUNDER (1972), dir. Martin Ritt
HESTER STREET (1975), dir. Joan Micklin Silver
SWEPT AWAY (1975), dir. Lina Wertmuller
ONE SINGS, THE OTHER DOESN'T (1977), dir. Agnes Varda
THE DEER HUNTER (1978), dir. Michael Cimino
APOCALYPSE NOW (1979), dir. Francis Ford Coppola
BLADE RUNNER (1982), dir. Ridley Scott
THE BIG CHILL (1983), dir. Lawrence Kasdan
MOSCOW ON THE HUDSON (1984), dir. Paul Mazursky
DESPERATELY SEEKING SUSAN (1985), dir. Susan Seidelman

Further Reading

Alloway, Lawrence. *Violent America: The Movies, 1946-1964.* New York: Museum of Modern Art, 1965.

Bogle, Donald. *Toms, Coons, Mulattoes, Mammies, and Bucks.* New York: Bantam, 1974.

Cripps, Thomas. *Slow Fade to Black: The Negro in American Film.* New York: Oxford University Press, 1977.

Eyles, Allen. *The Western.* Cranbury, N.J.: A.S. Barnes, 1975.

Folsom, James K., ed. *The Western.* Englewood Cliffs, N.J.: Prentice-Hall, 1979.

French, Philip. *Westerns.* New York: Viking, 1973.

Haskell, Molly. *From Reverence to Rape.* Baltimore: Penguin, 1974.

Houston, Beverle, ed. "Feminist and Ideological Criticism." *Quarterly Review of Film Studies* 3 (Fall 1978). [Special issue]

Kay, Karyn, and Gerald Peary. *Women and the Cinema.* New York: E. P. Dutton, 1977.

McConnell, Frank. *Storytelling and Mythmaking.* New York: Oxford University Press, 1979.

Mellen, Joan. *Women and Their Sexuality in the New Film.* New York: Dell, 1975.

Murray, James. *To Find an Image: Black Films from Uncle Tom to Superfly.* Indianapolis: Bobbs-Merrill, 1973.

Nachbar, Jack, ed. *Focus on the Western.* Englewood Cliffs, N.J.: Prentice-Hall, 1974.

Nichols, Bill. *Ideology and the Image.* Bloomington: Indiana University Press, 1981.

Parish, James R. *The Great Western Pictures.* Metuchen, N.J.: Scarecrow Press, 1974.

Schatz, Thomas. *Hollywood Genres: Formulas, Filmmaking, and the Studio System.* Philadelphia: Temple University Press, 1981.

Smith, Julian. *Looking Away: Hollywood and Vietnam.* New York: Charles Scribner's Sons, 1975.

Smith, Sharon. *Women Who Make Movies.* New York: Hopkinson and Blake, 1975.

Suid, Lawrence H. *Guts and Glory: Great American War Movies.* Reading, Mass.: Addison-Wesley, 1978.

Tyler, Parker. *Magic and Myth of the Movies.* New York: Simon and Schuster, 1944.

———. *Sex, Psyche, Etc. in the Films.* New York: Penguin, 1971.

Vogel, Amos. *Film as a Subversive Art.* New York: Random House, 1975.

Warshow, Robert. *The Immediate Experience: Movies, Comics, Theatre and Other Aspects of Popular Culture.* New York: Atheneum, 1975.

Wright, Will. *Six-Guns and Society: A Structural Study of the Western.* Berkeley: University of California Press, 1975.

Works Cited

Broeske, Pat H. "THE ROAD WARRIOR (MAD MAX II)." In *Magill's Cinema Annual 1983,* edited by Frank N. Magill, 277–82. Englewood Cliffs, N.J.: Salem Press, 1983.

Campbell, Joseph. *The Hero With a Thousand Faces.* 2d ed. Princeton: Princeton University Press, 1968.

———. *The Power of Myth.* New York: Doubleday, 1988.

Engelhardt, Tom. "Racism in the Media." *Bulletin of Concerned Asian Scholars* 3 (Winter-Spring 1971). Reprinted as a pamphlet by New England Free Press.

The Epic of Gilgamesh. Edited by N.K. Sandars. New York: Penguin, 1977.

Gledhill, Christine. "Recent Developments in Feminist Criticism." In *Film Theory and Criticism: Introductory Readings,* 3d ed., edited by Gerald Mast and Marshall Cohen, 817–45. New York: Oxford University Press, 1985.

Mancini, Marc. "ALIENS." In *Magill's Cinema Annual 1987,* edited by Frank N. Magill, 64–69. Englewood Cliffs, N.J.: Salem Press, 1987.

Mellen, Joan. *Women and Their Sexuality in the New Film.* New York: Dell, 1975.

Warshow, Robert. *The Immediate Experience: Movies, Comics, Theatre and Other Aspects of Popular Culture.* New York: Atheneum, 1975.

Character Relationships

Chapter 8 focuses on three kinds of character relationships frequently depicted in films: romantic relationships, power relationships, and family relationships. In order to explore some distinctive features of each of these types of relationships, we will treat them separately, even though in many films they are not easily separated from one another. We will compare and contrast examples of these relationships in Hollywood films of different periods, and analyze them from a social-historical perspective. Our purpose is to discover how character relationships reflect changing attitudes and values in American society.

Romantic Relationships

A textbook definition of romantic love is: a strong attraction to or infatuation with another person, which is founded upon an idealized image of the loved one or of the relationship. The following discussion focuses on romantic relationships in two popular Hollywood movies produced fifty-four years apart: IT HAPPENED ONE NIGHT (1934) and FATAL AT-TRACTION (1988). From these films, what can we learn about American attitudes toward romance in the 1930s and in the 1980s? How can we understand these films better by examining their character relationships from a historical perspective?

IT HAPPENED ONE NIGHT Versus FATAL ATTRACTION

IT HAPPENED ONE NIGHT swept all the major Academy Awards in 1934 and was immensely successful at the box office. The movie established director Frank Capra as the premier Hollywood filmmaker of the 1930s and made movie stars Clark Gable and Claudette Colbert international celebrities. And because it was so successful, IT HAPPENED ONE NIGHT institutionalized one of the most enduring models of romantic love that the Hollywood dream machine has ever produced (fig. 8.1).

In IT HAPPENED ONE NIGHT Ellie Andrews (Claudette Colbert) runs away from her wealthy father to join a flashy socialite, King Wesley, whom she has hastily married without her father's approval. Traveling incognita by bus from Miami to New York, she meets Peter Warne (Clark Gable), an unemployed newspaper reporter who discovers her identity and threatens to expose her unless she promises him an exclusive story. Despite considerable tension between them in the beginning, Ellie and Peter gradually fall in love on the journey. But a string of misunderstandings drives them apart until, thanks to her father's intervention, Ellie's marriage to King Wesley is annulled and she elopes with Peter.

How Do Films Reveal Characters?

a

b

Figure 8.1
(*a*) The "Walls of Jericho" between Ellie and Peter as they prepare for bed in IT HAPPENED ONE NIGHT. Sexuality lies beneath the surface in this scene. (*b*) Peter and Ellie on the road, broke and hungry. In this film true love emerges from shared misfortune.

FATAL ATTRACTION, directed by Adrian Lyne and starring Michael Douglas and Glenn Close, was one of the most popular movies of the 1980s. Within six months of its release, it had already earned more than $100 million. In FATAL ATTRACTION corporate attorney Dan Gallagher (Michael Douglas) has a passionate weekend affair with Alex Forrest (Glenn Close), an executive with a company he represents. Dan, who has a family (fig. 8.2), has no intention of continuing the affair but cannot extricate himself from it, especially after Alex announces that she is pregnant and wants the child. Alex, who turns out to be a seriously disturbed individual, harasses Dan and his family with increasingly dangerous attacks until Dan's wife Beth (Anne Archer) finally shoots her in self-defense.

In many ways the romantic relationships in these two films are completely antithetical. One relationship blossoms, the other withers; one ends happily, the other horribly. But perhaps the most salient difference between them is that one relationship is chaste and the other is adulterous.

In IT HAPPENED ONE NIGHT Ellie Andrews and Peter Warne never even kiss. In a memorable scene when they are stranded overnight in a motel room, Peter hangs a blanket across the room to separate their two beds (fig. 8.1a). He calls this makeshift divider the Walls of Jericho and assures Ellie that he has no trumpet up his sleeve to tumble them down. The Walls of Jericho remain between Peter and Ellie for the rest of the journey. They bed down together, but separately, twice more en route to New York—first in adjacent haystacks in an open field and once again in a motel room. Peter nearly kisses Ellie in the hayfield but draws away at the last moment. On their last night together Ellie circumvents the Walls of Jericho and asks Peter to take her away with him, but Peter, caught off guard, sends her back to her own side while he considers their relationship in this new light. Only at the end of the film, after Ellie's marriage has been annulled, do the Walls of Jericho finally fall. The last shot of the film shows the exterior of a motel cabin where Peter and Ellie are staying. A toy trumpet sounds within, the lights in the cabin go out, and the film ends.

In FATAL ATTRACTION, on the other hand, the relationship between Dan and Alex is physical from the outset, and most of the film deals with the consequences of their brief sexual liaison. Alex's hysteria surfaces as soon as Dan tries to draw away: She slashes her wrists to keep him from leaving her apartment (fig. 8.3a), and later tries to insinuate herself into Dan's life. He arrives home from work one day and finds Alex chatting with his wife. *Mise en scène* underscores the quiet

How Do Films Reveal Characters?

a

Figure 8.2
From FATAL ATTRAC-
TION, two images of Dan
Gallagher's happy home
life before his fatal affair
with Alex Forrest. The film
asserts family values with
a vengeance.

b

terror of this encounter: First Alex stands between Dan and Beth, facing her former lover; then Dan stands between the two women, facing Alex (fig. 8.3*b*). In both configurations Beth cannot see the silent hostility Dan and Alex exchange in her presence. This scene is Alex's first direct assault on Dan's happy family life; more terrifying attacks follow after the Gallaghers move to a house in the country. Eventually, Dan is forced to confide in Beth. The affair nearly shatters their marriage; but to protect the family Beth, too, joins the deadly battle with Alex and finally destroys her.

Subtext Analysis

What messages about romantic relationships do IT HAPPENED ONE NIGHT and FATAL ATTRACTION convey? What underlying values about sex, love, and family do they communicate? Think about these questions before reading the following comments.

The romantic relationships in these two films are, in one way, diametrically opposite: Peter and Ellie move from aversion to attraction; Dan and Alex move from attraction to aversion. But in other ways, the two relationships are remarkably alike. In both relationships, for example, the couples are "fatally" attracted to each other, in the sense that fate seems to bring them together. In IT HAPPENED ONE NIGHT Capra connects Peter and Ellie, even before they meet, in a shot at the Miami bus terminal that pans from Ellie receiving her bus ticket to Peter in a telephone booth being fired by his editor. They meet in the next scene when they are forced to share the last remaining seat on the bus, the first of many situations in which they must cooperate to survive. Later in the movie fate also thwarts their love, and Ellie, thinking Peter has rejected her, decides to marry King Wesley all over again in a formal wedding. But Ellie's father intervenes at the eleventh hour and persuades her, on the way to the altar, to run off with Peter.

Dan and Alex's relationship is also apparently fated from the outset. They meet by chance at a cocktail reception and again at an impromptu Saturday morning business meeting. After the meeting it is pouring rain outside, and they go to a restaurant for a drink until it stops. Dan happens to be free because his wife and child are house hunting in the country for the weekend. In the next scene, Dan and Alex are passionately embracing over Alex's kitchen sink. Later, when Alex announces she is pregnant, their destinies are further intermeshed. And just as Peter and Ellie are unable to commence their romantic relationship without her father's intervention, Dan and Alex are unable to terminate theirs without Beth's violent intervention at the end.

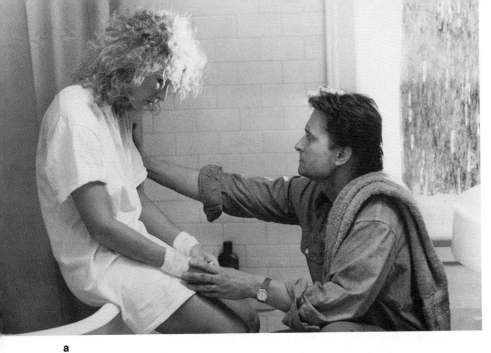

Figure 8.3
(*a*) Irrationality surfaces in FATAL ATTRACTION when Alex slashes her wrists to prevent Dan from leaving her apartment. (*b*) *Mise en scène* underscores the silent hostility between Dan and Alex as she tries to insinuate herself into his happy family life.

Character Relationships

The underlying messages about love and romance that IT HAPPENED ONE NIGHT and FATAL ATTRACTION deliver are also remarkably similar. At bottom, both films reinforce conventional notions about romantic love and uphold traditional values about the sanctity of marriage and family. How can this be so when the relationships in the two films are so opposite?

The moral of IT HAPPENED ONE NIGHT is fairly transparent: True love emerges from shared misfortune and flourishes when sexual urges are restrained until permanent commitments are made. The Walls of Jericho do not tumble until Ellie's marriage to King Wesley has been annulled and her relationship with Peter Warne has been sanctioned by her father.

It is less obvious how FATAL ATTRACTION upholds such traditional values, until we consider that the operative relationship in the film—the relationship that survives—is Dan and Beth's. Their relationship, after the strain it suffers because of Dan's affair, replicates the same pattern as Peter and Ellie's relationship in IT HAPPENED ONE NIGHT: The couple is forced to cooperate, despite animosity, to overcome misfortune that threatens to overwhelm them; and overcoming it together reinforces the bond between them.

Although she is not on screen as much as Dan and Alex, Beth is the pivotal character in FATAL ATTRACTION and the emotional centerpost of the film. She is the character whose feelings the audience identifies with most. Alex's feelings, on the other hand, become increasingly inconsequential as her behavior becomes more psychotic. As one reviewer points out, we are not meant to know how Alex feels; we are meant to hate her so much that we want to see her dead. But consider how appalling it would be, in another context, to want to see a pregnant woman shot to death. So what values is the film reinforcing in the climactic final scene when Beth shoots Alex? What judgment is the film making about these two women? Is there an underlying message that the independent working woman poses dangerous threats to family integrity? Consider the final image in the film: a framed family photograph of Dan and Beth, with their daughter Ellen, happy and secure at last in their country home.

Social-Historical Analysis: Two Critical Models
Contextual Criticism

What do we know about American life in 1934 that may explain the immense popularity of IT HAPPENED ONE NIGHT? Capra's movie was released at the height of the Great Depression, when people around the world were experiencing hard times. Many Americans were unemployed and living on meager incomes; some were destitute. People went to the movies to escape these harsh realities. So we can understand why a romantic relationship between a wealthy socialite and a common working man might catch viewers' attention. Ellie is "a spoiled brat" (as Peter dubs her) who has been insulated all her life from ordinary concerns and experiences: She's never ridden a bus or used a public shower; she doesn't know how to handle money or protect her belongings; she doesn't even know how to dunk a doughnut or ride piggyback. The clandestine bus trip is the first time Ellie has been out in the real world, removed from her wealthy father's influence and protection. Peter, on the other hand, is a practical, street-smart newspaper reporter who makes his own way in the world and who relishes the opportunity to show Ellie how the other half lives. In Capra's original script the male lead was a vagabond painter, but that character did not sit well with preview audiences. They wanted a common man in the role, someone they could recognize and identify with.

We can imagine how the 1930s audience must have enjoyed watching a spoiled rich girl fall in love with an unemployed newspaper reporter, how they must have cheered the transformation she undergoes as a result of rubbing elbows with ordinary folks. A little exposure to grit and hardship, however, reveals that Ellie is not a crusty socialite, nor a spoiled brat. She gives away Peter's last ten dollars to a famished woman and then goes hungry herself rather than call on her father for help (fig. 8.1*b*). She can be street-smart, too, as she proves in a famous hitchhiking scene where, after Peter fails dismally to thumb a ride for them, Ellie stops the first passing car by lifting her skirt above the knee.

IT HAPPENED ONE NIGHT was an unexpected success. Nobody, including the director, expected it to be a hit. When it was first released, critics mostly panned the movie as one of the trendy "bus stories" of the period, diverting perhaps but ordinary. A review in *The Nation* called it "entertaining" but said that "to claim any significance for the picture. . . would of course be a mistake." Audiences, however, loved the movie and flocked to theaters week after week to see it. Psychologically, the 1930s viewers must have found the happy ending in IT HAPPENED ONE NIGHT uplifting and reassuring, one that fostered a confident, optimistic view of the world. With historical hindsight it is easy to see why Peter and Ellie's story, on a subconscious level, makes a perfect fable for the Depression era.

Because FATAL ATTRACTION is a film of our own time, it may be harder to define how audiences respond to it on a subconscious level. But, besides reinforcing family values, does the film reflect the concerns of the times that produced it? If IT HAPPENED ONE NIGHT is a fable for the Great Depression, what is FATAL ATTRACTION for audiences of the 1980s?

Some critics have called FATAL ATTRACTION "a parable for the age of AIDS." In the mid-1980s, confronted with an epidemic spread by sexual contact, the sexual mores of the American people underwent marked changes. The sexual revolution withered, promiscuity became suspect, and "safe sex" was the new catch phrase. For a time, American public concern about AIDS bordered on mass hysteria; and this hysteria, some critics argue, is reflected in FATAL ATTRACTION, even though AIDS is not specifically mentioned in the movie. Let's consider some ways that FATAL ATTRACTION may reflect the AIDS scare of the 1980s.

From the film's early scenes, who would guess that FATAL ATTRACTION is a horror film? Yet there are subtle indications from the very beginning that FATAL ATTRACTION is a "domestic thriller." The opening shot, for instance, imitates the beginning of Alfred Hitchcock's PSYCHO: a slow **pan** of city buildings that gradually **zooms in** on the people inside one window of one building. In FATAL ATTRACTION the camera often searches out characters and traps them in closed, interior spaces (like bathrooms) so that "the viewer feels vulnerable and helpless while associating with the characters and constantly suspects that something dreadful is about to happen to them" (Konigsberg 119). Such claustrophobic horror is also characteristic of PSYCHO. Skillful **cross-cutting** in FATAL ATTRACTION builds up tension and dread until, in the climactic conclusion, events defy the laws of reason and probability and become pure psychological horror. What is the source of all this horror? What action has brought about such terrible consequences? One weekend of adulterous sex! A single infidelity jeopardizes the lives of the Gallagher family, and costs Alex hers. The underlying message of this parable is clear: Sex outside a monogamous relationship can kill you!

Dan's adulterous affair with Alex has such horrible impact partly because the consequences are so irrational. At the beginning of the film we are led to expect a casual one-night stand between two discreet adults. The sex is hot, so we can understand why Alex is miffed when Dan wants to return to his own apartment. But we are shocked, as Dan is, when Alex cuts her wrists to hold him there one night longer. These are not the rules for one-night stands. Thereafter, Alex's behavior becomes progressively more irrational, and Dan's efforts to deal with her reasonably, according to the rules of the game he expected, are utterly futile. Frustrated and angry, Dan also reacts irrationally, bursting into Alex's apartment and nearly choking her to death.

Alex's assaults on Dan's family become sicker and more bizarre: She leaves Ellen's pet rabbit boiling on the kitchen stove while the family is away; she kidnaps Ellen from school and takes her to an amusement park; and finally she breaks into the Gallagher home and attacks Beth in the bathroom with a knife. In this final scene, irrationality is pushed to absurdity when Alex, whom Dan has apparently drowned in the bathtub, suddenly rises out of the water to attack him again.

By immersing the viewer in a full-blown emotional enactment of irrationality, FATAL ATTRACTION recreates the hysterical atmosphere associated with the feared epidemic in the mid-1980s. Without directly alluding to AIDS, the film leads the viewer to associate horrible consequences with unrestrained sexual indulgence. It warns that, no matter how brief or how casual, sexual encounters may be fatal.

For some viewers this interpretation of FATAL AT-TRACTION as a "parable for the age of AIDS" may seem far-fetched. But it is a good example of how thoughtful **contextual criticism** can lead to deeper exploration of a film's meaning. Perhaps in fifty years, FATAL ATTRACTION's reflection of the 1980s will be as clear and telling as IT HAPPENED ONE NIGHT's reflection of the Great Depression is now.

Psychosocial Criticism

Psychotherapist Rollo May, in *Love and Will* (1969), suggests another kind of social-historical context for the relationships in IT HAPPENED ONE NIGHT and FATAL ATTRACTION. May argues that pressures on people in the postindustrial age have led to more impersonalized, dehumanized relationships. The heart of the problem, says May, is that *eros*—the powerful urge in human beings to create and procreate—has lost much of its original creative passion in the modern world and has become simply sex. May contends that eros today "stands not for the creative use of power—sexual, procreative, and other—but for the immediacy of gratification" (95). Whereas erotic love in the past was generally considered the *answer* to life's predicaments, today it has become the *problem* (13). Using Rollo May's model, we might argue that the relationship between Peter and Ellie in IT HAPPENED ONE NIGHT reflects the values of an era when erotic love still maintained its creative power and was seen as a solution to life's difficulties, and that the relationship between Dan and Alex in FATAL ATTRACTION reflects the values of an era when erotic love meant immediate sexual gratification that destroys rather than enhances life.

Comparing IT HAPPENED ONE NIGHT and FATAL ATTRACTION according to Rollo May's construct of erotic love, we may view the sexuality in the two films somewhat differently than we did earlier. Because Peter and Ellie's relationship is chaste, for example, does not mean it is bereft of sexuality. In fact, a good deal of sexuality surrounds their relationship from the beginning, but it is mostly subliminal. The scene where Peter first hangs the Walls of Jericho between their beds, for instance, contains strong sexual undercurrents. In 1934 it was risqué just to show an unmarried couple alone in a bedroom; and had there been a double bed instead of two single beds in the room, the scene would have faced objections from the Hays Office, which enforced the Hollywood Production Code in the 1930s. But Capra also employed cinematic devices to charge the scene with sexual energy. He photographed the medium-close shots of Ellie as she watches Peter undress in **soft focus,** blurring the image slightly and softening the edges to make her look more sensual. And, as Ellie undresses in the dark, Capra includes a provocative shot from Peter's point of view of Ellie draping her lingerie over the Walls of Jericho. Frank Capra knew that a scene like this could be very sexy without the couple ever touching. He wrote in his autobiography that sex scenes are better left to the audience's imagination. "Desire is the key," he wrote, "not fulfillment. The chase, not the catch" (249).

From Rollo May's perspective it is significant that the sexuality in IT HAPPENED ONE NIGHT lies beneath the surface while the sexuality in FATAL ATTRACTION is graphically depicted. In IT HAPPENED ONE NIGHT sexual gratification is the culmination of the romantic relationship in the film. In FATAL ATTRACTION the sexual gratification is over in a flash, producing destructive energy that ravages Dan's family and costs Alex her life. Moreover, this destructive energy only reaches full force with Alex's pregnancy.

Thus, FATAL ATTRACTION epitomizes the modern dehumanized relationship in which immediate sexual gratification replaces creative passion, in which the conception of new life marks a turning toward the destruction of life. IT HAPPENED ONE NIGHT, on the other hand, epitomizes the more human premodern relationship in which sexuality retains its creative power to enrich life, and in which life's harshness is ameliorated as barriers between people tumble.

The foregoing discussion of romantic relationships offers two models of how one might study movies within a social-historical framework. The underlying purpose is to illustrate how we can learn more about a society's attitudes and values by analyzing character relationships in its movies. Think about romantic relationships in recent American films you have seen. What kind of picture do they paint of love and sexuality, marriage and family, fidelity and adultery? What ideals do the characters strive for in these relationships? What makes these relationships thrive or die?

Power Relationships

WHITE HEAT Versus ONE FLEW OVER THE CUCKOO'S NEST

WHITE HEAT (1949), a gangster picture directed by Raoul Walsh, features one of Hollywood's most memorable movie endings. Cody Jarrett (James Cagney), a psychopathic killer gone mad, defies an army of police from atop a gas storage tank. Although shot several times, he refuses to buckle. He fires into the gas tank, and flames shoot up around him (fig. 8.4a). "Made it, Ma! Top of the world," he cries, just before the explosion blows him into oblivion.

United States Treasury agents in WHITE HEAT, who are pursuing the Jarrett gang for a train hijacking in which Cody killed four people, discuss Cody Jarrett's background in an early scene. They tell us that insanity runs in the Jarrett family and that Cody's father died raving in a mental institution. When Cody was a child, he faked headaches to get attention from his mother, until the fancied headaches became real. Now he suffers severe attacks, which, according to Cody, feel like a red-hot buzz saw inside his head. Ma Jarrett (Margaret Wycherly) nurses him through these headaches by massaging the back of his neck and flattering his megalomaniacal ego.

According to the T-men, Cody has a fierce psychopathic devotion to his mother. She is the only person he has ever cared about or trusted. Cody demonstrates this fierce devotion in nearly every scene; but the most dramatic example occurs when Cody, doing prison time for a lesser crime to avoid prosecution for the train murders, learns from a newly arrived inmate that his mother is dead. He goes berserk in the prison dining hall, crawling over tables and punching guards who try to subdue him, until a half dozen guards finally carry him out.

The treasury agents take advantage of Cody's mother fixation when they plant an undercover agent named Fallon (Edmond O'Brien) to spy on Cody in prison. Fallon's assignment is to get close to Cody and gain his trust—in short, to take Ma Jarrett's place. He accomplishes this task first by saving Cody's life in the prison machine shop and

a

Figure 8.4

(*a*) Cody Jarrett at the "top of the world" in WHITE HEAT, just before it blows up in his face. (*b*) Jarrett has a fierce psychopathic devotion to his mother. "Top of the world," he toasts her. "Don't know what I'd do without you, Ma."

later by helping him through a headache attack, massaging his head and feeding him praise, just as Ma used to do. As a result Cody takes Fallon along on a prison break and accepts him into the gang.

Cody Jarrett's relationship with his mother drives the story in WHITE HEAT. It explains Cody's psychopathic character, the source of his madness and his criminality, and the motivation for his actions throughout the film. To emphasize Cody's unusual dependency on his mother, director Raoul Walsh has Cody sit in Ma's lap in one scene, an image that immediately captures the psychological and physical bond between them. Afterwards, Ma pours Cody a drink (fig. 8.4*b*). "Top of the world," he toasts her. "Don't know what I'd do without you, Ma."

How Do Films Reveal Characters?

b

Walsh reinforces this relationship cinematically in a scene where Cody explains to his prison mates that he gets his share of the take on every job his gang pulls, even though he is in jail. "Ma takes care of that," Cody explains, as the scene **dissolves** to the gang's hideout where Ma is supervising the split from a recent robbery, setting aside one cut for Cody. During the **lap dissolve**, Cody's face and Ma's face occupy the same spot on the screen; and for a moment their features blend together, suggesting the close identification between them.

The bond between Cody and Ma apparently remains intact even after Ma's death. Hiding out in the mountains after the prison break, Cody reveals to Fallon that he has been talking to Ma in the woods. "All I ever had was Ma," Cody tells him. "When I'd start to slip, there she was behind me, pushing me back up to the top of the world." In confiding such personal information to Fallon, Cody reveals how much he has come to trust him. The final proof that Fallon has succeeded in taking Ma's place is that Cody accepts him as a partner, offering to split fifty-fifty with him, just as he did with Ma.

The ironic climax of this subterfuge occurs in the final reel when Cody discovers, in the middle of a payroll heist at a big chemical company, that Fallon is a federal agent. The shock of this betrayal drives Cody to madness as he tries to stand off the police single-handedly from atop the gas storage tank. Appropriately, Fallon is called upon to shoot Cody with a sniper's rifle. In the end Cody calls out to Ma that he's made it to the top of the world—just before it blows up in his face.

ONE FLEW OVER THE CUCKOO'S NEST (1975), directed by Miloš Forman, is another film story driven by a power relationship. CUCKOO'S NEST revolves around Randel P. McMurphy (Jack Nicholson), a prisoner transferred from a work farm to a mental institution for observation. McMurphy's free spirit and roguish humor threaten the iron discipline of a ward run by Nurse Ratched (Louise Fletcher). Consequently, they are at loggerheads from the outset. The antagonism between them is exacerbated because McMurphy has a therapeutic influence upon other patients and soon becomes a leader and role model on the ward. McMurphy especially influences Chief Bromden (Will Sampson), a huge Indian whom everyone believes is deaf and mute. McMurphy befriends Bromden, drawing him into ward activities, and eventually the chief speaks to him.

The first serious confrontation between McMurphy and Nurse Ratched occurs when she quashes his request to watch the World Series on television, whereupon he undermines her authority by rallying the men around the blank TV screen. But Nurse Ratched quickly regains the upper hand when, after a rowdy group therapy session that ends in a free-for-all, she sends McMurphy and Bromden for electroshock treatment. Realizing that the nurse will eventually destroy him, McMurphy plans to escape after a clandestine Christmas party. But he falls asleep. In the morning Nurse Ratched discovers the mayhem on the ward and browbeats one young patient, Billy Bibbit (Brad Dourif), so severely that he commits suicide; whereupon McMurphy tries to choke her to death. McMurphy is lobotomized for this violent attack and returns to the ward a vegetable. At the end of the film, Chief Bromden smothers McMurphy with a pillow before crashing out of the asylum.

The power relationship between McMurphy and Nurse Ratched is symbolized by a sliding glass window that separates the nurse's station and the ward (fig. 8.5). The men line up for medication at this

How Do Films Reveal Characters?

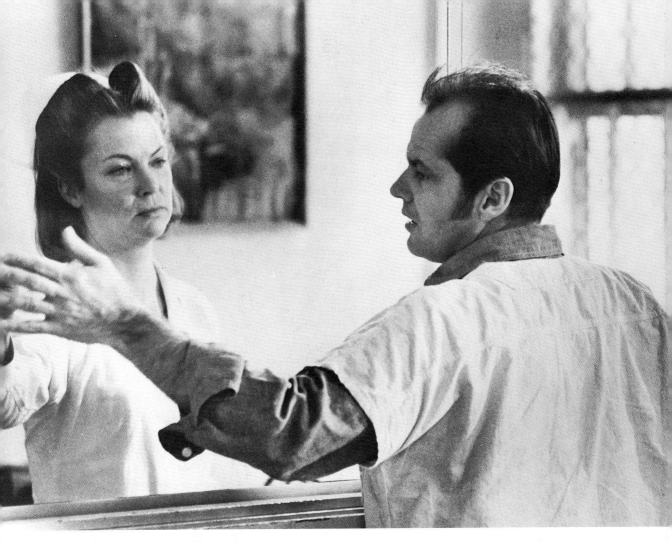

Figure 8.5

The power relationship between McMurphy and Nurse Ratched in ONE FLEW OVER THE CUCKOO'S NEST is symbolized by a sliding glass window that separates the nurse's station from the ward.

window, and through it the nurse keeps watch on her patients. Nurse Ratched likes this window to be spotless, and early in the film she admonishes McMurphy for smudging it. McMurphy's declaration of open war against Nurse Ratched occurs when he smashes his hand through the window to get cigarettes for one of the patients, insisting afterwards that the glass was so clean he forgot it was there.

Forman depicts the power relationship between McMurphy and Nurse Ratched cinematically by juxtaposing close-ups of their faces throughout the film. The two characters' facial expressions, more than action or dialogue, reveal the increasing hostility between them, beginning with mutual surveillance during McMurphy's first group therapy session and culminating with mutual loathing after Billy Bibbit's suicide.

The antagonism between McMurphy and Nurse Ratched precipitates the friendship between McMurphy and Chief Bromden. McMurphy's willingness to stand up to Nurse Ratched is a tonic that helps Bromden "grow"; for, although he is a giant of a man, the chief perceives himself as small and weak, dwarfed by Nurse Ratched's power. Thus, the fiercer McMurphy's battle with "Big Nurse" becomes, the more size and strength Bromden recoups. At the end of the film, after he dispatches McMurphy, the chief escapes by tearing a massive water fixture out of the floor and crashing it through a barred window.

Subtext Analysis

How would you compare and contrast the power relationships in WHITE HEAT and ONE FLEW OVER THE CUCKOO'S NEST? What underlying messages about power do they convey?

In both WHITE HEAT and ONE FLEW OVER THE CUCKOO'S NEST, dominant, aggressive women hold life-and-death power over men whom society has identified as deviants; and in the end these men, themselves forceful and aggressive individuals, are destroyed because of that power. But crucial differences between the character relationships in these two films make us respond very differently to Cody Jarrett and Randel P. McMurphy and the values they stand for.

The most obvious difference is that Cody fully accepts the power his mother holds over him, whereas McMurphy fights Nurse Ratched's power at every turn. Cody, in fact, does not even recognize that Ma dominates him; he simply behaves as he thinks a devoted son should. But the federal agents certainly recognize Ma's power over Cody, and they exploit it.

At first McMurphy does not recognize Nurse Ratched's power over him because he does not understand that he is *committed* to the mental institution, rather than just serving out his prison farm time there. But soon he realizes that by bucking her authority he is prolonging his own incarceration. Nevertheless, McMurphy repeatedly challenges Nurse Ratched because he cannot tolerate her manipulation of the other men on the ward, and each time he pays a greater price. Finally, when McMurphy attacks the nurse, he provides her with the cause she needs to destroy him.

Both Cody and McMurphy are deviant individuals, but we perceive and respond to their deviance very differently. Cody, shaped by Ma Jarrett's warped overindulgence, is a dangerous psychopathic killer, an enemy of society who destroys order in the world for his own material gain and ego gratification. McMurphy, shaped by dangerous

How Do Films Reveal Characters?

confrontations with Nurse Ratched, is a heroic champion who risks his own well-being for others less able to stand up for themselves.

Both Cody and McMurphy react to situations impulsively, without reflecting on the consequences of their actions. But Cody's typical impulse is to gun down anyone who stands in his way, whereas McMurphy's typical impulse is to hijack a busload of patients for a salmon-fishing expedition. Even when McMurphy tries to kill Nurse Ratched, his violence is motivated by concern for his friend Billy Bibbit.

Both Cody and McMurphy are finally destroyed by friendships that counterbalance these power relationships. In WHITE HEAT Fallon is assigned to befriend Cody, to insinuate himself into Cody's gang, to take Ma Jarrett's place. This is a false friendship, of course, one that ends in ultimate betrayal when Fallon shoots Cody. In CUCKOO'S NEST, on the other hand, McMurphy freely initiates the friendship with Chief Bromden and, in helping him grow back to health, acquires an ally in the struggle against Nurse Ratched. When the chief smothers McMurphy, it is an act of ultimate friendship that frees McMurphy from Nurse Ratched's power.

Social-Historical Analysis

What do the power relationships in WHITE HEAT and ONE FLEW OVER THE CUCKOO'S NEST reveal about American attitudes toward power in 1949 and in 1975? The key to the answer is how the audience reacts to the deaths of the two protagonists. How does the viewer feel when Cody Jarrett blows up in a spectacular fireball at the end of WHITE HEAT? There is bravado in his death, to be sure, but it is not tragic. Cody Jarrett unquestionably gets what he deserves in the end, and the world is better off without him. It is fitting that his existence is completely obliterated. This is the kind of justice Hollywood gangster pictures of the 1930s and 1940s dispense. The forces of good—personified by the army of cops that surrounds Cody at the end—resoundingly defeat the forces of evil and restore order in the world.

How does the viewer feel, on the other hand, about McMurphy's death? It is somber and tragic, a mercy killing to save a heroic individual from an ignominious life as a vegetable on Big Nurse's ward. It is painful to witness McMurphy's death because we have come to identify so much with his struggle. We do not feel that McMurphy gets what he deserves; we feel that Nurse Ratched has escaped what *she* deserves. We do not feel that order has been restored in the world, nor that the forces of good have triumphed; we feel frustrated that justice has *not* been dispensed.

In other words, we have dramatically different attitudes toward the institutions that destroy Cody Jarrett and Randel P. McMurphy. We applaud the authority that prevails, with a vengeance, at the end of WHITE HEAT and feel grateful that it has protected our security. We are impressed with the latest (for 1949) crime-fighting technology used to bring Cody Jarrett to justice—spectrographs, teletypes, radio car phones, tracking devices, etc.—which WHITE HEAT showcases in quasi-documentary fashion. This technology further reassures us that the authorities have the upper hand against criminals and that they use their power to defend law-abiding folks.

But we feel very differently about the power that destroys McMurphy. The authority Nurse Ratched personifies in CUCKOO'S NEST is dangerous, and its technology—electric shock treatment and lobotomy—is intimidating, not reassuring. We do not have blind faith in this authority; we question whether it protects our security and has the best interests of society at heart.

The power relationships in WHITE HEAT and ONE FLEW OVER THE CUCKOO'S NEST, therefore, reflect radically different attitudes toward authority. WHITE HEAT shows great trust in and respect for authority and a faith that powerful public institutions do serve society well. CUCKOO'S NEST, on the other hand, values individuality highly and expresses concerns that powerful institutions may encroach on personal freedom. Researching social and political conditions in the United States in 1949 and 1975 would undoubtedly produce some cogent explanations for these differing attitudes toward authority and institutional power. Can you offer any explanations from what you know of those years?

What attitudes toward authority do films since ONE FLEW OVER THE CUCKOO'S NEST reflect? How do more recent movies treat the balance of power between institutions and individuals? Have attitudes become even more jaded and cynical, as films like APOCALYPSE NOW (1979) and AND JUSTICE FOR ALL (1979) suggest? Or has the pendulum swung back to the opposite extreme, toward idolization of authority and the common good, as films like THE PRINCIPAL (1987) and LETHAL WEAPON (1987) suggest?

One way to approach questions like these is to analyze character relationships in contemporary films, as we did with WHITE HEAT and ONE FLEW OVER THE CUCKOO'S NEST, to determine which characters have power over others, how they use that power, and, most of all, how the audience is made to feel about the exercise of that power.

Family Relationships

Imagine that you are a sociologist studying family relationships and the only data at your disposal are photographs of families such as those in figure 8.6. What can you observe about the two families pictured? What can you infer about family structure and relationships from the arrangement of family members within each frame, and from the setting and tone of the photographs? Note your observations before reading further.

The eight family members in the first photograph (fig. 8.6a) represent several generations—an "extended family." The eldest couple in the family flanks the group on the extreme left and right. Something must be troubling the oldest male, seated on the far left, since everyone's attention is directed at him. Closest to him are two other males, likely his son and grandson, who treat him with great deference. But the most prominent member of this family is undoubtedly the stalwart, decisive-looking woman with the white hat standing in the middle of the group. The couple to her right is probably the latest branch of the extended family. The teenager standing in the back is the youngest person in the picture; he looks very absorbed in the situation but is apparently too young to have much say. The only anomaly in this photograph is the man with the cap kneeling in the foreground. He is of marriageable age and prominent in the family, since he is in closest contact with the family patriarch, yet there is no mate for him in the picture.

Judging from their clothes and appearance, this is a poor working family, probably farmers, since the setting is rural. The family is sandwiched between a ramshackle house on the left and a jalopy loaded with baggage and a mattress on the right. The door on the passenger side is open. It may be fair to assume that the crisis in the picture has to do with the family leaving home.

The family depicted in the second photograph (fig. 8.6b) is a "nuclear family"—one set of parents and their children. The most prominent member of this family is clearly the man with eyeglasses. He appears caught up in his own thoughts, while the rest of the family huddles around him, possibly looking for guidance or reassurance. His mate behind him, completely upstaged in the picture, appears to be consoling or placating him. The boy to the man's right is watching his father intensely; we sense a strong, complex relationship between them. The girl on the far right is more removed from and less focused on her father, but apparently quite attached to her brother. Another person, probably a third child, is obscured in the background. We can also see a

a

Figure 8.6

Families from two different films illustrate changes in American family structure over the years: (*a*) an extended family in THE GRAPES OF WRATH; (*b*) a nuclear family in THE MOSQUITO COAST.

black man in a cap, whose relationship to the family is unclear. The family members are disheveled and dirty, and their clothing seems inappropriate amid the dense tropical vegetation in the background. It appears they have fallen on hard times.

This exercise with family photographs illustrates how *mise en scène* in films can provide clues about character relationships within groups. (See chapter 1 and chapter 6 for more discussion of *mise en scène*.) But it also illustrates how films—like old photographs—can document developments in social institutions like the family. This last section of the chapter explores how Hollywood movies reflect important changes in American family structure and relationships since the 1930s.

b

THE GRAPES OF WRATH Versus THE MOSQUITO COAST

The first photo (fig. 8.6a) is a still from one of John Ford's most famous pictures, THE GRAPES OF WRATH (1940), based on John Steinbeck's novel of the same title, about the plight of migrant farm workers during the Great Depression. The film follows the Joad family, pictured in the still, on a trek from Oklahoma to California and recounts their frustrated efforts to find work there. A central theme in the film is the importance of the family. Ma Joad (Jane Darwell), the stalwart woman in the white hat, is appropriately positioned in the photograph because she is the backbone of the Joad family; her paramount concern throughout the story is to keep the family intact, which proves to be no easy task because both nature and society seem bent on tearing the family apart.

Family unity begins to disintegrate when the Joads, along with hundreds of other farmers in the Dust Bowl, are forced off their land to make way for corporate agriculture. In the scene in figure 8.7a, the Joads are about to set out for California, where, according to circulating handbills, hundreds of fruit pickers are needed. At the last minute, however, Grandpa Joad (Charley Grapewin) squats on the doorstep and refuses to leave his home. "It's my dirt," he cries, clutching a fistful of soil. "It's no good, but it's mine!" Tom Joad (Henry Fonda), kneeling in front, tries to persuade Grandpa to get on the truck, but Ma and Tom finally have to spike his coffee and carry him aboard unconscious.

Ma Joad cannot hold the family together. Grandpa and Grandma die on the odyssey to California; the new son-in-law runs off, leaving Tom's sister pregnant and despondent; and Tom himself is forced to flee after he kills a man in self-defense. Ma recognizes that the family's integrity is tied to the land in Oklahoma, which the family had worked for more than fifty years. "The family was whole and clear on the land," she tells Tom. "Ain't nothin' now to keep us clear. Pa ain't the head. We're crackin' up, Tom. We ain't no family now."

The second photograph (fig. 8.6b) is a still from THE MOSQUITO COAST (1987), directed by Peter Weir and based on a novel of the same title by Paul Theroux. In this film an eccentric inventor, Allie Fox (Harrison Ford), moves his family (wife, two sons, and twin daughters) from Massachusetts to Honduras to escape civilization's wanton exploitation of people and nature. In the jungle they build a small prosperous community from scratch. But Allie, who is obsessed with a dream to make ice from heat, becomes more and more tyrannical with his family, until gradually their faith in him erodes. A spectacular explosion at the ice plant he builds completely destroys their home, and the family is forced to start over again in another location, only to be wiped out in a flash flood. At this point the family is eager to return to civilization, but Father refuses to submit. "If it's on a map," he says curtly, "I can't use it." In the end the family stages a mutiny and walks out on Allie. But as they are leaving, a missionary whom Allie has antagonized shoots him, and the family drifts downriver to the sea with Allie dying.

The still of the Fox family is from the scene where they survey the rubble of their Robinson Crusoe home after the icehouse explosion. Thanks to the man in the background, Mr. Haddy (Conrad

How Do Films Reveal Characters?

Roberts), they escape downriver and start afresh; but the family's confidence in Father has been shaken. Tension begins to surface, particularly between Allie and his older son, Charley (River Phoenix), who previously idolized his father. At the beginning of the film, Charley, in **voice-over narration,** explains that he grew up believing that everything his father said was true. But gradually Charley begins to question his father's actions. The turning point in their relationship occurs when Father lies to the family, saying that they cannot return to the United States because it has been destroyed in a nuclear war. At the end of the film Charley persuades his mother that they must leave his father. After Allie's death, however, Charley finds a middle ground and comes of age. His last words in voice-over are: "Once I had believed in Father, and the world had seemed small and old. Now he was gone and I wasn't afraid to love him anymore, and the world seemed limitless."

Charley's mother (Helen Mirren)—never identified by name in the film, only as Mother—is completely subservient to her husband. She never questions, or participates in, his decisions. Until the end, she is trusting and loyal, even when Allie's decisions place the family in danger. "You must feel awful!" she says to Allie when their home is in ashes. Mother considers leaving Allie only after he shoves her violently and accuses her of disloyalty. As her sons help her up, she sees that the family cannot stay with Allie. Yet, to quiet him as he is dying, Mother lies to Allie, telling him their houseboat is headed upriver, where he dreamed of living free from civilization.

THE GRAPES OF WRATH and THE MOSQUITO COAST reflect important changes in American family structure and relationships since the 1930s. Indeed, as Christopher Lasch points out in *Haven in a Heartless World: The Family Besieged* (1977), "the family has been slowly coming apart for more than a hundred years" (xiv). In THE GRAPES OF WRATH when the Joads are removed from the land, they are cut off from their roots, from the values and traditions that bind them together. The family's patriarchal structure crumbles after Grandpa dies and Pa forfeits his position as head of the family, leaving the burden on Ma. Societal forces—poverty, unemployment, exploitation, politics—gradually splinter the family. The younger members, disillusioned and embittered, abandon the family for better opportunities or are driven away as fugitives. Ma recognizes the net result: the demise of the extended family.

The results are much the same for the nuclear family depicted in THE MOSQUITO COAST, except that the forces that tear the Fox family apart are mainly internal: Allie's obsessive and tyrannical control of the family. Allie dominates his family so completely that he stifles opportunities for individual growth. His sons are struggling for an identity of their own and resent their father's despotism; Mother is caught in the cross fire. In the end the family rebels against Father.

KRAMER VS. KRAMER

Changes in American family structure and relationships since the 1930s are strikingly evident if we introduce a third family photograph. We may be reluctant at first to accept figure 8.7 as an example of a family, since there is no mother in the picture, only a father and a child. Yet this still, taken from KRAMER VS. KRAMER (1979), reflects what a family means for many Americans today—the "single-parent family."

KRAMER VS. KRAMER, directed by Robert Benton, deals with the effects of divorce on family relationships. The first half of the film depicts the Kramers' broken marriage and focuses on Ted Kramer's (Dustin Hoffman) struggle to raise his seven-year-old son Billy (Justin Henry) while juggling a job and domestic responsibilities. The second half of the film concentrates on a bitter court battle for custody of Billy after Joanna Kramer (Meryl Streep) decides she wants her son back.

KRAMER VS. KRAMER could serve as a case study of a family broken by divorce. It raises provocative questions about the family responsibilities of men and women, and challenges some stereotyped notions about parenting, issues that are treated more humorously in movies like BABY BOOM (1987) and MR. MOM (1983). But KRAMER VS. KRAMER also raises a very thorny question about contemporary society: How do we define what a family is today? If the single parent and child in the third photograph constitute a family, then should other groups of people living together also be recognized as "nontraditional families"? For example, a growing number of unmarried couples, some of them homosexual, are claiming legal rights and social benefits as families. Are they families? Ultimately, the courts may have to answer this question. But meanwhile, films like ALIENS (1986) (discussed in chapter 7), RAISING ARIZONA (1987), and RAIN MAN (1989) bring unconventional family relationships to the public's attention; and films like the LA CAGE AUX FOLLES trilogy (1979, 1981, 1986) and THREE MEN AND A BABY (1988) (from the 1985 French original, THREE MEN AND A CRADLE) depict radically nontraditional familial situations.

Figure 8.7
A single-parent family in
KRAMER VS. KRAMER.

Figure 8.8
Bud Fox's loyalties are torn between (a) his father and (b) a financial high roller in WALL STREET. Tension between mutually exclusive character relationships in the film underscores messages about business ethics in our society.

a

b

How Do Films Reveal Characters?

Conclusion

This chapter has illustrated how character relationships in Hollywood films reflect changing American attitudes about social institutions. But these discussions are not presented as definitive studies of changes in American society. Other movies may depict romantic relationships, power relationships, and family relationships much differently. Films, after all, are only one indicator of social dynamics and, admittedly, not always a reliable indicator. Yet, character relationships in films sometimes provide fresh and insightful commentaries on social institutions. Look closely from a social-historical perspective at character relationships in the next Hollywood blockbuster you see. What do these relationships reveal, on the surface and underneath, about romance, power, and family in American society today?

Also look closely at how character relationships in a film play off one another. Popular movies often work around a **formula** in which a character is forced to choose between two mutually exclusive relationships. For example, in WALL STREET (1987), directed by Oliver Stone, the protagonist, Bud Fox (Charlie Sheen), is torn between two important people in his life who hold completely opposite business values—his father (Martin Sheen; fig. 8.8*a*) and an unscrupulous corporate raider named Gordon Gekko (Michael Douglas; fig. 8.8*b*), who becomes Bud's mentor. The tension in WALL STREET comes from Bud's dilemma about which relationship to choose, which set of values to follow. The film's message about business ethics is clear from the choice he makes.

General Study Questions

1. Analyze a film (such as JULES AND JIM, KNIFE IN THE WATER, or BROADCAST NEWS) that involves a love triangle. How does the film depict the interaction of the three characters? How does the film resolve the triangle? What attitude(s) does the film adopt toward love and marriage?
2. Study the shot-by-shot description of the sequence from AN OCCURRENCE AT OWL CREEK BRIDGE in chapter 2 and analyze how the filmmaker depicts the soldiers' power over the man who is to be hanged. Pay particular attention to *mise en scène* and editing.
3. Suppose you wanted to shoot a movie about your family. How would you depict family relationships cinematically? Create a detailed **film treatment** of one scene and tell how you would direct it.

4. Observe how films from another culture depict romantic relationships, power relationships, or family relationships. How are these relationships similar to and different from those in most Hollywood films? What attitudes and values about social institutions do character relationships in the foreign films reflect?

5. Identify a film that you think tries to *subvert* established social institutions. How do character relationships in the film help make it subversive? How do they help undermine conventional values and attitudes about institutions?

Additional Films for Study

JEZEBEL (1938), dir. William Wyler
THE AFRICAN QUEEN (1951), dir. John Huston
THE CRANES ARE FLYING (1957), dir. Mikhail Kalatozof
KNIFE IN THE WATER (1960), dir. Roman Polanski
THROUGH A GLASS DARKLY (1960), dir. Ingmar Bergman
JULES AND JIM (1961), dir. François Truffaut
TWO WOMEN (1961), dir. Vittorio De Sica
TO KILL A MOCKINGBIRD (1962), dir. Robert Mulligan
LOVES OF A BLONDE (1965), dir. Miloš Forman
PERSONA (1967), dir. Ingmar Bergman
BOB AND CAROL AND TED AND ALICE (1969), dir. Paul Mazursky
WOMEN IN LOVE (1970), dir. Ken Russell
CARNAL KNOWLEDGE (1971), dir. Mike Nichols
NIGHT PORTER (1973), dir. Liliana Cavani
SWEPT AWAY (1975), dir. Lina Wertmuller
TURNING POINT (1977), dir. Herbert Ross
COMING HOME (1978), dir. Hal Ashby
ON GOLDEN POND (1981), dir. Mark Rydell
SOPHIE'S CHOICE (1982), dir. Alan J. Pakula
EL NORTE (1983), dir. Gregory Nava
DESPERATELY SEEKING SUSAN (1985), dir. Susan Seidelman

A GREAT WALL (1986), dir. Peter Wang
HANNAH AND HER SISTERS (1986), dir. Woody Allen
RUNNING ON EMPTY (1988), dir. Sidney Lumet
SEX, LIES, AND VIDEOTAPE (1989), dir. Steven Soderbergh

Further Reading

Atkins, Thomas R., ed. *Sexuality in the Movies.* Bloomington: Indiana University Press, 1975.

Bergman, Andrew. *We're in the Money: Depression America and Its Films.* New York: Harper Colophon Books, 1972.

Capra, Frank. *The Name Above the Title: An Autobiography.* New York: Macmillan, 1971.

Glatner, Richard, ed. *Frank Capra.* Ann Arbor: University of Michigan Press, 1975.

Huaco, George A. *The Sociology of Film Art.* New York: Basic Books, 1965.

Jarvie, Ian C. *Movies and Society.* New York: Basic Books, 1970.

Mellen, Joan. *Women and Their Sexuality in the New Film.* New York: Dell, 1975.

Roffman, Peter, and Jim Purdy. *The Hollywood Social Problem Film.* Bloomington: Indiana University Press, 1981.

Thomson, David. *America in the Dark: The Impact of Hollywood Films on American Culture.* New York: William Morrow, 1979.

Trent, Paul. *Those Fabulous Movie Years: The Thirties.* New York: Crown, 1975.

Walker, Alexander. *Sex in the Movies.* London: Penguin, 1968.

Willis, Donald C. *The Films of Frank Capra.* Metuchen, N.J.: Scarecrow Press, 1974.

Works Cited

Capra, Frank. *The Name Above the Title: An Autobiography.* New York: Macmillan, 1971.

Konigsberg, Ira. "FATAL ATTRACTION." In *Magill's Cinema Annual 1988,* edited by Frank N. Magill, 118–21. Englewood Cliffs, N.J.: Salem, 1988.

Lasch, Christopher. *Haven in a Heartless World: The Family Besieged.* New York: Basic Books, 1977.

May, Rollo. *Love and Will.* New York: W.W. Norton, 1969.

How Do Films Depict Physical Reality?

The systematic study of any subject eventually demands the categorization of data and experience. So a systematic study of movies inevitably leads us to classify films into broad categories according to common characteristics. This unit will explore one way that film critics and historians have traditionally classified movies. Films, from the very beginning, have tended to separate themselves into two broad categories: One type of film depicts the physical world *realistically*; another type depicts it *expressionistically*—that is, distorts physical reality in some way in order to express strong feelings about it. Although these categories are by no means absolute, they do represent fundamentally different approaches to moviemaking and different ways of using images and cinematic techniques.

Chapter 9 first looks at the prototypes of cinematic realism and expressionism in the works of early filmmakers Louis Lumière and Georges Méliès, and then closely compares two futuristic movies that serve as models of realistic and expressionistic films: Fritz Lang's METROPOLIS and George Lucas's THX: 1138. Chapter 10 traces the development of the realistic tradition in cinema from Lumière forward, highlighting films directed by Edwin S. Porter, D.W. Griffith, Erich von Stroheim, Orson Welles, and Roberto Rossellini. Chapter 11 does the same for the expressionistic tradition, highlighting key films by Robert Wiene, F.W. Murnau, Luis Buñuel and Salvador Dalí, Jean Cocteau, Maya Deren and Alexander Hammid, and Federico Fellini.

Besides introducing a practical system for categorizing movies, the discussion of cinematic realism and expressionism in unit 3 also provides historical perspective by examining each tradition chronologically, focusing on how each tradition evolved over time, and provides theoretical perspective by introducing key issues and questions that film artists, critics, and historians have debated since the time of Lumière and Méliès.

WHO FRAMED ROGER RABBIT? (1988), dir. Robert Zemeckis.

Realism Versus Expressionism
in Narrative Film

C H A P T E R **9**

I magine you had the opportunity to make movies just before the turn of the twentieth century when the technology of photography first made motion pictures possible. What would you have done with a motion picture camera in 1895? Without models or precedents to follow, what kind of movies would you have made?

The Prototypes: Lumière Versus Méliès

From the very beginning, movies tended to follow one of two distinct directions, exemplified by two early French filmmakers, Louis Lumière and Georges Méliès. Their films became prototypes for realistic and expressionistic traditions in cinema. The discussion that follows will compare and contrast films by Lumière and Méliès in order to identify the basic characteristics and tendencies of cinematic **realism** and **expressionism**.

Lumière's *Actualités*

After Thomas Edison's Kinetoscope was demonstrated to the public at the Chicago World's Fair in 1893, inventors and impresarios in Europe and America were eager to develop the technical means to project "motion pictures" for a large audience. By 1895, Louis Lumière, a French inventor and pioneer in cinema, had built his own machine to compete with Edison's—the Cinématographe, a film camera and projector all in one, with a system of claws to move the film along. He patented the device jointly with his brother Auguste, and together they started making film *actualités*, which they hoped would catch the public's fancy. The Lumières' first public screening was in December 1895, a program of ten films that lasted twenty minutes altogether.

Since the film spool inside the Cinématographe held only fifty feet of film—about one minute's worth—that is how long an early Lumière film ran. Typically, each film recorded in a single shot an everyday event, which the title described: WORKERS LEAVING THE LUMIÈRE FACTORY (fig. 9.1*a*), TRAIN ENTERING A STATION (fig. 9.1*b*), A GAME OF CARDS, SWIMMING IN THE SEA, etc. Aside from deciding where to set up the camera, Lumière did not cinematically manipulate these *actualités*. The camera remained static, and the films were not edited, even in the camera. Siegfried Kracauer, a film critic and theorist who has written extensively about the contributions of Lumière and Méliès to cinema, points out that "the bulk of his [Lumière's] films

Figure 9.1
Frame enlargements from
two early Lumière
actualités: (*a*) WORKERS
LEAVING THE LUMIÈRE
FACTORY and (*b*) TRAIN
ENTERING A STATION.

a

b

Realism Versus Expressionism in Narrative Film

recorded the world about us for no other purpose than to present it" (*Theory* 31). A contemporary Parisian journalist, Henri de Parville, described Lumière's films as "nature caught in the act" (246).

On the other hand, most Lumière films arrange the action for the camera to some extent. On the simplest level, his films frequently show someone in the scene mugging for the camera, like the café waiter in A GAME OF CARDS, or exaggerated activity and enthusiasm, like the wrecking crew furiously at work with sledgehammers in DEMOLITION OF A WALL. Other Lumière films involve more direction. In SNOW-BALL FIGHT (1895), for example, two sets of action take place simultaneously: a snowball fight in the foreground and a man on a bicycle in the background pedaling toward it. The camera is positioned to photograph foreground and background action at the same time so that the audience can observe the snowball fight and watch the bicyclist approaching it. The highlight of the film occurs, naturally, when the bicyclist reaches the foreground and is pelted with snowballs. Selective camera positioning and careful timing of the action in SNOWBALL FIGHT indicate that this film is "directed." The snowball fight clearly was not a "found event."

Another Lumière film, WATERING THE GARDENER (1896), is one of the earliest **slapstick comedies** (fig. 9.2). A gardener looks into the nozzle of a hose to find out why the water has stopped. The reason is that a boy behind him is stepping down on the hose. The joke is obvious: When the boy steps up, the gardener gets splashed in the face. Once again, a purposeful combination of camera position and timing makes this **sight gag** work. Kracauer states that WATERING THE GAR-DENER represents "an imaginative attempt on the part of Lumière to develop photography into a means of story telling. Yet the story was just a real-life incident" (*Theory* 30–31).

Méliès's Trick Films

Georges Méliès, a stage designer and magician who owned the Theatre Robert-Houdin in Paris, was present at the Lumières' first public screening in December 1895. After seeing the Lumière program, he purchased an apparatus similar to the Cinématographe and, in April 1896, began showing films between stage acts. During that year, Méliès made seventy-eight films in the Lumière manner and built the first film studio in France at Montreuil, near Paris.

In 1898, however, Méliès began making a completely different kind of film after the **shutter** of his camera jammed. He accidently discovered how simple it is to make objects appear and disappear

Figure 9.2

This scene in Lumière's WATERING THE GARDENER is one of the first motion picture sight gags.

on film by stopping and starting the camera. Thereafter, Méliès specialized in **trick films** and developed many techniques to perform magical feats on film, including **multiple exposure, superimposition,** and **lap dissolves.**

Like Lumière's titles, Méliès's film titles also suggest their content: THE KINGDOM OF THE FAIRIES, JUPITER'S THUNDERBOLTS, THE MAGIC LANTERN, THE MERMAID. Méliès eventually made several hundred trick films that featured superimposed images and objects and characters appearing and disappearing. But his most famous film is A TRIP TO THE MOON (1902), which in its day was the most widely exhibited, and imitated, film in the world.

Figure 9.3
A scene from A TRIP TO
THE MOON, illustrating
Méliès's elaborate sets
and staging.

Based on a Jules Verne story, A TRIP TO THE MOON
depicts the comic adventures of a group of grandiose scientists who under-
take a voyage to the moon in a bullet-shaped rocket fired from an enormous cannon (fig. 9.3). The film is about ten times as long as the average
Lumière film and develops different scenes (fig. 9.4) so that the audience
follows the voyage through all its stages—the planning and spectacular
launching, adventures after the landing on the moon, and finally, a
perilous escape and return to Earth.

How does A TRIP TO THE MOON differ from a typical
Lumière film? Compare the stills from WATERING THE GARDENER
(fig. 9.2) and A TRIP TO THE MOON (fig. 9.3), and note major differences you observe.

One of the first things we notice about A TRIP TO THE
MOON is that Méliès staged the action much more than Lumière did in
WATERING THE GARDENER. It is apparent that A TRIP TO THE

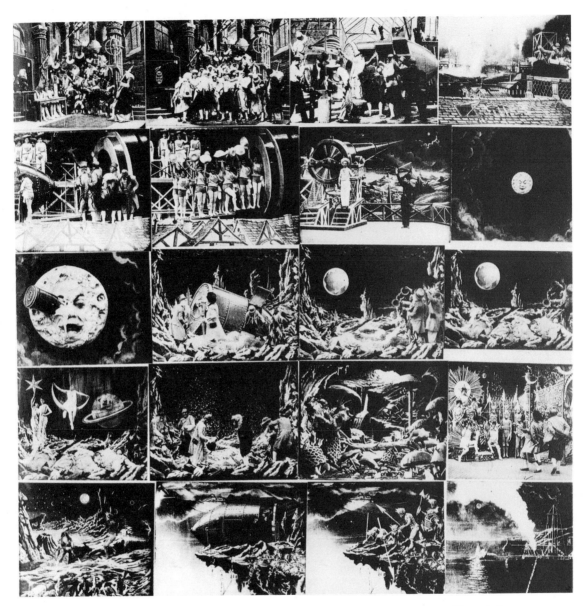

Figure 9.4

A composite of twenty scenes from Méliès's A TRIP TO THE MOON, which in its day was the most widely exhibited film in the world.

MOON was filmed in a studio and required considerable preparation and rehearsal. We see many costumed characters, probably stage actors, who perform on elaborate stage sets. The launching party, in scanty costumes, resembles a theatrical chorus line; and some of the "moon people" in the film execute acrobatic feats. Although it is a landmark in film history and often cited for its cinematic inventiveness, A TRIP TO THE MOON clings

Figure 9.5

Méliès created the first motion picture dream sequence in this scene from A TRIP TO THE MOON.

very closely to stage traditions. Its sets and costumes, its style of acting, its *mise en scène* are all very theatrical; the players even bow to the audience as in a stage production. Kracauer points out: "Much as his [Méliès's] films differed from the theater on a technical plane, they failed to transcend its scope by incorporating genuinely cinematic subjects. This also explains why Méliès, for all his inventiveness, never thought of moving his camera; the stationary camera perpetuated the spectator's relation to the stage" (*Theory* 33).

Besides being a more technically elaborate production than SNOWBALL FIGHT or WATERING THE GARDENER, Méliès's A TRIP TO THE MOON also presents a different kind of content than Lumière's films. Lumière depicts comic skits involving ordinary people in recognizable settings. The snowball fight could be filmed on any street;

the gardener could be your neighbor. Méliès, on the other hand, depicts a fantastic flight to the moon and strange, imaginary creatures and settings. Méliès's main contribution to cinema, says Siegfried Kracauer, "lay in substituting staged illusion for unstaged reality, and contrived plots for everyday incidents" (*Theory* 32).

But it is important to note that Méliès also uses cinematic techniques in A TRIP TO THE MOON to complement and reinforce the film's fantastic content. For example, in the scenes where the earth voyagers are chased and captured by the moon creatures, Méliès combines **stop motion** with theatrical pyrotechnics to make the aliens disappear in a puff of smoke. He also superimposes images to create a fantastic, other-worldly atmosphere. When they first arrive on the moon, the voyagers settle down for a nap, while in the heavens above them, stars turn into beautiful ladies—the first dream sequence in film history (fig. 9.5).

To summarize, Louis Lumière's films, both in content and technique, are early models for a realistic tradition that has a predilection for observation and attempts to record people and events much as they appear in the everyday world. Georges Méliès's films, on the other hand, are models for an expressionistic tradition that is inclined toward fantasy and illusion and that uses cinematic technique to distort people and events in order to express strong feelings.

A Model Comparison: METROPOLIS Versus THX: 1138

It is not difficult to distinguish between the realistic and expressionistic traditions in cinema when we compare Lumière *actualités* with Méliès trick films. But as motion pictures became longer and more complex, many filmmakers drew freely on both traditions. Today, for instance, many realistic films include expressionistic dream sequences. So how can we determine whether a film is realistic or expressionistic? What characteristics distinguish realism and expressionism in movies?

Since the Lumière and Méliès films can be divided so neatly into depictions of either everyday events or fantastic events, our first inclination might be to depend on a film's content to indicate whether it is realistic or expressionistic. Thus, a biographical film about Abraham Lincoln would be realistic, while a science fiction film about colonizing another galaxy would be expressionistic. But this approach simply does not work for all films. For example, some straightforward action mysteries in familiar contemporary settings, like Alfred Hitchcock's NORTH BY

NORTHWEST (1959) or Roman Polanski's FRANTIC (1988), are very expressionistic; whereas some science fiction fantasies set in the distant future, like Douglas Trumbull's SILENT RUNNING (1977) or Ridley Scott's ALIEN (1979), are startlingly realistic. Generally, therefore, cinematic realism or expressionism is better defined by visual appearance than by content.

The rest of this chapter will compare and contrast two futuristic films with similar stories, themes, and underlying messages: Fritz Lang's METROPOLIS (1927) and George Lucas's THX: 1138 (1971). One of these films is a clear-cut example of cinematic realism; the other, of cinematic expressionism. We will not try to determine whether the stories in these films are possible or even probable according to the world we know. Instead, we will compare how they depict the future and how they introduce and resolve problems about life in the future.

Both METROPOLIS and THX: 1138 are about monolithic societies of the future in which human freedoms are severely restricted. In METROPOLIS, workers are enslaved underground to work the engines that power the great city above for a privileged class of managers. The protagonist is a young man named Freder, whose father, John Fredersen, is Master of Metropolis. Freder falls in love with a saintly young woman, Maria, who preaches that a mediator will come to reconcile workers and managers. Meanwhile, John Fredersen commissions an evil inventor, Rotwang, to kidnap Maria and create a robot exactly like her in order to sow confusion and discord among the workers. After the robot incites the workers to rebellion, Fredersen orders the workers' underground homes flooded. Freder frees Maria from Rotwang's clutches; then together they rescue the workers' children from the flood. Afterwards, Freder pursues Rotwang to the roof of a cathedral from which, after a struggle, the evil inventor falls to his death. In the final shot of the film, Freder, the mediator, stands between his father and the workers' foreman and joins their hands together.

The title of THX: 1138 is the name of the protagonist in the film, a man who rebels against and escapes from a highly technological subterranean world in which human beings are routinely drugged and programmed to perform specialized mechanical jobs. Since children are artificially conceived, sex is forbidden and severely punished. But after THX and his computer-matched roommate, LUH: 3417, reduce their daily drug intake, they become sexually aware of each other and conceive a child. When THX's subnormal drug level is detected, he is arrested, convicted of drug evasion and sexual perversion, and imprisoned in a

How Do Films Depict Physical Reality?

desolate white void. Later he escapes and discovers that LUH is dead. Then he steals a jet-car and roars away, pursued by robot police on jet-bikes. THX eludes capture, climbs a ladder to a hatch that leads above ground, and escapes into open air and sunlight.

The following discussion will compare and contrast the imagery, setting, lighting, *mise en scène*, characters, and dramatic resolution in METROPOLIS and THX: 1138. Our thesis is that one of these films is realistic, and the other expressionistic. By exploring the differences between them, we will delineate more precisely the general characteristics of realism and expressionism.

Imagery

Since one of the dominant themes in both METROPOLIS and THX: 1138 is the relationship between human beings and machines, let us first consider the images of machines in each film. METROPOLIS opens with shots of actual machinery—large motors and pistons in operation—which **dissolve** to a studio set showing a colossal multitiered machine (fig. 9.6). Workers in identical drab coveralls and caps stand at their stations and sway methodically from side to side at their work (like machines themselves). One image in particular stands out: a gigantic control panel (fig. 9.7*a*) where a worker is spread-eagled in front of a large dial, moving three arms on the face of it to match lights flashing on the perimeter. His work appears senseless, but later it becomes clear that this dial regulates the pressure that is continually building up in the machine. The dial must be constantly attended, or the engine room will explode. In fact, Freder, the protagonist of the film, witnesses such an explosion in one of the early scenes.

The beginning of THX: 1138 is almost identical. It opens with images of computer-age machinery: digital gauges, CRT screens, and computer-generated voices. Workers wearing white coveralls and caps labor in closer, more sanitized quarters than the workers in METROPOLIS, but their machinery is no less dangerous. Again, a worker breaks down at his station, causing a dangerous buildup of radioactivity and an explosion. In this sequence we see THX, the film's protagonist, handling radioactive materials with an industrial robot (fig. 9.7*b*).

The machine in METROPOLIS is an obvious movie set. The most untechnical eye would not mistake it for a real machine—even a machine of the future. Why didn't Lang use an actual machine, or build a set that more closely resembles actual machinery? Why does he present such an exaggerated image?

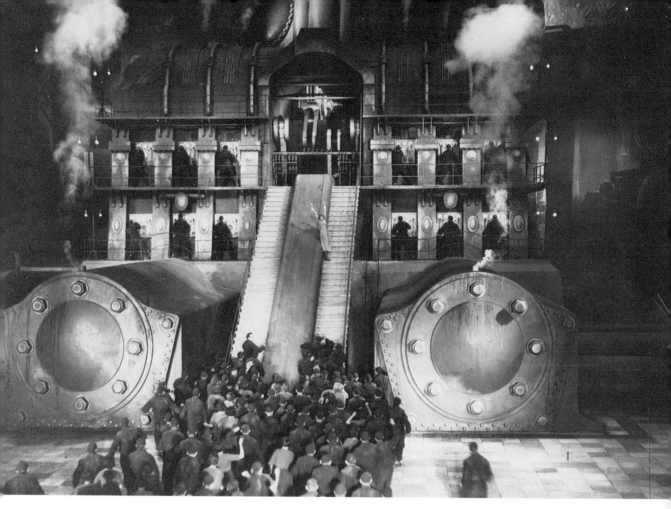

Figure 9.6

In METROPOLIS workers are slaves to a colossal multitiered machine in the city's underground.

The machine in METROPOLIS does not accommodate worker comfort or safety in any way. Workers are confined to their individual stations, spaced well apart from one another and permitted no human contact. After just a few moments of observing the machine, the viewer (like Freder in the film) perceives the dehumanized status of workers in this society. The exaggerated image of the machine, therefore, becomes a visual **metaphor** for the deadening (and deadly) working conditions in the engine room and in the whole society. Fritz Lang caricatures the machine in order to imbue it with strong emotional overtones.

Another dimension of the machine image in METROPOLIS is revealed when Freder witnesses the explosion in the engine room, which kills many workers. Suddenly, Freder has a vision in which the giant machine is transformed into the god Moloch, devouring the humans who are marched into his fiery maw. The film then cuts back to the aftermath of the explosion, as workers' bodies are carried away. Freder's

a

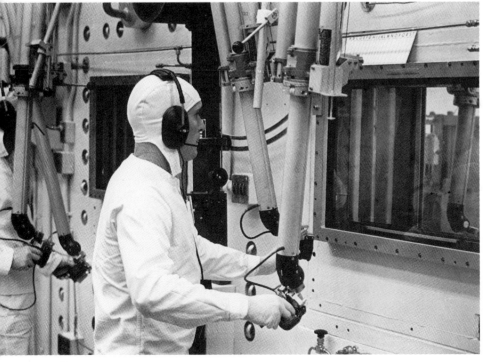

b

Figure 9.7
Contrasting images of machinery in METROPOLIS and THX: 1138. (a) The machine in METROPOLIS is obviously a studio set. Even the most untechnical eye would not mistake it for a real machine. (b) The machine in THX: 1138 is an actual industrial robot that George Lucas photographed on location in a high-tech factory.

Realism Versus Expressionism in Narrative Film

251

vision of Moloch, therefore, adds another layer of meaning to the machine, making it a **symbol** for the managers' destructive power, a bloodthirsty idol to which human lives are wantonly sacrificed.

Lang clearly does not intend the machine in METROPOLIS to be *representational*—that is, to look like an actual machine. Instead he intends it to be an image that strikes horror into people like Freder who witness how it exploits and dehumanizes the workers in Metropolis.

The machines in THX: 1138, on the other hand, are not constructed sets. Lucas found the kind of high-tech hardware he needed for the film and shot most of it **on location.** We see that the industrial robot THX controls is an actual machine because we watch him operate it. Although some machines in the film—like the robot police and the jet-cars—are fabricated or modified to look futuristic, Lucas convinces us that they are real because he surrounds them with technology that is already commonplace in the computer age. Therefore, even though they may not exist in our world the way they appear in the film, the robot police and the jet-cars are representational because Lucas makes them look like actual machines of the future.

Another kind of imagery in METROPOLIS has no counterpart in THX: 1138. In one scene, for example, Maria tells the workers the Biblical story of the Tower of Babel, which Lang depicts in tableau as she narrates. The story is a parable to help the workers (and the film viewers) understand the causes of social unrest in Metropolis. From this parable emerges the principal metaphor of the film: the "heart" that must mediate between the "brain" and the "hand"—that is, between the masters and the workers in Metropolis.

Setting

In METROPOLIS almost every setting is designed to evoke strong emotional responses: sensuous pleasure gardens for the elite in the upper world, the sweaty engine room, Rotwang's sinister laboratory, desolate underground catacombs. So that emotional overtones will not be missed, some sets, like the elevators to the lower city, are purposely oversized to dwarf individual human figures in the film; others, like the catacombs, are overlaid with emotionally charged images, such as human skulls or iron bars.

In THX: 1138, on the other hand, George Lucas shot many scenes on location—in modernistic West Coast buildings and labs, in underground parking garages and tunnels. He said in an interview: "I realized that we were already living in the future that everyone was talking and writing about in the 1930s—you know, rockets, television, glass skyscrapers, the world of the comics and '1984.' I thought, 'Hey, I can do a science-fiction movie using real locations'" (54). Lucas also shot some scenes for THX: 1138 in the studio and used constructed sets; but, as with the images of machines in the film, he was careful to make the sets appear authentic. Rather than err with too much detail, he preferred sets that were minimally decorated, often little more than bare white background, as in the barren prison setting.

Lighting

As with imagery and setting, there are also important differences between the lighting styles in METROPOLIS and THX: 1138. Look closely at the stills depicting the machines in each film (fig. 9.7a and b). What can you observe about the lighting effects and visual tone of each scene?

Fritz Lang's shot of the engine control panel (fig. 9.7a) employs **low-key lighting** that is diffused and softened with smoke to create a dim, oppressive atmosphere and to enhance the exaggerated and highly stylized set. Lang centers the panel in the background, squarely framed between two vertical ladders that draw the viewer's eye toward it. He sets it apart from the surroundings with soft **backlighting,** which illuminates the space around and above the panel and suggests its massive size and importance in the scene. **Spotlights** around the engine room further emphasize the object's significance. The focal point of the scene is the large dial with the spread-eagled worker, which is the most dramatic image in the frame. The luminous dial contrasts with the dark shape of the man grotesquely stretched before it.

George Lucas's shot of THX working the industrial robot (fig. 9.7b), on the other hand, employs **high-key lighting** that is straightforward and neutral. It does not attempt to cast evocative shadows or create an emotional atmosphere; it simply illuminates the scene the way we would expect in a sanitized, high-tech industrial setting where skilled workers perform delicate mechanical operations.

An even better example of Lang's lighting style in METROPOLIS is when Rotwang kidnaps Maria in the catacombs. In this scene Maria walks through the catacombs alone, carrying a single lighted candle, and Rotwang stalks her with a powerful flashlight. His light glances menacingly around the spooky vaults until it fixes Maria in its beam and finally corners her against the wall. The pursuit ends with a close-up of Rotwang's black-gloved hand snuffing out the flame of Maria's candle. The lighting in this scene is an effective narrative device that helps depict Maria's abduction, but it is also laden with emotional and symbolic overtones.

In THX: 1138 George Lucas also uses dramatic lighting to create special effects and atmosphere. For example, in the scene where THX is tried for drug evasion and sexual perversion, Lucas uses overhead spotlights to isolate the trial attorneys. The lighting effects are somewhat bizarre, but not especially laden with emotional or symbolic overtones because THX's guilt is a foregone conclusion. Rather, the scene is a curiosity, a glimpse into courtroom proceedings in the future. The lighting effects add to the visual texture of the scene, but they do not imbue it with conspicuous emotional overtones.

Mise en Scène

There are also important differences between the ways METROPOLIS and THX: 1138 depict people in their futuristic worlds, especially in group scenes. Siegfried Kracauer, in a landmark study of German cinema, *From Caligari to Hitler: A Psychological History of German Film*, observed that Fritz Lang has "a penchant for ornamentation" in METROPOLIS, both in the sets and in "the arrangements of the masses." Whether they are at work, on their way to and from the machines, or gathered together on their own time, "the workers form ornamental groups." "In his exclusive concern with ornamentation," says Kracauer, "Lang goes so far as to compose patterns for the masses who are desperately trying to escape the inundation of the lower city" (*Caligari* 149–50). And even in the aftermath of their frenzied rebellion against the city managers, "the workers advance in the form of a wedge-shaped, strictly symmetrical procession which points towards the industrialist standing on the portal steps of the cathedral [fig. 9.8a]" (Kracauer, *Caligari* 164).

In THX: 1138, however, the masses are not arranged into groups with any special symmetry or order; quite the opposite, in fact. Workers move singly and silently through antiseptic corridors between their jobs and their living quarters (fig. 9.8b). There is great symmetry and order in the sets of THX: 1138—for instance, in an apparently endless row of identical booths that dispense prerecorded religious platitudes; but this symmetry does not extend to groups of people in the film. People in THX: 1138 do not form groups; they live an isolated existence, working alone at their stations or sitting alone in front of video screens in their cubicles. Even sex is forbidden them. One scene, however, where a line of school children silently ascends an escalator, is a notable exception. Each child looks like all the others, with white clothes, a shaved

How Do Films Depict Physical Reality?

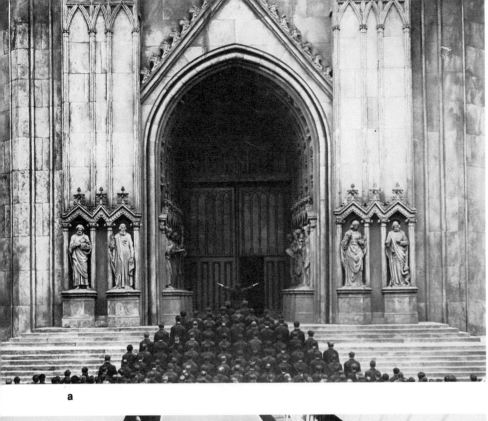

a

b

Figure 9.8
Contrasting images of people in METROPOLIS and THX: 1138.
(a) Workers in ME-TROPOLIS form ornamental groups.
(b) Workers in THX: 1138 move singly and silently through antiseptic corridors.

Figure 9.9
The frightful regimentation
of these school children in
THX: 1138 only under-
scores the isolation that
awaits them as adults.

How Do Films Depict Physical Reality?

Figure 9.10
Children of the workers in
METROPOLIS, reaching
desperately toward their
rescuers. The shot
simultaneously evokes
panic and hope, helpless-
ness and trust.

head, and a hypodermic bracelet to regulate drug intake (fig. 9.9). There is a frightful order in the regimentation of these children; but, within the larger context of the film, that order only underscores the isolation that awaits them as adults.

Does it make much difference that Lang arranges masses of people in METROPOLIS and that Lucas does not in THX: 1138? Consider how important choreography is for a dance performance. Dancers express themselves with their bodies, and choreographers arrange the dancers' body movements to music in order to evoke specific feelings. A film director who choreographs groups of characters, therefore, is externalizing feelings in the same way. For example, in the scene in ME-TROPOLIS where the workers' homes are flooded, Lang presents a series of shots of the children fleeing toward an alarm gong where Freder and Maria are waiting to rescue them. As the water rises in the streets and the children become more and more desperate, they encircle the platform, pressing in toward the center with arms outstretched to their rescuers. Finally, in a long, high-angle shot (fig. 9.10), Lang shows the pathetic circle of children, like so many iron shavings drawn to a magnet, reaching desperately toward Freder and Maria. The shot is emotionally powerful because it simultaneously evokes contradictory feelings: panic and hope, helplessness and trust.

The line of school children on the escalator proves that George Lucas also occasionally arranges groups of people to evoke specific emotions. But the crucial difference is that, as with sets, Lucas arranges groups so they appear natural and authentic within the story and setting, whereas Lang's "ornamental groups" are highly stylized and emotionally larger than life.

Characters

What about the protagonists of the two films? Both METROPOLIS and THX: 1138 present a heroic protagonist who struggles against the restrictiveness of his society and overcomes or escapes it in the end. But the struggles of the two protagonists are revealed very differently. Freder's inner experience, as with his vision of Moloch, is sometimes transmitted to us directly—not with a **point-of-view shot** of what one would see in Freder's place, but with a highly subjective depiction of Freder's innermost thoughts and feelings. For example, in one scene Freder discovers his father alone with Rotwang's robot, which looks exactly like Maria. To Freder, who does not yet know about the robot's existence, it appears that his father and Maria are lovers. Freder's emotions completely overpower him at this moment. Lights flash and explode in his mind, and distorted images of Maria's face spin around, intermixed with images of skulls from the catacombs. Lang rapidly **intercuts** close-ups of Freder, Maria, Rotwang, and statues of the Seven Deadly Sins. Finally, Freder collapses as the scene **fades out.**

In THX: 1138, on the other hand, very little of the protagonist's experience is presented subjectively. Lucas rarely uses even point-of-view shots in the film, so we observe THX's struggle objectively. In one scene, two medical technicians callously experiment with THX's pain tolerance. First we see THX in paroxysms of pain, for no apparent reason; then we see the same action on a video monitor, with indifferent, clinical commentary by the technicians on **voice-over.** Lucas does not depict THX's pain subjectively in this scene but rather lets the terrible contortions of his body communicate it. For irony, he further distances the audience from THX's torture by removing it to the video screen for clinical observation.

There are also important differences between the villains in these two films. In METROPOLIS John Fredersen is responsible for subjugating the workers. He is the Master of Metropolis who controls the machine room from his administrative tower. But even though Fredersen is an unsympathetic character throughout most of the film, he is not the ultimate villain. That distinction belongs to Rotwang, who has absolute disregard for human life. (Fredersen at least cares for his son.) When Rotwang reports to Fredersen that he has invented a machine that never tires or makes a mistake, he adds, "Now we have no further use for living workers." At the end of the film, therefore, it is the sinister Rotwang, appropriately identified by the black glove he wears on his right hand, who perishes. Only after Freder has defeated Rotwang and restored the true Maria to the workers does he reconcile his father and the workers.

In THX: 1138 no specific individual can be identified as the villain. The robot police who make arrests are not the villains because they are only machines; nor are the anonymous technicians, like THX himself, who operate the computers that track him throughout his life. THX's struggle in the film is against a nameless system. THX's enemy is the entire society.

Dramatic Resolution

METROPOLIS has a storybook ending: Evil is destroyed and good triumphs. Rotwang falls from the cathedral roof, and his robot is burned as a witch. Maria and Freder are reunited; they rescue the children from the flood; and they apparently live happily ever after. John Fredersen, his social consciousness raised, joins hands with the workers' foreman in front of the cathedral.

THX: 1138 ends with the rebellious hero outrunning the police and finally climbing out of the underground city in which he has spent his entire life. He emerges into sunlight and open air. In the sky the sun hangs near the horizon. Our feelings at the end of the film depend on how we perceive that sun. Is it rising or setting? On the one hand, after the tension of a high-speed chase through the tunnels of the underworld, we are relieved that THX has escaped his pursuers and the repressive technology of the society below. On the other hand, THX is now alone on the surface of a planet he has never seen. What kind of world has he climbed into? Is it safe or poisoned? Can he survive alone? As one critic noted, "It is an ambiguous conclusion, both liberating and a little frightening" (Farber 5).

Conclusion

Even though METROPOLIS and THX: 1138 offer similar underlying messages about human freedom in repressive societies, they differ significantly in how they communicate these messages. These differences are due to the kinds of images and settings the two directors present, how they light the settings and depict groups of people within them, how they delineate characters, and how they develop and finally resolve dramatic tension in the story. These differences are the principal reasons why one of these films is realistic and the other expressionistic.

If we keep in mind that the expressionistic tradition in cinema is rooted in fantasy and illusion and distorts people and events in order to express strong emotion, we recognize that METROPOLIS is the expressionistic film. Exaggerated settings, evocative lighting, and choreographed arrangements of people create a dreamlike world that we experience primarily through the highly subjective, emotionally charged perceptions of the film's protagonist, epitomized by Freder's vision of Moloch. As in dreams, the most important messages in METROPOLIS are communicated through metaphors and symbols; and the principal characters, like figures in a fable, personify pure good and evil. The film builds and resolves dramatic tension like a fairy tale.

On the other hand, if we keep in mind that the realistic tradition in cinema is rooted in a close observation of nature and an endeavor to show characters interacting with their surroundings in a true-to-life way, we recognize that THX: 1138 is the realistic film. Lucas's preference for shooting on location and his penchant for authentic detail create a world that we experience as representational, where objects and settings look real and characters react to stimuli around them in a believable way, as epitomized by THX's writhing under torture. Our position as objective observers of THX's struggle for freedom is more consistent with waking experience, where we try to understand people and situations according to our sense perceptions and reason. His experience is more like what we encounter in real life, where the opposition is not always a specific individual, where the best course of action is not always obvious, and where the resolution is often ambiguous.

The model comparison of METROPOLIS and THX: 1138 concentrates on characteristics of the two films that best distinguish them as realistic or expressionistic. But although they are not discussed specifically in this model, camera and editing techniques, sound, and color (or black and white) can also be employed realistically or expressionistically; so can costumes, makeup, and acting. A comparison of two other films might highlight different technical and stylistic features. In other words, there is no checklist that absolutely identifies a film as either realistic or expressionistic.

Moreover, it is not easy to isolate one technical or stylistic device as *the* indicator that a film is realistic or expressionistic. For example, in Lang's depiction of the engine room control panel in METROPOLIS, we cannot isolate the exaggerated image of the machine from the rest of the highly stylized set, nor from the "ornamental groups" of workers in the scene, nor from the evocative lighting. They complement one another and work together to create the scene's expressionistic appearance.

To develop a better critical sense about movies, it is useful to recognize whether a film falls in line with the realistic or expressionistic tradition in cinema. It is not fair, for example, to criticize METROPOLIS because it does not depict the future as realistically as SILENT RUNNING or ALIEN, when it is apparent that Fritz Lang did not intend a realistic depiction. In other words, recognizing films as realistic or expressionistic can help us understand and judge them better on their own terms.

The remaining two chapters in unit 3 will briefly delineate the realistic and expressionistic traditions in cinema and point out some of the major developments in each since the time of Lumière and Méliès.

General Study Questions

1. Imagine that you are a filmmaker. Choose a familiar incident or situation in your life and describe in detail how you might depict it realistically from your own point of view. Then describe how you might depict it expressionistically.
2. Choose a film that you think fits clearly into the realistic tradition in cinema. Describe a few scenes from the film in detail. What characteristics of these scenes make them realistic? What makes this film stand out for you as an example of realism?
3. Repeat the procedure in question 2 for a film that you think fits clearly into the expressionistic tradition in cinema.
4. Do you think that the most recent trend in American cinema is predominantly realistic or expressionistic? Support your answer with specific references to films you have seen during the last year.

5. In your own words explain to a friend the difference between realism and expressionism in films. Use examples from films you know to illustrate your explanation.

Additional Films for Study

See the list at the end of chapter 10 for additional realistic films for study and the list at the end of chapter 11 for additional expressionistic films for study.

Further Reading

Allen, Robert C., and Douglas Gomery. *Film History: Theory and Practice*. New York: Alfred A. Knopf, 1985.

Andrew, Dudley. *The Major Film Theories*. New York: Oxford University Press, 1976.

Armes, Roy. *Film and Reality*. New York: Penguin, 1974.

Baxter, John. *Science Fiction in the Cinema*. Cranbury, N.J.: A.S. Barnes, 1970.

Bazin, André. *What Is Cinema?* 2 vols. Translated and edited by Hugh Gray. Berkeley: University of California Press, 1967; 1971.

Brosnan, John. *Future Tense: The Cinema of Science Fiction*. New York: St. Martin's Press, 1978.

Cook, David A. *A History of Narrative Film*. New York: W.W. Norton, 1981.

Eisner, Lotte. *Fritz Lang*. New York: Oxford University Press, 1977.

Frazer, John. *Artificially Arranged Scenes: The Films of Georges Méliès*. Boston: Hall, 1980.

Hammond, Paul. *Marvelous Méliès*. London: Gordon Fraser Gallery, 1974.

Jensen, Paul M. *The Cinema of Fritz Lang*. Cranbury, N.J.: A.S. Barnes, 1969.

Kracauer, Siegfried. *From Caligari to Hitler: A Psychological History of the German Film*. Princeton: Princeton University Press, 1966.

———. *Theory of Film: The Redemption of Physical Reality*. New York: Oxford University Press, 1960.

North, Joseph H. *The Early Development of the Motion Picture, 1887–1909*. New York: Arno, 1973.

Tudor, Andrew. *Theories of Film*. New York: Viking, 1974.

Wenden, D.J. *The Birth of the Movies*. New York: E.P. Dutton, 1974.

Works Cited

de Parville, Henri. Quoted in *L'Invention du cinéma, 1832–1897*, by Georges Sadoul. Paris, 1946.

Farber, Stephen. "George Lucas: The Stinky Kid Hits the Big Time." *Film Quarterly* 27 (Spring 1974): 5.

Kracauer, Siegfried. *From Caligari to Hitler: A Psychological History of the German Film*. Princeton: Princeton University Press, 1966.

———. *Theory of Film*. New York: Oxford University Press, 1960.

Lucas, George. Quoted in "Man of the Future." *Newsweek* 31 May 1971: 54.

As movie experiences, the Lumière *actualités* would seem slow, uninteresting, and primitive to most modern audiences. But consider how a viewer at the turn of the twentieth century might have reacted to today's "realistic" movies, such as THE GODFATHER or TAXI DRIVER. Consider not only the length and complexity of today's movie stories, which might prove overwhelming for audiences accustomed to one-minute films, but also the degree of naturalistic violence that we take for granted, which would have shocked viewers who reportedly were startled by the first close-ups.

Camera, editing, and sound techniques have developed steadily over the eight decades since Lumière, and some of these developments have helped make movies look more realistic. How did these techniques come about? How did they come to be accepted as realistic when they are, in fact, blatant manipulations of time and space that would appear conspicuously unrealistic to viewers in Lumière's time? In short, how did the realistic tradition in cinema evolve?

Chapter 10 examines several key films that stimulated or enhanced realism in cinema.

Edwin S. Porter: THE GREAT TRAIN ROBBERY

It did not take moviemakers long to recognize that by constructing motion pictures with edited shots, they could make more dramatically interesting films than Lumière's *actualités* or Méliès's cinematic illusions. In 1902 Edwin S. Porter combined **stock footage** of a fire company answering an alarm with staged scenes of a mother and child being rescued from a burning building, thus creating a **fiction film** made up of ostensibly real events. The film was THE LIFE OF AN AMERICAN FIREMAN. Firefighting was just the sort of *actualité* Lumière liked to record, but Porter turned a "found event" into a film story by **dissolving** or **cutting** separate scenes together into a cohesive cinematic narrative. The film's significance in history is in dispute, however, because of a controversy over whether one version, which **cross-cuts** scenes inside and outside the burning building during the rescue (that is, uses **parallel editing** to create the illusion of separate actions happening simultaneously), is in fact the original.

There is no dispute, however, that Porter's next film, THE GREAT TRAIN ROBBERY (1903), introduced editing techniques that changed movies forever. THE GREAT TRAIN ROBBERY, the first

How Do Films Depict Physical Reality?

movie Western, was the longest film of its day (slightly longer than twelve minutes) and one of the most popular of the early story films. As described in the *Edison Catalogue* of 1904, the scenario consists of the following fourteen scenes:

> **Scene 1**: *Interior of railroad telegraph office*. Two masked robbers enter and compel the operator to get the "signal block" to stop the approaching train, and make him write a fictitious order to the engineer to take water at this station, instead of "Red Lodge," the regular watering stop. The train comes to a standstill (seen through window of office); the conductor comes to the window, and the frightened operator delivers the order while the bandits crouch out of sight, at the same time keeping him covered with their revolvers. As soon as the conductor leaves, they fall upon the operator, bind and gag him, and hastily depart to catch the moving train.

> **Scene 2**: *Railroad water tower*. The bandits are hiding behind the tank as the train, under the false order, stops to take water. Just before she pulls out, they stealthily board the train between the express car and the tender.

> **Scene 3**: *Interior of express car*. Messenger is busily engaged. An unusual sound alarms him. He goes to the door, peeps through the keyhole and discovers two men trying to break in. He starts back bewildered, but quickly recovering, he hastily locks the strong box containing the valuables and throws the key through the open side door. Drawing his revolver, he crouches behind a desk. In the meantime the two robbers have succeeded in breaking in the door and enter cautiously. The messenger opens fire, and a desperate pistol duel takes place in which the messenger is killed. One of the robbers stands watch while the other tries to open the treasure box. Finding it locked, he vainly searches the messenger for the key, and blows the safe open with dynamite. Securing the valuables and mail bags, they leave the car.

> **Scene 4**: This thrilling scene shows the tender and interior of the locomotive cab, while the train is running forty miles an hour. While two of the bandits have been robbing the mail car, two others climb over the tender. One of them holds up the engineer while the other covers the fireman, who seizes a coal shovel and climbs up on the tender, where a desperate fight takes place. They struggle fiercely all over the tank and narrowly escape being hurled over the side of the tender. Finally they fall, with the robber on top. He seizes a lump of coal, and strikes the fireman on the head until he becomes senseless. He then hurls the body from the swiftly moving train. The bandits then compel the engineer to bring the train to a stop.

> **Scene 5**: *Shows the train coming to a stop*. The engineer leaves the locomotive, uncouples it from the train, and pulls ahead about 100 feet while the robbers hold their pistols to his face.

Scene 6: *Exterior scene showing train*. The bandits compel the passengers to leave the coaches, "hands up," and line up along the tracks. One of the robbers covers them with a revolver in each hand, while the others relieve the passengers of their valuables. A passenger attempts to escape, and is instantly shot down. Securing everything of value, the band terrorize the passengers by firing their revolvers in the air, while they make their escape to the locomotive.

Scene 7: The desperadoes board the locomotive with this booty, compel the engineer to start, and disappear in the distance.

Scene 8: The robbers bring the engine to a stop several miles from the scene of the "hold up," and take to the mountains.

Scene 9: *A beautiful scene in a valley*. The bandits come down the side of a hill, across a narrow stream, mounting their horses, and make for the wilderness.

Scene 10: *Interior of telegraph office*. The operator lies bound and gagged on the floor. After struggling to his feet, he leans on the table, and telegraphs for assistance by manipulating the key with his chin, and then faints from exhaustion. His little daughter enters with his dinner pail. She cuts the rope, throws a glass of water in his face and restores him to consciousness, and, recalling his thrilling experience, he rushes out to give the alarm.

Scene 11: *Interior of a typical Western dance hall*. Shows a number of men and women in a lively quadrille. A "tenderfoot" is quickly spotted and pushed to the center of the hall, and compelled to do a jig, while bystanders amuse themselves by shooting dangerously close to his feet. Suddenly the door opens and the half-dead telegraph operator staggers in. The dance breaks up in confusion. The men secure their rifles and hastily leave the room.

Scene 12: Shows the mounted robbers dashing down a rugged hill at a terrific pace, followed closely by a large posse, both parties firing as they ride. One of the desperadoes is shot and plunges headlong from his horse. Staggering to his feet, he fires at the nearest pursuer, only to be shot dead a moment later.

Scene 13: The three remaining bandits, thinking they have eluded the pursuers, have dismounted from their horses, and after carefully surveying their surroundings, they start to examine the contents of the mail pouches. They are so grossly engaged in their work that they do not realize the approaching danger until too late. The pursuers, having left their horses, steal noiselessly down upon them until they are completely surrounded. A desperate battle then takes place, and after a brave stand all the robbers and some of the posse bite the dust.

Scene 14: *A life-size [close-up] picture of Barnes*, leader of the outlaw band, taking aim and firing point-blank at the audience. The resulting excitement is great. This scene can be used to begin or end the picture.

(In Jacobs, *Emergence* 28–30)

　　　　　　　　　　　　　　How Do Films Depict Physical Reality?

From the description, what you think of THE GREAT TRAIN ROBBERY? What are your impressions of the story in these fourteen scenes and the cinematic techniques Porter uses to tell it? Jot down your ideas before reading the comments that follow.

By today's standards THE GREAT TRAIN ROBBERY is not very cinematic. Lewis Jacobs points out in *The Emergence of Film Art*:

> The action of every scene was told in one shot instead of a number of shots. Every shot, moreover, was a long shot, its action being confined to the proscenium-limited stage area. . . . Foreground and middle ground were equally ignored, the background alone serving as the acting area. The camera never moved from eye level. Tension and excitement were achieved by a quickening of the players' movements rather than by a variation of the lengths of shots.
> (30)

Yet new dynamic possibilities for motion pictures were clearly emerging from the straightforward narrative structure and the rudimentary editing in THE GREAT TRAIN ROBBERY. Porter freely cut away from some actions before they were logically or dramatically complete and into others after they were already begun, thereby breaking away from one of the conventions of nineteenth-century theater and, more importantly, establishing the **shot** as the basic unit of meaning in the film, rather than the scene (as in Méliès) or the continuous unedited film strip (as in Lumière) (Cook 24).

Editing shots to tell a story was a major breakthrough for motion pictures and pushed them in a new direction after 1903. As Jacobs points out, "Editing propelled movies to a radical change in screen subject matter. Motion pictures, until then almost exclusively devoted to the film-of-fact's objective recording of unmanipulated actuality, now were suddenly opened up to the rearrangement and reconstruction of reality for narrative and dramatic purposes" (*Documentary* 3). After Porter, cuts and dissolves between shots were no longer simply trick devices for creating illusions and surprising audiences, as with Méliès; they became standard cinematic tools for telling film stories of all kinds. After THE GREAT TRAIN ROBBERY, the Lumière concept of the one-shot film of "nature caught in the act" was superceded forever as a yardstick of cinematic realism.

D.W. Griffith: THE BIRTH OF A NATION

After Edwin S. Porter, other cinematic innovations quickly followed, bringing more verisimilitude to fiction films. D.W. Griffith's THE BIRTH OF A NATION (1915), one of the most important movies in the history of cinema, pushed realism to new heights during the silent era. THE BIRTH OF A NATION, which tells a story of the American Civil War and Reconstruction from a Southern point of view, greatly influenced the way history has been depicted in motion pictures. Even though it aroused (and continues to arouse) indignation because of its blatant racism and its advocacy of the Ku Klux Klan, Griffith's film furnished a blueprint for future moviemakers attempting to popularize historical events. As Seymour Stern points out, "It [THE BIRTH OF A NATION] introduced an important new use for the motion picture: namely, the dramatic teaching and dramatization of history. It was the forerunner, and in some cases the inspiration, technical, exploitative or otherwise, of many historical and spectacle films which followed. . ." (59).

THE BIRTH OF A NATION set new standards of realism for narrative film in its time. It featured elaborate, realistic settings (both indoor and outdoor), authentic costumes, lavish spectacle, and naturalistic acting (for its day). To make battle scenes look more authentic, for example, Griffith shot them outdoors in spacious landscapes (with action sometimes as far as four miles from the camera), employed hundreds of extras costumed in replicas of Confederate and Union army uniforms, introduced night photography (for the first time in motion pictures) to show attacks and bombardments in the night, and used film tinting for dramatic and psychological effect (Stern 60–68). But Griffith's two greatest contributions to cinema in THE BIRTH OF A NATION were camera movement and innovative editing.

Before Griffith, the motion picture camera was basically static. Earlier filmmakers had **panned** and **tilted** the camera (Porter did both in THE GREAT TRAIN ROBBERY) to follow actors who strayed too far from the center of action. But in THE BIRTH OF A NATION Griffith used panning as a narrative device. For example, at the beginning of a scene depicting Sherman's march to the sea, the camera pans left, from an extreme long shot of the Union army on the march, to a medium-close shot of a destitute woman on a hilltop weeping in the wake of the destruction. The camera's panning emphasizes a causal relationship between the two images in the shot and arouses the audience's sympathy for the civilian refugees of the South.

Griffith also moved the camera itself for narrative purposes, and is generally credited with discovering **traveling shots.** As early as 1911, in THE LONEDALE OPERATOR, Griffith and his cameraman, Billy Bitzer, mounted a camera on a moving locomotive to dramatize a scene where a young woman is rescued from thieves. In THE BIRTH OF A NATION Griffith and Bitzer set up the camera on an automobile to

How Do Films Depict Physical Reality?

Figure 10.1

The climactic ride of the Klansmen in THE BIRTH OF A NATION, an example of D.W. Griffith's use of traveling shots for narrative purposes.

photograph prominent action scenes, notably the dramatic Confederate charge led by the film's protagonist, Col. Ben Cameron (Henry B. Walthall), and the ride of the Klansmen at the climax of the film (fig. 10.1).

Today, mounting the camera on a moving vehicle seems an obvious way to film action scenes; it is difficult to imagine that traveling shots had to be "discovered" as a cinematic technique. But the static camera in early motion pictures perpetuated one rudimentary feature of the theater experience—namely, that the spectator sits in a fixed position facing the stage. In the early movies the camera was simply sitting in for the spectator, offering everyone in the film audience a view from the best

The Realistic Tradition

seat in the house. Moving the camera was a startling innovation because the spectator's vantage point was no longer anchored in one spot relative to the action. Suddenly, the film audience could not only watch the action move, but could actually *move with the action.*

Griffith's innovative editing in THE BIRTH OF A NATION, which was used to tell the story and arouse the viewer's emotions, is probably his greatest contribution to cinema. Close examination of almost any scene in the film makes it apparent how modern Griffith's editing is—how much more intricate and sophisticated than Porter's fourteen scenes in THE GREAT TRAIN ROBBERY. Here, for example, is an excerpt from one of several "historical facsimiles" in THE BIRTH OF A NATION, depicting Abraham Lincoln's assassination:

TITLE
    "Time, 10:13
    Act III, scene 2"   2 feet

SCENE 471
    Long shot of theater   Iris at upper right of screen
    The gallery—man in shadows.   4 feet

SCENE 472
    Semi-close-up of Phil and Elsie
    Watching play—Elsie laughing behind fan—points with
        fan to man in balcony—asks who he is.   7 feet

TITLE
    "John Wilkes Booth"   (14)

SCENE 473
    Semi-close-up of Booth (circle iris)
    (Napoleon pose) in the shadows of gallery.   2(2)

SCENE 474
    As 472
    Elsie is amused by his mysterious appearance—laughs
        behind fan—looks at him through opera glasses.   6 feet

SCENE 475
    Booth waiting.   2(3)

SCENE 476
    Medium-long shot of gallery and audience (sides rounded)
    Booth waiting.   5 ¹/₂ feet

SCENE 477
    As 475
    Booth waiting.   4 feet

SCENE 478
    Medium shot of stage play
    Comedy line—man waves arms.   3 ¹/₂ feet

SCENE 479
  Medium shot of Lincoln's box
  They laugh—Lincoln feels draught—reaches for shawl.   6 ½ feet

SCENE 480
  As 477
  Booth watches.   3 feet

SCENE 481
  As 479
  The box—Lincoln drawing shawl around shoulders.   5 ½ feet

SCENE 482
  Long shot of theater as 471   *Iris opens*
  Booth goes to box door.   5 feet

SCENE 483
  Medium shot (circle)
  Guard in gallery—Booth opens door behind him.   1(7)

SCENE 484
  Medium shot of hall back of box (corners softened)
  Heavy shadows—Booth enters softly—closes and locks
      door—peeks through keyhole at box door—stands
      up majestically—pulls out pistol—tosses head
      back—actor-like—   12 ½ feet

SCENE 485
  Close-up of pistol (circle vignette)
  He cocks it.   3 feet

SCENE 486
  As 484
  Booth comes forward—opens door to box—enters.   9 feet

SCENE 487
  The box as 479
  Booth creeps in behind Lincoln.   4 ½ feet

SCENE 488
  The play as 478
  The comic chases woman out—cheers.   4 feet

SCENE 489
  Medium shot of box
  Lincoln is shot—Booth jumps from left side of box.
      [See figure 10.2a.]   4 ½ feet

SCENE 490
  Long shot of theater
  Booth jumps on stage—shouts.   2 ½ feet

TITLE
  "Sic semper tyrannis!"   2 feet

The Realistic Tradition   **271**

Figure 10.2
Two scenes from the "historical facsimile" of President Lincoln's assassination in THE BIRTH OF A NATION. (*a*) John Wilkes Booth jumps from the presidential box after shooting Lincoln (scene 489). (*b*) Pandemonium takes place in the theater after Booth flees across the stage (scene 496).

a

SCENE 491
> *Medium shot of Booth on stage*
> Holds arms out—limps back quickly.   3 feet

SCENE 492
> *Medium shot of box*
> Lincoln slumped down—Mrs. Lincoln calls for help.   2(6)

SCENE 493
> *Semi-close-up of Phil and Elsie*
> They hardly realize what has happened—rise.   4 ¹/₂ feet

SCENE 494
> *Long shot of theater*
> Audience standing up in turmoil—Elsie in foreground
>   faints—Phil supports her—   4 feet

SCENE 495
> *As 492*
> Man climbs up into box to Lincoln's aid.   5 feet

b

SCENE 496
 Medium-long shot of theater and boxes
 Audience agitated. [See figure 10.2*b*.]   3 ¹/₂ feet

SCENE 497
 Long shot of excited throng
 Phil and Elsie leave.
 Fade-out   11 ¹/₂ feet

SCENE 498
 Medium shot of box
 They carry Lincoln out.
 Fade-out   10 ¹/₂ feet

(From a shot-by-shot description of THE BIRTH OF A NATION by Theodore Huff, in Cook 84–86.)

This segment of the Lincoln assassination sequence contains thirty-one shots (including titles) and runs about two and a half minutes on the screen. ("The figure at the right of each scene is the footage; it also can be taken as the number of seconds the scene lasts. When scenes were under three feet, they were measured exactly—the figure in parentheses being the number of *frames*" [Huff, quoted in Cook 82].) Closely examine the editing in this scene. What cutting techniques does Griffith employ to narrate the action? How does the editing create tension and arouse the viewer's emotions? What is the overall effect of the editing in these thirty-one shots? You will get more from the comments that follow if you address these questions before reading on.

In the Lincoln assassination segment, D.W. Griffith creates a great deal of visual tension by isolating several spheres of action and briskly **intercutting** them. Notice, for instance, that after he introduces John Wilkes Booth in scene 473, Griffith cuts away to Elsie Stoneman (scene 474), to the stage play (scene 478), to Lincoln in his box (scenes 479 and 481), to the theater (scene 482), and finally, to the guard in the gallery (scene 483), while Booth is waiting to enter Lincoln's box. After Booth draws his weapon (scene 484), Griffith cuts to a close-up of the pistol as Booth cocks it (scene 485), and then cuts back to a continuation of the medium shot to show Booth opening the door to Lincoln's box. Next Griffith **reverses the angle** to show Booth creeping in behind Lincoln (scene 487) and cuts away one last time to the play (scene 488) before Booth shoots Lincoln. To appreciate Griffith's achievement with the editing in this sequence we only have to consider that Edwin S. Porter would probably have depicted the entire scene in one shot.

With action scenes, Griffith's parallel editing is very explosive. For example, he constructed a rousing climax in THE BIRTH OF A NATION by intercutting three simultaneous dramatic actions, each of which builds toward its own climax. The first action is the "Summoning of the Clans," which begins with only two Night Hawks calling out the Klansmen. In successive shots more and more hooded horsemen flow together until they pour across the screen, as Vachel Lindsay says, like an "Anglo-Saxon Niagara" (41). The second action is the rioting in the streets of Piedmont, where one of the film's heroines, Elsie Stoneman, is abducted by Silas Lynch, a villainous mulatto carpetbagger. The third action centers around a cabin in the woods where a party of whites is surrounded and besieged by black Union soldiers.

Griffith creates tension by intercutting among these three dramatic spheres of action, and he resolves the tension in two stages. First the Klansmen ride into Piedmont, clear the streets, and rescue Elsie

Stoneman from Lynch. Then they rush to the surrounded cabin, where the situation is desperate. The men in the cabin are about to dispatch two white women, lest they fall into the hands of the blacks, just as the Klan comes to the rescue. Griffith creates frenzied tension at the end of the sequence by cross-cutting between the cabin and the Klansmen with increasingly quicker and more kinetic shots.

Thus, for the climax of THE BIRTH OF A NATION, writes Seymour Stern, "Griffith builds a structure from which he can engineer three-way cutting at will and unleash the maximum emotional potential from each of the three separate but converging dramas. The pattern of suspense suggests a spiralling series of interlocking triangles, mounting toward a common apex. . ." (78). The climax is so effective because "its unfolding has been prepared well in advance through a mounting series of cumulative dramatic crises, out of which the climax itself flows logically and organically, like a dam-burst" (Stern 79).

Griffith's parallel editing at the climax of THE BIRTH OF A NATION significantly influenced the way filmmakers edited action scenes thereafter. The chase sequence from RAIDERS OF THE LOST ARK discussed in chapter 4, for example, illustrates that Griffith's editing techniques are still evident in movies today.

Erich von Stroheim: GREED

GREED (1924), directed by Erich von Stroheim, is a film version of Frank Norris's naturalistic novel *McTeague*, which tells the grim story of a man who completely degenerates because of his lust for money (fig. 10.3a–c). *Naturalism* in literature is basically nineteenth-century scientific determinism applied to fiction, a doctrine that views human beings as animals in the natural world, responding to environmental forces and internal drives over which they have neither control nor full knowledge. Von Stroheim tried to follow Norris's novel as closely and completely as possible and to translate its literary naturalism into cinematic images. After von Stroheim edited the finished footage himself early in 1924, GREED was more than ten hours long. To make it more marketable, von Stroheim cut it to about four hours—the bare minimum, he felt, to maintain the film's continuity. Later, however, MGM studios took the film out of the director's hands for further editing and reduced it again by almost half. Understandably, therefore, GREED was criticized by contemporary reviewers for its choppy story and abrupt development. Yet most critics recognized that GREED was a seminal film.

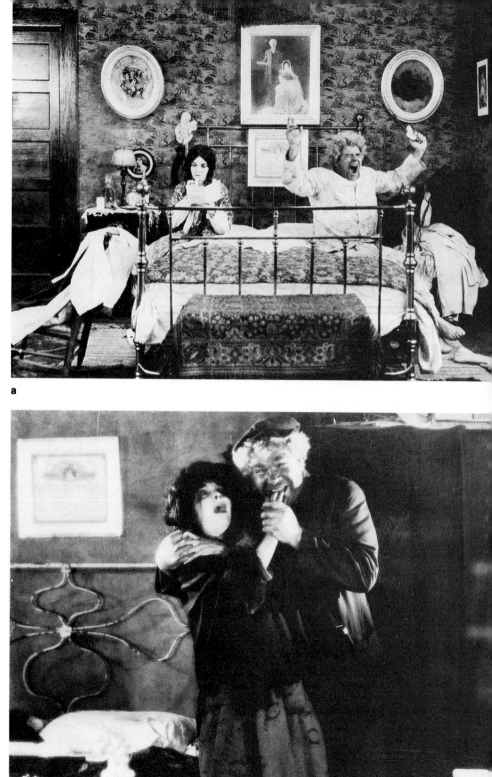

Figure 10.3
In GREED director Erich von Stroheim depicts the grim story of McTeague, a man who completely degenerates because of his lust for money.

a

b

How Do Films Depict Physical Reality?

c

     Von Stroheim tried to reproduce the settings and atmosphere in GREED as realistically as Norris had described them in *McTeague*. He shot the film entirely **on location** in San Francisco, the California mountains, and Death Valley. Both city and wilderness scenes are strikingly authentic. Whether McTeague, the protagonist, is working at dentistry or gold mining (fig. 10.4), von Stroheim's settings capture subtle nuances and completely immerse the viewer in the scene. No studio set could recreate the overpowering barren landscape of Death Valley that dominates the screen at the end of GREED (fig. 10.5).

     Von Stroheim and his cinematographer, William H. Daniels, used camera techniques that complemented these realistic settings. They developed a realistic photographic style in which **long takes** build up tension within shots rather than between them by cutting, and in which the viewer's experience of time and space closely corresponds to that of characters in the film (Cook 228). They photographed most scenes in **deep focus** to reveal layers of detail in the middleground and background of the shot. This style of cinematography became a model for realistic filmmakers who followed von Stroheim, including director Orson Welles and cinematographer Gregg Toland, who further refined deep-focus and long-take techniques in CITIZEN KANE. (See the next section of this chapter.) Other more recent directors to employ a camera style like

Figure 10.4

The naturalistic settings in GREED, both interior and exterior, were photographed in deep focus to reveal layers of details as realistically as possible. (*a*) Interior scene in a dentist's office. (*b*) Exterior scene in a gold mine.

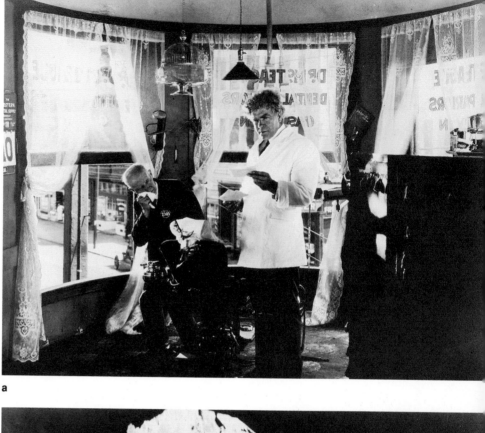

a

b

How Do Films Depict Physical Reality?

Figure 10.5
(*a*) Director Erich von Stroheim (seated under the umbrella) shot GREED's final scenes on location in Death Valley. (*b*) The overpowering, barren landscape as it appeared on the screen.

a

b

The Realistic Tradition

that in GREED include Michelangelo Antonioni (in L'AVVENTURA), Roman Polanski (in KNIFE IN THE WATER), and Robert Altman (in MCCABE AND MRS. MILLER).

Perhaps GREED's most significant influence on later films was that it changed "the feeling that motion pictures must always be pretty pictures" and featured naturalistic depiction of violence and brutality on the screen (fig. 10.6). A contemporary review in *Exceptional Photoplays* pointed out:

> There is and should be a place for a picture like GREED. It is undoubtedly one of the most uncompromising films ever shown on the screen. There have already been many criticisms of its brutality, its stark realism, its sordidness. But the point is that it was never intended to be a pleasant picture. It is a picture that is grown up with a vengeance, a theme for just those adults who have been complaining most about the sickening sentimentality of the average film.
> ("GREED" 155–56)

Terms like "brutality," "stark realism," and "sordidness" frequently appear in film reviews today, too. Regarding violence, we live in an era when motion pictures have indeed "grown up with a vengeance." Technical developments in cinematography, makeup, and special effects enable filmmakers today to depict physical violence as graphically as they wish. For example, most Westerns and action movies since the 1960s commonly depict the full effects of gunshot wounds on the human body; some films, like Arthur Penn's BONNIE AND CLYDE (1967) or Sam Peckinpah's THE WILD BUNCH (1969), even show them in slow motion. Public mores have changed since the silent film era, and the "brutality" of GREED is not very shocking by today's standards. Yet the issue is still very alive; how violence in the movies affects our behavior is a hotly contested perennial question. Von Stroheim's GREED is a significant film, therefore, because it paved the way for successive generations of "grown-up" movies, as well as for an ongoing debate about the social consequences of stark realism in such movies.

Orson Welles: CITIZEN KANE

Like D.W. Griffith's THE BIRTH OF A NATION, Orson Welles's CITIZEN KANE (1941) is a landmark film in the history of cinema, replete with cinematic techniques that were years ahead of their time. Scenes from CITIZEN KANE have been used in previous chapters to illustrate lessons on setting and costumes (chapter 1), lighting (chapter 3), sound

Figure 10.6

One significant influence
of GREED was that it
paved the way for
naturalistic depiction of
violence and brutality in
later films.

(chapter 5), and flashbacks (chapter 6). But this chapter will concentrate
specifically on CITIZEN KANE's most significant contributions to realistic cinema: **deep-focus photography** and multilayered sound.

Gregg Toland, one of Hollywood's most highly paid and
sought-after cinematographers during the 1930s and 1940s, was the **lighting cameraman** on CITIZEN KANE. For two years Toland had been
developing a technique for deep-focus photography (also called **pan-focus
photography**), which could record objects twenty inches or several hundred feet away from the lens with equal clarity, an unprecedented range
for sharp focus in motion pictures. To achieve this **depth of field,** Toland
shot with **fast film** (one highly sensitive to light) and used a 24mm **wide-
angle lens** with the **aperture** stopped down to about f5.6 (an opening that
drastically reduces the amount of light the lens admits) (Cowie 268). He

The Realistic Tradition

Figure 10.7
Two examples show how Orson Welles employed deep-focus photography in CITIZEN KANE to reveal foreground, middleground, and background details in a shot. In (*b*) the background is reflected in the *Inquirer*'s plate glass window.

a

b

How Do Films Depict Physical Reality?

also coated the lens with a clear plastic substance that reduced glare and enabled him to shoot scenes lit with high-intensity **arc lights.** Using this deep-focus technique in CITIZEN KANE, Welles and Toland were able to photograph scenes where objects and characters were in clear focus all at once in the foreground, middleground, and background (fig. 10.7).

       A good example of the deep-focus technique in CITIZEN KANE occurs in a scene at the Kane boardinghouse in Colorado when Charles Kane is a boy. In the foreground on the right of the frame Mrs. Kane is signing papers that will place her son and his fortune under the guardianship of Mr. Thatcher, a banker, who is seated beside her (fig. 10.8). On the left stands Mr. Kane, half-heartedly protesting that his son is being sent away. Deep in the background, through the window at the back of the room, young Charlie can be seen frolicking in the snow.

Figure 10.8
Cinematographer Gregg Toland developed a technique of deep-focus photography for CITIZEN KANE that could record objects twenty inches or several hundred feet away from the lens with equal clarity.

Welles employs depth of field in this scene to convey important narrative information. Using the window as a focal point, he depicts a power struggle between Kane's parents: When Mr. Kane closes the window, grumbling about his wife's decision to send Charlie off to the East, Mrs. Kane immediately strides to the back of the room and raises it again. She is clearly the more dominant personality. Deep focus helps Kane and Toland sustain the tension in this scene because it allows them to shoot the scene in a long take—that is, without editing the action or changing the camera position. With deep focus, Welles and Toland also create dramatic tension between the action inside and outside the boardinghouse, since the audience sees that the boy romping in the snow does not know yet that his mother is signing him away for life.

A shot later in the film illustrates how immediately and economically deep-focus photography can present narrative information. In the extreme foreground, prominently lit, we see a glass with a spoon in it and an open medicine bottle (fig. 10.9). In the dark middleground Susan Alexander is lying in bed. And in the background Kane and another man are rushing into the room toward her. What meaning is this shot trying to convey? How do you "read" it? Describe your reaction to it.

The shot with the medicine looming in the foreground introduces a brief scene in which Kane discovers that his wife has tried to kill herself. To convey that meaning, Welles presents three "layers" of images in the shot, which interconnect visually and logically to show Susan's attempted suicide without words. There is a clear cause-and-effect relationship between the medicine bottle that appears oversized in the foreground and the comatose woman in the shadows beyond it, which, in turn, explains the urgency of the two men breaking into the room to reach her.

In *The Making of CITIZEN KANE*, Robert Carringer points out that this shot is technically not an example of deep-focus photography but an in-camera **matte shot**. "First, the foreground was lighted and focused, and shot with the background dark. Then, the foreground was darkened, the background lighted, the lens refocused, the film rewound, and the scene reshot" (82). Nevertheless, the shot illustrates very effectively how Welles and Toland employ depth of field as a narrative device in CITIZEN KANE.

To complement the deep-focus photography in CITIZEN KANE, Welles developed a sound track that features overlapping layers of sound in many scenes. During a gala banquet Kane throws for the staff of his newspaper, for instance, Bernstein and Leland, Kane's two closest

How Do Films Depict Physical Reality?

Figure 10.9

An example of an in-camera matte shot in CITIZEN KANE, illustrating how Orson Welles uses layers of images for storytelling. This scene conveys Susan Alexander's suicide attempt without words.

associates, discuss their boss in the foreground of the shot while Kane dances with a line of chorus girls in the background. Although both layers of sound are distinctly audible, the conversation in the foreground, because it is closer to the viewer's vantage point, is more pronounced than the song and dance in the background, just as the medicine bottle in the foreground of Susan's suicide attempt appears larger than the figures more distant from the camera.

A simple yet striking example of how Welles matches deep-focus photography with layered sound is a scene where Kane finishes writing Jed Leland's bad review of Susan Alexander's operatic debut. Kane clacks away steadily at a typewriter in the left foreground as Leland, who is passed out drunk, awakens and staggers slowly toward him from far back in the newsroom. As he advances from the background to the foreground, Leland's footsteps advance from "background" to "foreground" on the sound track—from barely audible to about as loud as the typewriter keys. Thus, Welles creates a precise correspondence between visual and aural "space" (Cook 352). The shot ends with a brief, sharp exchange between the two characters, punctuated finally by the sound of Kane's typewriter carriage:

KANE: Hello, Jedediah.
LELAND: Hello, Charlie, I didn't know we were speaking.
KANE: Sure we're speaking, Jedediah. You're fired.
He swings the carriage back and continues typing.

In a few instances, sound effects in CITIZEN KANE are expressionistic—for example, when a screeching cockatoo punctuates the highly charged moment when Susan Alexander walks out on her husband. Even deep-focus photography is used expressively in this scene "to create metaphors for things cinema cannot represent directly on the screen," as Susan walks away from Kane through doorways that recede toward a vanishing point deep in the background (Cook 349). Nevertheless, the use of deep-focus photography and multilayered sound in CITIZEN KANE help anchor it solidly within the realistic tradition in cinema. David Cook points out:

> Through deep-focus photography, it [CITIZEN KANE] attempts to technically reproduce the actual field of vision of the human eye in order to structure our visual perception of screen space by means of composition in depth. Through its innovative use of sound, it attempts to reproduce the actual aural experience of the human ear and then to manipulate our aural perception of screen space by distorting and qualifying this experience.
>
> (366)

André Bazin observes that D.W. Griffith's classical editing "separated reality into successive shots which were just a series of either logical or subjective points of view of an event," but that Orson Welles in CITIZEN KANE "restored to cinematic illusion a fundamental quality of reality—its continuity" (28). Bazin elaborates:

> Whereas the camera lens, classically, had focused successively on different parts of the scene, the camera of Orson Welles takes in with equal sharpness the whole field of vision contained simultaneously within the dramatic field. It is no longer the editing that selects what we see, thus giving it an *a priori* significance, it is the mind of the spectator which is forced to discern, as in a sort of parallelepiped of reality with the screen as its cross-section, the dramatic spectrum proper to the screen. It is therefore to an intelligent use of a specific step forward that CITIZEN KANE owes its realism. Thanks to the depth of focus of the lens, Orson Welles restored to reality its visible continuity.
>
> (28)

What is Bazin saying in this statement? What does he mean by expressions like "*a priori* significance" and a "parallelepiped of reality"? What does it mean to say Welles "restored to reality its visible continuity"?

Bazin is arguing that CITIZEN KANE has contributed significantly to the realistic tradition in cinema because its deep-focus camera technique brought to motion pictures "a fundamental quality of reality," namely, that the viewer can see every phase of the action simultaneously. For example, the in-camera matte shot that Orson Welles and Gregg Toland created to depict Susan Alexander's suicide attempt may be pure cinematic illusion; but on the screen it becomes a "parallelepiped [a six-sided prism with parallel surfaces] of reality." Itself a single shot with multiple "surfaces," the matte shot brings into focus a whole, immediate experience (the attempted suicide) even as it separates the parallel components (the medicine, the victim, the rescuers). André Bazin's point is that there is more reality than illusion in a shot like this because viewers must discern its meaning for themselves, experiencing it as a *continuous action*, unedited and uninterrupted, just as an event in real life.

Roberto Rossellini: OPEN CITY

A great resurgence of cinematic realism occurred in Italy during and after World War II, where politically progressive filmmakers and critics were pushing for a popular, realist national cinema. In 1942 Marxist screenwriter Cesare Zavattini called for a new kind of cinema that would depict the dignity of everyday life in films shot in the streets, without professional actors and contrived plots. In 1943 film critic Umberto Barbaro coined the term that came to designate the new Italian film movement—**neorealism.**

The first neorealist film to have international impact was Roberto Rossellini's OPEN CITY (1945), from a script by Cesare Zavattini. In OPEN CITY, a story of the Gestapo's efforts to wipe out underground resistance in occupied Rome, Rossellini tried to recreate as accurately as possible the heroic struggle of ordinary people during the Nazi occupation. Working with minimal resources, he shot nearly the entire film on location in the streets and apartments of Rome, where only months before incidents like those in the film had actually taken place. Shot on scavenged low-quality black-and-white **film stock,** and mainly with **available lighting,** OPEN CITY looks like a contemporary **documentary** or **newsreel.** Some scenes, in fact, contain candid footage shot from cameras concealed on rooftops or in traveling cars.

OPEN CITY is about a handful of ordinary people—a woman, her son, her common-law husband, a Catholic priest—who, risking torture and execution, resist the Nazis in their day-to-day lives. Anna Magnani, who plays the woman (fig. 10.10), and Aldo Fabrizi, who plays the priest (fig. 10.11), are the only professional actors in the film.

Even from this brief description, it is evident that Rossellini and Zavattini have very strong sentiments about what a film story is and how it should be depicted. In an interview in 1952, Cesare Zavattini stated one of the basic premises of neorealist cinema:

> . . . the question today is, instead of turning imaginary situations into "reality" and trying to make them look "true," to make things as they are, almost themselves, create their own special significance. Life is not what is invented in "stories"; life is another matter . . . . The true function of cinema is not to tell fables . . . .
> (219)

In OPEN CITY Rossellini and Zavattini set out to depict life in Nazi-occupied Rome. The film shows things as they were during the Occupation: ordinary citizens performing mundane activities, which assume special significance because the consequences may be torture and death. Zavattini says:

> In life, in reality today, there are no more empty spaces. Between things, facts, people, exists such an interdependence that a blow struck for the cinema in Rome could have repercussions all over the world. If this is true, it must be worthwhile to take any moment of a human life and show how "striking" that moment is: to excavate and identify it, to send its echo vibrating into other parts of the world.
> (221)

Filmmakers who perceive the purpose of cinema this way have an implicit moral responsibility that takes precedence over other concerns. In an interview in *Cahiers du Cinéma*, Roberto Rossellini said, "For me it [neorealism] is above all a moral standpoint from which to view the world. Afterwards it becomes an aesthetic standpoint, but the point of departure is definitely moral" (261). Rossellini's moral standpoint is clearly reflected in OPEN CITY, where the heroism of the characters transcends ideology. The Catholic priest and the Communist revolutionary find a common enemy in fascist inhumanity, and both sacrifice their lives to free their city from Nazi repression. Ultimately, the heroic actions of the characters in OPEN CITY become inspirational models for others seeking the courage to resist. The priest's execution at the end of the film emblazes the spirit of resistance upon the boys who witness it; from his death they will gather strength to carry on the fight.

Figure 10.10
OPEN CITY, the first neorealist film to have international impact, recreates the heroic struggle of ordinary people against the Nazis during the occupation of Rome.

Figure 10.11
The priest on the left (Aldo Fabrizi) is one of only two roles in OPEN CITY played by professional actors. Neorealist films were typically shot on location, using available lighting, an unobtrusive camera style, and nonprofessional actors.

The Italian neorealists offered filmmakers around the world a new way of looking at reality. Film critic André Bazin writes:

> Neo-realism is a description of reality conceived as a whole by a consciousness disposed to see things as a whole. Neo-realism contrasts with the realist aesthetics that preceded it, and in particular with naturalism [as in Erich von Stroheim's GREED] and verism [as in slice-of-life films like Lumière's *actualités*], in that its realism is not so much concerned with the choice of subject as with a particular way of regarding things. . . . To put it still another way, neo-realism by definition rejects analysis, whether political, moral, psychological, logical, or social, of the characters and their actions. It looks on reality as a whole, not incomprehensible, certainly, but inseparably one.
>
> (97)

For this reason, says Bazin, neorealism is "basically antitheatrical" and stands in opposition to other kinds of realism in literature and cinema that went before it. Bazin's statement explains, in theoretical terms, why neorealism has had such tremendous impact on films that followed it, not only in Italy, but all over the world.

But in practical terms, why is it so significant that the neorealists perceived "reality as a whole" or that their films were basically "antitheatrical"? How did the neorealist concept of cinema affect the way movies were made afterwards?

First of all, the neorealist directors demonstrated that films need not be spectacular to be impressive. By discarding standard practices of the film industry up to that time—like shooting in the controlled environment of a studio and employing "stars"—the neorealists showed it is possible to make significant pictures on small budgets. Their films spawned other national film movements that also sought alternatives to big-budget studio productions. The French New Wave directors of the 1960s, for example, acknowledge the influence of postwar Italian films on their work. The Indian director Satyajit Ray says that Vittorio De Sica's THE BICYCLE THIEF (see chapter 1), another influential neorealist film, largely determined the visual treatment of Ray's well-known Apu trilogy. Czech filmmakers Miloš Forman and Ivan Passer gained worldwide recognition during the Prague Spring in the 1960s by depicting ordinary people and events in films like LOVES OF A BLONDE (1965), FIREMEN'S BALL (1968), and INTIMATE LIGHTING (1965). In the United States recent movies are as likely to be filmed on location in New York or San Francisco as on Hollywood back lots. And some American filmmakers, like Paul Mazursky and John Cassavetes, have preferred to produce "small" films independently rather than work through Hollywood studios.

Secondly, the neorealists bridged the gap between fiction film and nonfiction film and paved the way for a freer mix of documentary and narrative styles in movies. OPEN CITY, shot hastily under the noses of the retreating Nazis, could easily be mistaken for a documentary account of the Resistance in Rome; indeed, many viewers in 1945 reportedly believed it was a documentary. OPEN CITY became a prototype for "fictional documentaries," like Gillo Pontecorvo's THE BATTLE OF ALGIERS (1966), a film about the Algerian rebellion against the French in the 1950s, and Robert M. Young's ALAMBRISTA (1976), a film about a migrant worker who crosses illegally into California from Mexico. On the other hand, documentaries like Albert and David Maysles's SALES-MAN (1969) (see chapter 12), about a door-to-door Bible salesman, and Barbara Kopple's HARLAN COUNTY, U.S.A. (1976), about a bloody coal miners' strike in Kentucky, are examples of nonfiction films with narrative continuity and dramatic structure similar to OPEN CITY and THE BICYCLE THIEF. This blend of fiction and nonfiction styles often shows up today in movies that are based on a true story, like Alan Parker's MIDNIGHT EXPRESS (1978), a film about a young man's degradation in a Turkish prison, or Bruce Beresford's BREAKER MORANT (1979), a film about three Australian soldiers in the Boer War in South Africa.

Finally, the neorealist sensibility reinforced a more realistic treatment of social issues in commercial films. Social/political awareness in Hollywood productions in the early 1940s is typified by two popular films John Ford directed: THE GRAPES OF WRATH (1940) (see chapter 8), from John Steinbeck's novel about displaced farmers from the Dust Bowl who migrate to California during the Depression, and HOW GREEN WAS MY VALLEY (1941), from Richard Llewellyn's novel about a family breaking up in an economically depressed Welsh mining town. In comparison with the unflinching neorealists, however, these films are conspicuously optimistic (THE GRAPES OF WRATH) or nostalgic (HOW GREEN WAS MY VALLEY). Yet, only a few years later, Hollywood took a more hard-boiled view of issues like alcoholism, as in Billy Wilder's THE LOST WEEKEND (1945), and anti-Semitism, as in Elia Kazan's GENTLEMAN'S AGREEMENT (1947). After neorealism, filmmakers everywhere found it more difficult to gloss over despair and pessimism in the human experience or to contrive upbeat endings for grim stories. Consequently, a compelling psychological realism is the rule rather than the exception today for dramatic films that depict suffering individuals and communities.

David Cook succinctly summarizes the impact of Italian neorealism on world cinema:

> It is clear that neo-realism was a great deal more than a localized national phenomenon; its formative influence extended well beyond the Italian cinema. There can be no question today that, whatever its limitations of vision and form, Italian neo-realism was one of the great innovative movements in the history of cinema. . . .
> (393)

Conclusion

The films discussed in this chapter are by no means the only ones that influenced the development of realism in cinema, but they do highlight some important milestones along the way from Lumière's *actualités* to films we consider realistic today. It is important to recognize the contributions of these key films to realistic cinema; but it is more important to recognize the common characteristics and the common aesthetic values shared by films in the realist tradition. A whole body of film theory and criticism, from writers like André Bazin, aligns itself with the realist aesthetic. Quotations from Bazin and others in this chapter suggest the kinds of connections thoughtful viewers can find between movies and real life.

In the next chapter we will examine the expressionistic tradition from Georges Méliès onward—some of its milestones and some of its key aesthetic issues.

General Study Questions

1. David Cook points out that Edwin S. Porter's THE GREAT TRAIN ROBBERY established the *shot* as the basic unit of meaning in the film, rather than the scene or the continuous unedited filmstrip. Why was this development so important to cinema? For cinematic storytelling, why is it better to have the shot rather than the scene as the basic unit of meaning?
2. Seymour Stern writes that D.W. Griffith's THE BIRTH OF A NATION introduced to movies "the dramatic teaching and dramatization of history." How is history "taught" and "dramatized" in films you know? How does a filmmaker persuade the viewer to sympathize more with one view of history than another?
3. According to the definition of naturalism in literature, human beings are basically animals in a natural world, responding to environmental forces and internal drives over which they have neither control nor full knowledge. Can you identify recent films in which characters fit this description? Analyze the characters and character relationships in one naturalistic movie.

4. André Bazin says that deep-focus photography in Orson Welles's CITIZEN KANE "restored to cinematic illusion a fundamental quality of reality—its continuity." What does he mean by this statement? Use the statement to explicate another film that features deep-focus photography.

5. Cesare Zavattini argues that the function of cinema is "to make things as they are, almost by themselves, create their own special significance." What does this statement mean? Illustrate the explanation with examples from recent films you know. Evaluate a recent movie according to how well it fulfills this function of cinema.

Additional Films for Study

OUR DAILY BREAD (1934), dir. King Vidor
PAISAN (1946), dir. Roberto Rossellini
SHOESHINE (1946), dir. Vittorio De Sica
LOS OLVIDADOS (THE YOUNG AND THE DAMNED) (1950), dir. Luis Buñuel
ON THE WATERFRONT (1954), dir. Elia Kazan
PATHER PANCHALI (1954), dir. Satyajit Ray
THE VIRGIN SPRING (1959), dir. Ingmar Bergman
HUD (1962), dir. Martin Ritt
A MAN FOR ALL SEASONS (1966), dir. Fred Zinnemann
THE SHOP ON MAIN STREET (1966), dir. Jan Kadár and Elmar Klos
THE BATTLE OF ALGIERS (1967), dir. Gillo Pontecorvo
RAMPARTS OF CLAY (1970), dir. Jean-Louis Bertucelli
MCCABE AND MRS. MILLER (1971), dir. Robert Altman
BADLANDS (1973), dir. Terrence Malick
THE AUTOBIOGRAPHY OF MISS JANE PITTMAN (1974), dir. John Korty
HESTER STREET (1974), dir. Joan Micklin Silver
THE STORY OF ADELE H. (1975), dir. François Truffaut
MIDNIGHT EXPRESS (1978), dir. Alan Parker
STEVIE (1978), dir. Robert Enders
NORMA RAE (1979), dir. Martin Ritt
GALLIPOLI (1981), dir. Peter Weir
THE RETURN OF MARTIN GUERRE (1983), dir. Daniel Vigne
THE KILLING FIELDS (1984), dir. Roland Joffe
ELENI (1985), dir. Peter Yates
MATEWAN (1987), dir. John Sayles

Further Reading

Aitken, Roy E. THE BIRTH OF A NATION. Middleburg, Va.: William W. Denlinger, 1965.

Armes, Roy. Patterns of Realism: Italian Neo-Realist Cinema. Cranbury, N.J.: A.S. Barnes, 1971.

Bazin, André. Orson Welles: A Critical View. Translated by Jonathan Rosenbaum. New York: Harper & Row, 1978.

Carringer, Robert L. *The Making of CITIZEN KANE*. Berkeley: University of California Press, 1985.

Curtis, Thomas Quinn. *Von Stroheim*. New York: Farrar, Straus & Giroux, 1971.

Finler, Joel. *Stroheim*. Berkeley: University of California Press, 1968.

Gottesman, Ronald, ed. *Focus on CITIZEN KANE*. Englewood Cliffs, N.J.: Prentice-Hall, 1971.

———. *Focus on Orson Welles*. Englewood Cliffs, N.J.: Prentice-Hall, 1976.

Guarner, José Luis. *Rossellini*. New York: Frederick A. Praeger, 1970.

Higham, Charles. *The Films of Orson Welles*. Berkeley: University of California Press, 1970.

Huff, Theodore. *A Shot Analysis of D.W. Griffith's THE BIRTH OF A NATION*. New York: Museum of Modern Art Film Library, 1961.

Jacobs, Lewis, ed. *The Emergence of Film Art*. New York: Hopkinson and Blake, 1974.

Kael, Pauline. *The CITIZEN KANE Book*. Boston: Little, Brown, 1971.

McBride, Joseph. *Orson Welles*. New York: Viking, 1972.

Overbey, David, ed. *Springtime in Italy: A Reader on Neorealism*. New York: Archon, 1979.

Silva, Fred, ed. *Focus on THE BIRTH OF A NATION*. Englewood Cliffs, N.J.: Prentice-Hall, 1971.

Weinberg, Herman G. *The Complete GREED*. New York: E.P. Dutton, 1972.

———. *Stroheim: A Pictorial Record of His Nine Films*. New York: Dover Books, 1975.

Williams, Martin. *Griffith: First Artist of the Movies*. New York: Oxford University Press, 1980.

Zavattini, Cesare. *Sequences from a Cinematic Life*. Translated by William Weaver. Englewood Cliffs, N.J.: Prentice-Hall, 1970.

Works Cited

Bazin, André. *What is Cinema?* Vol. II. Translated by Hugh Gray. Berkeley: University of California Press, 1971.

Carringer, Robert L. *The Making of CITIZEN KANE*. Los Angeles: University of California Press, 1985.

Cook, David A. *A History of Narrative Film*. New York: W.W. Norton, 1981.

Cowie, Peter. "The Study of a Colossus: *CITIZEN KANE*." In *The Emergence of Film Art,* edited by Lewis Jacobs, 262–74. New York: Hopkinson and Blake, 1974.

"GREED." In *American Film Criticism: From the Beginnings to CITIZEN KANE,* edited by Stanley Kauffmann, 155–57. New York: Liveright Press, 1972.

Jacobs, Lewis, ed. *The Documentary Tradition*. New York: W.W. Norton, 1979.

———. *The Emergence of Film Art*. New York: Hopkinson and Blake, 1974.

Lindsay, Vachel. *The Art of the Moving Picture*. New York: Liveright Press, 1970.

Rossellini, Roberto. Quoted in *Light and Shadows: A History of Motion Pictures*. 3d ed. Edited by Thomas W. Bohn and Richard L. Stromgren. Palo Alto: Mayfield Publishing, 1987.

Stern, Seymour. "THE BIRTH OF A NATION: The Technique and Its Influence." In *The Emergence of Film Art,* edited by Lewis Jacobs, 58–79. New York: Hopkinson and Blake, 1974.

Zavattini, Cesare. "Some Ideas on the Cinema." In *Film: A Montage of Theories,* edited by Richard Dyer MacCann, 216–28. New York: E.P. Dutton, 1966.

When film critics speak about expressionism, they often mean **German Expressionism,** a very influential style of filmmaking in Germany after World War I, which characteristically depicted unstable mental and emotional experiences. German Expressionism, because it established new patterns for fantasy films after Méliès, advanced the expressionistic tradition in cinema as much as D.W. Griffith's THE BIRTH OF A NATION advanced the realistic tradition.

We have already examined one important German Expressionistic film, Fritz Lang's METROPOLIS (see chapter 9). In this chapter we will cover two more: Robert Wiene's THE CABINET OF DR. CALIGARI and F.W. Murnau's NOSFERATU. These two films, each in its own way, helped realign the tradition of moviemaking that Georges Méliès began.

Robert Wiene: THE CABINET OF DR. CALIGARI

In Germany just after World War I, Robert Wiene directed THE CABINET OF DR. CALIGARI (1919), one of the most influential and famous expressionistic films in the history of cinema. The story centers on a string of murders in a small town, which coincide with the arrival of a carnival sideshow run by Dr. Caligari and featuring the somnambulist Cesare (fig. 11.1*a*). An investigation leads to a mental asylum, from which Cesare has reportedly escaped, where Dr. Caligari is the mad director. This story is narrated by Francis, a character who pursues Dr. Caligari after Cesare murders his friend and abducts his sweetheart (fig. 11.1*b*). At the end of the film, however, it is revealed that Francis is a patient in the asylum and that his doctor is the Caligari figure from the fantastic story he narrates. Thus Francis, not Caligari, is the madman who is subdued in a straightjacket at the end of the film.

What usually strikes the viewer first about THE CABINET OF DR. CALIGARI are the sets, which were designed by three prominent expressionist painters, Hermann Warm, Walter Röhrig, and Walter Reimann (fig. 11.1). How are we supposed to react to these stylized, grotesque sets? By comparison, the obviously nonrepresentational sets in METROPOLIS look almost lifelike.

The word *distortion* inevitably comes to mind in describing the sets in THE CABINET OF DR. CALIGARI: distortion in the odd angles of walls, windows, roofs, and chimneys; in the exaggerated

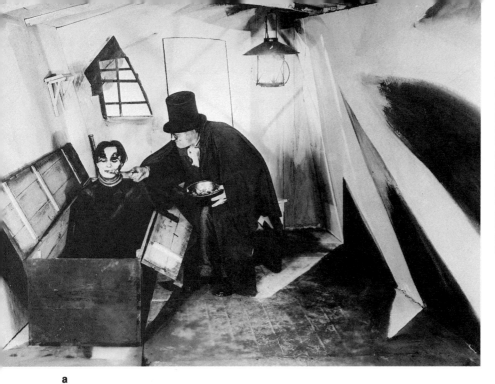

a

b

Figure 11.1
Two examples of the
conspicuously
nonrepresentational sets
in THE CABINET OF DR.
CALIGARI, designed by
three prominent expres-
sionist painters. The
stylized sets reflect the
narrator's demented
perception of people and
events. (*a*) Dr. Caligari
grooms the somnambulist
Cesare. (*b*) Cesare
abducts the narrator's
sweetheart.

dimensions of objects and furniture; in the unusually sharp contrast between light and dark; and in the hard-edged division of space. Why all this distortion? Why did Wiene use such stylized sets?

One reason was that economic hardships in Germany after the war made building materials and energy resources scarce. With limited electricity at hand for lighting, it was more efficient to paint scenery with black and white paint to look heavily shadowed, as in the set with the hanging lantern (fig. 11.1a), than to light the scene for that effect. But clearly there were also aesthetic reasons for the distortions in these sets. They are so conspicuously nonrepresentational, so unreal. As a contemporary reviewer of CALIGARI pointed out, "the picture has the quality of a weird, horrible nightmare" (Sherwood 122). Considering the twist at the end of the story, what reasons do you see for the distorted sets—as well as the bizarre costumes, makeup, and acting style—in this film?

As Gerald Mast points out, the striking effect of CALIGARI's design is not just the *look*, but the unnatural *feel* of it. In real life, such distorted buildings, without stabilizing horizontals and verticals, could never stand, and their jagged patterns fracture normal spacial proportions. Windows and furniture are designed in impossibly grotesque shapes. Conspicuously heavy makeup turns actors' faces into masks. And most unnatural of all, says Mast, is that CALIGARI is a world without sunlight:

> Shadows of light and dark, shafts where the sun would normally cast its shadow, have been painted on the [CALIGARI] sets. To use paint to make a shadow where the sun would normally make one emphasizes the fact that no sun exists. The outdoor scenes feel as if they were shot indoors. And they were. . . . The deliberate unnaturalness of the film is so striking that it is difficult to tell if the acting is intentionally or unintentionally stilted. It is expressionistically appropriate.
> (138–39)

Thus the sets, costumes, and makeup in Wiene's film are deliberately distorted to give concrete, physical form to moods and feelings. The expressionistic sets and **mise en scène** reflect the demented narrator's perception of people and events. As David Cook observes, "the creators of CALIGARI. . . made a deliberate effort to portray subjective realities in objective terms, to render not simply narrative but states of mind, moods, and atmosphere through the medium of photographic image" (115).

The tale-within-a-tale narrative structure in THE CABINET OF DR. CALIGARI complements the film's expressionistic design. Using the device of a madman as a storyteller, Wiene first presents the story's bizarre events, then fits them into a rational perspective at the end by revealing that they are, in fact, Francis's delusions. The ending does not completely restore rationality, however. For example, when the kindly doctor puts on his glasses at the end of the film, he looks no different than the demented Dr. Caligari; and the scene at the asylum looks no more natural from a supposedly healthy, objective point of view than it does from Francis's psychotic point of view (Mast 139). Nevertheless, these ambiguities enrich the film's expressionistic qualities because they underscore the fine dividing line between objectivity and subjectivity, between rationality and irrationality, which lies at the heart of THE CABINET OF DR. CALIGARI.

Robert Wiene's innovative approach to cinematic storytelling became a model for other German directors and the cornerstone of German Expressionism, which "attempted to express interior realities through the means of exterior realities, or to treat subjective states in what was widely regarded at the time as a purely objective medium of representation" (Cook 115). Cook believes that such an approach to moviemaking "was perhaps as radical an innovation for the cinema as Porter's discovery of the shot, since it added a non-narrative and poetic dimension to what had been, even in the hands of Griffith, an almost wholly narrative medium" (115).

Film theorists who ascribe to a realist view of cinema (like Erwin Panofsky, Siegfried Kracauer, and André Bazin), have commented that THE CABINET OF DR. CALIGARI is uncinematic, that it resembles a photographed stage play. The film has even been described as a filmed painting, since it so resembles the unsettling distortions in cubist and expressionist paintings. Nevertheless, THE CABINET OF DR. CALIGARI immensely influenced later filmmakers, both in Germany and abroad, and broke the ground for a wide range of fantasy and "art" films on the theme of "the human soul in search of itself" (Cook 116).

F.W. Murnau: NOSFERATU

Unlike THE CABINET OF DR. CALIGARI, F.W. Murnau's NOSFERATU, A SYMPHONY OF HORROR (1922), cannot be criticized for being uncinematic. CALIGARI's expressionism is primarily *graphic*; but NOSFERATU's is almost purely *cinematic*, relying on camera angles, lighting, and editing rather than production design to express moods and feelings (Cook 120).

**Figure 11.2
(facing page)**

Almost sixty years after
F.W. Murnau's
NOSFERATU (1922),
Werner Herzog directed
NOSFERATU THE
VAMPYRE (1979),
recreating some of
Murnau's most memo-
rable shots. Top: Low-
angle shots of Nosferatu,
as depicted (a) by Murnau
and (b) by Herzog,
featuring his grotesque
makeup and fingernails.
Middle: (c) Murnau and
(d) Herzog depict
Nosferatu crouching
beside Lucy Harker.
Bottom: Special effects
dramatize Dracula's
annihilation in Lucy's
bedroom with the first
light of day, as envisioned
by (e) Murnau and (f)
Herzog.

Based loosely on Bram Stoker's novel *Dracula*, NOSFERATU depicts how Count Dracula victimizes an unsuspecting young man, Jonathan Harker, who has traveled from Wismar, Germany, to the count's castle in Transylvania to present a real estate contract. Dracula, along with an army of rats carrying the plague, later transports himself by ship to Wismar, where the population is quickly decimated. Jonathan's wife, Lucy, reads in a book about vampires that if a woman of pure heart detains Nosferatu, the undead, until after cockcrow, the first light of day will destroy him. She then sacrifices herself to annihilate Dracula.

Whereas CALIGARI's stylization was deliberately un-natural looking, NOSFERATU has a remarkable naturalness, despite its preternatural story and atmosphere. The main reason is that Murnau, unlike Wiene in CALIGARI and Lang in METROPOLIS, shot much of NOSFERATU on location and made extensive use of landscapes. Another reason is that Fritz Arno Wagner's cinematography employs **low-key lighting** in many scenes, which distributes light and dark tones more evenly than the **high-contrast lighting** in CALIGARI. Consequently, there is a softer, grainier quality to NOSFERATU, particularly in the night scenes, which looks less distorted than CALIGARI.

Murnau and Wagner employ an array of cinematic de-vices and special effects in NOSFERATU. For instance, to establish an evil atmosphere around Count Dracula's castle, they use **fast-motion, negative images** to reverse dark and light, and **stop-action photography** to produce **pixilation.** The camera exaggerates Dracula's hideous appear-ance by occasionally photographing him in an extreme **low angle shot** (fig. 11.2*a*). Later in the film, Dracula's long, menacing shadow is used to symbolize his sinister power. As he stands above Lucy's bed, the shadow of his clawlike hand, with its grotesquely long fingernails, passes over her body and tightens on her heart.

One way to appreciate the impact of Murnau's brand of expressionism on later filmmakers is to compare the original NOSFERATU with a remake almost sixty years later by the German director Werner Herzog. Except for a twist at the end, Herzog's NOSFERATU THE VAMPYRE (1979) follows Murnau's story faithfully. And Klaus Kinski, who plays Dracula in Herzog's film, imitates the costume, makeup (in-cluding the fingernails), and gestures of the character played by Max Schreck in Murnau's film (fig. 11.2). Herzog arranges many scenes ex-actly as they appear in the original and even recreates some of Murnau's most impressive shots, such as an extreme low-angle shot of Dracula looming above the ship's deck (fig. 11.2*a* and *b*) or a tightly framed shot of

How Do Films Depict Physical Reality?

a

b

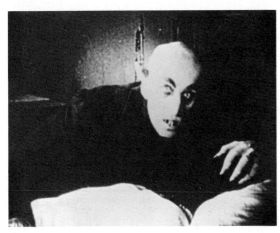

c

d

e

f

him crouching beside Lucy's bed and staring up toward the camera (fig. 11.2*c* and *d*). The special effects to show Dracula's annihilation with the first light of day are also remarkably similar in the two films (fig. 11.2*e* and *f*).

The new NOSFERATU is shot in color and with sound, two technical innovations unavailable to Murnau in 1922; nevertheless, Herzog's version is remarkably compatible with Murnau's silent, black-and-white original. Herzog, for example, softens and understates color in his film. Lush mountain landscapes are shrouded in mist that tones down the colors and gives a **graininess** like Murnau's. Interiors are mainly white (in Dracula's castle) or neutral pastels (in the Harker house); costumes are predominantly dark, earthy shades; and the makeup, appropriately, is pale. Yet, occasional splashes of bright color in Herzog's NOSFERATU provide lively visual counterpoint. For instance, after Harker's first night in Dracula's castle, he awakens beside the cold fireplace and finds a banquet table laid for him—slices of rare beef, wedges of red melon, delicacies nestled under a feathered chicken—all in bright colors that contrast sharply with Harker's bloodless face and Dracula's lifeless decor. And in the climactic scene, as dawn breaks in Lucy's bedchamber, the curtains flush with rich amber sunlight that destroys Dracula.

The sound track for Herzog's NOSFERATU is minimal. Two recurring musical themes are a simple, repetitious folk melody and a few bars of resonant chords from Richard Wagner's opera *Das Rheingold*. In most scenes dialogue is sparse. Otherwise, the sound track is dominated by realistic background sounds—doors creaking, wolves howling, clocks chiming, and bells tolling.

Herzog, however, has added several expressionistic devices of his own to Murnau's NOSFERATU. He opens the film with shots of mummified bodies and slow-motion footage of a bat in flight, images from a horrible dream that awakens Lucy Harker at the beginning of the story. Some scenes in Herzog's film, although shot in completely realistic settings, take on an eerie, dreamlike quality when Dracula is present. Once Dracula sets foot in Wismar, for instance, rats proliferate everywhere. In one scene, at the height of the plague Dracula brings to the city, a group of elegantly dressed men and women sit down to a banquet in the street while hundreds of rats scurry around their feet. One of the gentlemen invites Lucy to share a toast with them. "We have the plague," he explains, "and we rejoice in each remaining day." A **jump cut** then shows the banquet table later, covered with rats devouring the remains of the feast.

Herzog has also added dimensions to Dracula's character that are not evident in Murnau's NOSFERATU. The first evening Harker spends with the count, as "the children of the night" howl "their music" outdoors, Dracula admonishes Harker for being just like the small-minded villagers who cannot project themselves "into the soul of a hunter." He asks Jonathan to imagine enduring centuries without growing old, repeating the same tedium day after day. To Jonathan, and later again to Lucy, he comments that death is not the worst experience, alluding to the perpetual plight of the undead. Finally, in a scene that Herzog added to Murnau's story, Dracula enters Lucy's bedroom, introduces himself, and complains to her that "the absence of love is the most abject pain."

It appears that F.W. Murnau's brand of expressionism remains quite viable for modern filmmakers and audiences. Allowing for technological developments with color and sound over nearly sixty years and for more character development and motivation, there is not much difference stylistically between Murnau's NOSFERATU and Herzog's. At the heart of these films is an atmosphere of horror that the filmmakers created by depicting an unnatural story within natural settings using evocative camera techniques and special effects. Murnau's expressionism is an attractive model for modern directors like Herzog because it makes more direct connections with physical reality than Wiene's expressionism. Few modern films look as purely expressionistic and stylized as THE CABINET OF DR. CALIGARI.

Luis Buñuel and Salvador Dalí: UN CHIEN ANDALOU

Besides German Expressionism, another important influence on the expressionistic tradition in cinema was **surrealism,** a movement in the arts—primarily painting, literature, and cinema—that flourished in Paris in the 1920s. André Breton, a French poet and the leader of the surrealists, defined surrealism in *Manifeste du surréalisme* (1924) as "pure psychic automatism by which an attempt is made to express, either verbally, in writing, or in any other manner, the true function of thought." Surrealists considered "the true function of thought" to be the expressiveness of imagination unfettered by conscious control, which is best typified by and realized in dreams. Surrealistic artists, therefore, tried to create (as in dreams) fantastic or irrational images by combining or juxtaposing them incongruously.

Surrealistic filmmakers in the 1920s—including Fernand Léger, Man Ray, Salvador Dalí and Luis Buñuel—were vehemently against conventional narrative cinema, and in favor of purely visual "films without subjects." Thus it is generally pointless to summarize what happens in surrealistic films because they have no plot. For example, in the film often cited as the best example of cinematic surrealism, UN CHIEN ANDALOU (AN ANDALUSIAN DOG) (1928), filmmakers Luis Buñuel and Salvador Dalí deliberately tried to avoid logical connections and associations between scenes and to disrupt continuity of time, place, and action. They presented instead a succession of grotesque images and visual gags that defy rational explication: a woman's eyeball dispassionately slit with a straight razor, ants crawling from a hole in a man's hand, a drooling man fondling a woman's buttocks, two clerics pulling a grand piano and putrefied donkey carcasses.

What is the purpose of such grotesque images? How does a viewer accustomed to movies with stories approach a film like UN CHIEN ANDALOU? How are we meant to react?

First, we can observe that the images in UN CHIEN ANDALOU are apparently intended to shock the audience, to affront conventional sensibilities. The brutal, erotic images in the film, even though they appear within an absurdly unreal and essentially humorous context, can be very disturbing and offensive. Buñuel's famous comment about UN CHIEN ANDALOU is that the film is "nothing less than a despairing, passionate appeal to murder."

Second, we can surmise that the bizarre images in the film apparently reflect the unconscious mind where, as in dreams, thoughts take shape without conscious control or ordinary waking logic, often revealing basic, unrestrained urges. Some gags in UN CHIEN ANDALOU look like they could be dream scenarios straight from Sigmund Freud's journals. In one scene, for instance, hair under a young woman's arm suddenly becomes a beard on a young man's face; in another, a young man dresses in a woman's clothes. Surrealist art was, in fact, greatly indebted to Freud's work with the unconscious. Surrealism was the artistic counterpart of psychoanalysis in that it attempted to bypass the corrupting "censorship" of logic and morality in order to tap the primeval sources of "creativity" (Neiman 105). "Using such methods as automatic writing and self-induced trance, the surrealists tried to consciously reconstruct the unconscious, much as Freud had done with patients via free-association and the interpretation of dreams" (Neiman 105).

Third, we can appreciate that the images in UN CHIEN ANDALOU mock the narrow, stereotypical perception of human experience reflected in many commercial movie formulas for the masses. Buñuel and Dalí, as avant-garde artists, were offering a radically new perception of cinema, one in which the individual spectator, not the filmmaker, decides what a film means. As with a troublesome dream, therefore, the viewer is ultimately the one who must create order from UN CHIEN ANDALOU's systematized confusion, discover a dream logic that explains its grotesque images, and find significance in seeming nonsense.

The surrealist cinema of the 1920s was not a popular success. It appealed primarily to artists, intellectuals, and filmmakers who viewed surrealist films in specialized theaters and *ciné clubs* that had sprung up in France in the mid-1920s. These were the first people in Europe, according to Georges Sadoul, "to assert the stature of the film as an art—the equal (or even the superior) of music, literature and the theatre—and to obtain recognition for it as such" (33). Yet, as often happens when avant-garde filmmakers introduce innovations, mainstream directors and critics recognized that surrealistic films offered fresh, sensational material that could be adapted successfully for commercial movies. Thus, indirectly, surrealism made its mark on the film industry.

Commercial films commonly employ surrealistic sequences to recreate a character's dreams or visions. For instance, Alfred Hitchcock's SPELLBOUND (1945) presents a purely surrealistic dream sequence, designed by Salvador Dalí, as the key to the film's murder mystery. (See chapter 6.) In JULIET OF THE SPIRITS (1965) Federico Fellini uses a stylized, dreamlike scene to depict a psychological trauma the protagonist suffered during a grade school play in which she was grilled alive as a martyr. Surrealistic sequences also appear frequently in popular movies that depict psychotic or hallucinatory experiences, as in EASY RIDER (1969), when the protagonists consume LSD, or in STEPPENWOLF (1974), when the schizophrenic protagonist loses touch with reality.

Some film critics contend, however, that the surrealist sensibility is far more pervasive in films than occasional dream sequences or acid trips. Carl Belz, for example, argues that Alfred Hitchcock's THE BIRDS (1963) fails as a conventional thriller because "the total work must be viewed as a fantasy which uses reality only as a sort of convenient launching pad, going beyond it into a sur-real sphere of human existence" (146). Behind the film's conventional situations and characters, Belz sees a "dramatic fantasy" in which, as in surrealistic paintings by Giorgio de

Chirico and others, "individually understandable elements form a whole which remains a series of tenuously related fragments" and in which conventional logic must give way to "the logic of the absurd" (146–47).

Michael Gould in *Surrealism and the Cinema* contends that the surrealist film experience arises from an intense emotional response to either irrationality or exaggeration in a movie. Gould argues that there are surrealistic qualities—such as the dramatic juxtaposition of "ideal" and "real" images or the exaggerated use of color—in films as diverse as Alfred Hitchcock's THE BIRDS (1963), Walt Disney's PINOCCHIO (1939), and Michelangelo Antonioni's THE RED DESERT (1964) (Gould 38).

Gould's broad definition of surrealism suggests that a wide range of movies may be, at least in part, strongly aligned with the expressionistic tradition in cinema. Consider how many commercial movies, aimed both at serious audiences (A CLOCKWORK ORANGE, CRIES AND WHISPERS, THE TIN DRUM) and at mass audiences (THE OMEN, THE AMITYVILLE HORROR, HALLOWEEN), employ irrationality and exaggeration that push them far beyond reality. We may not label these films surrealistic today, but we can certainly recognize the influence of surrealist filmmakers like Buñuel and Dalí who, in UN CHIEN ANDALOU, used cinema to create "a subterranean voyage through the recesses of the unconscious mind" (Cook 328).

Jean Cocteau: THE BLOOD OF A POET

Many film critics and historians consider Jean Cocteau's THE BLOOD OF A POET (1930) a surrealist film, even though avant-garde artists in France repudiated it as a parasite on the body of surrealism and Cocteau himself declared that the film had nothing whatsoever to do with surrealism. Like UN CHIEN ANDALOU, Cocteau's film is a bizarre exploration of the unconscious that shatters conventional notions of cinematic narration. But THE BLOOD OF A POET differs from UN CHIEN ANDALOU in that it is an intensely personal film, "a documentary of the imagination," in André Bazin's words. This characteristic made its influence on later filmmakers much different than that of UN CHIEN ANDALOU.

At the beginning of THE BLOOD OF A POET, a tall industrial chimney begins to topple. But the film cuts away from the chimney before it falls and presents three extended surrealistic episodes in which Cocteau explores his personal and artistic identity through dream imagery and personal symbolism, after which the film cuts back to the chimney as it crashes to the ground. In the first episode a young painter draws a face reminiscent of Picasso's early style. The drawing's mouth suddenly begins to move, and when the painter tries to erase it, it sticks to the palm of his hand. He kisses it and caresses himself with it, then swoons. In the second episode the artist passes through a mirror into a hotel corridor where he peeks through keyholes and observes a man and a statue destroyed by a firing squad, a young girl learning to fly, a Chinese preparing an opium pipe, and an hermaphrodite arguing between its male and female halves. The third episode begins with a snowball fight in which a statue of a poet is destroyed.

The images in THE BLOOD OF A POET are highly personal and autobiographical. The snowball fight, for instance, was recalled from Cocteau's childhood, and the hermaphrodite arguing with itself suggests Cocteau's sexual ambivalence. But the film's images are also mythical, reflecting universal experience as much as Cocteau's personal experience. The opium den in the second episode, for example, alludes directly to Cocteau's experimentation with that drug, but also indirectly to an artist's deliberate cultivation of dreams (Johnson 275). The artist's narcissism in the film, his wish to fly above traditional constraints, his need to destroy (and perhaps be destroyed by) bourgeois culture are more than Cocteau's personal recollections; they are the psychological underpinnings of creativity expressed as archetypal dream images. Thus, in that frozen moment of time between the two shots of the toppling chimney, Cocteau's psycho-mythic images, drawn from personal experience, reflect upon the nature of creative consciousness.

THE BLOOD OF A POET served as a blueprint for Cocteau's later semiautobiographical films, such as ORPHEUS (1950) and THE TESTAMENT OF ORPHEUS (1959). It also became the prototype for so-called **trance films** produced by avant-garde filmmakers in the United States during the 1940s and 1950s. Trance films are highly personal psychodramas in which the filmmaker (often the protagonist in the film as well) depicts dreams and fantasies that reveal his or her inner self. For the artist, the trance film itself becomes a process of self-realization (Sitney 3–19, 33–36). One of the most commonly cited examples of the trance film is Maya Deren and Alexander Hammid's MESHES OF THE AFTERNOON (1943), which is the next film to be discussed in this chapter.

But THE BLOOD OF A POET also influenced some mainstream films. Some of the world's best-known directors have produced autobiographical films built around imagery and symbolism that is at once personal and mythic. For example, Federico Fellini's 8 ½ (1963), to be discussed in the last section of this chapter, is a highly

a
b

Figure 11.3
Seven frame enlarge-
ments from a sequence of
fifteen shots in MESHES
OF THE AFTERNOON,
depicting a nightmarish
incident when a woman
with a knife attacks her
sleeping double.
MESHES is an example
of a trance film that
recreates "the interior
experiences of an
individual."

autobiographical work in which the filmmaker probes his personal and artistic identity in archetypal situations. 8 ½ is also "a documentary of the imagination," except that it employs more conventional imagery and narrative structure than does THE BLOOD OF A POET.

Maya Deren and Alexander Hammid: MESHES OF THE AFTERNOON

MESHES OF THE AFTERNOON (1943), produced and directed by Maya Deren and Alexander Hammid, is recognized as a landmark in the history of American experimental cinema and "one of the best examples of the cinema's ability to recreate the actual experience, and oblivion, of dreaming" (Neiman 79). MESHES is, in fact, essentially a filmed dream.

As in a dream, the story MESHES OF THE AFTER-NOON presents is tenuous, incompatible with waking logic, and laden with bizarre images and symbols. A woman (Maya Deren) picks up a flower in the street, walks up a flight of stairs, and lets herself into a house. But surreal circumstances transform these rather mundane activities into nightmarish experiences. Once inside the house, the woman cautiously explores the living area downstairs and a bedroom upstairs, then falls asleep in a living room chair and dreams of herself entering the house three more times, until there are three of her, exactly alike, seated around the dining room table. Each of them in turn draws the house key from the center of the table. Nothing happens for the first two women (fig. 11.3*a*), but for the third woman the key suddenly changes into a kitchen knife (fig. 11.3*b*), and she rises with the knife poised to attack (fig. 11.3*c* and *d*) the sleeping woman in the living room (fig. 11.3*f*). Just as the knife is about to cut into her upturned throat (fig. 11.3*g*), the sleeping woman is startled awake by a man's kiss, depicted from her point of view.

c

d

e

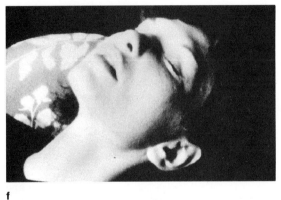

f

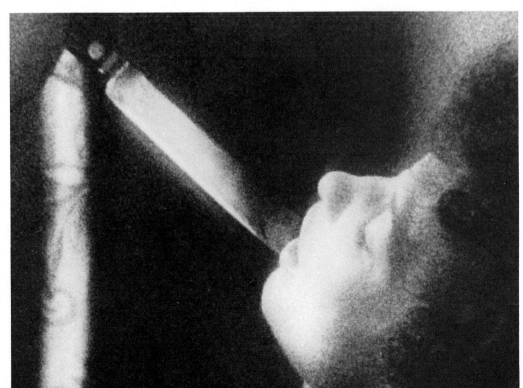

g

Now begins the only segment of the film without surreal effects. A man (Alexander Hammid) draws the woman up from the chair and leads her upstairs, carrying a flower, which he places on a pillow in the bedroom. The woman lies down on the bed, her head next to the flower, and closes her eyes.

As the man leans toward her, apparently to kiss her again, the dream mode recurs. The flower changes into the knife, and the woman uses it to strike at the man's face, which is reflected in a mirror that the knife shatters. There is an abrupt cut to a beach where broken glass falls on wet sand and is washed over by waves.

In the final sequence of the film, the man enters the house and finds the woman dead in the living room chair, strewn with broken glass and seaweed.

In MESHES OF THE AFTERNOON Deren and Hammid are not so interested in creating dream incidents, as Alfred Hitchcock does with the dream sequence in SPELLBOUND (see chapter 6), as in recreating feelings associated with the incidents. In Maya Deren's earliest program note for MESHES, she writes:

> This film [MESHES] is concerned with the interior experiences of an individual. It does not record an event which could be witnessed by other persons. Rather, it reproduces the way in which the subconscious of an individual will develop, interpret and elaborate an apparently simple and casual incident into a critical emotional experience. . . . The makers of this film have been primarily concerned with the use of the cinematic technique in such a way as to create a world: to put on film the feeling which a human being experiences about an incident, rather than to accurately record the incident.
> (In Neiman 78–79)

How do Deren and Hammid use cinematic technique in MESHES to create this feeling? How does cinematic technique help them reproduce the individual's subconscious reaction to the event rather than simply record the event?

There are so many interesting camera and editing devices in MESHES that almost any sequence can illustrate how the film employs cinematic technique to reproduce subconscious feeling. One straightforward example is when the protagonist pursues an elusive black-veiled figure upstairs to the bedroom. As Deren moves up the stairs, the staircase appears to pitch from side to side, throwing her against first one wall and then the other. This effect, which Deren calls "the moving frame," was created with simple maneuvering of the **hand-held camera**: While Maya Deren lurched from side to side as she staggered up the stairs, Alexander Hammid tilted the camera each time in the opposite direction, thus creating "movement of the frame," which is, in effect, "transferred to the objects within the frame" (Deren, in Neiman 96).

Maya Deren writes that in this sequence "it was necessary to convey the idea that even the ostensibly inanimate staircase in the house conspired (as do other objects in the film) to frustrate the girl in her effort to catch up with a figure she was pursuing" (in Neiman 96). But the feeling that this scene conveys is really intimidation, not frustration. "The ostensibly inanimate staircase" buffets her so violently that the woman on the stairs must struggle to maintain her balance and reach the top. Moreover, the narrow confines of the enclosed staircase make the setting very claustrophobic, a feeling that is further reinforced by the high camera angle used for the shot. Within the dream reality that MESHES creates, the woman seems "the prisoner of the stairs" (Neiman 82). For some people this scene even creates an unpleasant physical sensation. Deren writes that "at times members of the audience who are particularly susceptible to sea-sickness, have had to close their eyes" (in Neiman 96).

Despite Maya Deren's repeated assertions that there are no symbols or hidden meanings in MESHES OF THE AFTERNOON, the film seems to cry out for psychoanalysis. It is difficult in the post-Freudian era not to interpret the significance of objects like a flower, a key, a knife, and a mirror within such a conspicuously dreamlike setting. Clearly, MESHES OF THE AFTERNOON, like Jean Cocteau's THE BLOOD OF A POET, contains very fertile psycho-mythic imagery. Maya Deren herself, commenting on the film, has identified and explained some of this imagery. For example, regarding the nightmarish moment in the film when the woman with the knife rises from the table to attack her sleeping double (fig. 11.3), Deren writes:

> As the girl with the knife rises, there is a close-up of her foot as she begins striding. The first step is in sand (with the suggestion of sea behind) [fig. 11.3e], the second stride (cut in) is in grass, the third is on pavement, and the fourth is on the rug, and then the camera cuts up to her head with the hand with the knife descending towards the sleeping girl. What I meant when I planned that four stride sequence was that you have to come a long way—from the very beginning of time—to kill yourself, like the first life emerging from the primeval waters. Those four strides, in my intention, span all time.
>
> (In Neiman 98–99)

The sleeping woman is awakened from her nightmare at the last moment by the man's kiss. But the final shot of MESHES makes us wonder whether the woman has succeeded in destroying herself after all. Is the woman in the easy chair at the end of the film dead or just dreaming that she is dead? Has one part of her personality been destroyed or consumed by another part? Is she perhaps imagining how the man might react to finding her dead? MESHES does not provide answers to such questions, but rather forces the viewer to grapple with the film experience, as with a dream, and to discover its meaning through careful explication of the images there and the feelings the images evoke.

On account of its surrealistic imagery, MESHES OF THE AFTERNOON is very similar to UN CHIEN ANDALOU and THE BLOOD OF A POET, but the structure of MESHES is very different from that of the two earlier films. Buñuel and Dalí deliberately tried to avoid logical connections and associations in UN CHIEN ANDALOU, and Cocteau completely disregarded conventional notions of cinematic narrative in THE BLOOD OF A POET. Deren and Hammid, on the other hand, maintain a tight structural integrity from shot to shot throughout MESHES, sequencing images as coherently as any meaningful dream (Neiman 104). Film critic Rudolf Arnheim even asserts that the images in the film are "logical": "They are never arbitrary nor absurd. They follow the letter of a law we never studied on paper; but guided by our eyes, our minds conform willingly" (in Neiman 104). Catrina Neiman, in *The Legend of Maya Deren*, summarizes why the structure of MESHES is noteworthy:

> The persuasive continuity of MESHES OF THE AFTERNOON is unique among the early film-makers' attempts to abandon the narrative form. Deren and Hammid transformed the notion of plot, as dreams do, without destroying the dramatic function it serves. MESHES is not a mockery of the mind. Rather, it accurately reproduces the momentum of human anxiety.
> (104)

Therefore, one important contribution MESHES OF THE AFTERNOON made to the expressionistic tradition in cinema was to introduce narrative continuity, derived from the structure and logic of dreams, to the purely visual, surrealistic depiction of the unconscious mind. We should keep in mind that the purpose behind MESHES, according to Maya Deren, is to reproduce the way "the subconscious of an individual will develop, interpret and elaborate . . . an incident into a critical emotional experience." "If MESHES were scrutinized as a document of the imagination," says Neiman, "it could be as much a contribution to the field of psychology as it has been to the cinema as an art form" (105).

Federico Fellini: 8¹/₂

It is apparent by now that the dividing line between the expressionistic tradition and the realistic tradition in cinema is not always hard-edged. A mystery thriller like Hitchcock's SPELLBOUND features a surrealistic dream sequence; a horror movie like Herzog's NOSFERATU is shot on location with naturalistic settings; and a trance film like MESHES OF THE AFTERNOON can be called "logical." It is appropriate, therefore, to conclude this unit on realism and expressionism with a film by director Federico Fellini, who once stated, "I see no dividing line between imagination and reality." Fellini's 8¹/₂ (1963) is a good example of a film that interweaves realistic and expressionistic images, themes, and techniques.

8¹/₂ is about an established, middle-aged filmmaker named Guido (Marcello Mastroianni), who is unable to decide how to proceed with his new movie. He wants the film to be very autobiographical, incorporating important experiences and people (particularly women) from his own life; yet he is frustrated artistically because his personal life is in such disarray and because he is unable to reconcile his relationships with women. Guido wants to make a truthful film, but he cannot face his own life truthfully.

But, as Timothy Hyman points out, 8¹/₂ is also about "interior events" in Guido's life, which happen "outside time, in fantasy, dream and vision" (121). The "exterior events" surrounding Guido's movie serve as a vehicle for exploring unconscious, "interior events" expressed in his dreams and fantasies. 8¹/₂ shifts freely back and forth between these exterior and interior events—that is, between realistic and expressionistic depictions of Guido's experience—and finally weaves them together so inextricably that distinctions between them blur.

8¹/₂ opens in the expressionistic mode, with a dark claustrophobic dream in which Guido is trapped in his car on a ferry, hemmed all around by motionless automobiles. He pounds and kicks at the closed windows as smoke rises around him, choking him, but he is unable to break out. Strangers in nearby cars stare at him but do nothing to help. Then he is floating above and away from the cars, sailing like a kite with a rope tethered around his leg down to the ground. Suddenly, he is falling. As he is about to crash to earth, Guido wakes up from the dream.

What is the significance of Guido's dream? What does it reveal about Guido and his dilemma?

Guido's dream suggests a severe psychological impasse and a struggle to be free of it. In the dream he breaks free at first but eventually comes crashing down, a recurring pattern that defines Guido's behavior in $8\frac{1}{2}$ (Hyman 123). Immediately after the dream, for instance, the same pattern of crisis, liberation, and fall is reenacted in waking reality, in the realistic mode, at a lavish spa hotel where Guido is struggling with his screenplay. Guido wakes from the dream in a hotel room, surrounded by people making demands on him. Then, alone in the bathroom, he is momentarily free of pressure and demands, corresponding to his flight in the dream. Finally, just as the rope brought him crashing down to earth, the telephone rings and brings him down to mundane responsibilities again. Hyman points out that "corresponding sequences" like this occur throughout $8\frac{1}{2}$ (123). Thus, from the very beginning of the film, Fellini juxtaposes dream and waking experiences with a common pattern to depict Guido's psychological predicament.

It is enlightening to observe the transitions Fellini uses to carry $8\frac{1}{2}$ back and forth between the realistic and expressionistic modes. The transitions frequently hinge on a specific association in Guido's mind that triggers a flashback or a fantasy. For example, early in the film a mind reader at the spa prints seemingly unintelligible words on a chalkboard: ASA NISI MASA. Fellini immediately cuts to a **flashback** in which Guido as a young boy is bathed and bundled off to bed by his mother. Not until the very end of the flashback, when Guido's cousin chants the magical words ASA NISI MASA, do we understand the specific connection with the mind reader at the spa, who picked up these words in Guido's mind.

In another scene, as he is discussing his film script with an aged Catholic cardinal, Guido is distracted by a woman descending the hillside behind him. Her skirt rides up, and Guido catches a glimpse of her muscular legs. The film flashes back to Guido's schoolboy days when he danced the rumba with a massively built harlot named Saraghina. This memory ends unpleasantly because priests from his school caught Guido with Saraghina and shamed him before a tribunal of doddering clerics. A double association, therefore, connects Guido's present and past experience at this moment: the woman's sturdy legs and the senile cardinal.

Besides being blocked as an artist, Guido is also blocked in his relationships with women. $8\frac{1}{2}$ concentrates on four women in his life: Luisa, his wife; Carla, his current mistress; Claudia, the beautiful star for his new movie; and Saraghina, the harlot. Much is revealed about these women, and about Guido's perception of them, by their physical appearance. What can you observe about them, for example, from the way each of them is dressed and made up in figure 11.4? What is your reaction to Luisa's dark-rimmed glasses? To Carla's glamorous hat and

a

b

c

Figure 11.4

In the film 8½ Guido's psychological impasse, as a man and as a film director, is reflected in his relationships with four women: (*a*) Luisa, his wife; (*b*) Carla, his current mistress; (*c*) Claudia, the idealized woman in his new movie; and (*d*) Saraghina, a harlot remembered from his school days.

d

veil? What do their costumes suggest about Guido's associations with these four women? You will find the following discussion more interesting if you address these questions before reading on.

In 8½ Guido interacts with his wife and his mistress primarily in the real world and is faced with mundane problems in dealing with them. He invites both of them to the spa and must contend with the embarrassing consequences when they meet each other. He sets Carla up in an out-of-the-way hotel to avoid causing a scandal, but is called back there in the middle of the night to nurse her through a fever. He lies repeatedly to his wife to cover his tracks and feigns sleep to avoid making love to her.

Saraghina and Claudia, on the other hand, belong primarily to Guido's fantasy world. For Guido, Claudia is a symbol of purity, a smiling, graceful angel dressed all in white. Guido does not listen to Claudia when she tells him the flaw in his movie (and, by inference, in his life) is that "the man does not know how to love." Such practical advice from Claudia does not register on Guido because he has idealized her beyond everyday concerns. Saraghina, on the other hand, is Claudia's opposite: the woman in black, the embodiment of sensuality and sin, the source of both sexual excitement and shame. The costumes that the four women wear identify their dominant characteristics from Guido's perspective and situate them either in his real world or his fantasy world.

In 8½, however, Guido's experiences do not remain purely real or fantastic. There is too much crossover between exterior and interior events in his life. Luisa, for instance, appears in Guido's "harem fantasy" (one of the most memorable sequences in 8½), looking much softer and more becoming. With a white turban on her head and without her black-rimmed glasses, Luisa is transformed from an abrasive, suspicious wife into a charming hostess who manages Guido's exotic household with elegance and humor.

Guido's real and fantasized conceptions of women also intermesh during a scene where screen tests for Guido's film are projected. Except for Claudia, whose role as Ideal Woman is settled, Guido is casting for the parts of Luisa, Carla, and Saraghina. The actresses testing for these roles appear in the makeup and dress of wife, mistress, and harlot, and attempt to reproduce their characteristic gestures and movements, apparently with Guido's personal coaching. Ironically, Luisa is present in the screening room, shocked to see a caricature of herself on the screen. Someone whispers, "Why, that's his own life!"

Shortly after the screen tests, Guido's film collapses completely, and he fantasizes about committing suicide. But this mental

How Do Films Depict Physical Reality?

breakdown is necessary, it seems, along with the corresponding demolition of his film's monumental, useless set, for Guido to recognize the faults in himself, both artistic and personal, which are blocking him. Liberated at last from his psychological impasse, Guido immediately begins to direct another film in his mind. This time he experiences no doubt or hesitation. The new film, in which Guido himself participates, is bursting with energy and celebration. All the people in Guido's life, now dressed in white, join hands and dance around him in the center of an arena. Guido directs them confidently and, finally, joins the circle and dances with them. The final image of 8½ is a caped Guido-as-schoolboy, also entirely in white, spotlighted in the center of the arena.

In 8½ Federico Fellini masterfully interweaves exterior and interior experience, reality and fantasy, and realistic and expressionistic film techniques to present a penetrating psychoanalysis of his protagonist. In the opening dream sequence he establishes a pattern of behavior for Guido and applies it throughout the film to both real and fantastic situations. Events at the spa trigger memories and fantasies; and characters in Guido's life, particularly the four women, exist simultaneously for him in reality and fantasy. Finally, in the resolution of 8½, Fellini allows Guido insight that helps him unite reality and fantasy, life and art, in a different kind of autobiographical film than he first envisioned. Guido uses that enlightenment to stop dreaming about his life and his art and to start directing them—if only in his imagination. At the end of 8½, Guido can aptly testify, in Fellini's own words, "I see no dividing line between imagination and reality."

Conclusion

The expressionistic tradition in cinema, like the realistic tradition, has key films, directors, and movements that advanced it conceptually and technically after Georges Méliès. Expressionistic films have tended to probe beneath conscious experience into unconscious experience, to depict dream reality rather than waking reality. We viewers have come to accept, and expect, these distinctions. We have little difficulty, for example, accepting an expressionistic dream in a realistic movie if the filmmaker clearly sets that sequence apart from waking events, as Alfred Hitchcock does in SPELLBOUND. We have more difficulty dealing with a film like 8½, which blurs distinctions between real and fantastic events. Knowing how the realistic and expressionistic traditions in cinema developed, however, makes it easier to understand how films like 8½ can depict both conscious and unconscious reality at once.

General Study Questions

1. Analyze a film that, like THE CABINET OF DR. CALIGARI, deals with madness. From how many points of view is madness depicted? Does the film communicate how it *feels* to be demented? How?
2. Critique a film that, like NOSFERATU, depicts preternatural horror. How does the filmmaker employ narrative and cinematic techniques to horrify the audience?
3. Explicate a film that, like THE BLOOD OF A POET or MESHES OF THE AFTERNOON, explores the human psyche through images from dreams and fantasies. How do images and cinematic techniques work together to reveal the subconscious feelings of the protagonist (or of the filmmaker)?
4. Write a shot-by-shot description of a dream sequence and analyze its logic. How does the editing of the sequence reinforce its meaning?
5. Evaluate a film that, like 8½, recognizes "no dividing line between imagination and reality." How does the film combine conscious and unconscious events? How does it make transitions between them?
6. Compare and contrast two films from the list of Additional Films for Study at the end of this chapter as models of cinematic expressionism.

Additional Films for Study

CRAZY RAY (1922), dir. René Clair
THE MAN WITH A MOVIE CAMERA (1928), dir. Dziga Vertov
ZERO FOR CONDUCT (1933), dir. Jean Vigo
THE TESTAMENT OF DR. MABUSE (1933), dir. Fritz Lang
BEAUTY AND THE BEAST (1946), dir. Jean Cocteau
INVASION OF THE BODY SNATCHERS (1956), dir. Don Siegel
THE TESTAMENT OF ORPHEUS (1959), dir. Jean Cocteau
SHADOWS OF FORGOTTEN ANCESTORS (1964), dir. Sergei Parajanov
HOUR OF THE WOLF (1965), dir. Ingmar Bergman
A REPORT ON THE PARTY AND THE GUESTS (1966), dir. Jan Němec
THE KING OF HEARTS (1967), dir. Philippe de Broca
IF (1968), dir. Lindsay Anderson
THE NIGHT OF THE LIVING DEAD (1968), dir. George Romero
THE DISCREET CHARM OF THE BOURGEOISIE (1972), dir. Luis Buñuel
STEPPENWOLF (1974), dir. Fred Harris
THE MAN WHO FELL TO EARTH (1976), dir. Nicolas Roeg
THAT OBSCURE OBJECT OF DESIRE (1976), dir. Luis Buñuel
THE TENANT (1976), dir. Roman Polanski
THE TALL BLOND MAN WITH ONE BLACK SHOE (1978), dir. Yves Robert
THE TIN DRUM (1979), dir. Volker Schlöndorff
ALTERED STATES (1980), dir. Ken Russell
POLTERGEIST (1982), dir. Tobe Hooper
KISS OF THE SPIDER WOMAN (1985), dir. Hector Babenco
BRAZIL (1986), dir. Terry Gilliam
SOMETHING WILD (1986), dir. Jonathan Demme

How Do Films Depict Physical Reality?

Further Reading

Buache, Freddy. *The Cinema of Luis Buñuel.* Cranbury, N.J.: A.S. Barnes, 1973.

Durgnat, Raymond. *Luis Buñuel.* Berkeley: University of California Press, 1970.

Eisner, Lotte. *The Haunted Screen: Expressionism in the German Cinema and the Influence of Max Reinhardt.* Berkeley: University of California Press, 1973.

————. *Murnau.* Berkeley: University of California Press, 1973.

Fellini, Federico. *Fellini on Fellini.* Translated by Isabel Quigley. New York: Delacorte Press, 1976.

Fraigneau, André. *Cocteau on Film.* New York: Dover Books, 1972.

Gilson, René. *Jean Cocteau.* New York: Crown Publishers, 1974.

Gould, Michael. *Surrealism and the Cinema.* Cranbury, N.J.: A.S. Barnes, 1976.

Jacobs, Lewis, ed. *The Emergence of Film Art.* New York: Hopkinson and Blake, 1974.

Kracauer, Siegfried. *From Caligari to Hitler: A Psychological History of the German Film.* Princeton: Princeton University Press, 1966.

Kyrou, Ado. *Luis Buñuel.* New York: Simon and Schuster, 1963.

Matthews, J. H. *Surrealism and Film.* Ann Arbor: University of Michigan Press, 1971.

Mellen, Joan, ed. *The World of Luis Buñuel: Essays in Criticism.* New York: Oxford University Press, 1978.

Neiman, Catrina. "Chambers (1942–47)." *The Legend of Maya Deren.* Vol. I, pt. 2. New York: Anthology Film Archives/Film Culture, 1988.

Perry, Ted. *Filmguide to 8 1/2.* Bloomington: Indiana University Press, 1975.

Rosenthal, Stuart. *The Cinema of Federico Fellini.* Cranbury, N.J.: A.S. Barnes, 1976.

Steinbrunner, Chris. *Cinema of the Fantastic.* New York: Saturday Review Press, 1972.

Wollenberg, Hans H. *Fifty Years of German Film.* Edited by Roger Manvell. New York: Arno Press, 1972.

Works Cited

Belz, Carl. "The Terror of the Surreal." In *Focus on the Horror Film,* edited by Roy Huss and T.J. Ross, 144–48. Englewood Cliffs, N.J.: Prentice-Hall, 1972.

Cook, David A. *A History of Narrative Film.* New York: W.W. Norton, 1981.

Gould, Michael. *Surrealism and the Cinema.* Cranbury, N.J.: A.S. Barnes, 1976.

Hyman, Timothy. "8 1/2 as an Anatomy of Melancholy." In *Federico Fellini: Essays in Criticism,* edited by Peter Bondanella, 121–29. New York: Oxford University Press, 1978.

Johnson, Lincoln F. *Film: Space, Time, Light, and Sound.* New York: Holt, Rinehart and Winston, 1974.

Mast, Gerald. *A Short History of the Movies.* 4th ed. New York: Macmillan, 1986.

Neiman, Catrina. "Chambers (1942–47)." *The Legend of Maya Deren.* Vol. I, pt. 2. New York: Anthology Film Archives/Film Culture, 1988.

Sadoul, Georges. *French Film.* London: Falcon Press, 1953.

Sherwood, Robert E. "THE CABINET OF DR. CALIGARI." In *American Film Criticism From the Beginnings to CITIZEN KANE,* edited by Stanley Kauffmann, 121–22. New York: Liveright, 1972.

Sitney, P. Adams. *Visionary Film: The American Avant-garde.* New York: Oxford University Press, 1974.

How Do Films Inform, Persuade, and Indoctrinate?

   The lessons in *Frameworks* so far have dealt primarily with narrative films—films that tell a story. But this unit, which focuses more on nonfiction films, covers some other important functions of motion pictures, addressing the question, "How do films inform, persuade, and indoctrinate?" Of course, narrative films can also inform, persuade, and indoctrinate the viewer (sometimes even more effectively than nonfiction films), but they are not usually produced solely for these purposes, as many nonfiction films are.

   The term *nonfiction film* here does not mean only documentary film. Chapter 12, "Film as Reportage," discusses both *journalistic* reporting (recording real-life situations and events as news) and *poetic* reporting (recording real-life experience more personally or artistically than is usual in news documentaries). The main purpose of the chapter is to distinguish between objective and subjective reportage and to identify where filmmakers can use each most effectively and appropriately.

   Chapters 13 and 14 examine subtle distinctions between film as education and film as propaganda. Chapter 13 looks at why cinema is such an effective educational medium in the modern world and how films can educate the public about important problems and issues, including the role of cinema as a communications medium.

   To illustrate how films can be used for indoctrination, chapter 14 examines three classic propaganda films: Sergei Eisenstein's THE BATTLESHIP POTEMKIN, Leni Riefenstahl's TRIUMPH OF THE WILL, and Frank Capra's PRELUDE TO WAR. The purpose of the chapter is to investigate what film propaganda is, how it works, and how it affects the viewer.

NANOOK OF THE NORTH (1922), dir. Robert Flaherty.

F ilm reporting is not simply a synonym for **documentary film.** Many kinds of **nonfiction films,** and even some **fiction films,** employ documentary techniques to report on real-life situations or events in some way. This chapter examines several types of cinematic reportage.

Objectivity Versus Subjectivity

Many lessons in *Frameworks* highlight how filmmakers employ cinematic techniques to manipulate our perceptions and our reactions. The first question we might ask about a film that reports, therefore, is how much the filmmaker is manipulating our response to the events being documented. Does a film about the plight of whales, for instance, favor one viewpoint over others? Does it play heavily on emotions? Does it primarily inform or persuade the viewer? Does the film report the issue objectively or subjectively?

The discussion in this chapter is based on the assumption that objectivity is not necessarily more desirable than subjectivity in film reporting, but rather that, depending on the filmmaker's purposes, varying degrees of objectivity or subjectivity may be appropriate.

In *Documentary in American Television*, A. William Bluem distinguishes between journalistic and poetic film reporting. He writes:

> Television documentary divides its purposes into the journalistic, which falls within those "lower reaches" of communication, and the poetic, where the "world of imagination" can be stimulated and represented while firmly anchored in life's realities. The first allows for the precision and impartiality of description, with emphasis upon the detached and dispassionate in techniques of presentation; the other frees its techniques and approaches to advance the subjective purpose of the poet in his presentation of those universal themes of life and humanity which he senses in the documents themselves.
> (89–90)

We can use Bluem's differentiation between the *journalistic* and the *poetic* in documentary film to distinguish degrees of objectivity and subjectivity more clearly in all kinds of film reporting: from detached and dispassionate accounts of life's realities to imaginative interpretations of the universal themes those realities suggest; from straight news coverage to a work of art. Let us consider journalistic reporting first, then poetic reporting.

Journalistic Reporting

The following four nonfiction films illustrate a range of objectivity/subjectivity in journalistic reporting.

 1. PRIMARY (1960), a film made for television by Richard Leacock, Robert Drew, D.A. Pennebaker, and Albert Maysles, is about the 1960 Democratic presidential primary election in Wisconsin between Hubert H. Humphrey and John F. Kennedy. Employing a **hand-held camera**, PRIMARY follows the two candidates as they campaign (fig. 12.1) and records both the public appearances—speeches and hand-shaking—and the behind-the-scenes politicking that go into a presidential primary. It presents Humphrey and Kennedy candidly and at times intimately, and compares their campaigns evenly. Richard Meran Barsam observes in *Nonfiction Film: A Critical History*:

> PRIMARY comes as close to balanced, objective reporting as a film about politics can. The film makers leave everyone to judge for himself, and attach no labels through editing that might have distorted the words or actions of either side. . . . The sequences are well balanced between the two campaigns; the narration is impartial, and there is little of it in comparison to the amount of direct sound recording. The candidates act out their own scenarios and tell their own stories; the film makers are there to record and to reveal, not to interpret.
> (257)

 PRIMARY will serve as our baseline for determining levels of objectivity in the discussion of journalistic reportage that follows. But it will be useful if each student also has a particular film in mind as a clear-cut example of objective reporting. What documentary have you seen recently on television or in class that presents a balanced, objective account of an event and allows viewers to judge that event for themselves? You may also consider the journalistic reporting on television feature news programs, such as "60 minutes" or "20/20."

 2. SALESMAN (1969), directed by Albert and David Maysles and edited by Charlotte Zwerin, is about a door-to-door Bible salesman named Paul Brennan who uses his easy banter to sell expensive Bibles to people who are too vulnerable or unhappy to resist his sales pitch. Shot without a script, the film simply follows the salesman's day-to-day life as he works his territory out of motel rooms. Paul's anecdotes and commentaries throughout the film provide intimate glimpses into his life and personality, and ultimately reveal his loneliness and desperation.

Figure 12.1

PRIMARY, a documentary about the 1960 Democratic presidential primary campaign, "comes as close to balanced, objective reporting as a film about politics can," in the words of one critic.

SALESMAN is often cited as an example of *cinéma vérité* (literally, "cinema truth"), a style of filmmaking that records action and events as they occur, without arranging them for the camera; in other words, this style does not use the camera to shape reality but simply to photograph it truthfully. Nevertheless, there is a thin line between fact and fiction in SALESMAN because the film "gives dramatic shape and structure to the words and actions of real people" and because "Paul is a natural actor, unaware of the camera, able to spin yarns, to reminisce, to laugh at adversity" (Barsam 284–85).

Reviewers of SALESMAN have compared Paul Brennan to Willy Loman, the fictional protagonist of Arthur Miller's play *Death of a Salesman*, because Paul, like Willy, is basically a sympathetic man losing his grip on life and his life's work. Consistently bleak images in

SALESMAN (dreary motels, Paul's pathetic colleagues, the gaudy Bible they sell for $49.95) encourage the viewer to sympathize with Paul and his disheartening occupation. In a review for *The New Leader* John Simon suggests that the advertisement for the film (which shows Jesus Christ, complete with halo, carrying two salesman's cases) epitomizes such imagery (Simon 467). Thus, although it is not easy to isolate precisely where and how the Maysles are guiding our responses in SALESMAN, they are certainly not leaving us to judge entirely for ourselves, as the makers of PRIMARY did.

How does SALESMAN compare with your own baseline example of objective reporting? Do you know other films that might be examples of *cinéma vérité*? How do they compare with SALESMAN? Is a film like Robert Flaherty's NANOOK OF THE NORTH (1922) an example of *cinéma vérité*? Why, or why not? How objective is the reporting in NANOOK OF THE NORTH?

3. THE TITICUT FOLLIES (1967), directed and edited by Frederick Wiseman, candidly depicts conditions at the state hospital for the criminally insane in Bridgewater, Massachusetts. The title of the film is taken from a variety show staged by patients and staff at the institution each year. Wiseman opens and closes his film with scenes from the follies and **cross-cuts** them with everyday incidents at the institution. But THE TITICUT FOLLIES is anything but light entertainment. It is an **exposé** that relentlessly points out the degrading conditions at the hospital and the inhuman treatment of the patients. Richard Schickel, reviewing the film for *Life*, writes:

> The Bridgewater atmosphere is one of aimless hopelessness
> punctuated by outbursts of unthinking, almost ritualized violence.
> A psychiatrist turns an interview into a sadistic assault on such
> shreds of sanity as his inmate-victim may still retain; or, with
> malicious cheerfulness, he force-feeds an old man—already near
> death—while we wonder whether the ash from the doctor's
> carelessly dangling cigarette is really going to fall into the glop
> being funneled into the convulsively shuddering throat, or the
> guards will vary their routine by tormenting—with words and a
> slap—a naked inhabitant of the violent ward who has soiled his
> cell in the night.
>
> (459)

In THE TITICUT FOLLIES it is certainly not difficult to put a finger on where and how Wiseman manipulates our emotional responses. The film is rife with scenes in which carefully juxtaposed images, without any verbal commentary, overpower us with the horrible conditions at the Bridgewater asylum. Most memorable perhaps is the force-feeding scene Schickel describes. Wiseman matches close-ups of the frightened old man with a feeding tube up his nose and the psychiatrist with his cigarette ash hanging over the open funnel. The feeding tube and the cigarette ash become the focal points of the horror we feel in this scene, and our attention is drawn to them almost more than to the faces of the two men. The doctor's neglect of basic hygiene reveals his disregard for the patient and makes the force-feeding all the more dehumanizing. Wiseman's editing leaves little room for moral ambiguity. We feel outraged at such atrocities and driven to do something about them, which is the purpose of an exposé.

There is considerable artistry in Wiseman's editing of the force-feeding which, notwithstanding the grisliness of the scene, pushes it much closer to the subjective side of A. William Bluem's model. THE TITICUT FOLLIES is a long way from the detached, dispassionate film reporting in PRIMARY.

Think of a recent television news report or news program that you consider an exposé. Does the report attempt to provoke the viewer or to arouse a strong emotional reaction, as Wiseman does in the force-feeding scene in THE TITICUT FOLLIES? Do you observe any camera or editing techniques that manipulate the viewer's responses or judgments? How objective is this report in comparison with your baseline example?

4. HEARTS AND MINDS (1974), directed by Peter Davis, is a film that criticizes American involvement in Vietnam. It pieces together interviews, news and **archive footage** about the war, *cinéma-vérité* accounts of war-related incidents (both in Vietnam and in the United States), and clips from commercial Hollywood war movies in order to search out the causes of the Vietnam War in American culture and to show that it was unjust. Included in the film are familiar images of Vietnam that have been popularized by the news media (a Vietnamese officer shooting a prisoner in the head, napalmed children running naked in the street [fig. 12.2]) as well as images that seem far removed from the war (for instance, a high school football coach priming his players in the locker room to "go out and kill" their opponents on the field). The interviewees include famous people associated with Vietnam (General William Westmoreland, Clark Clifford, Daniel Ellsberg) as well as ordinary people affected by the war (a former POW who receives a hero's welcome in his New Jersey hometown, the parents of a Harvard graduate killed in action, a Vietnamese coffin maker).

HEARTS AND MINDS makes no attempt to disguise or dilute its bias, and in fact repeatedly uses "coercive" editing to drive its point home. In one of the film's most memorable sequences, Davis cross-

Figure 12.2
HEARTS AND MINDS
incorporates familiar
images of Vietnam, such
as this shot of napalmed
children running naked in
the street, which was
popularized by the news
media.

cuts an interview with General Westmoreland, former commanding general of American forces in Vietnam, with a Vietnamese child weeping uncontrollably over his dead father. As the child hugs a photograph of the father to his heart and doubles over with grief (fig. 12.3), Westmoreland comments that "the Oriental doesn't put the same high price on life as does the Westerner." This editing does more than simply highlight opposing images within a scene, as with the feeding tube and the cigarette ash in THE TITICUT FOLLIES; it juxtaposes images that are physically unrelated (occurring at different times and places) in order to manipulate the viewer. The filmmaker intercuts shots of the mourning Vietnamese child expressly to deprecate Westmoreland's statement about the price of life in the East and to insure that the viewer will be outraged by the blatantly racist attitude behind it. Clearly, this kind of manipulative editing shapes reality even more conspicuously than Wiseman's force-feeding scene in THE TITICUT FOLLIES, and it places HEARTS AND MINDS at the extreme subjective end of our objectivity/subjectivity continuum, making it the polar opposite of the detached, dispassionate account of politics in PRIMARY.

Figure 12.3
Director Peter Davis uses coercive editing in HEARTS AND MINDS to drive home his opposition to the Vietnam War. He intercuts this shot of a child weeping for his slain father with a statement by General William Westmoreland that "the Oriental doesn't put the same high price on life as does the Westerner."

In films like HEARTS AND MINDS, the filmmaker's deep personal commitment to political issues makes objective reporting unthinkable. In *American Film Now* James Monaco explains:

> HEARTS AND MINDS is at once so deeply felt and so insistently rational that it almost transcends its subject. . . . Certainly [Peter] Davis. . . doesn't pretend to the specious objectivity of **Direct Cinema.** Most of the nonfiction filmmakers who have come to the fore in the seventies have been devoted to a cinema that is more personal and passionate than seemingly objective.
> (259–60)

Some fiction films also adopt documentary techniques as a means of reporting historical incidents or realities along with a fictional story. In OPEN CITY (1945), for example, director Roberto Rossellini wanted to recreate as accurately as possible the underground resistance against the Nazis during their occupation of Rome. To do so he shot a simple story with ordinary people in the streets and apartments of Rome. He used **available lighting** and an unobtrusive camera style, sometimes photographing candidly from cameras concealed on rooftops or in traveling cars. The result is a film that almost looks like a documentary. (For more discussion of **neorealism** and OPEN CITY, see chapter 10.)

Other narrative films include actual documentary footage to provide a historical context for the story. THE UNBEARABLE LIGHTNESS OF BEING (1988), for example, includes **newsreel** footage of the Soviet invasion of Prague in 1968 to depict the background of Czech characters in the film who are torn between their homeland and life abroad afterwards. The film deftly incorporates the two main characters into the footage of the invasion—one of whom is an aspiring photographer snapping shots of Russian tanks in the center of Prague. Thus, the scene is a moving film report on the 1968 Russian invasion of Czechoslovakia, couched within a story about people who were displaced by it.

A noteworthy example of cinematic reportage in narrative film is MEDIUM COOL (1969), written, photographed, and directed by Haskell Wexler. MEDIUM COOL is a loosely constructed story about a Chicago television cameraman, John Cassellis (Robert Forster), whose consciousness is raised about politics and the media. But the film also graphically depicts the riots in Chicago during the Democratic National Convention in August 1968.

Wexler shot and recorded MEDIUM COOL entirely on location in Chicago during the weeks before the Democratic Convention. The narrative structure of the film was left open-ended in order to incorporate developments in the streets as the convention approached. Wexler shot twenty hours of footage covering the riots and the events that led up to them, and included lengthy segments of this footage in the film. In some scenes he photographed the film's characters amidst actual demonstrations (fig. 12.4). He also placed the characters in street situations where they were forced to improvise. In one scene, for instance, a group of black militants confronts Cassellis about his responsibilities as a member of the white media establishment. The scene, shot with minimal preparation, placed Forster in a situation almost identical to that of the character he was playing. "The result," says one reviewer, "is as honest a political confrontation as has yet been captured by a commercial American film" (Roddick 1559).

In MEDIUM COOL Wexler set out to achieve a unique combination of story and reportage, a "wedding between features and *cinéma vérité*," by melding largely improvised situations with actual footage of the Chicago riots. The result is an honest picture of a society in turmoil and a biting commentary on the interrelationship between film journalism and politics.

Figure 12.4
In MEDIUM COOL
director Haskell Wexler
photographed fictional
characters amidst actual
demonstrations in
Chicago at the Demo-
cratic National Conven-
tion in August 1968. The
woman in the foreground
with the light-colored
dress (*a* and *b*) and the
sound technician (*b*) are
actors improvising in
street situations.

a

b

Poetic Reporting

A. William Bluem concludes his discussion of objectivity and subjectivity in film reportage by stating that in news documentary "life must always be in control of art" (91). But in another kind of film reporting art is in control of life; that is, the filmmaker presents highly subjective and imaginative depictions of reality more for aesthetics than for information. Let us now consider poetic film reporting. The following nonfiction films illustrate a range of objectivity/subjectivity in poetic reporting.

1. RAIN (1929), directed by Joris Ivens, is "a film of atmosphere" that tries "to show the changing face of a city, Amsterdam, during a shower" (Ivens 60). RAIN opens with a clear sky over the city. Gradually, a wind rises and the first raindrops splash in the canals. The shower comes down harder, and people scurry around with umbrellas and raincoats. Then it ends, leaving the houses and streets glistening.

RAIN has neither titles nor dialogue. "Its effects were intended as purely visual," says Ivens. "The actors are the rain, the raindrops, wet people, dark clouds, glistening reflections moving over wet asphalt, and so forth. The diffused light on the dark houses along the black canals produced an effect that I never expected" (60–61). When it was first screened in Paris, French reviewers called RAIN a *ciné-poem*, an appropriate description since, like the imagist poems popular in the 1920s, the film uses concentrated images to suggest subtle moods and emotions. Ivens writes:

> In RAIN I consciously used heavy, dark drops dripping in big, pear-shaped forms at long intervals across the glass of the studio window, to produce the melancholy feeling of a rainy day. The opposite effect of happiness or gaiety in a spring shower could be produced by many bright, small, round drops pounding against many surfaces in a variety of shots.
>
> (63)

Ivens himself likens the overall effect of RAIN to specific lines of poetry: "And the whole film gives the spectator a very personal and subjective vision. As in the lines of Verlaine:

> *Il pleure dans mon coeur*
> *Comme il pleut sur la ville.*"
> (61)

(Translated freely, the lines mean: "My heart weeps/As it rains on the city.")

In this section of the chapter RAIN will serve as a baseline example of poetic reporting that is relatively straightforward and presents images basically as they appear in reality, even though the film artist employs them very subjectively to recreate moods and feelings. Again, it will be useful if each student can identify a poetic film as his or her own baseline example. One place to find such films is public broadcasting television, which periodically screens short films by independent filmmakers.

2. REPORT (1965), an **underground film** by Bruce Conner, is an example of poetic film reportage where the filmmaker conspicuously reshapes images from the real world. REPORT dramatically juxtaposes sound and images to create a highly subjective account of President John F. Kennedy's assassination. It begins with a short **film loop** of the Kennedy motorcade in Dallas before the shooting, which is repeated over and over and accompanied by a **sound track** of a radio broadcaster's coverage of the actual event. But the assassination itself is not depicted. Instead, Conner presents a flickering blank screen, **film leader,** newsreel clips of Lee Harvey Oswald's rifle and Jacqueline Kennedy entering an ambulance, and evocative archive footage (a bullfight, a bullet bursting a light bulb in slow motion, a bomb exploding, etc.), which complement the broadcaster's emotional on-the-scene report.

From the preceding description, what do you think Conner is hoping to accomplish with REPORT? Why does he create such startling disparity between the audio and video accounts of Kennedy's assassination? How does this disparity affect us as we witness this report of the assassination?

On the one hand, the immediacy of the radio broadcaster's live account rivets our attention to the grim events in Dallas; on the other hand, the film images distance us from the physical scene of the assassination and depict it symbolically. The film loop of President Kennedy and his companions in the open convertible lasts only a few seconds but is repeated many times. By dwelling on those few seconds before the gunshots, freezing them in time, Conner creates an atmosphere of dreadful anticipation. On which repetition of the loop will the smiling Kennedy be annihilated? As the screen pulsates with white light, each viewer must envision the horror in Dallas from the broadcaster's description of it.

Many of the images that appear later in the film are ironically matched with the broadcaster's words rather than with the actual assassination. For example, as the reporter comments that the "doors fly open" on the presidential car, Conner inserts a snippet from a television commercial in which refrigerator doors magically fly open by themselves.

In short, even though a report on a historical event like an assassination is the very stuff of journalism, and even though Bruce Conner employs an actual radio report of the assassination as the film's sound track, REPORT is not at all journalistic because it uses images contrived by the film artist to depict a highly subjective, associative reaction to President Kennedy's assassination rather than the event itself. REPORT is an example of film reporting in which art is decidedly in control of life.

3. Jonas Mekas's autobiographical film, DIARIES, NOTES AND SKETCHES (1964–69), is an example of another kind of subjective film reporting. Mekas, a prominent spokesperson for **independent film**, explains how he accumulated and organized footage for DIARIES, a film he describes as "a series of personal notes on events, people (friends) and Nature (Seasons)":

> Since 1950 I have been keeping a film diary. I have been walking around with my Bolex and reacting to the immediate reality: situations, friends, New York, seasons of the year. On some days I shot ten frames, on others ten seconds, still on others ten minutes. Or I shoot nothing. When one writes diaries, it's a retrospective process: you sit down, you look back at your day, and you write it all down. To keep a film (camera) diary, is to react (with your camera) immediately, now, this instant: either you get it now or you don't get it at all. To go back and shoot it later, it would mean restaging, be it events or feelings.
>
> (In *Visionary Film* 398–99)

Besides being highly personal, film diaries like Mekas's are perhaps the most spontaneous kind of film reporting. As he says, "Either you get it now or you don't get it at all." Such filming requires of the filmmaker a special kind of improvisation that Mekas says is "the highest form of concentration, of awareness, of intuitive knowledge, when the imagination begins to dismiss the pre-arranged, the contrived mental structures, and goes directly to the depths of the matter" (in *Film: A Montage* 337).

In a later autobiographical film, REMINISCENCE OF A JOURNEY TO LITHUANIA (1971–72), Mekas recorded his experiences during a visit to his homeland after twenty-five years.

4. The films of Stan Brakhage, another independent filmmaker, are also very autobiographical. Most of Brakhage's films are shot at his mountain home in Colorado and feature himself, his wife, children,

friends, and even pets. For example, in WINDOW WATER BABY MOV-ING (1959) and THIGH LINE LYRE TRIANGULAR (1961), Brakhage records the births of two of his children; and in several films—NIGHTCATS (1956), CAT'S CRADLE (1959), and PASHT (1965)—he features the family cats. Brakhage's films, however, are by no means simple home movies. He describes how he photographed an argument with his wife Jane that appears in WEDLOCK HOUSE: AN INTER-COURSE (1959):

> One day in midst of quarrel I felt the necessity to take the camera and photograph her again and again. I grabbed the lights and began letting her face emerge in and out of black and white flashes in order that as much as I could see be immediately pitched into expression. I moved the light with one hand—painting her image as it moved over her and away into darkness—and photographed her with the other hand. . . . At a crucial moment out of some graciousness that I did not fully compre-hend; (I kept feeling a little guilty wondering what Jane's view of me would be.) I sensed that my view, or what I would cast upon her, was becoming too dominant. So I handed her the camera and she took it very quickly. We were trying to reenact the quarrel, trying to comprehend it.
> (*Metaphors on Vision*)

Brakhage is preoccupied with "the art of vision," and in most of his work, the people and events he photographs are less significant than the visual experiences he creates with them. To create "levels of vision" that "can *only* exist *in* the eye of the viewer" Brakhage usually augments or distorts the subjects he photographs in various ways: He scratches the **film stock** or paints on it; he uses multiple superimpositions, distorting lenses, and fuzzy focus; he employs what he calls "plastic cutting" to connect shots so that the flow of images on the screen is not conspicuously interrupted.

Nevertheless, the domestic events Brakhage records in his films are principally the material from which his aesthetic vision derives as well as the source of his inspiration. For example, in one of his longest films, SCENES FROM UNDER CHILDHOOD (1969), which is 144 minutes long in its complete version, Brakhage attempts to recreate how his children perceive the world. His own description of the film is: "A visualization of the inner world of foetal beginnings, the infant, the baby, the child—a shattering of the 'myths of childhood' through revelation of the extremes of violent terror and overwhelming joy of that world dark-ened to most adults by their sentimental remembering of it" (*Canyon* 31).

Conclusion

Clearly, there are many ways for filmmakers to convey real-life experiences and events to the viewer and many types of film reportage—news coverage, *cinéma vérité*, exposé, *ciné-poems*, film diaries, autobiographical films. Between PRIMARY and SCENES FROM UNDER CHILDHOOD there is a tremendous range of objectivity and subjectivity in cinematic reportage. A film report on any issue or event, such as the plight of whales, may fall anywhere along this range, depending on whether the filmmaker's tendencies are journalistic or poetic. Naturally, it is important for a visually literate viewer to discern whether the film leans more toward journalism or poetry—whether life is in control of art or art is in control of life.

General Study Questions

1. What does A. William Bluem mean when he says that in news documentary "life must always be in control of art"? Do you agree with this statement? Explain why or why not.
2. How can we tell whether life or art is in control in a nonfiction film? Draw up a list of indicators to serve as guidelines. Illustrate with examples from films discussed in this chapter or from other nonfiction films you know.
3. Keep a log of film reports you see on television. Using A. William Bluem's distinction between journalistic and poetic reporting, categorize the reports according to how objective or subjective they are.
4. Choose an important current issue or event as the subject for a nonfiction film. Describe in detail how you would present this issue or event in a journalistic film report. Then describe how you would present it in a poetic film report.
5. Many schools and organizations today are producing video yearbooks. Evaluate one of these as an example of cinematic reportage. Identify specific examples of journalistic and poetic reporting and determine whether this particular yearbook leans more toward one or the other. Critique how effective and appropriate it is as film reportage.

Additional Films for Study

NANOOK OF THE NORTH (1922), dir. Robert Flaherty
À PROPOS DE NICE (1930), dir. Jean Vigo
SONG OF CEYLON (1935), dir. Basil Wright
THE QUIET ONE (1949), dir. Sidney Meyers
NIGHT AND FOG (1955), dir. Alain Resnais

THE BATTLE OF ALGIERS (1960), dir. Gillo Pontecorvo
POINT OF ORDER! (1964), dir. Emile de Antonio and Daniel Talbot
THE ANDERSON PLATOON (1967), dir. Pierre Schoendorffer
MONTEREY POP (1967), dir. Richard Leacock and D.A. Pennebaker
HIGH SCHOOL (1969), dir. Frederick Wiseman
WOODSTOCK (1970), dir. Michael Wadleigh
GIMME SHELTER (1970), dir. David and Albert Maysles, Charlotte Zwerin
THE SELLING OF THE PENTAGON (1971), dir. Peter Davis
MARJOE (1972), dir. Howard Smith and Sarah Kernochan
VISIONS OF EIGHT (1973), dir. Arthur Penn, Miloš Forman, Kon Ichikawa, Claude Lelouch, Juri Oserov, Michael Pfleghar, John Schlesinger, Mai Zetterling
HARLAN COUNTY, U.S.A. (1976), dir. Barbara Kopple
PUMPING IRON (1976), dir. Robert Fiore and George Butler
JUST ANOTHER MISSING KID (1982), dir. John Zaritsky
FACES OF WAR (1985), dir. Nick Allen and Gil Friend
DOWN AND OUT IN AMERICA (1986), dir. Lee Grant
SALVADOR (1986), dir. Oliver Stone
BROADCAST NEWS (1987), dir. James Brooks

Further Reading

Barsam, Richard Meran. *Nonfiction Film: A Critical History.* New York: E.P. Dutton, 1973.
Beveridge, James. *John Grierson: Film Master.* New York: Macmillan, 1978.
Bluem, A. William. *Documentary in American Television.* New York: Hastings House, 1965.
Brakhage, Stan. *Metaphors on Vision.* New York: Film Culture, 1963.
Fielding, Raymond. *The March of Time.* New York: Oxford University Press, 1978.
Grierson, John. *Grierson on Documentary.* Edited by Forsyth Hardy. New York: Praeger, 1971.
Issari, M. Ali. *Cinéma Vérité.* East Lansing: Michigan State University Press, 1971.
Ivens, Joris. *The Camera and I.* New York: International Publishers, 1969.
Jacobs, Lewis, ed. *The Documentary Tradition: From Nanook to Woodstock.* New York: Hopkinson and Blake, 1979.

Jowett, Garth, and James M. Linton. *Movies as Mass Communication.* Beverly Hills: SAGE Publications, 1980.

Levin, G. Roy, ed. *Documentary Explorations.* Garden City, N.Y.: Doubleday, 1971.

Lovell, Alan, and Jim Hillier. *Studies in Documentary.* New York: Viking, 1972.

Mamber, Stephen. *Cinéma Vérité in America: Studies in Uncontrolled Documentary.* Cambridge, Mass.: M.I.T. Press, 1973.

Monaco, James. *American Film Now.* New York: New American Library, 1979.

Rosenthal, Alan. *The New Documentary in Action.* Berkeley: University of California Press, 1971.

Rotha, Paul, in collaboration with Sinclair Road and Richard Griffith. *Documentary Film.* New York: Hastings House, 1970.

Works Cited

Barsam, Richard Meran. *Nonfiction Film: A Critical History.* New York: E.P. Dutton, 1973.

Bluem, A. William. *Documentary in American Television.* New York: Hastings House, 1969.

Brakhage, Stan. Quoted in *Canyon Cinema, Catalogue 5,* 21–41. San Francisco: Canyon Cinema, 1982.

———. *Metaphors on Vision.* New York: Film Culture, 1963.

Ivens, Joris. "The Making of RAIN." In *The Documentary Tradition,* 2d ed., edited by Lewis Jacobs, 60–63. New York: W. W. Norton, 1979.

Mekas, Jonas. "Notes on the New American Cinema." In *Film: A Montage of Theories,* edited by Richard Dyer MacCann, 333–40. New York: E. P. Dutton, 1966.

———. Quoted in *Visionary Film: The American Avant-Garde,* by P. Adams Sitney. New York: Oxford University Press, 1974.

Monaco, James. *American Film Now.* New York: New American Library, 1979.

Roddick, Nick. "MEDIUM COOL." In *Magill's Survey of Cinema,* 2d series, edited by Frank N. Magill, 1557–60. Englewood Cliffs, N.J.: Salem Press, 1981.

Schickel, Richard. "Sorriest Spectacle: THE TITICUT FOLLIES." In *The Documentary Tradition,* 2d ed., edited by Lewis Jacobs, 459–61. New York: W.W. Norton, 1979.

Simon, John. "A Variety of Hells." In *The Documentary Tradition,* 2d ed., edited by Lewis Jacobs, 466–68. New York: W. W. Norton, 1979.

Film As Education

Most people watch films for entertainment and are conversant with current box-office hits, Hollywood movie stars, and big-name directors. Yet, each year many more films are produced to educate and inform rather than to entertain, and they are made by film companies and filmmakers whose names are largely unknown to the public. Included in this category are educational films for schools; training films for business, industry, and the military; self-help films of all kinds; documentaries that disseminate information or examine topical issues; and public service television commercials. Today, films and videotapes are commonly used for many purposes, such as teaching sex education in high school, training business executives in management techniques, informing industrial workers about job safety, indoctrinating military personnel, educating farmers in developing countries about agricultural technology, and demonstrating all kinds of skills—from how to prepare sushi to how to win at craps.

Educating the Public *With* Films

Documentary Films

John Grierson, a film critic and the leader of a group of documentary filmmakers in England in the 1930s, was one of the first to recognize the importance of film as a means of educating the public. In the late 1920s Grierson supervised the film unit of the Empire Marketing Board, an organization established to promote trade and improve public relations for Great Britain. A strong nationalist cinema in the Soviet Union during the 1920s had been aggressively promoting Soviet political and economic ideology with films like Eisenstein's POTEMKIN (1925) and Pudovkin's STORM OVER ASIA (1928). England hoped to counteract that influence by highlighting the British working class in socially conscious **documentary films**—a movement that came to be identified in the 1930s as the British School of Documentary.

     In 1933 Grierson became film officer of the General Post Office and established a film unit in London to carry on public relations for the British government. With money and the latest movie equipment at his disposal, Grierson attracted talented filmmakers, artists, and musicians to work together on politically oriented films; he also enticed them by offering freedom to experiment with subject matter and cinematic techniques. The earliest G.P.O. films are short, realistic documentaries that unpretentiously explain various General Post Office functions, like collecting and sorting mail (SIX-THIRTY COLLECTION), maintaining underground utility lines (UNDER THE CITY), and broadcasting weather

Figure 13.1
NIGHT MAIL, which
focuses on postal workers
on a train who sort mail
through the night,
represents the 1930s
British School of Docu-
mentary at its best.

reports (WEATHER FORECAST). Some of these films are noteworthy for their technical innovations in sound recording and for the way they effectively combined sound effects and narration with visual images.

The most significant of the early G.P.O. films is NIGHT MAIL (1936), written and directed by Basil Wright and Harry Watt, with poetic narrative by W.H. Auden and music by Benjamin Britten. The film is about an express train that carries mail overnight from London to Glasgow, and it focuses primarily on postal workers aboard the train who load and sort the mail through the night (fig. 13.1), highlighting their dedication and efficiency. In *Nonfiction Film: A Critical History*, Richard Meran Barsam observes:

> The film [NIGHT MAIL] derives its power from several
> sources. First, it handles ordinary people in ordinary situations in such a
> way that they appear to be special. Second, it keeps the speed and sound
> of the train as an important part of the sound track; underscored with a
> mix of Britten's music and Auden's staccatolike poem, the film moves

with an almost breathtaking rhythm. Third, it emphasizes the importance
and dignity of a job well done, as well as the emotional importance of mail
to the lives of everyday citizens. . . . There is power in NIGHT MAIL, the
power of sight and sound, and there is also charm, and a particularly
British feeling for detail, for efficiency, and, finally, for the working man,
that gives this film a very special quality. . . . NIGHT MAIL represents
the British documentary school in the early 1930s at its best, for it
combines social purpose with cinematic experimentation.
(53)

As early as the 1920s, Grierson argued that documentary
film should have a major role in education—indeed, that the purpose of
documentary film is fundamentally educational. He pointed out that the
documentary film movement in England was developed expressly "to
'bring alive' to the citizen the world in which his citizenship lay, to 'bridge
the gap' between the citizen and the community" (220–21). Clearly, this
concept of education is much broader than conventional instruction for
children and young adults in school. Grierson argues that documentary
film has an important place not only in the classroom but in the community center and the union hall as well. He sees responsible citizenship as a
primary goal of education.

How, then, does documentary film promote good citizenship? Grierson writes:

When we talk of bridging the gap between the citizen and the
community and between the classroom and the world without, we are
asking for a kind of educational shorthand which will somehow give
people quick and immediate comprehension of the highly complex forces
which motivate our complicated society. . . . That is why the documentary
film has achieved unique importance in the new world of education. It
does not teach the new world by analyzing it. Uniquely and for the first
time it *communicates* the new world by showing it in its corporate and
living nature.
(199)

What does Grierson mean when he says that film "communicates" rather than teaches the new world? What does it mean to show
the new world "in its corporate and living nature"? Can you cite films that
illustrate these concepts? Can you think of recent films that give us quick
and immediate comprehension of our complicated society?

Grierson wrote these comments about education long before the television set was a common household item, before satellite
communications and video cassettes even existed; so he could not have
imagined how extensively the world in its corporate and living nature
appears on viewing screens in today's society, nor how instantaneously

accessible visual communication has now become to almost every citizen in the industrialized world. Political events, wars, and even natural disasters from anywhere in the world appear on our living room screens *in progress*. Indeed, the visual media today are themselves highly complex forces that motivate and complicate our society. Nevertheless, John Grierson accurately identified in the 1930s what makes film a uniquely important educational tool in the modern world: its immediacy, its drama, its power to communicate directly.

For Grierson, "education is activist or it is nothing." He believed that education should establish "patterns of thought and feeling" to help citizens manage the flood of information confronting them in the modern world, and that government should exert strong leadership in determining these patterns. In other words, he believed that educating the public is essentially a matter of propaganda.

Thus, Grierson points up a fundamental concern about documentary film as an educational instrument—namely, that there is often a very thin line between information and persuasion, between instruction and propaganda. (This concern will be taken up more extensively in the next chapter, "Film as Propaganda.")

Commercial Films

But documentaries are not the only films useful for educating the public. Many commercial narrative films also have great educational value. Films made from the works of Shakespeare, for instance, or from classic novels, like MOBY DICK (1956), TOM JONES (1963), and BARRY LYNDON (1975), introduce important works of literature to audiences who might otherwise not experience them. In fact, there are some indications that movies stimulate reading, since book sales often skyrocket after a movie popularizes a work of fiction. Much is written today about the relationship between film and literature, including theories suggesting that the development of film and the development of the novel in the twentieth century closely complement one another. In *Novels into Film*, for example, George Bluestone observes that "the rise of the film, which preempted the picturing of bodies in nature, coincides almost exactly with the rise of the modern novel, which preempted the rendition of human consciousness" (61).

Similarly, commercial movies about historical people and events, like LAWRENCE OF ARABIA (1962), A MAN FOR ALL SEASONS (1966), REDS (1981), and GANDHI (1982), educate audiences about history. But even though many historical films employ researchers and scholarly consultants to insure historical accuracy and take care to reproduce settings, costumes, and **props** authentically, there is a legitimate concern about how accurately commercial movies depict history. For example, in a documentary film entitled BLACK HISTORY: LOST, STOLEN OR STRAYED (1968), narrator Bill Cosby argues that generations of white Americans have formed their impressions and attitudes about black people largely from Hollywood movies that stereotyped blacks as stupid and inferior. One of the principal offenders Cosby cites is D.W. Griffith's THE BIRTH OF A NATION (1915), a romanticized fictional account of the American Civil War and Reconstruction, which strongly influenced how blacks (and history) were depicted in Hollywood movies for many years afterwards. (For more discussion of THE BIRTH OF A NATION, see chapter 10.)

However, some commercial movies about historical events are remarkably effective educational films as John Grierson envisioned they should be—that is, immediate communications about responsible citizenship in the modern world and experiences that ultimately raise the viewer's social and political consciousness. For example, THE KILLING FIELDS (1984), directed by Roland Joffe, provides a moving and insightful historical account of one of the most chilling atrocities in recent history. Based on a 1980 article by journalist Sydney Schanberg in *The New York Times Magazine*, THE KILLING FIELDS chronicles the real-life experiences of Schanberg (Sam Waterston) and his Cambodian assistant, Dith Pran (Haing S. Ngor) during the takeover of Cambodia by the Khmer Rouge guerrillas in the 1970s. The film's title comes from a Cambodian phrase used to describe the terror-ridden land where more than a million inhabitants perished in a genocidal war. In one gripping scene, Dith Pran, having just escaped from a Khmer Rouge forced labor camp, finds himself knee-deep in "the killing fields" where, numbed by exhaustion and horror, he falls asleep amidst countless decomposing bodies of fellow Cambodians who have not survived Pol Pot's execution squads (fig. 13.2). THE KILLING FIELDS effectively shows how the political upheaval in Cambodia engulfed the lives of individuals like Schanberg and Dith Pran, and dramatically reveals the torment Cambodian people have suffered and continue to suffer in our own time.

Commercial films, therefore, play a significant role in educating the public, and perhaps an even greater role than documentaries because they attract much larger audiences. Moreover, since we expect a documentary to be educational and a feature movie to be entertaining, we tend to be less discriminating about the lessons that commercial films deliver, intentionally or inadvertently, about history and social institutions.

Figure 13.2
THE KILLING FIELDS is an example of a commercial film that educates the public with its historical account of political upheaval in Cambodia during the 1970s.

In the 1920s John Grierson recognized that film could become the premier educational instrument of the modern age. Today, when television has become such an all-pervasive communications medium, there is more concern than ever about the power of films—not only documentaries, but all kinds of films and videos—to instill "patterns of thought and feeling" in audiences. Psychologists, educators, journalists, political and religious leaders, and concerned citizens ask: What are films teaching us about our new world? What values are they inculcating? How are they affecting our behavior? (See chapters 7 and 14 for more discussion of how films influence and manipulate values, attitudes, and behavior.)

a

b

Figure 13.3
Dziga Vertov depicts everyday occurrences as the camera perceives them in THE MAN WITH A MOVIE CAMERA. (*a*) Special lenses are among the camera features he demonstrates in this "cinegraphic" film. (*b*) Vertov shows frequent, sometimes amusing, glimpses of the camera operator at work. (*c*) The superimposed image of the camera lens and a human eye perfectly demonstrates and symbolizes the Kino-Eye principle. (*d*) Vertov includes a basic demonstration of film editing in the film.

Educating the Public *About* Films

Many films educate the public *about* films and filmmaking. Documentaries and television specials on movies or moviemakers often present sophisticated information and background about cinema. Short, behind-the-scenes films like THE MAKING OF BUTCH CASSIDY AND THE SUNDANCE KID (1969), THE MAKING OF STAR WARS (1977), and GREAT MOVIE STUNTS: RAIDERS OF THE LOST ARK (1981), offer general film audiences practical lessons about filmmaking techniques. And many feature films themselves focus on the subject or the process of filmmaking.

Dziga Vertov: THE MAN WITH A MOVIE CAMERA

Sometimes a filmmaker sets out to educate people about films in a revolutionary way. Dziga Vertov, a director and film theorist in the Soviet Union who referred to himself as "a cinépoet," developed a theory called "Kino Eye" during the 1920s, which is best illustrated in THE MAN WITH A MOVIE CAMERA (1929). The basic premise of Vertov's theory is "the utilization of the camera as a cinema eye—more perfect than a human eye for purposes of research into the chaos of visual phenomena filling the universe" (82). For Vertov, a Kino-Eye production does not create theatrical scenes or literary stories on film but rather "writes something cinegraphic" with recorded shots and organizes film frames into "a ciné-thing" (102). Vertov was not at all interested in making fashionable commercial movies like those being produced in Hollywood and Europe in the twenties.

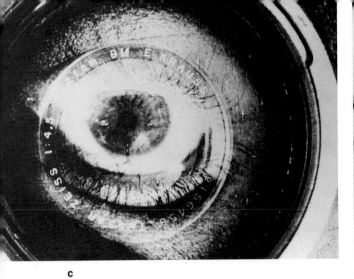

c   d

THE MAN WITH A MOVIE CAMERA is neither a story film nor a documentary. Instead, Vertov presents everyday occurrences as the camera perceives them in order to demonstrate cinematically his Kino-Eye theory. The camera itself is the star of the film. Vertov introduces it to the audience in a **split-screen shot,** showing the camera in close-up on the bottom half of the screen and the operator setting it on a tripod in the top half. He illustrates how the camera works by comparing basic camera functions, like **focusing** and **irising,** with the workings of the human eye. For example, to demonstrate the physical similarity between an eyelid and the camera **shutter,** he juxtaposes a close-up of a woman blinking and a shot of the camera shutter opening and closing. Vertov also demonstrates **panning** and **tracking, slow motion** and **fast motion, freeze-frame shots** and split-screen shots, and special lenses (fig. 13.3*a*). He makes us aware of the camera's presence throughout the film and frequently shows glimpses of the camera operator at work (fig. 13.3*b*), sometimes unexpectedly reflected in a storefront or in the camera lens itself. Finally, Vertov regularly **superimposes** the camera lens and a human eye throughout the film (fig. 13.3*c*), an image that perfectly demonstrates and symbolizes his Kino-Eye principle.

After he introduces the camera in the split-screen shot at the beginning, Vertov shows a movie theater where a screening is about to begin. The projector is set up, the doors open, and spectators file into their seats. The lights fade and a movie begins on the theater screen: motionless images of a sleeping woman, vacant streets, store mannequins, window displays, shut-down machines. The first movement on the screen is an automobile slowly winding through the streets. A man with a movie camera and tripod steps into the car and sets off to photograph the city coming to life. The sleeping woman awakens; the streets fill with people and vehicles; factories, offices, and businesses start up their work; and a flurry of activity gradually fills the screen. Thus, even with the film's visual content—sleeping images that awaken to activity, static images that become kinetic—Vertov highlights an essential characteristic of the movie camera: its capacity to reproduce *motion* pictures. And with the film-within-a-film structure, he reminds us from the outset that, like the audience filing into the theater, we too are witnessing a "cinegraphic" event: the camera's perception of everyday experiences.

Near the end of THE MAN WITH A MOVIE CAMERA, the camera gives a solo performance. In a brief **animated** sequence, the camera mounts itself on the tripod and runs through the mechanics of focusing, panning, tilting, etc. Then Vertov changes the scene back to the movie theater depicted at the beginning and concludes the film-within-a-film with images that move and change at a frantic pace. Masses of people and vehicles scurry in fast motion across the screen as the rhythm of the montage accelerates. Some shots from the beginning are repeated, but greatly speeded up. Like the finale of a fireworks display, the screen bursts with movement and activity. In the final shot of the film Vertov superimposes the camera eye and the human eye one last time and lets the camera iris out.

Vertov also includes basic lessons about film editing in THE MAN WITH A MOVIE CAMERA. In one vignette, for example, the cameraman photographs a group of people in a horse-drawn carriage from an open automobile traveling beside it. The scene alternates long shots (both the carriage and the car are in the frame) with closer shots from the cameraman's point of view (only the carriage is in the frame). In other words, we see the man shooting film as well as the film he shoots. About midway through the scene, Vertov interrupts these traveling shots with sequences, inserted like parenthetical comments in a written text, which illustrate principles and techniques of film editing. Each insert opens with a medium-to-close shot of one of the carriage group—a lady with a parasol or the horse pulling the carriage—and freezes that subject in the frame. Next, Vertov shows the freeze-frame shot as a strip of film on an editing table where an editor cuts it apart from the next shot (fig. 13.3*d*). To close each insert Vertov repeats the freeze-frame shot and activates it, so the action of the carriage ride resumes where it left off earlier.

What does Vertov teach us about the editing process in this scene? How does he make us look at this carriage ride?

a

In this brief scene with the carriage Vertov identifies the basic elements of cinematic language—the single **frame** and the **shot**—and demonstrates how connecting individual shots creates continuous action on the screen. He shows a film editor at work and illustrates the rudiments of film cutting. By focusing our attention on the editing process, Vertov makes us look at an ordinary carriage ride *cinematically*. And, as with the workings of the movie camera, he makes us more aware of **montage** and how it functions in movies.

Michael Snow: WAVELENGTH

In the tradition of Dziga Vertov, avant-garde filmmakers sometimes create films that challenge conventional ways of perceiving and understanding movies. Bruce Conner, for example, in a short film appropriately entitled A MOVIE (1958), examines movie content as assiduously as Vertov examined movie technique. Composed entirely of **archive footage** excerpted from newsreels, documentaries, and commercial films, A MOVIE is a collage of generic movie scenes: cowboys chasing Indians, race cars crashing in flames, airplanes dropping bombs, a diver exploring a sunken hull, etc. But the way Conner juxtaposes these scenes and synchronizes them with the music on the sound track makes us consider them in a new light and question our usual reactions to such movie images.

Other avant-garde filmmakers experiment more radically with cinematic form and structure. Michael Snow shot a forty-five-minute film entitled WAVELENGTH (1967), in which the camera gradually **zooms in** to a picture on a wall (fig. 13.4). WAVELENGTH is frequently

b

Figure 13.4
(*a*) A still and (*b*) a film strip from Michael Snow's WAVELENGTH, which employs static images to suggest how we perceive and know reality.

cited as an example of **structuralist** cinema, a style of filmmaking that employs basically static images to suggest how we perceive and know reality, allowing film structure to determine, rather than conform to, film content. Snow describes WAVELENGTH in very specific technical terms:

> The film [WAVELENGTH] is a continuous zoom which takes 45 minutes to go from its widest field to its smallest and final field. It was shot with a fixed camera from one end of an 80 foot loft, shooting the other end, a row of windows and the street. This, the setting, and the action which takes place there are cosmically equivalent. The room (and the Zoom) are interrupted by 4 human events including a death. The sound on these occasions is sync sound, music and speech, occurring simultaneously with an electronic sound, a sine-wave, which goes from its lowest (50 cycles per second) note to its highest (12,000 c.p.s) in 40 minutes. It is a total glissando while the film is a crescendo and a dispersed spectrum which attempts to utilize the gifts of both prophecy and memory which only film and music have to offer.
> (249)

For viewers accustomed to conventional fictional and documentary films, Michael Snow's cinematic statement in WAVELENGTH, and perhaps his verbal description of it as well, seem incomprehensible. What purpose can there be in a film without story, characters, and action? How does one respond to such methodical documentation of apparently random, static events in a studio loft?

Snow says that in WAVELENGTH he was "trying to make a definitive statement of pure Film space and time, a balancing of 'illusion' and 'fact', all about seeing. The space starts at the camera's (spectator's) eye, is in the air, then is on the screen, then is within the screen (the mind)" (249). Although this comment may still not satisfactorily explain WAVELENGTH, it shows that Michael Snow, like Dziga Vertov, is keenly interested in exploring the relationship between the camera eye and the human eye in his film and in examining the fundamental nature and function of cinema. Like Vertov, Snow is also educating film audiences—from a structuralist perspective—about how the camera perceives reality.

François Truffaut: DAY FOR NIGHT

Not all films about the nature and function of cinema are as theoretical as Dziga Vertov's THE MAN WITH A MOVIE CAMERA or Michael Snow's WAVELENGTH. François Truffaut's DAY FOR NIGHT (1972) is a narrative film that demonstrates from a film director's perspective how a commercial movie is made. We watch the director, played by Truffaut himself, work day by day through a shooting schedule, contending with financial and contractual delays, the emotional problems of leading actors and actresses, and even the accidental death of one of the principals. Sometimes the director, as if in an interview, describes his responsibilities or comments on them in **voice-over narration,** but mostly we just observe him at work. DAY FOR NIGHT depicts what happens on a shooting set and how the director works with actors and technicians during a shoot. Truffaut even features some of the less celebrated members of a film crew—the hairdresser, the wardrobe attendant, the script girl, the properties master, the stuntman, etc.—and shows how they contribute to a movie.

Like Vertov in THE MAN WITH A MOVIE CAMERA, Truffaut occasionally shows the viewer both how a scene is shot and how it appears on screen. DAY FOR NIGHT opens with a tense scene where a man is about to kill someone on a crowded street. Suddenly, the director yells "Cut!", and we find ourselves situated among the cast and crew filming the street scene (fig. 13.5*a*). The director calls for another **take;** then we follow the action again, but this time from behind the scene, observing the camera crew on a **studio crane** and hearing the director instruct the actors and extras on the set.

Also like Vertov, Truffaut demonstrates the mechanics of filmmaking throughout DAY FOR NIGHT. He shows camera, lighting, and sound crews at work and displays the equipment they use (fig. 13.5*b*). He presents a lesson in film cutting when the director and the editor review a stunt scene on a **moviola.** They study the footage, run it rapidly backwards and forwards, mark with a grease pencil where to cut it. We watch the editor fine-cut the scene and attach the sound track, as the frame counter ticks away and film piles up on the floor. This editing lesson is itself a polished montage, cut with lively music, which illustrates how a skillfully edited sequence looks when finished.

Unlike Vertov, however, Truffaut delves more deeply into the emotional and psychological energy that goes into moviemaking. In DAY FOR NIGHT the director has a recurring dream that depicts the tension and isolation he feels during the filming. Photographed in somber black and white, the dream contrasts visually with the breezy atmosphere and color photography of the rest of the film.

The director's dream recurs three times in DAY FOR NIGHT, and each time it advances further toward completion: A boy is walking alone at night on a deserted street. He carries a cane and taps on the sidewalk as he goes, looking back over his shoulder. The second time

a

Figure 13.5

DAY FOR NIGHT demonstrates from a film director's perspective how a commercial movie is made and depicts what happens on a shooting set. (*a*) The cast and crew filming a street scene. (*b*) The director with some of his crew and equipment.

the dream occurs, the boy walks further along, toward a metal gate that bars his way. As he approaches the gate, the dream fades to black, but there is a loud crash on the sound track. The third time, the director's dream completes itself, and all the earlier mysterious business falls into place. With his cane the boy reaches through the gate, which closes off the entrance to a cinema, pulls a bulletin board on rollers within reach, and then climbs on the gate to remove glossy promotional stills from CITIZEN KANE. At the end of the dream the boy has collected a stack of filched pictures.

Likewise, the director in DAY FOR NIGHT also succeeds in "collecting scenes" for his movie by overcoming the problems that arise during filming. For example, the leading lady, on the verge of a nervous

b

breakdown that may wreck the film, makes a dramatic, despairing statement that the director incorporates verbatim into the script, thus bolster-
ing both her self-esteem and a crucial scene in the movie. By such inspiration in the midst of adversity, the director, like the boy in the dream, piles
up a stack of memorable scenes. His film is finally "in the can" and,
though perhaps not a masterpiece like CITIZEN KANE, appears headed
for success. Therefore, by the end of DAY FOR NIGHT, Truffaut trium-
phantly fulfills the director's dream, both in sleep and in waking reality.
He also takes the viewer step-by-step through the experience of making a
commercial movie.

Conclusion

Thus, all kinds of films—fictional and nonfictional, commercial and avant-garde—can educate the public about what movies are, how they are made, and how they affect the viewer. Although they regard cinema from drastically different perspectives, films such as THE MAN WITH A MOVIE CAMERA, WAVELENGTH, and DAY FOR NIGHT ultimately help us better understand the complex role motion pictures play in today's world and their great power to educate as well as to entertain.

General Study Questions

1. To what extent have films been a part of your education up to now? Apart from film studies, how often were films shown in your classes at school? What kinds of films were they? For which courses were they especially valuable?
2. Name a film that has been important to your education. Using that film as a model, identify some characteristics of an effective educational film.
3. John Grierson says that "education is activist or it is nothing." Do you agree with this statement? Use examples from films you have seen to explain your position.
4. Name a film that made you think about the filmmaking process or about the nature and function of cinema. How did this film present movies differently than you were used to? Explain with examples.
5. Look back at the discussion of Fellini's 8½ in chapter 11. Compare and contrast 8½ with Truffaut's DAY FOR NIGHT as examples of movies about filmmaking. How does each film comment on the role of the director and the creativity he or she brings to filmmaking?

Additional Films for Study

COAL FACE (1936), dir. Alberto Cavalcanti
THE PLOW THAT BROKE THE PLAINS (1936), dir. Pare Lorentz
THE RIVER (1937), dir. Pare Lorentz
THE CITY (1939), dir. Ralph Steiner and Willard Van Dyke
THE FORGOTTEN VILLAGE (1941), dir. Herbert Kline and Alexander Hammid
THE JAMES DEAN STORY (1957), dir. Robert Altman
GLASS (1958), dir. Bert Haanstra
THE HUNTERS (1958), dir. John Marshall and Robert Gardner
DEAD BIRDS (1963), dir. John Gardner

WORLD WITHOUT SUN (1964), dir. Jacques Cousteau
RAMPARTS OF CLAY (1970), dir. Jean-Louis Bertucelli
THE SORROW AND THE PITY (1971), dir. Marcel Ophuls
THE HELLSTROM CHRONICLES (1971), dir. Walon Green
RIVERS OF SAND (1974), dir. John Gardner
AMERICA AT THE MOVIES (1976), prod. George Stevens, Jr.
THE NILE (1979), dir. Jacques Cousteau
GENOCIDE (1981), dir. Arnold Schwartzman
THE LAST EPIDEMIC (1981), dir. Eric and Ian Thiermann
THE ATOMIC CAFE (1982), dir. Kevin Rafferty
HE MAKES ME FEEL LIKE DANCIN' (1983), dir. Emile Ardolino
BROKEN RAINBOW (1985), dir. Maria Florio and Victoria Mudd
INCAS REMEMBERED (1986), dir. Peter Jarvis
SWIMMING TO CAMBODIA (1987), dir. Jonathan Demme
THE LAST EMPEROR (1987), dir. Bernardo Bertolucci

Further Reading

Allen, Don. *Truffaut*. New York: Viking, 1974.

Battcock, Gregory, ed. *The New American Cinema: A Critical Anthology*. New York: E.P. Dutton, 1967.

Beveridge, James. *John Grierson: Film Master*. New York: Macmillan, 1978.

Curtis, David. *Experimental Cinema*. New York: Universal Books, 1971.

Feldman, Seth R. *The Evolution of Style in the Early Works of Dziga Vertov*. New York: Arno Press, 1977.

Geduld, Harry M., ed. *Film Makers on Film Making*. Bloomington: Indiana University Press, 1967.

Grierson, John. *Grierson on Documentary*. Edited by Forsyth Hardy. New York: Praeger, 1971.

Low, Rachel. *The History of British Film, 1929–1939: Documentary and Educational Films of the 1930s*. London: George Allen & Unwin, 1979.

————. *The History of British Film, 1929-1939: Films of Comment and Persuasion of the 1930s*. London: George Allen & Unwin, 1979.

Manvell, Roger, ed. *Experiment in the Film*. London: Gray Walls Press, 1949.

Renan, Sheldon. *Introduction to the American Underground Film*. New York: E.P. Dutton, 1967.

Sitney, P. Adams, ed. *Film Culture Reader*. New York: Praeger, 1970.

————. *Visionary Film: The American Avant-Garde*. New York: Oxford University Press, 1974.

Stauffacher, Frank, ed. *Art in Cinema*. New York: Arno Press, 1969.

Truffaut, François. *The Films in My Life*. New York: Simon and Schuster, 1979.

Tyler, Parker. *Underground Film: A Critical History*. New York: Grove Press, 1969.

Youngblood, Gene. *Expanded Cinema*. New York: E.P. Dutton, 1970.

Works Cited

Barsam, Richard Meran. *Nonfiction Film: A Critical History.* New York: E.P. Dutton & Co., 1973.

Bluestone, George. *Novels into Film.* Berkeley: University of California Press, 1973.

Grierson, John. *Grierson on Documentary.* Edited by Forsyth Hardy. London: Collins Press, 1946.

Snow, Michael. Quoted in *Canyon Cinema, Catalogue 5,* 249–50. San Francisco: Canyon Cinema, 1982.

Vertov, Dziga. "Kinoks-Revolution." In *Film Makers on Film Making,* edited by Harry M. Geduld, 79–105. Bloomington: Indiana University Press, 1967.

Despite John Grierson's contention that the proper end of educational film is propagandistic—that is, to direct public thought and feeling toward what is best for the whole community—the word *propaganda* today carries strong negative connotations. It suggests a blatant manipulation of emotions that undermines rationality and provokes mass reactions. We tend to believe that education opens minds, while propaganda closes them. Yet many people who are quick to condemn the propaganda of groups that threaten their beliefs fail to recognize their own group's propaganda. Most Americans, for instance, would not consider films that spread American values to be propagandistic, even though such films may undermine the ideals other societies believe in.

What is film propaganda? How does it work? How can we recognize and see through propaganda when we encounter it?

The first task is to define film propaganda. Paul Rotha distinguishes between *indirect* and *direct* propaganda—that is, between a film "which wields influence by reason of its incidental *background* propaganda" and a "*specifically designed* propaganda film, sponsored as an advertisement for some industry or policy" (7). T.H. Qualter offers a definition of propaganda that includes more about its methodology:

> Propaganda is thus defined as the deliberate attempt by some individual or group to form, control, or alter the attitudes of other groups by the use of the instruments of communication, with the intention that in any given situation the reaction of those so influenced will be that desired by the propagandist.
>
> (27)

Jacques Ellul emphasizes that modern propaganda is based on scientific analysis, especially from psychology and sociology, and that it addresses itself at once to the individual and to the masses. Ellul writes:

> The individual is of no interest to the propagandist; as an isolated unit he presents much too much resistance to external action. To be effective, propaganda cannot be concerned with detail, not only because to win men over one by one takes much too long, but also because to create certain convictions in an isolated individual is much too difficult. Propaganda ceases where simple dialogue begins . . . . Conversely, propaganda does not aim simply at the mass, the crowd. A propaganda that functioned only where individuals are gathered together would be incomplete and insufficient. Also, any propaganda aimed only at groups as such. . . would be an abstract propaganda that likewise would have no effectiveness. Modern propaganda reaches individuals enclosed in the mass as participants in that mass, yet it also aims at a crowd, but only as a body composed of individuals.
>
> (3)

How Do Films Inform, Persuade, and Indoctrinate?

The propagandist, therefore, reduces individuals to an average and addresses messages to that average while maintaining the impression of individuality.

Finally, Ellul stresses that to be effective, modern propaganda must be total, utilizing every available communication medium to its best advantage. He says:

> Propaganda tries to surround man by all possible routes, in the realm of feelings as well as ideas, by playing on his will or on his needs, through his conscious and his unconscious, assailing him in both his private and his public life. It furnishes him with a complete system for explaining the world, and provides immediate incentives to action.
> (6)

Robert Vas reiterates this last point. "The real propaganda film," he says, "can't stand half-measures. It cannot really afford to let us think, and is consequently a totalitarian form of expression. After the final fadeout we are supposed to go straight into action, to seize the nearest spade and begin to dig. . ." (10).

This chapter examines three classic films that were specifically produced as propaganda and have been especially successful at it: Sergei Eisenstein's THE BATTLESHIP POTEMKIN, Leni Riefenstahl's TRIUMPH OF THE WILL, and Frank Capra's PRELUDE TO WAR. These films are radically different from one another in the messages they impart as well as in the format, visual style, and cinematic techniques they employ to convey their messages; but together they effectively illustrate the essential characteristics of film propaganda.

Sergei Eisenstein:
THE BATTLESHIP POTEMKIN

Sergei Eisenstein's THE BATTLESHIP POTEMKIN (1925) is a landmark in cinema history and one of the most renowned propaganda films ever made. The film is the culmination of systematic political propaganda in the Soviet Union after the 1917 Bolshevik Revolution. Vladimir Ilich Lenin and the leaders of the revolution recognized that cinema was the most mobile, flexible, and reliable means to communicate revolutionary ideology across the vast Russian lands where 150 million people, most of them illiterate, spoke more than one hundred different languages. "The cinema," proclaimed Lenin, "is for us the most important of the arts." Consequently, cinema in the Soviet Union after the revolution geared itself toward political indoctrination and developed a new kind of film, called the *agitka*, expressly for political agitation and propaganda, or "agit-prop." When the Soviet film industry was nationalized in 1919, the State Film School in Moscow was established (the first school of its kind in the world to train film actors and technicians), primarily to prepare filmmakers to make agit-prop.

Commissioned to commemorate the twentieth anniversary of an unsuccessful revolution against Czarism in 1905, POTEMKIN recreates a mutiny that occurred during that revolution when an officer on the battleship *Potemkin* shot a deckhand who complained about maggots in the meat and was in turn shot and thrown overboard by rebellious sailors. A seaman named Matyushenko led the mutineers, who seized weapons from the ship's armory, killed the captain and several officers, and flung the rest of them alive into the sea. These historical events are dramatically reconstructed in POTEMKIN's first two parts, "Men and Maggots" and "Drama on the Quarter Deck."

POTEMKIN's fourth part, "The Odessa Steps," contains the film's *tour de force*, one of the most admired and studied sequences of all time: a scene where Cossacks massacre a crowd of citizens who gather on the steps overlooking the Odessa harbor to welcome the *Potemkin*. Eisenstein was reportedly so fascinated by these 240 magnificent steps (twelve flights of twenty steps each, twenty-five yards wide, with broad landings between flights) and the cinematic possibilities they offered that he incorporated them as the centerpiece of his film.

Let us examine the Odessa Steps Sequence as an example of film propaganda. How does Eisenstein attempt to form, control, or alter the attitudes of the audience with this depiction of the massacre on the Odessa Steps? How does he use the incident to impress political ideology?

Historical Adaptation

Eisenstein's depiction of the massacre on the Odessa Steps is based on historical events. According to historian Richard A. Hough's *The Potemkin Mutiny*, workers had paralyzed the city of Odessa with a general strike the day before the *Potemkin* sailed into port, and violent demonstrations had taken place in which workers fought with police and Cossacks. When the *Potemkin* arrived, the workers thought at first that the battleship had been sent to enforce order; but when they learned of the mutiny on board, they became bolder in their fight, believing that the ship's tremendous firepower would back them. In the meantime, the Czar telegraphed military leaders in Odessa that a state of war was in effect in the city and placed it under martial law. Shortly after midday on June 28, 1905, General Kokhanov dispatched one hundred Cossacks against a mass of demonstrators assembled on the Odessa Steps (Hough 75–78). Hough's historical account of the attack reads like a **film treatment** of Eisenstein's massacre scene:

> At the head of the steps a party of Cossacks had dismounted and formed up with rifles raised. At the command of an officer, they aimed the barrels and fired point-blank into the panic-stricken, fleeing crowd of men and women, drew back the bolts of their rifles, descended three steps, crouched on one knee—all in perfect unison—and fired again.
>
> The dead and the wounded rolled down step by step, some by their posture gathering speed and tripping and carrying the living with them, others sprawling limp and inert across the steps. The weight and momentum of descent increased as the line of Cossacks advanced, rolling up the great stair carpet of humanity; squatting, firing, striding down three more steps over limbs and torsos, firing again; pausing to fix bayonets, then pacing down step by step in their high black boots, thrusting the long blades into the crowd.
>
> The second party of Cossacks galloped along the quayside and caught the delayed recoil from the rear of the crowd at the base of the steps. The alarm was still fresh and uncertain when the clatter of hoofs on the cobbles caused the crowd to turn. At once it was clear that this was no simple dispersal of a demonstration: this was a killing operation. Sabers were raised high and came slashing down as contact was made with the first of the fleeing crowd. Men, women, a youth or two, fell to the cobbles, sometimes screaming. From above, the volleys of gunshots confirmed the reality: this was a massacre.
>
> (78–79)

Eisenstein's Odessa Steps Sequence, however, is not an exact historical reenactment of the massacre that took place there. For instance, the people on the steps are not depicted as demonstrators but as peaceful citizens, dressed for a promenade, who have turned out to welcome the *Potemkin* to their city. Among them are small children, respected elders, and a young mother with a child in a baby carriage. The people on the steps are orderly and decorous, smiling and waving hand-kerchiefs at the sailors on the battleship, before the Cossacks appear.

More importantly, Eisenstein freely adapts some of the historical events that took place in Odessa. For example, at the end of the scene, the *Potemkin*'s turret guns bombard the Czarist military head-quarters in the Odessa theater, apparently an immediate devastating retaliation for the atrocities committed on the steps. But according to Richard Hough's historical account, the shelling occurred about thirty hours later, on the evening of the day after the massacre, and only after much wavering among the mutineers. One of the *Potemkin*'s six-inch guns fired two salvos (after three blank warning shots) at the Odessa theater, where a group of senior military officers were meeting. Both salvos fell long, damaging buildings near the theater. The headquarters was not hit, and no one was hurt (Hough 80–82). Thus, it is apparent that, although Eisenstein is at times meticulous about historical detail in POTEMKIN, he is also capable of disregarding or distorting historical accuracy when it interferes with the film's ideology.

Imagery

Eisenstein does not feature the traditional individual hero or heroine in the Odessa Steps scene but presents people as an "aggregate protagonist" (Cook 147). None of them is more valuable or expendable than another. Whether they survive or die, together they face the horror of the Cossacks' sudden attack. The villains are even less individualized. Until the end of the scene, not one Cossack is shown in close-up or from a camera angle that reveals his face. The soldiers are so many white caps and tunics moving in unison down the steps, so many ranks of shadows cast across the landings. Employing **synecdoche** (a figurative device whereby a part is used to indicate the whole), Eisenstein sometimes depicts the Cossacks by isolating their boots or their rifles in the frame. At the end of the sequence we see just one grimacing Cossack's face, menacingly photographed in a **low-angle shot,** a face that embodies all the cruelty of this killing operation. (See chapter 4.)

In an essay entitled "The Structure of the Film" Eisenstein discusses the pathos POTEMKIN evokes, one of the features of the film most remarked upon when it was released. Eisenstein defines pathos as "whatever 'sends' the spectator into ecstasy," (literally, from the Latin *ex stasis*, meaning "standing out of oneself")—whatever moves one "to leave oneself, to remove oneself from one's customary equilibrium and condition, and to pass over into a new condition" (Eisenstein 167). In the Odessa Steps Sequence, Eisenstein tries to move viewers out of themselves and into the condition of the ordinary people who are, collectively, the victim of the Cossack attack. The audience identifies with the group, not with particular individuals, and feels compelled to seek collective redress for the atrocities witnessed. At the same time Eisenstein depicts the Czarist oppressors as a faceless, mechanical organization, bereft of human compassion, which evokes unmitigated rage and desire for revenge.

To appreciate the subtle effects of Eisenstein's collective psychology on the viewer, contrast POTEMKIN with films like DEATH WISH or RAMBO in which a highly individualized hero single-handedly avenges atrocities perpetrated by specific villains or criminals. Rambo's struggle is a superhuman personal victory against a corrupt political system represented by one amoral man. (For more discussion of RAMBO: FIRST BLOOD PART II, see chapter 7.) In the end, Rambo's personal heroics barely affect that system, but when the guns of the *Potemkin* level the Czarist military headquarters, it is a great collective victory for all the masses oppressed by the Czar and a big step toward overthrowing his power. Thus, Eisenstein's depiction of victims and oppressors in the Odessa Steps Sequence reinforces the revolution's ideals that the common welfare supercedes the welfare of the individual and that collective action is the answer to political and economic oppression. The pathos Eisenstein creates in this scene engages the viewer as an emotional participant in that common welfare and collective action.

Editing

One of Eisenstein's most important contributions to film theory is his concept of "dialectical montage." Karl Marx described history as a dynamic process, or a dialectic, in which continual conflict between a force (the *thesis*, in Marxist terms) and an opposing counterforce (the *antithesis*) produce results (a *synthesis*) greater than and different from the two original forces. Consistent with the principles of the Marxist dialectic, Eisenstein conceived of film editing as a dialectical process in which images "in collision" produce meaning greater than and different from the sum of their parts. (See the discussion of dynamic montage in chapter 4.) To illustrate the basic mechanics of dialectical montage, Eisenstein described how Chinese ideograms combine separate hieroglyphs to create new meaning:

> For example: the picture for water and the picture of an eye signifies "to weep"; the picture of an ear near the drawing of a door = "to listen";
> a dog + a mouth = "to bark";
> a mouth + a child = "to scream";
> a mouth + a bird = "to sing";
> a knife + a heart = "sorrow," and so on.

(30)

It is important to note here that the combination of *eye* plus *water* does not create *tears* but *to weep*; a *mouth* plus a *bird* does not equal a *bird beak* but *to sing*. As Eisenstein points out, "by the combination of two 'depictables' is achieved the representation of something that is graphically undepictable" (30). Two combined hieroglyphs of objects yield not another object but a concept, an abstraction, associated with those objects. This is montage, says Eisenstein. "It is exactly what we do in the cinema, combining shots that are *depictive*, single in meaning, neutral in content—into *intellectual* contexts and series" (30).

a

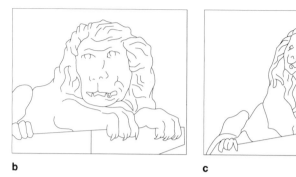

b

c

Figure 14.1
Line drawings from a scene in POTEMKIN where Sergei Eisenstein cuts together shots of three separate stone lions to create the illusion of a living lion arising.

One striking example of dialectical montage in POTEMKIN is a three-shot series of sculptured lions (fig. 14.1) which Eisenstein inserts after the *Potemkin* bombards the Czar's military leaders in the Odessa theater. When these stationary shots of three separate statues are cut together, they create the illusion of a living lion awakened by the din of the shelling.

Two of the most stirring examples of Eisenstein's dialectical montage in POTEMKIN occur at the climax of the Odessa Steps Sequence: ". . . the young Cossack savagely swinging his saber collides with the bloodied face of the woman with the pince-nez to produce the synthesis: rage [fig. 14.2]. Then, the guns of the *Potemkin* collide with the generals' headquarters to produce the ultimate synthesis: collective action" (Cook 175). The visual and psychological intensity of these syntheses clearly illustrates how Eisenstein's montage in the Odessa Steps scene reinforces the political messages POTEMKIN delivers: public rage at the oppression of the masses and collective action as the antidote to it. The editing in this scene, therefore, effectively demonstrates how Eisenstein, with his dialectical montage, uses Marxist principles to propagate Marxist ideology.

Leni Riefenstahl: TRIUMPH OF THE WILL

Many film critics regard TRIUMPH OF THE WILL (1935) as the most perfectly crafted propaganda film ever made. According to the opening titles, the film is "The Document of the Reich Party Rally [in] 1934 at Nuremberg," produced "by order of the Führer" and "fashioned by Leni Riefenstahl." But, in fact, TRIUMPH OF THE WILL is a blatant propaganda film that glorifies Nazism and its leader, Adolf Hitler. Hitler himself coined the film's title. He also gave Riefenstahl his full cooperation and an almost unlimited budget. According to her own account in *Behind the Scenes of the Party Rally Film*, Riefenstahl had 120 personnel at her

How Do Films Inform, Persuade, and Indoctrinate?

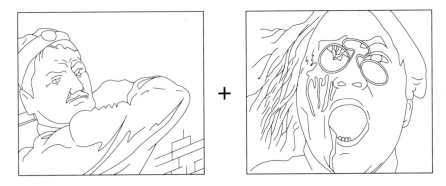

+ ⟨image⟩ = RAGE

Figure 14.2
An example of
Eisenstein's dialectical
montage: The Cossack
swinging his saber
collides with the woman's
bloodied face to produce
"rage."

disposal for filming TRIUMPH OF THE WILL, including sixteen camera
operators and sixteen assistant operators; thirty cameras; four complete
sound equipment trucks; numerous lights; twenty-two chauffeur-driven
cars; and an airplane and an airship for **aerial shots.** She had twenty-nine
newsreel cameramen, dressed inconspicuously in SA uniforms, to back up
the regular camera operators, and thirty-seven genuine SA and SS officers to maintain order. In six days Riefenstahl's film crews shot more than
sixty hours of footage which, over an eight-month period, she edited into a
two-hour film.

In *Behind the Scenes of the Party Rally Film*, Riefenstahl
calls TRIUMPH OF THE WILL "a heroic film of facts." And in an
interview in 1965 in which she tried to disassociate herself from Nazism,
she said:

> But you will notice, if you see the film [TRIUMPH OF THE
> WILL] today, that it doesn't contain a single reconstructed scene.
> Everything in it is real. And there is no tendentious commentary for the
> simple reason that the film has no commentary at all. It is history. A
> purely historical film.
>
> (In Leiser 138)

These statements certainly need clarification. TRIUMPH OF THE WILL
is by no means a documentary "film of facts," and the reality it depicts is
not history as most of us understand it. The Nuremberg rally was, in fact,
largely staged for the camera. Some scenes were rehearsed beforehand;
nothing was left to chance. Riefenstahl herself wrote that "the preparations for the party congress were made in concert with the preparations
for the camera work" (in Sadoul 383). The city of Nuremberg was at the
director's disposal. Bridges and towers were constructed and tracks laid
down to secure the best vantage points for cameras photographing the
Nazi ceremonies and demonstrations in the city. Such preparations for
shooting, while routine for studio films, are unusual for documentaries.

"The result," as historian David Welch points out, "was a transfiguration of reality which purported to assume the character of an authentic documentary" (148).

Imagery

One reason for TRIUMPH OF THE WILL's success as propaganda is Riefenstahl's careful manipulation of film images. In the opening scene, for example, she introduces images suggesting that Hitler is a godlike savior of his people: An airplane descends through the clouds toward Nuremberg and casts its shadow on the city below, where ranks of party faithful are marching in the streets. A blatantly chauvinistic commentary from program notes that accompanied TRIUMPH OF THE WILL at its premiere in Berlin suggests the impression this scene was expected to make on the audience:

> Sunlight floods the land of the Germans. Clouds gather into clusters, rise up to form gigantic mountains surrounded by silver and golden rays, they subside, flow, scatter. . . like a fantastic eagle, an aeroplane glides through the air. Spreading its wings wide, it plunges forward, its propellers grinding themselves howling into the wind. It is the aeroplane that carries the Führer towards the city, in which the great, proud, heart-stirring spectacle of a new Germany will be consummated. Onwards rushes the mighty machine. The roaring rhythm of the motor shouts into the wind: 'Nuremberg . . . Nuremberg . . . Nuremberg . . .'
>
> Far below the city is radiating. Boundless masses of people stare into the sky. There!—as close as the clouds, on the sun-golden firmament, the speeding shadow becomes larger, approaches. Thundering, it circles over the city. An aeroplane. *The* aeroplane! The Führer is arriving.
>
> (Program notes 149–50)

How do the images in this opening scene suggest that Hitler is godlike? How does Riefenstahl combine them for the greatest emotional impact on the audience?

White billowy clouds, like gigantic mountains, are the first image in the scene, viewed from inside the cockpit of the führer's airplane. But the clouds scatter, and the sun breaks through as the führer's presence brightens the heavens. Hitler comes to his people like a god out of the sky and, like the shadow of his plane gliding over the city, watches over them from above.

The airplane itself is a very important image in the opening scene. The program notes compare the plane to "a fantastic eagle," an association with the eagle symbolizing the German Reich, which is the first image to appear in TRIUMPH OF THE WILL—even before the opening titles. But the airplane is also a symbol of the new German technology, a mighty machine roaring and thundering over the land. The airplane, therefore, associates Hitler both with Germany's glorious heritage and with its mighty technology.

The third important image in the opening scene is the "boundless masses of people." The aerial shots of the party faithful marching in the streets of Nuremberg, under the führer's watchful eye, establish from the outset Hitler's dominion over masses of devoted followers. Sharing his bird's-eye view of them, the viewer senses the führer's power over the people in the streets below.

Thus, although Hitler does not appear in person in the opening scene, the viewer is keenly aware of his presence as the airplane breaks through the clouds over Nuremberg. A powerful leader is arriving; a savior of the people is descending from the heavens to consummate a great ritual among his faithful followers.

It is no accident that a *rally film* is the format Hitler and Riefenstahl chose for TRIUMPH OF THE WILL and that scene after scene depicts ritualized mass meetings and demonstrations. Hitler wrote in *Mein Kampf*:

> Mass assemblies are necessary for the reason that, in attending them, the individual. . . now begins to feel isolated and in fear of being left alone as he acquires for the first time the picture of a great community which has a strengthening and encouraging effect on most people. . . . And only a mass demonstration can impress upon him the greatness of this community. . . while seeking his way, he is gripped by the force of mass suggestion.
> (Quoted in Welch 148–49)

One measure of the führer's greatness in TRIUMPH OF THE WILL is the ever-increasing size of the masses he appears to control. The crowd gathered at the Nuremberg airfield to welcome Hitler is negligible compared with the gathering of 52,000 workers from the German Labor Force who salute him a few scenes later. That rally, in turn, is dwarfed by an outdoor memorial service where a vast assembly, in ranks that extend beyond the edges of the frame, stands at attention while Hitler lays a wreath to honor those who died for the party (fig. 14.3). An **extreme long shot** showing the führer amidst this boundless sea of party faithful provides overwhelming visual testimony to his power over the masses. Finally, near the end of TRIUMPH OF THE WILL, as Hitler salutes endless ranks of goose-stepping Nazi elite who parade past him, the führer's image as a powerful leader is complete. Erwin Leiser observes: "After TRIUMPH OF THE WILL there was no need to make

Figure 14.3
One measure of Hitler's greatness in TRIUMPH OF THE WILL is the ever-increasing size of the masses he appears to control.

another film about Hitler, and none was commissioned. He had been seen once and for all the way he wanted to be seen; and no actor was ever asked to represent him" (29).

Editing

A second important reason for TRIUMPH OF THE WILL's success as propaganda is Riefenstahl's editing. With so many camera crews at her disposal, Riefenstahl was able to photograph each event at the Nuremberg rally from many vantage points and in great detail. She had a tremendous amount of material to select from and could piece together the most visually interesting and psychologically stimulating footage. In editing the

How Do Films Inform, Persuade, and Indoctrinate?

film, Riefenstahl strove to construct compact scenes that build up and release emotional excitement, gradually increasing the level of excitement as the film progressed. Consider, for example, the following twenty-shot sequence in which Riefenstahl introduces Hitler when his plane lands at Nuremberg. The average length of the shots in this sequence is less than three seconds; the entire sequence runs less than one minute.

1. LS (establishing shot). The camera pans left along the crowd of people awaiting Hitler at the airfield. (The sound track features stirring background music mixed with the crowd's cheering, which continues throughout the sequence.)

2. LS. The camera tracks the airplane from behind as it lands, moving from right to left across the frame.

3. MS. Slight L/A. The camera pans left along the crowd. The people, facing toward frame right, raise their arms in the Nazi salute.

4. XLS. H/A. The crowd in f/g at the bottom of the frame and the airplane in b/g taxiing into the frame from the right.

5. MLS. L/A. A crowd of children in the bleachers, saluting away from the camera toward frame left.

6. MLS (detail). The nose of the airplane moving left to right across the frame.

7. MS. Children in the bleachers, saluting toward frame right.

8. MLS (detail). The camera focuses on one wheel of the airplane and pans with it from left to right across the frame.

9. MS. Officers (out of focus) in f/g running to meet the airplane in b/g. The airplane wheel is detailed on the right side of the frame.

10. MS (detail). The wheel of the airplane moving from right to left across the frame.

11. MS. H/A. The crowd of people saluting away from the camera toward frame left.

12. MLS. Officer opens the door of the airplane, which is dark inside.

13. MS. People in the bleachers saluting toward frame right.

14. MLS. Hitler, on the right side of the frame, emerges from the airplane and salutes.

15. XLS (same position as shot #4). The cheering crowd in f/g and the airplane in b/g with Hitler emerging.

16. MCU. The crowd, facing away from the camera, salutes toward frame right and surges forward in that direction.

17. MLS. Two more men emerge from the plane. The second one is Joseph Goebbels, the Nazi minister of propaganda.

How Do Films Inform, Persuade, and Indoctrinate?

18. MS. Two smiling young women in the crowd are featured in f/g, saluting toward frame right.

19. MCU. Hitler, smiling, looks to frame left.

20. MS (shot #18 continued). The camera pans left to reveal a third woman, who is pointing to the right.

Before reading the comments that follow, take a few moments to note your observations about the editing in these twenty shots. How does Riefenstahl create emotional excitement here? How does she set up Hitler's appearance in shot #14?

In this sequence, Riefenstahl stirs the viewer's emotions, in less than one minute, by presenting a rapid succession of visually and psychologically exciting images that build up to Hitler's appearance in shot #14. In the opening shots she introduces the crowd and the airplane, the two emotionally charged images in the scene, and connects them in shot #4 when the airplane rolls into the frame where the crowd is gathered. Thereafter, the crowd's excitement escalates as the plane taxies nearer. The people cheer and salute, their arms outstretched toward the führer's airplane. Using a **telephoto lens**, Riefenstahl creates the impression that the airplane is physically very close to the viewer. The camera isolates first the nose of the plane (shot #6) and then one wheel (shots #8 through #10) rolling steadily closer. At last, in shot #12 the plane stops and the door opens. But Riefenstahl makes us wait yet to see the führer; she cuts back once more to the ecstatic crowd in the bleachers. When Hitler steps out of the airplane, the emotional excitement in the sequence peaks, and the tension is released in shot #16 as the crowd surges forward. But again Riefenstahl makes us wait—until shot #19—for a clear, unhurried look at the führer.

The direction in which Hitler's airplane is taxiing in the sequence seems confusing. In shot #4 the plane enters the frame from the right and travels left. But in shots #6 and #8 it moves across the frame in the opposite direction, from left to right. In shot #10 its direction is once again right to left. Why? Isn't changing the airplane's direction a flaw in the editing, a violation of basic visual continuity? Shouldn't the plane move consistently in one direction across the frame?

Looking more closely at the sequence, we see that the airplane's movement is not the only directional inconsistency. Sometimes, for instance, the crowd at the airfield is shown from the front, sometimes from behind; and the direction of bodies and arms within the frame changes from shot to shot. In shot #5 the children in the bleachers are leaning toward the left, but in shot #7 they are saluting toward the right. In shot #11 the crowd salutes to the left, but in shot #16 it surges toward the right. Finally, camera movements within the sequence seem at odds with one another. The camera tracks with the airplane from right to left in shot #2 but pans with it from left to right in shot #8; the camera pans left along the crowd in shot #3, while their bodies are strongly inclined to the right. Why does there seem to be so much visual confusion in this sequence?

The answer is partly that Riefenstahl, like Eisenstein in POTEMKIN, is creating tension by juxtaposing conflicting images on the screen. But intellectual montage is not what Riefenstahl is striving for; she wants to create *emotional* montage that will glorify Hitler's image. She wants to recreate for the viewer the excitement of the crowd at the airfield when the führer arrives—exuberant, contagious excitement that is unrestrained by logic or by ordinary perception of time and space. So the airplane seems at first distant (in shot #4), then very close (in shots #6, #8, and #10), then distant again (in shot #15); it seems to arrive from one direction and then from another. The viewer is situated in the midst of this ecstatic crowd, which stretches and surges, now left and now right, for a glimpse of the führer as he steps off the plane. All of this action unfolds in shots lasting only two or three seconds. Notice, however, that Riefenstahl juxtaposes bits of action from many angles to stimulate, not confuse, the viewer and that she carefully matches the shots in the sequence to focus the viewer's attention at every moment on what is most important in the frame. For example, the saluting crowd controls most of the directional changes in the sequence by pointing out where important visual information will appear on the screen in the next shot: The arms point to the right in shot #3, and Hitler's airplane rolls into the frame from the right in shot #4; they point to the left in shot #5, and the airplane moves from left to right in shot #6; they point to the right in shot #13, and Hitler disembarks on the right side of the frame in shot #14. Thus, by combining meticulously controlled doses of physical disorientation and mass hysteria, Riefenstahl makes the viewer feel just as ecstatic about Hitler's arrival as his fanatical supporters do.

Compared to the rest of the sequence, the final four shots seem quite low-keyed. Shot #17 of Goebbels stepping off the plane is anticlimactic after Hitler's appearance. And the last three shots are emotionally flat compared with the highly charged images earlier. Why does the sequence reach its climax in shot #16 rather than at the end?

In the last four shots of the sequence Riefenstahl deliberately pulls back from the emotional peak achieved in shot #16 and lets the excitement level ease down so that she can build it up again in the next scene. This is just the beginning of TRIUMPH OF THE WILL; there are nearly two hours of film yet to come. Riefenstahl must pace the audience's emotional energy, not exhaust it too quickly.

The final three shots of the sequence depict a more sub-
dued, congenial Hitler than we might expect after such a dramatic buildup.
Is this gentle-looking man the powerful savior of the German people?
Notice that Riefenstahl juxtaposes the smiling Hitler with three young
women in the crowd, the only time in the sequence when people in the
crowd are so individualized. Why? What does the director accomplish
with these three shots? Hitler and the two young women in shot #18 are cut
together to suggest eye contact between them—an **eyeline match** (see
chapter 4). Riefenstahl is intimating here that, despite his tremendous
power, Hitler is a modest, personable man who cares for the people he
leads. When Hitler smiles at the young women, each person viewing the
film also receives the führer's warm personal attention for a moment.
Thus, Riefenstahl gives each individual in the audience the "impression
that *he* is being looked at, that *he* is being addressed personally"—an
essential characteristic of modern propaganda, according to Jacques
Ellul (4).

To this day, Leni Riefenstahl's TRIUMPH OF THE WILL
remains a devastating example of film propaganda and a model of how
cinema can manipulate emotions. As Erwin Leiser points out, filmmakers
who wanted to mount a counterattack against Riefenstahl's film had to
acknowledge its effectiveness: "TRIUMPH OF THE WILL is repeatedly
quoted in anti-Nazi films as a representative example of the process of
transforming the individual into a soulless, anonymous part of the great
mass, blindly following their führer" (29).

Frank Capra: PRELUDE TO WAR

The tremendous effectiveness of TRIUMPH OF THE WILL and, in
general, the resources that Nazi Germany and its allies were devoting to
propaganda in World War II compelled the United States to produce its
own propaganda films.

> Propaganda and information were indeed sorely needed when
> the war began. After Pearl Harbor, the American authorities were faced
> with the tricky problem of curing the population of the after-effects of
> isolationism. A will to fight had to be fostered; the aims of the war needed
> clarifying; arguments had to be developed and anchored to generally
> accepted values. There was a need to instill solidarity with the allies and
> hatred for the enemy.
>
> (Furhammar 64)

Even before the United States became involved in the war, its film industry was making movies that tried to persuade Americans to support a fight against Germany. Charles Chaplin (THE GREAT DICTATOR), Anatole Litvak (CONFESSIONS OF A NAZI SPY), Alfred Hitchcock (FOREIGN CORRESPONDENT), and other Hollywood directors urged a tough stand against the Nazis. Documentary filmmakers like Joris Ivens (THE SPANISH EARTH) and Herbert Kline and Alexander Hammid (CRISIS and LIGHTS OUT IN EUROPE) reported on the spread of fascism and emphasized the moral responsibility of free nations to oppose it. After Pearl Harbor, the United States government established the Office of War Information (OWI) to produce films that would promote the American image at home and abroad, and the military itself went to work producing war propaganda films. Some of Hollywood's top directors—Frank Capra, John Ford, John Huston, Anatole Litvak, William Wyler, and others—served in the United States armed forces during World War II and worked on films that sustained the war effort. Walt Disney placed his staff and studio at the Army's disposal to make instructional propaganda films, and at the same time used his cartoon characters in **animated films** that satirized Hitler and the Nazis.

The best-known and most effective United States film propaganda during World War II was a series of seven films called WHY WE FIGHT, produced between 1942 and 1945 by Frank Capra. Capra was one of the most successful Hollywood directors in the 1930s. Three of his comedies—IT HAPPENED ONE NIGHT (1934), MR. DEEDS GOES TO TOWN (1936), and MR. SMITH GOES TO WASHINGTON (1939)—won Academy Awards and were among the most popular movies of the decade. (See chapter 8 for a discussion of IT HAPPENED ONE NIGHT.) During World War II, Capra was a major in the Army and was commissioned by the chief of staff, General George C. Marshall, "to make a series of documented, factual-information films" that would explain to civilians being inducted into the military "*why* we are fighting, and the *principles* for which we are fighting" (Capra 327). Capra supervised seven films, each about one hour long, which covered in rough chronological sequence the phases of World War II.

Although the WHY WE FIGHT films were primarily made by the Army for the Army, they became standard training films for the Navy, the Marine Corps, and the Coast Guard, and were also used in training the armed forces of Great Britain, Canada, Australia, and New Zealand. They were translated into French, Spanish, Portuguese, and Chinese, and were shown to armies of American allies in China, South

America, Africa, and Europe. Some of the films were also screened for the general public in the United States, Great Britain, and the Soviet Union (Capra 336).

Imagery

Frank Capra began the WHY WE FIGHT series realizing that TRIUMPH OF THE WILL was the propaganda film he had to match. In his autobiography, *The Name Above the Title*, Capra wrote:

> Shortly after General Marshall ordered me to make the WHY WE FIGHT films for our servicemen, I saw Leni Riefenstahl's terrifying motion picture, TRIUMPH OF THE WILL. . . . It was at once the glorification of war, the deification of Hitler, and the canonization of his apostles. Though panoplied with all the pomp and mystical trappings of a Wagnerian opera, its message was as blunt and brutal as a lead pipe: We, the Herrenvolk, are the new invincible gods!
>
> TRIUMPH OF THE WILL fired no gun, dropped no bombs. But as a psychological weapon aimed at destroying the will to resist, it was just as lethal. . . . I sat alone and pondered. How could I mount a counterattack against TRIUMPH OF THE WILL; keep alive *our* will to resist the master race?
>
> (328–29)

Capra needed one basic, powerful idea around which to organize his counterattack, "an idea from which *all* ideas flowed":

> Well, it was obvious to me that the Nazis of Germany, the warlords of Japan, and the Fascists of Italy were out to deliberately take over the free nations by force, so they could stamp out human freedom and establish their own world dictatorships. If that statement was the truth, free men everywhere would fight to the death against it.
>
> But how did *I* know that statement was true? Who proved it to *me*? Why the enemy *himself* proved it to me, in his acts, his books, his speeches, his films.
>
> That was the key idea I had been searching for. . . . Let the *enemy* prove to our soldiers the enormity of his cause—and the justness of ours.
>
> (330–31)

Capra's first order of business was to scour film archives, collecting footage from enemy films that he could twist into meanings contrary to those originally intended. Many sequences in the WHY WE FIGHT films were lifted straight from Leni Riefenstahl's TRIUMPH OF THE WILL and from German, Italian, and Japanese newsreels and documentaries (fig. 14.4). Putting the enemy's own propaganda to work against him became both the goal and the format of the WHY WE FIGHT films.

How Do Films Inform, Persuade, and Indoctrinate?

a

Figure 14.4
Putting the enemy's
propaganda to work
against him became both
the goal and the format of
PRELUDE TO WAR.
Frank Capra twisted
(*a*) Nazi and (*b*) Facist
newsreels and documen-
taries to show how
militaristic societies
turned individuals into "a
human herd."

b

The first WHY WE FIGHT film, PRELUDE TO WAR (1942), which Capra himself directed, is representative of the whole series. In it Capra sets down the format and style for all seven films and addresses the fundamental "why we fight" question behind the war. It is highly patriotic and plays on viewers' emotions in order to stir up support and enthusiasm for a committed struggle against the enemy. Since it was the first film of the series, PRELUDE TO WAR had to arouse viewer interest and convincingly establish the justness of the American cause. It had to emphasize the immediacy of the war and the dire consequences of a totalitarian victory.

At the beginning of PRELUDE TO WAR, a commentator poses the question, "Why are Americans on the march?" The question is answered visually with three sets of images showing Pearl Harbor, British cities burning, and a catalogue of countries invaded by the Axis powers. But Capra wants the film's audience—men and women in transition from civilian life to military service—to understand not only the immediate causes of the war but also the underlying principles for which they will be fighting. To illustrate these principles, Capra contrasts "the free world" and "the slave world," and shows the war as a struggle to the death between two mutually exclusive ways of life. The basic structure of PRELUDE TO WAR is to juxtapose images of these two worlds and the values they stand for. The free world is founded on religious principles and a firm belief in individual freedoms, like those outlined in the Declaration of Independence; it has produced "men of vision" who uphold human values—not only Washington, Jefferson, and Lincoln, but also Garibaldi, Lafayette, and Bolivar. The slave world, on the other hand, is a godless, militaristic society in which people must give up their rights as individual human beings and become part of a mass, "a human herd"; it has produced unscrupulous dictators—Hitler, Mussolini, Hirohito. Capra implies that it was inevitable that the slave world would "gang up on us" and try to destroy the free world we have built "only by a long and unceasing struggle." That is why we must fight. "It's us or them," says the commentator at the end of the film. "The chips are down."

Capra dramatizes the radical differences between the free world and the slave world with sharply contrasting images. For example, to stress the importance of religion in the free world, he focuses on the founders of four great world religions (Moses, Confucius, Jesus, and Mohammed), depicts contributions these religions have made to humankind, and shows close-ups of their holy books. These are settling,

How Do Films Inform, Persuade, and Indoctrinate?

reassuring images that reinforce for the audience a message that in the free world one can count on diversity and the right to choose freely what to believe and how to live. On the other hand, this is how Capra depicts religion in the slave world: People are kneeling and praying inside a church. Sunlight streams through a large, stained-glass window, and religious music plays on the sound track. The camera tilts up to an inscription on the wall, "I am the light of the world. He that followeth me shall not walk in darkness." The camera continues to tilt further up to an image of Jesus in the stained glass. The commentator says, "The word of God and the word of the Führer cannot be reconciled." A harsh voice answers back, "Then God must go!" A rock smashes through the stained-glass window, revealing a poster of Hitler behind it, inscribed "Heil Hitler!"

How do you imagine this scene affected American service-men and servicewomen in the 1940s? Clearly, it was meant to be very disturbing, suggesting religious desecration. The quiet religious music and the camera's steady upward movement, pausing at the inscription on the wall, create a peaceful mood and rhythm that are suddenly shattered when the rock crashes through the window and Hitler's image appears. The scene dramatizes how tenuous religious freedom is in Nazi Germany; but it also suggests how suddenly the slave world, if not checked, can shatter sacred institutions in the free world.

Contrasting images of ordinary people also figure signifi-cantly in PRELUDE TO WAR. The typical American, Mr. John Q. Public, is presented as the backbone of freedom. (The script consistently employs "we" and "our" when referring to the people of the free world and frequently includes patriotic phrases like "we the people" and "gov-ernment of the people.") At a particularly emotional moment, the com-mentator proclaims, "This isn't just a war, this is the common man's life-and-death struggle against those who would put him back into slavery. We lose it and we lose everything." Over a shot of children singing "Onward Christian Soldiers," the commentator states that the typical American "got a kick out of seeing his kids grow up." There follows a **montage** of shots of American children playing innocently, from which Capra cuts to shots of highly regimented German and Japanese children fanatically saluting and drilling, and Italian children in gas masks playing a war game. The commentator adds: "Yes. . . while their children were being trained to kill. . . John Q.'s kids were giving pennies to help them have life."

Narration

Unlike POTEMKIN and TRIUMPH OF THE WILL, PRELUDE TO WAR employs a **voice-over narrator** to complement the images on the screen and to reinforce their persuasive power. Eric Knight and Anthony Veiller, along with Capra, wrote the script for PRELUDE TO WAR; Walter Huston narrated it. They tailored the commentary to fit the images in the film; employed language that was simple, direct, and hard-hitting; and allowed plenty of time between statements for both the words and the images to sink in. Describing the leaders of the slave world, for example, the commentator explains that the war in Italy began when "an ambitious rabble rouser" came to power; in Japan it was "not one man but a gang" who "took advantage" of the people's worship of the emperor; "the third gangster" gained control in Germany. But in all three countries "no matter how you slice it, it was plain old-fashioned military imperialism." Later, with portrait shots of Hitler, Mussolini, and Tojo on the screen, the commentator admonishes the audience: "Remember these faces, remember them well. If you ever meet them, don't hesitate!" In contrast, the commentator characterizes the American public as tolerant, peace-loving people who unfortunately held on too long to the belief that Europe should fight its own battles: "We let our hopes for peace become so strong that they grew into a determination not to fight unless directly attacked." Thus, the commentary in PRELUDE TO WAR, and Walter Huston's delivery of it, is "a combination of a sermon, a between-halves pep talk, and a barroom bull session" (MacCann 216).

Animation

Along with the spoken commentary, PRELUDE TO WAR also employs captions and animation to complement documentary footage selected from enemy films. There are fifty-four shots with titles or captions and fifty-six shots with animation (Bohn 210). The most effective captions are blatant propaganda statements from Axis leaders, which Capra overlays as ironic commentary on scenes from enemy films (fig. 14.4a). Over a shot of Nazi children goose-stepping, for example, he insets a quotation from Hitler: "I want to see in youth again the gleam of the beast of prey." Thus, Capra uses Hitler's own words to twist the scene into a sinister picture of Nazi mind control.

The animation in PRELUDE TO WAR (produced in the Walt Disney Studios) is primarily used for maps, diagrams, and charts that reinforce the historical information the film introduces. For example, animated maps illustrate Germany's systematic takeover of neighboring territories and Japan's Tanaka plan for world conquest. But in presenting historical information, the animation also produces considerable emotional impact. To show how a country is invaded by Nazis, for example, a huge dagger plunges like a bolt of lightning into that land on the map. In other scenes, black swastikas drip like blood into Austria and Czechoslovakia, and little swastika projectiles shoot out of Germany and explode in the Low Countries, turning them black.

Editing

Careful editing is the key to assembling excerpted footage from many different films into one coherent, persuasive propaganda film. But there is not much straight cutting in PRELUDE TO WAR. Instead, Capra and the film's editor, William Hornbeck, mostly use **dissolves** and **wipes** to smooth transitions between shots. For example, to show the immediate cause of America's entry into World War II, Capra dissolves from a shot of enemy soldiers marching to a shot of a burning ship at Pearl Harbor; to depict Italy's invasion of Ethiopia, the scene dissolves from Mussolini to a map of Ethiopia. The Nazi occupation of Paris is indicated by a series of images—the swastika flying on a flagpole, German boots marching, and Nazi troops parading through the Arc de Triomphe—which dissolve from one to another. In PRELUDE TO WAR Capra employs wipes both to change scenes and to maintain continuity. In one scene seven consecutive wipes are used to introduce prominent Nazis whose ideas collectively characterize the threat that Nazism poses to free societies.

Capra also uses **superimposition** extensively to present several layers of visual information or contrasting images within one shot. Sometimes Capra tries to shock the viewer with superimposed images that are especially incongruous or inimical, as in a shot where Japanese troops seem to parade on Pennsylvania Avenue in Washington, D.C. With superimposition, Capra can include, and therefore twist, more choice enemy propaganda footage in the fifty-three minutes PRELUDE TO WAR runs.

Most critics agree that PRELUDE TO WAR was a very persuasive film in its day, with hefty visual and psychological impact. Richard Dyer MacCann summarizes PRELUDE TO WAR's effect on the audience for whom it was intended:

> There can be no doubt of the effectiveness of such a film as
> this for young men and women who had lived through the thirties—simply
> as a reminder, for some, but more particularly as a forceful organizing of
> loose thoughts for those who had never bothered to work things out in
> their minds. This single film may not have deeply affected fighting

motivation. Research Branch reports, using questions of doubtful relevance, tended to discredit the effect of the film. But it strengthened those who were most in agreement with the opinions of waverers. A propaganda film could not expect to do much more. And the most typical comment on PRELUDE TO WAR was: "It's propaganda all right, but it's good propaganda."
(218)

Conclusion

The three classic propaganda films discussed in this chapter— POTEMKIN, TRIUMPH OF THE WILL, and PRELUDE TO WAR— exhibit very different ideologies, visual styles, and persuasive techniques. Yet each of them in its own way systematically attempts to reach "individuals enclosed in the mass" and to manipulate, both consciously and unconsciously, their attitudes and beliefs (Ellul 3). Each film, at a specific time and place in history, furnished the viewer with "a complete system for explaining the world" and provided "immediate incentives to action" (Ellul 6). But the cinematic techniques Eisenstein, Riefenstahl, and Capra used to create these masterpieces of propaganda transcend time and place. A careful examination of today's television commercials will reveal how thoroughly contemporary film propagandists have learned from past masters how to sell ideology—or merchandise—to mass audiences.

General Study Questions

1. Explain what Jacques Ellul means when he says that modern propaganda furnishes a person "with a complete system for explaining the world, and provides immediate incentives for action." Provide examples from films you know.
2. What does Robert Vas mean when he says that "the real propaganda film can't stand half-measures"? Explain this statement with examples from either the Odessa Steps Sequence in POTEMKIN or the Airfield Sequence in TRIUMPH OF THE WILL.
3. Use the still in chapter 4 (fig. 4.4) from Sergei Eisenstein's OCTOBER (TEN DAYS THAT SHOOK THE WORLD) (1928) to explain and illustrate Eisenstein's concept of *dialectical montage.* What new meaning emerges in the shot when the dangling horse and the open drawbridge are juxtaposed? How does the combination of two "depictables" in the shot yield an "undepictable" intellectual concept?
4. Suppose you were commissioned to produce a propaganda film about an important political issue or event that interests you. Like Frank Capra with the WHY WE FIGHT series, find "one basic, powerful idea" around which

to organize your film and then outline its essential structure. Decide who will be the audience for the film and plan how best to address that audience.

5. Write a shot-by-shot analysis of one scene or sequence from a film that is generally considered propaganda. Point out how the filmmaker forms, controls, or alters the viewer's attitudes.

6. Study one of the popular commercial movies from the 1970s or 1980s about American involvement in the Vietnam War. Identify the film's viewpoint of the war and how it articulates that viewpoint to the audience. Is the movie propaganda according to T.H. Qualter's definition in this chapter? Why, or why not?

7. Consider television commercials as propaganda films. How do they attempt to manipulate consumers? Support your answer with specific examples.

8. Write a shot-by-shot analysis of a television commercial. Analyze it as an example of film propaganda.

9. Study a paid political announcement on television that promotes a candidate for public office. What cinematic techniques are employed to enhance the candidate's image? Does the announcement direct a political message to "individuals enclosed in the mass"? Does it attempt to manipulate the viewer unconsciously?

Additional Films for Study

ALL QUIET ON THE WESTERN FRONT (1930), dir. Lewis Milestone
EARTH (1930), dir. Alexander Dovzhenko
QUE VIVA MEXICO! (1931–32), dir. Sergei Eisenstein
OLYMPIA (1936–38), dir. Leni Riefenstahl
THE GRAND ILLUSION (1937), dir. Jean Renoir
SPANISH EARTH (1937), dir. Joris Ivens and Ernest Hemingway
ALEXANDER NEVSKY (1938), dir. Sergei Eisenstein
SABOTEUR (1942), dir. Alfred Hitchcock
THE BATTLE FOR THE UKRAINE (1942–43), dir. Alexander Dovzhenko
THE NAZIS STRIKE [WHY WE FIGHT SERIES] (1943), dir. Frank Capra and Anatole Litvak
BATTLE OF MIDWAY (1944), dir. John Ford
THE BATTLE OF SAN PIETRO (1944), dir. John Huston
LIFEBOAT (1944), dir. Alfred Hitchcock
OPEN CITY (1945), dir. Roberto Rossellini
WAR COMES TO AMERICA [WHY WE FIGHT SERIES] (1945), dir. Anatole Litvak
THE CRANES ARE FLYING (1957), dir. Mikhail Kalatozov
HIROSHIMA MON AMOUR (1959), dir. Alain Resnais
THE GREEN BERETS (1968), dir. John Wayne
JOHNNY GOT HIS GUN (1971), dir. Dalton Trumbo
GALLIPOLI (1981), dir. Peter Weir

ASHRAM (1981), dir. Wolfgang Dobrowolny
ALSINO AND THE CONDOR (1983), dir. Miguel Litten
FULL METAL JACKET (1987), dir. Stanley Kubrick

Further Reading

Barna, Yon. *Eisenstein*. Boston: Little, Brown, 1973.

Berg-Pan, Renata. *Leni Riefenstahl*. Boston: Twayne, 1980.

Bohn, Thomas W. *An Historical and Descriptive Analysis of the WHY WE FIGHT Series*. New York: Arno Press, 1977.

Capra, Frank. *The Name Above the Title: An Autobiography*. New York: Macmillan, 1971.

Eisenstein, Sergei. *Film Form*. Translated and edited by Jay Leyda. New York: Harcourt Brace Jovanovich, 1969.

———. *The Film Sense*. Translated and edited by Jay Leyda. New York: Harcourt Brace Jovanovich, 1969.

Furhammar, Leif, and Folke Isaksson. *Politics and Film*. Translated by Kersti French. New York: Frederick A. Praeger, 1971.

Hough, Richard. *The Potemkin Mutiny*. Englewood Cliffs, N.J.: Prentice-Hall, 1960.

Hull, David Stewart. *Films in the Third Reich*. Berkeley: University of California Press, 1969.

Infield, Glenn. *Leni Riefenstahl: The Fallen Film Goddess*. New York: Thomas Y. Crowell, 1976.

Jones, Ken D., and Arthur F. McClure. *Hollywood at War*. Cranbury, N.J.: A.S. Barnes, 1973.

Kagan, Norman. *The War Film*. New York: Pyramid, 1974.

Leiser, Erwin. *Nazi Cinema*. Translated by Gertrude Mander and David Wilson. New York: Collier, 1974.

Leyda, Jay. *Kino: A History of the Russian and Soviet Cinema*. London: George Allen & Unwin, 1960.

MacBean, James Roy. *Film and Revolution*. Bloomington: Indiana University Press, 1975.

Manvell, Roger. *Films and the Second World War*. Cranbury, N.J.: A.S. Barnes, 1974.

Marshall, Herbert, ed. *Sergei Eisenstein's THE BATTLESHIP POTEMKIN*. New York: Avon Books, 1978.

Mayer, David. *Eisenstein's POTEMKIN*. New York: Grossman Publishers, 1972.

Maynard, Richard A., ed. *Propaganda on Film: A Nation at War*. Rochelle Park, N.J.: Hayden, 1983.

Minton, David B. *The Films of Leni Riefenstahl*. Metuchen, N.J.: Scarecrow Press, 1978.

Taylor, Richard. *Film Propaganda: Soviet Russia and Nazi Germany*. New York: Barnes & Noble, 1979.

———. *The Politics of the Soviet Cinema, 1917–1929*. London: Cambridge University Press, 1979.

Vogel, Amos. *Film as a Subversive Art*. New York: Random House, 1975.
Welch, David. *Propaganda and the German Cinema: 1933–1945*. Oxford: Clarendon Press, 1983.

Works Cited

Bohn, Thomas W. *An Historical and Descriptive Analysis of the WHY WE FIGHT Series*. New York: Arno Press, 1977.

Capra, Frank. *The Name Above the Title: An Autobiography*. New York: Macmillan, 1971.

Cook, David A. *A History of Narrative Film*. New York: W.W. Norton, 1981.

Eisenstein, Sergei. *Film Form: Essays in Film Theory*. Translated and edited by Jay Leyda. New York: Harcourt Brace Jovanovich, 1969.

Ellul, Jacques. "Characteristics of Propaganda." In *Propaganda on Film: A Nation at War*, edited by Richard A. Maynard, 1–7. Rochelle Park, N.J.: Hayden, 1983.

Furhammar, Leif, and Folke Isaksson. *Politics and Film*. Translated by Kersti French. New York: Praeger, 1971.

Hitler, Adolf. Quoted in *Propaganda and the German Cinema: 1933–1945*, by David Welch. Oxford: Clarendon Press, 1983.

Hough, Richard A. *The Potemkin Mutiny*. Englewood Cliffs, N.J.: Prentice-Hall, 1960.

Leiser, Erwin. *Nazi Cinema*. Translated by Gertrude Mander and David Wilson. New York: Collier, 1974.

MacCann, Richard Dyer. "World War II: Armed Forces Documentary." In *The Documentary Tradition*, 2d ed., edited by Lewis Jacobs, 213–23. New York: W.W. Norton, 1979.

"Program Notes for TRIUMPH OF THE WILL." Quoted in *Propaganda and the German Cinema: 1933–1945*, by David Welch. Oxford: Clarendon Press, 1983.

Qualter, T.H. Quoted in *Film Propaganda: Soviet Russia and Nazi Germany*, by Richard Taylor. New York: Barnes & Noble, 1979.

Riefenstahl, Leni. *Behind the Scenes of the Party Rally Film*. Quoted in *Nazi Cinema*, by Erwin Leiser. Translated by Gertrude Mander and David Wilson. New York: Collier, 1974.

———. Quoted in *Dictionary of Films*, by Georges Sadoul. Translated and edited by Peter Morris. Berkeley: University of California Press, 1972.

Rotha, Paul. Quoted in *Propaganda on Film: A Nation at War*, edited by Richard A. Maynard. Rochelle Park, N.J.: Hayden, 1983.

Vas, Robert. "Sorcerers or Apprentices: Some Aspects of the Propaganda Film." Quoted in *Propaganda on Film: A Nation at War*, edited by Richard A. Maynard, 7–15. Rochelle Park, N.J.: Hayden, 1983.

Welch, David. *Propaganda and the German Cinema: 1933–1945*. Oxford: Clarendon Press, 1983.

Appendix
Writing About Films

How to Take Notes on a Film

Two good reasons to take notes during a film screening are to help you remember what you've seen and to keep you interacting with the film as you watch it. A good film usually stays fresh and alive in your mind for a few days as you relive it and think about it. But how fresh will it be several weeks later when you wish to discuss it or write about it, perhaps in connection with another film? During the interval you may have seen a dozen other movies that interfere with or blur your recollections.

Note taking not only helps you recall what you observed in a film; it usually helps you observe the film better to begin with. Most people watch films quite *passively*. They want easy entertainment or escape from mundane concerns. They do not care how or why a movie excites them, only that it does. But those who seek more than entertainment want to know how and why movies affect them; therefore, they train themselves to watch films *actively*. For film study, it is important to look at a movie for more than its plot—to become more conscious of camera and editing techniques, subtleties of lighting and visual tone, metaphorical nuances, and the interplay of sound and image. Taking notes can help you become a more active film spectator. If you find that you haven't consciously noted anything about a film for ten minutes, chances are that you have lapsed into passive viewing. If so, nudge yourself to write down something about the shot on the screen at that moment and get back to interacting with the film.

What should you write down about a film? Because note taking is generally associated with reading or lectures, many students find themselves jotting down lines of dialogue. But although spoken language is important in most films, cinematic language is usually more important.

Don't concentrate so much on *words*; pay attention to *images* and how they are presented. Watch with two fundamental questions in mind: What am I seeing, and what does it mean? Remember that the filmmaker has purposefully selected and prepared whatever you see on the screen; everything contributes to the overall experience of the film.

There are two big problems with note taking during screenings. The first is that movies are shown in the dark. How can you take notes if you can't see to write? There are several remedies for this problem. You can sometimes find enough light in a theater or screening room by sitting near an aisle lamp or an exit sign, or you can carry a penlight with you. For classroom screenings, many professors dim but do not extinguish the lights, or they allow time after important scenes or between reels for students to take notes. When you screen a film on a viewing table or a VCR, you can stop the film yourself for notes.

The second problem with note taking is that it draws your eyes away from the screen. For this reason some film instructors advise their students to take notes after the screening rather than during it, but there are other possible solutions. Some people find that a very minimal note—a phrase, a simple diagram, a single word—is enough to recall an entire scene or sequence; others write notes without looking at the page and decipher them later. During the film keep your notes laconic. If you space them down the page, they won't run together and will follow the film's chronology. Your observations during the screening do not need to be lengthy or profound; what is important is that you consciously *note* them. You can organize your observations and flesh them out later.

How to Keep a Film Journal

Keeping a film journal often leads effortlessly to wonderful discoveries. Journal writing is free writing. You don't need to know where you are going or what you want to say when you begin. With free writing, ideas take shape and find direction *as you write*. A film journal, therefore, is a good way to discover what you think about the movies you see. After a film you may be teeming with impressions and feelings, thoughts and questions. A film journal is the place to give free rein to them, to sort out your reactions to the film, to develop a personal connection with it, to relate it to other experiences.

Just because journal writing is free writing does not mean it is necessarily an unfocused stream of consciousness. In fact, sometimes a clear focus develops as soon as you begin writing. You can also choose a focus for your writing. If you're interested in camera techniques, or visual symbols, or gender stereotyping in films, keep that focus in mind as you write. Free writing in a journal is a good way to ease into a more formal paper about films; and sometimes, with a little revising, a journal entry can be turned into a good reaction paper, film review, or expository essay.

Some people find it a good psychological incentive to select an attractive notebook for a journal; others prefer to collect individual entries in a folder or loose-leaf binder. Some people write immediately after a screening; others let a movie settle in their minds before writing. It is best to establish a routine for keeping the journal and not to wait too long before writing about the films you see.

Some film instructors require their students to keep a film journal; others strongly advise it. But students who catch the knack of writing freely in a journal usually find it a self-rewarding activity.

How to Write a Reaction Paper About a Film

When a professor asks you to write a reaction paper about a film, she or he is looking for a written response that is more structured than free writing but not a formal expository essay. The purpose of a reaction paper is to articulate your thoughts and impressions about a film in a way that brings its significance into focus.

How should you go about writing a reaction paper? One way to begin is with free writing. (See the previous section.) Write down quickly whatever you found memorable in the film. Then go back and select the most promising observations to elaborate upon in the reaction paper. Another way to begin is to articulate how you felt immediately after the film. Did you feel angry or intimidated? Depressed or exhilarated? Fired up or indifferent? Confused or enlightened? Try to describe your reaction as precisely as possible; consult a dictionary or thesaurus if necessary to find the right words. Avoid stating whether you liked or disliked the film unless you can attach a clause that succinctly explains why—for example, "I disliked this film intensely because it made me feel how cruel men and women can be to each other" or "I loved the film because it made me feel like a child again." At this stage of the paper, however, it is best to avoid making a judgment about the film; just describe your feelings about it.

Whether you begin with free writing or by describing your immediate reaction, the next step is to expand and substantiate your first impressions with details and examples from the film. Trace your feelings about the film to specific images, shots, or scenes that made you feel angry, exhilarated, or enlightened. Again, try to be precise; don't settle for vague recollections. Recall pertinent details and include them in the paper. You don't have to cover everything in the film; select a few key examples and develop them fully. You may wish to include a shot-by-shot description for a sequence or scene in which camera or editing technique is crucial. (See the following section.)

Conclude the reaction paper by making a statement about the film based on your feelings about it. A statement at this stage must be more than a gut reaction and more than a personal opinion about how much you liked or disliked the movie. Now, after some reflection on the film, you want to take a thoughtful position about the film's meaning and significance, a position that invites further discussion and perhaps debate. What does the film want to say? What problems or issues does it raise? What is controversial about the film?

A few additional suggestions:

1. Write the reaction paper soon after the screening. Short-term memory loss is appreciable. Write while your impressions of the film are fresh.
2. Plan from the outset to revise your paper. Then you can write the first draft without inhibition. Revise the paper to clarify and structure your thoughts, to polish sentences, to make corrections.
3. Don't plan the concluding statement before your thoughts develop through the middle of the paper. Let there be an element of surprise for yourself at the end of the paper.
4. Avoid plot summary. You will not discover much about a film's meaning by retelling the story. If you need to comment on plot, summarize concisely, in a sentence or two, whatever is important for your purpose.

Examine the following sample reaction paper about François Truffaut's DAY FOR NIGHT (1972). (See chapter 13 for more discussion of the film.) In this paper the writer, based on her own experience as a movie extra, responds to the "mechanics" and the "magic" of moviemaking that Truffaut depicts in DAY FOR NIGHT. The numbers in the left margin correspond to comments at the end of the paper.

DAY FOR NIGHT: A Film Artist's Valentine

by Cindy Tierney

1   Back in 1962, Arthur Penn shot part of THE MIRACLE WORKER at the old train station in Peapack-Gladstone. My mother's players group and their families were invited to be extras. I remember that I got a purple bonnet but I didn't get to be in the scene (I always swore that it was because the bonnet was so damned purple); however, my

cousin was the conductor and my mother was the shadow of a woman on the train. A scene inside the train had been shot the day before. Now we were shooting the train pulling out and the hustle and bustle around the station. We shot all day. We did the scene over and over. It seemed to me that it was perfect the first time. And it was so difficult to set up because there were horses and babies and the sun kept moving.

2   I think that this is why I loved DAY FOR NIGHT. When Truffaut kept saying "Lady with the dog, move a little faster," I was reminded of Penn saying "Lady with baby, step quickly." What was

3   wonderful was that the mechanics did not dim the magic. I looked around and saw bonnets and carriages that evoked another era and cameras and makeup and chairs with names that evoked another world. That other world was magic, too. I think that is what Truffaut was saying in DAY FOR NIGHT. All the dispassionate discussions can't break the spell. Poor Alphonse doesn't know which world he's in. He wants life to play like the movie script. He needs more than one shot to get it right.

There is something wonderfully childlike, too. Can this be

4   adult work: Pick a gun! Pick a wig! Pick a car! Don't crash that one, it's white . . . let's smash up this one. Take this vase . . . it's perfect . . . we'll put it in our movie. Find a cat that likes milk. We can have snow and rain and guns that go pow and nobody gets hurt.

5   But at the same time Truffaut [as Ferrand, the fictional movie director in the story] is reminded constantly that if his magical little

6   film goes over budget, he loses everything. He sees his film people as human beings but is not above using even their most intimate revelations to intensify his film. Julie laments that she must live alone and finds the line, verbatim, in her new script. Good or bad. . .who knows. . . maybe Truffaut [Ferrand] is showing her a way to use her

7   pain in her craft. Acting may well be exorcism.

8   We get a fine glimpse of the aging female star also. She is bigger than life and scared stiff. Looking at the beautiful Julie, she sees herself a decade ago. Perhaps she took the place of an aging star. Perhaps Julie has come to take her place. Her looks were her trade. Even if we can't see the wrinkles, she knows them by heart. She has given everything for this life in the movies and will have nothing if she loses it.

9   Jacqueline Bisset [Julie] is the exquisite flower in search of

10   roots. She, too, is rather simple and childlike. She needs to be tended if she is to flourish. Her vulnerability and sadness play well on the screen and for this reason she feels used. She feels invisible, like some sort of vessel or empty receptacle waiting for lines or instructions. Poor Julie needs a road map for the real world. She is lucky to have her doctor-husband with the kind eyes, but we have to wonder just how far she will push him before his patience runs out.

11   And then there's Alphonse who needs a keeper not a wife. Women are supposed to be magical. "I prefer to suffer," he says. When he is not in a movie, he is going off to see one. Alphonse is celluloid; he does not exist off the screen.

    Alexandre instantly commands our respect as does any good craftsman. He has been around and is a pro. His voice is velvet and his movements are fluid and natural. He seems to have a sense of himself. With Julie he is paternal, and with Alphonse he is indulgent. He is playful and supportive of the aging star. Alexandre is a man for all seasons; he shows us exactly what we want to see and gives us exactly what we need—the consummate actor. But who is Alexandre? He may have forgotten.

    The man who holds the whole eccentric, talented group together is Truffaut [Ferrand]. I doubt that an elephant walking down Main Street would shock Truffaut [Ferrand]. He has seen it all. He accepts, as if it were perfectly normal, his hysterical star's request for country butter. He will always be that little boy who collected the pictures from CITIZEN KANE. He'll use everything and everyone at his disposal to make magic. He cares for them, but as he said to Alphonse, "Tomorrow is work, work is more important than anything." He is no prima donna, nor is he a creative egotist. When he is told that his film must be shot in 35 days, he accepts the news. He figures a way around Stacy's pregnancy and Alexandre's death. He is pragmatic when necessary and has few illusions about himself. When he begins a film, he wants the best film possible; later on he just wants to finish it.

12   Truffaut [Ferrand] loves his craft (note the books delivered to the set), his actors, and even his difficulties. He will find a way to make those difficulties work for him creatively. DAY FOR NIGHT is a Valentine to all film artists, and the rest of us can enjoy it, too.

Comments:

1. The writer describes her own experience on a film set in the first paragraph in order to establish a personal connection with DAY FOR NIGHT and to arouse the reader's interest.

2. In the second paragraph the writer presents her reaction to DAY FOR NIGHT. The pronoun "this" in the first sentence is too vague. A more specific reference to her experience as an extra would clarify why she loved Truffaut's film.

3. In the third sentence the writer introduces the "magic" of movies and moviemaking, a major theme in the paper.

4. The writer employs informal language and writing style in this paragraph (and, generally, throughout the paper), which is very effective in a reaction paper but may not be appropriate in a more formal essay or research paper.

5. Using "Truffaut" in this paper may be a source of confusion because François Truffaut, who directed DAY FOR NIGHT, also plays the role of a movie director named Ferrand in the film. Since the writer identifies all the other characters by their movie names, she should use "Ferrand" in the paper whenever she refers to the character Truffaut plays.

6. The writer makes a general statement in the second sentence of this paragraph and immediately substantiates it in the following sentence with a specific example from the film. In any kind of writing it is important to support generalizations with examples or explanations.

7. The writer ends several paragraphs with comments and opinions about characters in DAY FOR NIGHT, which add zest to a reaction paper but, without further substantiation, may not be appropriate in a more formal paper.

8. In the next five paragraphs the writer reacts to the principal characters in DAY FOR NIGHT, presenting a few essential details that characterize each of them. She builds toward the discussion of Truffaut's character, Ferrand, who "holds the whole eccentric, talented group together."

9. For consistency, the writer should refer to actress Jacqueline Bisset by her character name in the film—Julie.

10. The writer compares Julie to an "exquisite flower," which provides insight into her character and adds flourish to the writing; but she should be wary of mixing metaphors later in the paragraph.

11. The writer quotes a line of dialogue from the film to delineate a character. Quoting dialogue is usually a good way to reinforce impressions and opinions about a film in a reaction paper, but the quotes should be succinct and used judiciously.

12. The concluding paragraph could be developed more. Comparing DAY FOR NIGHT to a valentine is a worthy conclusion for this reaction paper, but the writer could introduce the "love of the craft" motif earlier in the paper to set up the ending better. Perhaps she could find a way to tie in "magic," too.

How to Write a Shot-by-Shot Analysis

Except for actually making or cutting a movie, there is no better way to learn how films are constructed than by writing a shot-by-shot analysis of a well-crafted scene or sequence. A shot-by-shot analysis generally has two steps: The first is to number and describe every shot in the sequence in complete detail; the second is to examine the interrelationship of those shots and comment on the overall purpose and meaning of the sequence. Shot-by-shot analysis is somewhat inconvenient with films on celluloid since it requires a viewing table or a projector that can freeze individual frames, but with the recent proliferation of VCRs, it has become much easier to do shot analyses of films on videotape.

Formats and abbreviations for shot-by-shot descriptions vary somewhat from author to author. The following abbreviations are used in shot analyses in this text:

For Camera Positions
XLS extreme long shot
LS long shot
MLS medium long shot
MS medium shot
MCU medium close-up
CU close-up
XCU extreme close-up

For Camera Angles
XL/A extreme low angle
L/A low angle
H/A high angle
XH/A extreme high angle

Other Abbreviations
POV point-of-view shot
R/A reverse angle
FX special effects
f/g foreground
m/g middleground
b/g background

A shot-by-shot description generally includes the following information:

1. The number of each shot.
2. The opening of each shot. If not specified, it is understood that the shot begins as a straight cut from the previous shot. Otherwise, the opening is described as **fade in, dissolve in, or iris in.**
3. The camera position (from XLS to XCU) and the camera angle (from XL/A to XH/A) at the beginning of each shot. If not specified, the camera angle is assumed to be level.
4. Special characteristics of each shot, especially POV or R/A, but also special devices such as "circle iris" and "corners rounded" (as in Theodore Huff's shot analysis of THE BIRTH OF A NATION in chapter 10).
5. Camera movements within each shot: **panning** and **tilting, tracking, crane shots** and **aerial shots, zooming.**
6. A description of the visual content of each shot, including what appears in f/g, m/g, and b/g; the placement and movement of actors; significant actions and events.

7. Spoken dialogue or screen titles in each shot.
8. A description of the sound track for each shot (usually in parentheses).
9. The ending of each shot (fade-out or iris-out) or the transition to the next shot (dissolve to or **wipe to**). If no transition is specified, it is understood that the shot ends with a straight cut. Sometimes even unusual cuts are identified, such as **jump cut** or **cut on action**.
10. A shot-by-shot description may also include the length of each shot, measured in feet and/or frames (as in Huff's analysis of THE BIRTH OF A NATION in chapter 10).

The first step of the shot-by-shot analysis, the description of the shots, delineates what happens in the sequence. The second step explores why it happens; this is the step where one tries to analyze how all the cinematic elements in the sequence fit together and create meaning. For example, the shot analysis of Robert Enrico's AN OCCURRENCE AT OWL CREEK BRIDGE in chapter 2 explores how the director employs the camera at the beginning of the film to set the scene, how the camera angles and movements reinforce the predicament of the prisoner about to be hanged, and how the camera foreshadows the prisoner's fantasized escape. The overall objective of the shot analysis is to demonstrate the active narrative role the camera plays in the sequence.

The first time one undertakes a shot-by-shot analysis, the task may seem overwhelming, but the benefits gained from the exercise are usually more than adequate compensation. After completing a shot-by-shot analysis, most students understand the craft and technique of moviemaking much better and see more in movies than they did before.

How to Write an Expository Paper About a Film

An expository paper is the kind of assignment most professors have in mind when they ask you to answer a question in a well-organized essay. The word *expository* is derived from the Latin verb *exponere*, which means to set forth or expound. An expository paper, therefore, is one in which the writer sets forth or explains ideas in an orderly, detailed manner. Unlike a reaction paper, an expository paper is generally not written in the first person.

An essential characteristic of an expository paper is that it focuses on and develops a central idea, called a *thesis*, which is clearly identified for the reader in a *thesis statement*. A thesis statement does not just tell what the paper is about (its subject or theme), but also presents a specific position on the subject, which the writer expounds or argues in the essay. A good thesis statement is clearly defined and limited, frequently indicating the writer's main arguments or supporting evidence. A thesis statement usually (though not always) occurs in the opening paragraph in order to let the reader know early on what to expect in the essay.

Another essential characteristic of an expository paper is that it is structured to explain and support the thesis. Paragraphs organized around *topic sentences* develop the thesis methodically in the body of the paper; *transitional words and phrases* indicate the flow and interconnection of ideas between paragraphs. The wording of a thesis statement often suggests (or even dictates) the structure of an essay. For this reason, it is to the writer's advantage, as well as the reader's, to formulate a thesis that will serve as a clear blueprint for an expository paper.

The key to good expository writing is revising. Often a writer must produce several drafts of a paper before the thesis becomes clear. Many writers only discover their thesis statement in the final paragraph of the first draft. Then they move that paragraph to the beginning and restructure the next draft around it. In any case, the more you revise the ideas and the language in an expository paper, the clearer and more polished they will become.

The expository paper that follows contains many sound observations and comments about the use of cinematic techniques in CITIZEN KANE, but the essay needs revision. Read it with an eye toward refining its thesis and structure in the next draft. Comments, corresponding with the numbers in the left margin, follow the essay.

Cinematic Techniques in CITIZEN KANE
by Thomas McGreevy

In his landmark film, CITIZEN KANE, Orson Welles created a work that utilized basic filmmaking techniques like no other film before. His use of camera, editing, lighting, and sound provided a wealth of cinematic variety, and has spawned continual review to this day. An examination of each of the four techniques will demonstrate some of the specific methods used by Welles which make this film so unique.

The camera work in CITIZEN KANE provided a great variety of shots, a few of which were used repeatedly with powerful effect. One of these is the first shot of the film, a low-angle shot of the gate at Xanadu, with an iron "K" in the foreground, and the mansion itself in the background. This shot is used three times to establish the location: in the beginning, when we first learn of Kane's death; later in the film during a flashback; and in the final shot, as Kane's possessions are being burned and smoke billows from Xanadu like a funeral pyre. Another repeated shot is the one that introduces Susan

1

2

3

4

Alexander. It opens with a bolt of lightning illuminating Susan's face on a billboard. It then moves up to the roof, through a flashing neon sign of her name, and down to a rainsoaked skylight. The next shot then picks up on the other side of the glass and moves down to a table where she sits. This not only introduces the character, but once again indicates the location. When the story is finished with her character, the exact opposite shot is taken, with the camera moving out the skylight and back through the sign on the roof. It effectively "closes the book" on Susan Alexander. A third repeated shot, one which makes the viewer feel that he is about to see some private information, is that of a door closing on the camera. In both the Thatcher Library and Xanadu, a shot is abruptly cut off by a door closing, which then gives the impression that the camera has been shooting from a point-of-view of sorts. When the next shot places the viewer inside the room, the "closed door" action is revealed.

Another interesting technique Welles uses in the film is deep focus, where the camera layers the action going on in the shot. A good example of this would be the shot at the Chicago *Inquirer*, when Kane is finishing Leland's dramatic review. Kane is shown in the foreground at the typewriter, Leland appears in the middleground, and Bernstein is silhouetted in a doorway in the background. These three characters appear again, in a similar way, for the shots taken during the newspaper party. Bernstein and Leland are in the foreground this time, with Kane and the dancers shown through the middle and background as reflections in a window.

Just as fascinating as the camera is the editing done in CITIZEN KANE. One of the most common techniques is the lap dissolve. It is used repeatedly for transitions, and is the key to making the flashbacks so successful. As the reporter reads Thatcher's memoirs in the library, the words dissolve to Kane's childhood. As Leland tells the story of Kane's marriage, a lap dissolve keeps his old face narrating in the frame for quite a while as the Kanes sit eating their breakfast. This is an interesting series of shots which shows the relationship of Emily and Kane disintegrate simply by displaying their changing attitudes at the breakfast table over time. Just a few simple shots properly edited commented on an entire marriage. Transitions, through the use of shock cuts, also figure prominently throughout the film. Examples would include the cut to "News on the March" (and its accompanying documentary style editing) and the cut to Susan Alexander's face on the billboard during the lightning storm. Finally, Hollywood montage is repeated on numerous occasions, with newspaper headlines (quite appropriate for a newspaper magnate like Kane) showing the passage of time and events.

Welles uses lighting to set the mood throughout the entire film. By never showing the reporters' faces, whether in the screening room, during interviews, or at the end at Xanadu, he relegates them

5

6

7

8

9

to a position of secondary importance. They are just a "means to an end" and exist simply to tell Kane's story. There are also shots that keep Kane's visage in the dark. During the reading of the "Declaration of Principles" Kane's disembodied voice comes at the viewer,

10   making him concentrate on what is being said, while also foreshadowing the destruction of these principles later. During the sequence when Kane faces his political rival both men are shown silhouetted in a doorway, antagonizing each other, with Emily between them brilliantly lit. Moments later a shadowy Kane bursts into the light as he decides to stay with Susan, a turning point he may later regret. The control Kane later has over Susan is emphasized with lighting, as in the shot when Kane's shadow engulfs her as they argue about her

11   singing career. By and large, the film uses shadow and lighting contrast throughout to reinforce feelings and sentiments.

12   The final technique, sound, also plays an important role in CITIZEN KANE. It is used as a transition, as when the cockatoo screeches at Xanadu as Susan leaves, or when the thunder claps as Susan's face is first shown on the billboard. Welles also layers the sound, allowing several bits of dialogue or sound effects to run simultaneously. The reporters' rapid banter or the scene in the tent with Kane arguing with Susan while someone screams in the background both demonstrate this concept. Impressions of immensity and emptiness are also accomplished with sound. By using an echo effect, Welles makes both the Thatcher Library and the Xanadu great hall become huge, forbidding rooms. A sound effect also aids the visual narrative in the scene where the sound of a splash is followed by a shot of Kane covered with mud. Another interesting use of sound is in the scene when Kane screams at Gettys and Emily as they leave

13   Susan's building. His cry is cut off when they close the door but is finished by the sound of a car horn in the street. Subtle nuances such as this show how carefully Welles used sound techniques in CITIZEN KANE.

            The examples presented here give a taste of the great variety of cinematic techniques Welles incorporated into CITIZEN KANE. The camera, editing, lighting, and sound are all special in their own

14   right; but put together in the film they are extraordinary. They make CITIZEN KANE always a fresh viewing experience, as new, subtle details are discovered each time the film is examined.

Comments

1.   The opening paragraph has the makings of a good thesis statement, but the language is too fuzzy. What does the writer mean by "a wealth of cinematic variety"? This phrase, if clarified, could provide a more precise focus on cinematic technique in CITIZEN KANE and redefine the paper's structure. How would you revise the second sentence to make the thesis sharper?

2. The first paragraph clearly indicates the structure of the paper: The writer will discuss camera, editing, lighting, and sound in CITIZEN KANE.

3. The writer makes a good observation that some shots are repeated in CITIZEN KANE, but the point would be much stronger if he were more specific about the "powerful effect" of this repetition.

4. The writer's example of the opening shot is described well and effectively supports the generalization in the first sentence of the paragraph. But the writer should specify why it is significant that the shot is repeated "to establish the location" (especially since he reiterates this point later in the paragraph). It looks like the writer has a more specific point in mind but does not see it clearly enough yet.

5. This observation looks very promising, but the writer needs to pinpoint it, to find more precise language for "of sorts." Perhaps if the writer connects this point with "powerful effect" in the opening sentence, he will be able to close this paragraph with a bang.

6. The writer provides a transition into the new paragraph (with "another"), but the sentence lacks substance. How would you revise here to lead more forcefully into "deep focus"? Consider carrying over "powerful effect" from the previous paragraph and taking it to the superlative. Thus, deep focus might be "the most powerful camera technique" instead of just "another technique."

7. There are good examples in this paragraph, but the writer should also point out what these deep-focus shots accomplish—how they affect the viewer.

8. Again, how could the writer make the transition here and still say something substantial about editing?

9. Would you begin a new paragraph here with "transitions"? Why, or why not?

10. This paragraph contains an excellent observation about the use of shadows in the "Declaration of Principles" scene. Notice how much clearer the writer's language is here than in his observation about the "point-of-view of sorts" at the end of the second paragraph.

11. This paragraph ends with a summary generalization that is well prepared for by examples within the paragraph. But the writer should push himself to tone up the vague language about "feelings and sentiments" and give this comment more punch.

12. It is clear by now that this writer needs to beef up the first and last sentence of each paragraph. Excellent details and examples are given throughout the paper, but the writer should use them to support gutsier statements about cinematic techniques in CITIZEN KANE.

13. This observation about the use of sound effects is excellent, but wouldn't you say this is more than just "another interesting use of sound"? Wouldn't you like to see the writer follow up this observation with comment or analysis?

14. The conclusion is adequate but doesn't push the discussion of cinematic techniques to a higher level. The writer tells us that, "put together," the cinematic techniques in CITIZEN KANE are "extraordinary," but (unlike the other paragraphs) he does not show us that this is true. Perhaps one more detailed example would tie together some loose threads in this paper. Perhaps the writer might clarify for himself what "extraordinary" means and rebuild this paragraph as the opening paragraph for the next draft. How would you advise the writer to revise this expository paper? How would you revise it if it were your own?

How to Write a Research Paper About a Film

A research paper is a formal, expository paper that includes documentation and bibliography. It is a paper in which, ideally, the writer contributes something original to the body of knowledge that already exists about a given subject. But in most college classes the object of a research paper is to allow the student to demonstrate competent independent scholarship on a specialized topic.

The purpose of this section of the appendix is to offer a few basic suggestions about how to plan and write a research paper about films. It is not meant to explain how to conduct research or how to formulate reference citations and bibliographies. Many good research guides thoroughly cover these tasks, and most college English handbooks include extensive information about how to organize and write a research paper.

1. The first problem in writing a research paper is choosing a topic. Most professors would agree that a common weakness of student research papers is that they are too general. At the outset of a project many students fear that they will not find enough material to develop their topic, and consequently, they choose topics that are too broad. (Actually, it is more difficult to research a broad topic than a narrow one because there is more material to gather and sort through.) When choosing a research topic, you should define it as specifically as possible to begin with, and then continue to narrow it down as you are researching. This means, for example, that you don't try to take on "Fellini's $8^1/_2$" as a topic, or even "dream imagery in $8^1/_2$." Timothy Hyman developed an essay around "the pattern of Crisis, Liberation, and Fall in Guido's behavior in $8^1/_2$" (cited in chapter 11). With a limited topic like this, you can combine scholarship with your own observations, and focus in depth on a single aspect of a film.

2. Next, you must shape your topic into a thesis statement that identifies your position on the film. Remember that good expository writing needs a clearly delineated thesis statement to pull ideas together and give them direction. Scholarship should address some problem or controversy. Look for the controversy in your topic; that is where you'll find a thesis statement. Carl Belz, for example, took a controversial stance on Hitchcock's THE BIRDS (cited in chapter 11). He stated that THE BIRDS is not a conventional thriller but a "dramatic fantasy" that is basically surrealistic. A controversial thesis like Belz's is more engaging and challenging to write about than one that is safe and innocuous.

3. Good writing on any subject is specific. As you are preparing your research paper, plan to include your own commentary and descriptive illustrations. But use good judgment. You do not want to assume that the reader is completely familiar with the film(s) you are writing about because if you fail to describe important scenes specifically enough, your best observations may be lost on the reader. However, you also do not want to overwhelm the reader with tedious, superfluous description. You must find a balance: Describe the film specifically, but use the description to underscore the points you want to make. Notice, for example, how David Cook includes details about THE JAZZ SINGER (cited in chapter 5) as he explains why it is the first talking picture. The reader understands the gist of the film and picks up quite specific information about a few scenes, but there are no extraneous details. Cook makes every detail relevant to the main point of the paragraph. For your research paper, carefully select details that will strengthen, not dilute, your arguments.

4. Cinema is a visual medium, so why not include visual illustrations in your research paper? A few simple drawings or photocopies from books or magazines may help your reader visualize the scenes you discuss and accept your observations about them more readily. Consider, for example, how stills from METROPOLIS and THX: 1138 in chapter 9 illustrate the differences between those two films. The pictures and the written text complement each other and make the lesson about realistic and expressionistic films more comprehensible. But, again, be cautious not to include pictures gratuitously. Use visuals to reinforce your arguments, not to decorate them.

5. Finally, in preparing your research paper, remember that you are the one who must weave together all the information you gather. Ultimately, you must sort the raw material, find the common threads, create a woven fabric. Don't be afraid to let your hand show in the work. A research paper is formal writing, but it needn't be stuffy or humorless. Cinema is supposed to be the liveliest art; writing about it should be lively as well.

Examine the following short research paper about animation in television advertising. Once again, the numbers in the left margin correspond with comments that follow the paper.

"That Sells Folks!"
Animation in Television Advertising
by Donna Weaver

1   What do Metropolitan Life, Coca-Cola, and the California Raisin Advisory Board have in common? They are all using animation to advertise their products on television. Animation has become

2   a fast-growing medium in the commercial television advertising business. Claymation [clay animation], object animation, cel animation, and computer animation are the forms used to advertise

3   products.

4   "Last November, the ads for the California Raisin Advisory Board were mentioned most often when a survey was done. People were asked what television advertisement came to mind first and the doo-wopping raisins took top honors" (Franz 3). The California Raisins have become a household name, and advertisers are using them to the fullest. They can be seen on commercials for General Food's Post Natural Raisin Bran and for the Hardee's Cinnamon and Raisin Biscuits. The success of the Raisins has turned them into their own corporation.

5   But Will Vinton's creative genius hasn't stopped there.

6   Claymation has caught on quickly. Domino Pizza's "Noid," Kentucky

7   Fried Chicken's transforming fowl, and "The Mouths," newly created for General Food's Tang and Kool-Aid commercials, have all been successful at selling products.

8   Object animation is also used often in advertising. How else could you see New York Seltzer bottles dancing in Times Square? "Using stop motion animation with a motion control camera the bottles dance on a 20' by 20' square foot model of New York City with the Trade Center about six feet tall" (Turner 77). The Golden Grain company has also used object animation with mechanical models of a "Potato Family." This family sings and dances to promote Rice-a-Roni by telling consumers to "Save a Potato, Eat Rice-a-Roni." Both the thirty-second spot and the fifteen-second spot use stop-motion

9   animation (Cuneo 42).

10   Computer animation hit it big in advertising with the creation of Max Headroom. A computer graphics simulation, Max Headroom

11   was signed on as a "spokesthing" for Coca-Cola. "In signing him, Coca-Cola has harnessed the modern-day equivalent of Superman. When you see Max, you want to salute him, because he's red, white,

and blue. He looks typically American, and that's what the Coca-Cola company was after" (Skeanzy 64). Computer animation in commercials is now primarily a special effects generator, but then you could call Max the ultimate computer animated special effect.

12

Cel animation, or classic cartoon-style animation, has drawn up many characters to advertise products. Everybody remembers Tony the Tiger, Toucan Sam, Keebler Elves, Campbell Kids, and Snap, Crackle, and Pop. These characters were created especially for certain products, but now advertising has cartoon and comic strip characters endorsing products. "Snoopy, Charlie Brown, Dennis the Menace, and Cathy are only a few of the many cartoon characters that have found themselves taking on jobs that in the past were reserved for members of the Actors Equity Association" (Busch S-6).

13

Why are cartoon characters becoming such a popular alternative to a human spokesperson? They have an established following, wide appeal, work at a fraction of the cost, and aren't going to embarrass the sponsor with things like divorce or a drug problem. The selection of a character to endorse a product is very difficult. A specific character, like Cathy, can't endorse anything they want her to. Even cartoon characters have standards and images to uphold. One good example is using Garfield the Cat to endorse Embassy Suites Hotels. Garfield's motto is "Eat, Sleep, and Rest," all of which he can do at Embassy Suites. Licensing cartoon characters for advertising has become very profitable. "With performances like this, and barring any sudden submission to drug addiction by Charlie Brown and the gang, these and other animated characters will continue to find advertising a rewarding outlet for their talents" (Busch S-6).

14

15

16

Animation has become a popular way to advertise on television. In New York alone over 170 commercials are produced, but there are problems of client and agency approval and tight deadlines. "Even though some of the best animation has shown up in advertisements, many commercial animators would rather tell a story without having to sell soap or cat food, and to make films that would last more than thirty or sixty seconds" (Solomon 148). Despite all these problems the animated commercial industry will continue to grow, because it sells.

17

Works Cited

Busch, Anita. "Advertiser Draws Cartoon into Endorsements." *Advertising Age* 9 June 1986: S-6.

Cuneo, Alice. "Against the Grain." *Advertising Age* 9 May 1988:42.

Franz, Julie. "Clay Crooners Raisin' Interest." *Advertising Age* 29 Feb. 1989:3.

Skeanzy, Lenore. "Taking Mythology to the Max." *Advertising Age* 15 Sept. 1986:64.

Solomon, Charles, and Ron Stark. *The Complete Kodak Animation Book*. Rochester: Eastman Kodak Company, 1983.

Turner, Jean. "Dancing Bottles Take New York." *American Cinematographer* Oct. 1988:76–78.

Comments

1. The introductory paragraph is direct and engaging. Opening with a question is often a good way to begin a research paper.

2. The writer's thesis statement is clear but rather superficial. If it suggested *why* animation has become a fast-growing advertising medium, the thesis would provide the writer more opportunity to explore the topic in depth and to incorporate some of her own ideas into the paper. As it is, this thesis statement is setting up a research paper that will be informational but not argumentative.

3. The last sentence of the paragraph delineates the types of animation the writer will discuss in the paper.

4. In a research paper it is important to integrate direct quotations with the rest of the text. Usually it is best to introduce a quote, rather than begin a paragraph with it, so the reader will understand its context. How might the writer revise the second paragraph to use this quotation more advantageously?

5. The writer should identify people mentioned in the paper. Who is Will Vinton, and what is his connection with animated advertising?

6. The writer should define, at least briefly, important terms and concepts used in the paper, such as "claymation" and "object animation."

7. One of the strong points of this research paper is that the writer supports generalizations with plentiful examples.

8. This sentence makes a clear transition to "object animation," but it does not add anything substantial to the paper. The sentence could be expanded to define object animation or to distinguish it from clay animation.

9. The writer cites a reference for this information, even though she did not quote it, because the material is not general knowledge and is attributable to a specific source.

10. The writer should follow the order of topics delineated in the opening paragraph; cel animation should be discussed next.

11. This quotation is well integrated with the text. Notice how the writer uses "signed on" in the second sentence to set up the quote.

12. The writer presents her own comments and observations too sparingly. A good research paper is not simply a compilation of quotes.

13. This is a good question to ask. The writer should pose more questions like this. This paragraph is the most substantive and interesting part of the research paper.

14. The writer does a good job here of supporting a generalization with an example.

15. Be wary of vague pronoun references in quotations. The writer should use brackets to insert a specific reference to Garfield the Cat after "this": "With performances like this [Garfield's]. . . ." The previous sentence, "Licensing cartoon characters. . . ," should be the last sentence in the paragraph.

16. This sentence is unclear and confusing. Problems with animation in advertising should be a major concern in this research paper; the writer should certainly expand here.

17. The writer concludes the paper with a flourish, alluding back to the play on words in the title.

A Glossary of Film Terms

A

aerial shot
An **overhead shot,** usually taken from a helicopter or airplane.

American montage
A style of editing typical of many Hollywood films, which condenses time or summarizes many events in a few shots. Also called **Hollywood montage.**

anamorphic lens
A camera lens that allows a wider image to be photographed on a standard-sized frame. See also **aspect ratio** and **Cinemascope.**

animation
The process in which inanimate objects or individual drawings are photographed frame-by-frame in order to create an illusion of movement on the screen when the film is projected at the standard speed of 24 frames per second (fps). By manipulating the objects or drawings minutely for each frame, the filmmaker can make objects or characters appear to move. Also called **animated film.**

aperture
An adjustable opening that limits the amount of light passing through a camera lens. Also called the **lens aperture.**

arc light
A high-intensity studio lamp that uses a carbon arc discharge as its source of illumination.

archetype
A character in literature or film who is a universal representation of human behavior or experience.

archive footage
See **stock footage.**

area lighting
Lighting that illuminates a specific area of a film set rather than the entire set, usually with **spotlights** rather than **floodlights.**

aspect ratio
The ratio between the width and the height of the frame. The standard aspect ratio for motion picture film is 1.33:1. Using an **anamorphic lens** on the camera and projector can produce an aspect ratio of 2.35:1, where the projected image is 2.35 times wider than it is high. See also **Cinemascope.**

asynchronous sound
Film sound that is not synchronized with the screen image. See also **nonsynchronous sound** and **synchronous sound.**

auteur theory
A theory popularized by French film critics in the 1950s, which argues that the director is the "author" of a film, having artistic control and the power to imbue the work with his or her personal vision.

available lighting
The illumination that actually exists on location during filming, either natural (sunlight) or artificial (street lamps, candles, fires, etc.).

avant-garde film
See **underground film**.

B

baby spot
A **spotlight** with 500 to 1,000 watts of illuminating power.

back lighting
A style of film lighting in which light comes from behind objects or people being photographed, producing halo-like highlights around the subject (as in portraits by Rembrandt van Rijn) or, when the light is especially intense, showing the subject in silhouette. Also called **Rembrandt lighting**.

background light
Light that illuminates background areas of a film set and adds depth to a shot.

background music
Film music whose source is not apparent in the scene. See **foreground music**.

bird's-eye view
A view of a scene photographed from directly overhead; an **overhead shot**.

blimp
A soundproof camera housing that prevents the noise of the camera's motor from being recorded on the sound track.

boom
A pole used to extend a microphone above a film set, permitting **synchronous sound** recording without interfering with actors. Also called a **boom microphone**.

C

camera angle
The position of the camera in relation to the subject during filming. It may be straight (**eye-level shot**), tilted up at the subject (**low-angle shot**), tilted down at the subject (**high-angle shot**), or tilted off the vertical axis to either side (**Dutch-angle shot**).

camera movement
Any movement of the camera during a shot. For examples, see **panning, tilting, dollying, tracking, craning**.

camera speed
The rate at which film is run through a motion picture camera in frames per second (fps) or feet or meters per minute. The normal speed for sound film is 24 fps; for silent film, 18 fps. See also **overcrank** and **undercrank**.

cels
Transparent plastic sheets on which animators draw or letter images to be photographed frame-by-frame for an animated film or to be superimposed over live action. Animation done from such drawings is called **cel animation**.

Cinemascope
The trade name for wide-screen films photographed and projected with **anamorphic lenses** on the camera and the projector.

cinematographer
A film's director of photography who is responsible for the lighting and often for the actual shooting of film scenes. Also called a **lighting cameraman**.

cinéma vérité
In French, literally, "cinema truth." A style of documentary filmmaking in which the filmmaker interferes as little as possible with events being filmed. *Cinéma vérité*, also called **direct cinema**, is characterized by direct and spontaneous use of the camera (usually hand-held), long takes, naturalistic sound recording, and in-camera editing.

Cinerama
A wide-screen motion picture process that employs three cameras and three projectors, a wide, curved screen, and **stereophonic sound**. Three separate images are projected simultaneously onto the curved screen, widening the picture into the viewer's peripheral vision.

close-up shot (CU)
A close view of an actor or an object, featuring details isolated from their surroundings. A close-up of an actor typically shows only his head.

compilation film
A film composed largely of **stock footage** or clips from other films.

contextual criticism
A type of criticism that evaluates a film within the context in which it was created and/or screened.

continuity
The appearance of a continuous temporal flow of events in a film. Editing for continuity means to cut smoothly and unobtrusively between shots that condense time.

crane shot
A shot taken from a **studio crane.**

cross-cutting
Editing together shots of two or more actions occurring simultaneously. Also called **intercutting, parallel editing,** or **parallel action.**

cutaway shot
A shot of an image or an action in a film scene that is not part of the main action; sometimes used to cover breaks in a scene's continuity.

cutting
See **editing.**

cutting on action
Editing two shots at a point where a gesture or movement in the first one is not yet completed and a gesture or movement in the second one has already begun.

D

dadaism
An avant-garde movement in the arts during the 1920s that, like **surrealism,** stressed the unconscious and the irrational in human experience, incongruity, spontaneity, and irreverent wit.

deep-focus photography
A cinematographic technique that keeps objects in a shot clearly focused from close-up range to infinity. Also called **pan-focus photography.**

depth of field
The distance in front of the camera lens within which objects appear in sharp focus.

diagonal
A shot where the camera pivots both horizontally and vertically; a combination of **panning** and **tilting.**

dialogue
Lip-synchronous speech between two or more characters in a film, with the speaker usually, but not always, visible. See **monologue.**

direct cinema
See *cinéma vérité.*

dissolve
A transition between two shots during which one shot fades out at the same time that a second shot fades in. Also called **lap dissolve.**

documentary film
A **nonfiction film,** usually photographed on location, using nonactors rather than actors and actual events rather than scripted stories.

Dolby sound
The trade name for a system that reduces the noise level of a tape or optical recording in order to achieve better sound fidelity.

dolly shot
See **traveling shot.**

double exposure
The superimposition of two (or more) images on a single filmstrip. Also called **multiple exposure.**

dubbing
Adding sound to a film after shots have been photographed and edited. Also, inserting dialogue, sometimes foreign, into a film after it has been shot.

Dutch angle
A tilted camera angle that shows images obliquely slanted to the frame's vertical axis. Also called **oblique angle.**

dynamic montage
Editing, often in scenes with much action or movement, intended to evoke strong emotional reactions. See **Russian montage.**

E

editing
The process of connecting one shot to another. Also called **cutting.** See **montage.**

emulsion
The chemical coating on **film stock** that contains light-sensitive particles of metallic silver.

epic
A film genre characterized by sweeping historical themes, heroic action, spectacular settings, period costumes, and a large cast of characters.

establishing shot
A camera shot, usually at long range, that identifies, or establishes, the location of a scene.

ethnographic film
An anthropological film that records, and perhaps comments on, an ethnic group and its culture.

experimental film
See **underground film.**

exposé
An investigative **documentary film** that reveals, often in shocking ways, discreditable information or events.

expressionism
A style of filmmaking that distorts physical reality in some way in order to express strong feelings about it. Typical expressionistic techniques include the use of distorting lenses, extreme camera angles, bizarre lighting and sound effects, and fragmented editing. See **realism.**

extreme close-up (XCU)
A very close view of an actor or an object featuring minute details. An extreme close-up of an actor typically shows only his eyes or part of his face.

extreme long shot (XLS)
A panoramic view of a film scene, photographed from a great distance.

eyeline match
Editing shots that are aligned, or matched, to suggest that two characters in separate shots are looking at each other.

F

fade
An optical effect in which the screen gradually brightens as a shot opens (**fade-in**) or gradually darkens as a shot goes to black or another blank color (**fade-out**). Sound also fades in or out when the sound track gradually changes from silence to sound, or from sound to silence.

fast film
Film stock that is highly sensitive to light, usually with an exposure index of 100 or higher. Also called **fast-speed film.** See **slow film.**

fast motion
Shots photographed slower than the standard speed of 24 frames per second (fps) so that the action on the screen appears faster than normal when projected at standard speed. See **slow motion.**

feature film
A full-length motion picture produced for commercial distribution.

feminist film criticism
Film analysis and criticism from a feminist perspective, concerned primarily with the social and political implications of how women are depicted in films.

femme fatale
In French, literally, "fatal woman." An irresistibly attractive woman in a dramatic story who leads men to destruction.

fiction film
Any film that employs invented plot or characters; also called narrative film.

fill light
Illumination for a camera shot that opposes and softens shadows thrown by the **key light.**

film criticism
The analysis and evaluation of films, often according to specific aesthetic or philosophical theories.

film leader
Film footage with visual calibrations, usually in one-second intervals, used to lead into the film proper.

film loop
Film footage spliced tail to head in order to run continuously. **Looping** is sometimes used when actors dub lip-sync sound to scenes that have already been photographed.

film noir
In French, literally, "black film." A type of film, mainly produced in Hollywood during the 1940s and 1950s, that depicts dark themes, such as crime and corruption in urban settings, in a visual style that features night scenes and **low-key lighting.**

filmography
A bibliographic listing of a film artist's body of work.

film stock
Unexposed motion picture film with variable characteristics, such as **gauge**, color, and light sensitivity.

film treatment
A written description of a film story that may later be developed into a script.

filter
A piece of glass or plastic fitted in front of the lens to control the color or quality of light entering the camera.

final cut
The edited version of a film as it will be printed and released for exhibition. See **rough cut**.

first-person shot
See **point-of-view shot**.

fisheye lens
A wide-angle lens that distorts a film image so that straight lines appear rounded at the edges of the frame.

fiver
See **senior spot**.

flashback
A shot or sequence depicting action that occurred before the film's present time.

flash-forward
A shot or sequence depicting action that will occur after the film's present time or will be seen later in the film.

flash pan
See **swish pan**.

floodlight
A studio lamp that illuminates a relatively wide area by flooding it with light. Also called a **flood**. See **spotlight**.

focal length
The distance from the center of the lens to the point on the film plane where light rays meet in sharp focus. A **wide-angle lens** has a short focal length; a **telephoto lens** has a long focal length.

focus
The sharpness or definition of a film image.

following shot
A shot in which the camera pans or travels to keep a moving figure or object within the frame.

footage
Exposed **film stock**.

foreground music
Music that emanates from a source within the film scene, such as a live orchestra or a radio. Also called **source music**. See **background music**.

formalism
An approach to filmmaking or film criticism that emphasizes form over content. A formalist would argue that the meaning of a film emerges from the way its content is presented.

formula
A familiar plot or pattern of dramatic action that is often repeated or imitated in films—for example, in genres like gangster films or Westerns.

frame
Each individual photograph recorded on motion picture film. The outside edges of a film image on the screen.

frame enlargement
A photograph of one motion picture frame reproduced from actual footage, not to be confused with a still photograph taken during the shooting of a scene.

framing
The visual composition of a shot within the frame.

freeze-frame shot
A shot in which one frame is printed repeatedly in order to look like a still photograph when projected. Also called a **freeze shot**.

full shot
A **long shot** that includes the human body in full within the frame.

G

gauge
The width of **film stock** in millimeters (16mm, 35mm, 70mm).

genre
A type of motion picture. The films within a particular genre employ similar plots, narrative conventions, character types, and formulas—for example, Westerns or science-fiction films.

genre criticism
A type of film criticism that examines genre films to determine how they reflect or comment on social values.

German Expressionism
A film movement in Germany from 1919 through the mid-1920s that used bizarre decor, lighting, and camera techniques to express strong feelings and depict inner experiences.

grain
Minute crystals of light-sensitive silver halide within the **emulsion** on the **film stock**. Graininess is the speckle-like appearance in a film image caused by coarse clumps of individual silver grains.

H

hand-held camera
A camera supported and moved by the camera operator, rather than by a tripod or a mechanical vehicle.

hard lighting
Illumination that creates stark contrast between light and shadow. See **high-contrast lighting**.

high-angle shot (H/A)
A shot in which the camera is tilted down at the subject.

high-contrast lighting
A style of film lighting that creates a stark contrast between bright light and heavy shadow.

high-key lighting
A style of film lighting that creates bright, even illumination and few conspicuous shadows. See **low-key lighting**.

Hollywood montage
See **American montage**.

I

in-camera editing
Editing done within the camera itself by selectively starting and stopping the camera for each shot.

independent film
Any motion picture produced apart from a commercial film studio. Sometimes called **avant-garde film, experimental film,** or **underground film.**

indigenous sound
Sound or music originating from a source apparent within a film scene. See also **foreground music**.

ingenue
A naive girl or young woman in a dramatic story.

insert
A shot of a detail edited into the main action of a scene. Also called an **insert shot**. See also **cutaway**.

intellectual montage
Editing intended to convey an abstract or intellectual concept by juxtaposing concrete images that suggest it.

intercutting
See **cross-cutting**.

interior monologue
See **monologue**.

invisible editing
Editing made unobtrusive by carefully **cutting on action** or **matching action** between shots. Also called **invisible cutting**.

iris
A circular **masking** device around the camera lens that blacks out the edges of the image. Like the iris of the human eye, an iris on the camera may be opened up or shut down during a shot.

irising
To open a camera iris gradually at the beginning of a shot (iris-in) or close it gradually at the end of a shot (iris-out).

Italian Neorealism
See **neorealism**.

J

jump cut
An abrupt transition between shots that disrupts (often deliberately) the continuity of time or space within a scene.

K

key light
The primary source of illumination for a camera shot.

L

lap dissolve
See **dissolve.**

leader
See **film leader.**

lens
A ground or molded piece of transparent glass or plastic through which light rays are focused to create a photographic image on film. See **normal lens, telephoto lens, wide-angle lens, zoom lens.**

lens aperture
See **aperture.**

lighting cameraman
See **cinematographer.**

limbo lighting
A style of film lighting that eliminates background light and isolates the subject against a completely dark (or neutral) field.

lip sync
Dialogue or narration that is precisely synchronized with the lip movements of a character or narrator on the screen. See **synchronization.**

live action
Film action with living people and real things, rather than action created by **animation.**

location shooting
Filming in an actual setting, either outdoors or indoors, rather than in a motion picture studio.

long shot (LS)
A shot that shows a fairly broad view of a subject within its setting. A long shot of an actor typically includes his entire body and much of his surroundings.

long take
A take, or shot, of lengthy duration.

looping
See **film loop.**

low-angle shot (L/A)
A shot in which the camera is tilted up at the subject.

low-key lighting
A style of film lighting that produces less illumination than high-key lighting, and

therefore a darker atmosphere and tone. See **high-key lighting.**

M

magnetic sound track
A sound track that is recorded on an iron oxide stripe at the edge of the film opposite the sprocket holes.

mask
To block out part of a film image, usually at the edges of the frame, thus altering the size or shape of the frame projected on the screen.

master shot
A single shot, usually a **long shot** or a **full shot,** which provides an overview of the action in an entire scene.

matching action
Cutting together different shots of an action on a common gesture or movement in order to make the action appear continuous on the screen. Also called a **matched cut.** See **invisible editing.**

matte shot
A type of **process shot** in which part of a scene is masked so that other action or background/foreground images, photographed separately, can be added later with an **optical printer.** See **traveling matte.**

medium shot (MS)
A relatively close shot that shows part of a person or object in some detail. A medium shot of an actor typically shows his body from the knees or waist up.

melodrama
A play or film based on a romantic plot and developed sensationally, with little regard for convincing motivation and with strong appeal to the emotions of the audience.

metaphor
An implied comparison between two objects or images, usually achieved in films by **montage.**

method acting
A naturalistic style of acting taught by the Russian actor-director Konstantin Stanislavsky, in which the actor identifies closely with the character to be portrayed. Also called the **Stanislavsky Method.**

Mickey Mousing
Creating music that mimics or reproduces a film's visual action, as in many Walt Disney cartoons. Also called **Mickey Mousing the music.**

mise en scéne
In French, literally, "placing in scene." A theatrical term, carried over to cinema, which refers to the arrangement of everything physical in a camera shot, including scenery, props, and actors.

mix
To combine sound from two or more sources onto a single sound track. Also called **sound mix.**

monologue
A character speaking alone on screen or, without appearing to speak, articulating his or her thoughts in **voice-over** as an **interior monologue.**

montage
To assemble film images by editing shots together, often rapidly, to condense passing time or events. In Europe, montage means **editing.** See also **American montage, Russian montage, dynamic montage, narrative montage.**

motif
A recurring subject, theme, or image in a film.

Moviola
Trade name of an American film editing machine. With lowercase "m" (**moviola**), a generic term for a film editing machine.

multiple exposure
See **double exposure.**

multiple-image shot
A shot that includes two or more separately photographed images within the frame.

multiscreen projection
Projecting motion picture images simultaneously on more than one screen.

musical
A film genre that incorporates song and dance routines into the film story.

N

narration
Information or commentary spoken directly to the audience rather than indirectly through dialogue. Narration is often delivered by an anonymous off-screen voice. See **voice-over.**

narrative montage
Editing that constructs a story with film images by arranging shots in carefully sequenced order. See **montage.**

naturalism
A style of filmmaking that is starkly realistic and avoids any semblance of artifice.

negative image
A photographic image in which dark and light tones are reversed on the screen, with dark areas appearing light and light areas appearing dark.

neorealism
A film movement in Italy after World War II characterized by starkly realistic, humanistic stories and documentary-like camera style. Neorealistic films were generally shot on location, using available lighting and nonprofessional actors.

newsreel
A short film that presents a compilation of timely news stories.

nonfiction film
Any film that does not employ invented plot or characters. See **documentary.**

nonsynchronous sound
Sound whose source is not apparent in a film scene or sound that is detached from its source in the scene; commonly called **off-screen sound.** See **synchronous sound.**

normal lens
A camera lens that shows a subject without significantly exaggerating or reducing the **depth of field** in a shot. For 35mm films, a normal lens is 35–50mm long.

O

oblique angle
See **Dutch angle.**

off-screen sound
See **nonsynchronous sound.**

off-screen space
Space beyond the camera's field of vision that the audience is aware of nevertheless.

on location
See **location shooting**.

optical printer
Elaborate film laboratory equipment, consisting of a projector and a camera, which can reduce or enlarge film images and create special effects, such as fades, dissolves, and superimposition, in a printed film.

optical sound track
A sound track consisting of photographed sound modulations at the edge of the film opposite the sprocket holes.

out-take
Any footage deleted from a film during editing; more specifically, a shot or scene that is removed from a film before the **final cut.**

overcrank
To run film stock through the camera faster than the standard speed of 24 frames per second (fps), producing **slow motion** on the screen when the film is projected at standard speed. See **undercrank.**

overhead shot
A camera shot from directly above the action. See **bird's-eye view.**

overlapping editing
Cutting that repeats part or all of an action.

P

pan
Short for "panorama." A shot in which the camera pivots horizontally, turning from left to right or from right to left.

parallel editing, parallel action
See **cross-cutting.**

pixilation
A type of film animation in which real objects or people are photographed frame-by-frame in order to make them appear to move abruptly or magically when the film is projected. See also **stop-motion photography** and **trick shot.**

point-of-view shot (POV)
A shot taken from the vantage point of a character in a film. May also be abbreviated as **p.o.v. shot.** Also called a **first-person shot** or **subjective camera.**

postsynchronized sound
Sound added to images after they have been photographed and assembled; commonly called **dubbing.**

process shot
A shot in which live foreground action is photographed against a background image projected on a translucent screen.

property
Any movable item used on a theater or film set. Usually called a **prop.**

puppet film
An animated film in which inanimate objects or figures are manipulated and photographed frame-by-frame in order to make them appear to move when the film is projected.

pure film
A type of **experimental film** that explores the purely visual possibilities of cinema rather than the narrative possibilities. Also called **pure cinema.**

R

rack focus
To change the focus of the lens during a shot in order to call attention to specific images. Also called **selective focus** or **shift focus.**

reaction shot
A shot that shows a character's reaction to what has occurred in the previous shot.

realism
A style of filmmaking that endeavors to depict physical reality much as it appears in the everyday world. Typical realistic techniques include the prominent use of long shots, eye-level camera angles, lengthy takes, naturalistic lighting and sound effects, and unobtrusive editing. See **expressionism.**

Rembrandt lighting
See **back lighting.**

reverse angle (R/A)
A shot where the camera is placed opposite its position in the previous shot, reversing its view of the scene.

reverse motion
Action that moves backward on the screen, achieved by reversing film footage during editing or by reverse printing in an **optical printer**. Also called **reverse action**.

rough cut
An early version of a film in which shots and sequences are roughly assembled but not yet finely edited together for the **final cut**.

running time
The duration of a finished film, including the credits.

Russian montage
A style of editing, typical of that used by prominent Soviet filmmakers in the 1920s, which employs dynamic cutting techniques to evoke strong emotional, and even physical, reactions to film images.

S

scene
A unit of film composed of one shot or several interrelated shots unified by a single location, incident, or set of characters.

science-fiction film
A film genre characterized by plot and action involving scientific fantasy. Also called **sci-fi film**.

screenplay
See **script**.

screwball comedy
A type of Hollywood comic film characterized by zany characters, incongruous situations, and fast-breaking events.

scrim
A translucent sheet of material used to soften or diffuse light on a shooting set.

script
A set of written specifications for a motion picture production, usually delineating the film's settings, action, dialogue, camera coverage, lighting and sound effects, and music. Also called a **screenplay**.

selective focus
See **rack focus**.

selective sound
A sound track that selectively includes or deletes sounds.

semiology
A theory of film criticism that views cinema as a language, or linguistic system, that conveys meaning via signs or symbolic codes. Also called **semiotics**.

senior spot
A **spotlight** with 5,000 watts of illuminating power; also called a **fiver**.

sequence
A unit of film composed of interrelated shots or scenes, usually leading up to a dramatic climax.

setting
A location for a film or a film scene.

setup
The positioning of the camera and lights for a specific shot.

shift focus
See **rack focus**.

shock cut
A jarring transition between two actions occurring at different times or places. Also called a **smash cut**.

shooting ratio
The amount of film footage shot compared to the length of the film's **final cut**.

shooting script
The script that the director and the actors follow during filming.

short lens
See **wide-angle lens**.

shot
A single, continuous run of the camera. The images recorded on a strip of exposed film from the time the camera starts until the time it stops.

shot-by-shot analysis
Close and thorough study of the separate shots that make up a scene, sequence, or entire film. Also called **shot analysis**.

shutter
The mechanical device on a motion picture camera that shields the film from light at the **aperture** during filming.

sight gag
A visual joke; a piece of nonverbal comic business in a film.

single-frame cinematography
Shooting film one frame at a time to speed up normal motion, make lifeless objects appear to move, or do **time-lapse photography**. Also called **single framing**.

slapstick comedy
Broad comedy characterized by violent physical action.

slow film
Film stock that is relatively insensitive to light and produces finer-grained images than **fast film**. Also called **slow-speed film**.

slow motion
Shots photographed faster than the standard speed of 24 frames per second (fps), so that the action on the screen appears slower than normal when projected at standard speed. See **fast motion**.

smash cut
See **shock cut**.

soft focus
Blurring the sharpness of a film image with a special lens or with a gauze over the lens in order to diffuse or soften hard edges; used especially for close-ups to make the human face look more sensual or glamorous.

sound bridge
Sound continuing across two shots that depict action in different times or places, thus providing an aural transition between the two scenes.

sound effect
Any sound in a film other than dialogue, narration, or music.

sound track
The optical or magnetic strip at the edge of the film that carries the sound; the audio component of a motion picture.

source music
See **foreground music**.

special effects (FX)
Shots that are unobtainable by straightforward motion picture filming techniques and therefore require special models, matting, multiple exposure, or the like. The term also applies to most pyrotechnic and ballistic effects in a film.

splice
To join two pieces of film.

split-screen shot
Division of the film frame into two or more areas for photographing images separately, done either by masking the camera lens or in the laboratory with an **optical printer**. Also called a **split-screen image**.

spotlight
A studio lamp that illuminates a relatively small, specific area. Also called a **spot**. See **floodlight**.

Stanislavsky Method
See **method acting**.

star system
A system developed in the early days of Hollywood to market movies based on the appeal of popular actors and actresses (movie stars) who were under contract with commercial motion picture studios to play leading roles in their productions.

stereophonic sound
Sound recorded on separate tracks with two or more microphones and played back on two or more loudspeakers to reproduce and separate sounds more realistically.

stereotype
A character in literature or film who is an oversimplified, standardized representation of a group of diverse individuals, such as a race or an ethnic group.

still
A photograph taken of a film scene, often for promotional purposes; not to be confused with a **frame enlargement** reproduced from actual film footage.

stock footage
Motion picture footage from previously existing films, which is filed in film libraries or archives and may be incorporated into a new film, usually for scenic background or for stock situations and settings, such as war scenes or foreign locations. Also called **archive footage**. See **compilation film**.

stop-motion photography
Filming real objects or live action by starting and stopping the camera, rather than by running the camera continuously, in order to create **pixilation**, **trick-film** effects, or **time-lapse photography**. Also called **stop-action photography**.

storyboard
A pictorial outline of a film scene or sequence using drawings or photographs to illustrate how each shot should look on the screen.

straight cut
Two shots edited together without optical effects.

structuralism
A theoretical approach to filmmaking and film criticism that focuses on how visual codes or signs are structured to convey meaning in a film, a **genre**, or the works of a particular filmmaker. See **semiology**.

studio crane
A large mechanical arm that can move the camera and its operator smoothly and noiselessly in any direction. See **crane shot**.

subjective camera
See **point-of-view shot**.

subtext
Implicit meaning that lies beneath the language of the text in a play or film.

subtitle
A written caption superimposed over the action in a film, usually at the bottom of the frame, to identify a scene or to translate dialogue from a foreign language.

superimposition
An optical technique that allows two or more images to appear in the frame, one over another; produced by **double exposure** or by multiple printings in an **optical printer**.

surrealism
An avant-garde movement in the arts during the 1920s that endeavored to recreate unconscious experience with shocking, dreamlike images. Surrealistic films rejected traditional notions of causality and emphasized incongruous, irrational action instead.

swish pan
Panning the camera so rapidly across a scene that the image blurs on the screen. Also called **flash pan, whip pan,** or **zip pan**.

symbol
An object or image in a dramatic story that has significance beyond its literal meaning.

synchronization
A precise match between film image and sound. Also called **sync**.

synchronous sound
Sound that matches the action in a film scene and whose source is apparent in the scene. See **nonsynchronous sound**.

synecdoche
A type of **metaphor** that employs a part to represent the whole, or the whole to represent a part. In a film, for example, a shot of boots may represent a soldier; a shot of city hall may imply the mayor.

T

take
The shot resulting from one continuous run of the camera. A filmmaker generally films several takes of the same scene and then selects the best one.

telephoto lens
A camera lens of long **focal length** that, like a telescope, magnifies the size of distant objects. For 35mm films a telephoto lens is 75mm or longer. Also called a **long lens**.

three-shot
A medium **shot** featuring three actors.

360-degree pan
A panning shot that turns around a complete circle.

tilt
A shot in which the camera pivots vertically, turning from top to bottom or from bottom to top.

time-lapse photography
A type of cinematography in which the camera intermittently photographs the same object or scene over an extended time period in order to speed up on the screen a lengthy process or action, such as the growth of a flower from a seed. Also called **time-lapse cinematography**.

tracking shot
See **traveling shot**.

trance film
A type of expressionistic film in which a character, frequently the filmmaker, experiences a personal revelation by playing out a psychological drama in dreamlike surroundings.

traveling matte
A process for combining separately photographed images in a single shot using an **optical printer**. See **matte shot.**

traveling shot
A shot in which the camera, mounted on a vehicle, moves while filming. Traveling shots are sometimes identified more specifically according to the kind of vehicle used to move the camera (a **dolly shot** or a **trucking shot,** for example). When tracks are laid down for the camera to roll on, the shot is usually called a **tracking shot.**

treatment
See **film treatment.**

trick film, trick shot
A film or a shot created by special camera or optical techniques, such as **stop-motion photography** or **double exposure.** See also **pixilation.**

trucking shot
See **traveling shot.**

two-shot
A **medium shot** featuring two actors.

typecasting
Selecting an actor or actress for a film role because of his or her physical type, manner, or personality, or according to a public image created by previous roles he or she has performed.

U

undercrank
To run film stock through the camera slower than the standard speed of 24 frames per second (fps), producing **fast motion** on the screen when the film is projected at standard speed. See **overcrank.**

underground film
An **independent film** that emphasizes the filmmaker's self-expression rather than commercial success. Underground films frequently challenge or experiment with traditional cinematic form and technique, hence they are also called **avant-garde films** or **experimental films.**

V

voice-over narration
An off-screen narrator's voice accompanying images on the screen. Also called **voice-over,** for any off-screen voice.

W

whip pan
See **swish pan.**

wide-angle lens
A lens of short **focal length** that enables the camera to photograph a wider area than a normal lens. For 35mm films a wide-angle lens is 30mm or shorter. Also called a **short lens.**

wipe
An optical effect in which one image replaces another by pushing, or wiping, it off the screen.

work print
A duplicate of film footage, used during the editing process in order to preserve the original intact until the **final cut.**

Z

zip pan
See **swish pan.**

zoom lens
A camera lens of variable **focal length** that allows the camera to photograph from wide-angle to telephoto range in the same shot.

zoom shot
A shot with a **zoom lens,** which can make a film image appear to move closer (to **zoom in**) or farther away (to **zoom out**) by varying the **focal length** of the lens.

Credits

Illustrations

Line art on the following pages generated by Precision Graphics: 31, 32, 33, 35, 36, 37, 54, 55, 56, 57, 58, 95, 100, 108, 109, 110, 111, 136, 366, 367.

Quoted Material

Chapter 1

Page 20: (Source) Mankiewicz, Herman J., and Orson Welles. *CITIZEN KANE: The Shooting Script*. In *The Citizen Kane Book*. Boston: Little, Brown and Company, 1971 (95, 97).

Chapter 4

Pages 108-10: (Source) Eisenstein, Sergei. POTEMKIN. Translated by Gillon R. Aitken. New York: Simon and Schuster, 1968 (14).

Page 112: Reprinted from A HISTORY OF NARRATIVE FILM by David A. Cook, by permission of W.W. Norton & Company, Inc. Copyright © 1981 by W.W. Norton & Company, Inc. (168).

Chapter 5

Page 120: Reprinted from A HISTORY OF NARRATIVE FILM by David A. Cook, by permission of W.W. Norton & Company, Inc. Copyright © 1981 by W.W. Norton & Company, Inc. (240).

Page 126: From Kerr, Walter. "In Praise of Silence in Films." *The New York Times Magazine*. 30 September 1984:42-44. Copyright © 1984 by The New York Times Company. Reprinted by permission.

Page 129: (Source) RKO Cutting Continuity of the Orson Welles Production of CITIZEN KANE. In *The Citizen Kane Book*. Boston: Little, Brown, 1971 (351-52).

Chapter 6

Page 159: Reprinted from A HISTORY OF NARRATIVE FILM by David A. Cook, by permission of W.W. Norton & Company, Inc. Copyright © 1981 by W.W. Norton & Company, Inc. (124).

Page 165: (Source) Bergman, Ingmar. WILD STRAWBERRIES. Translated by Lars Malmström and David Kushner. New York: Simon & Schuster, 1960 (38-39).

Chapter 7

Pages 190-91: From Engelhardt, Tom. "Racism in the Media." *Bulletin of Concerned Asian Scholars*. 3(Winter-Spring 1971). Reprinted as a pamphlet by New England Free Press (2, 3, 7). Used by permission.

Chapter 10

Pages 270-73: From Huff, Theodore. Quoted in A HISTORY OF NARRATIVE FILM by David A. Cook. Reprinted by permission of Department of Film, Museum of Modern Art (84-86).

Page 286: (Source) RKO Cutting Continuity of the Orson Welles production of CITIZEN KANE. In *The Citizen Kane Book*. Boston: Little, Brown, 1971 (394-95).

Page 286: Reprinted from A HISTORY OF NARRATIVE FILM by David A. Cook, by permission of W.W. Norton & Company, Inc. Copyright © 1981 by W.W. Norton & Company, Inc. (366).

Page 292: Reprinted from A HISTORY OF NARRATIVE FILM by David A. Cook, by permission of W.W. Norton & Company, Inc. Copyright © 1981 by W.W. Norton & Company, Inc. (393).

Chapter 11

Pages 298-99: Reprinted from A HISTORY OF NARRATIVE FILM by David A. Cook, by permission of W.W. Norton & Company, Inc. Copyright © 1981 by W.W. Norton & Company, Inc. (115, 116).

Chapter 14

Page 363: Reprinted by permission from Hough, Richard A. *The Potemkin Mutiny.* Englewood Cliffs, N.J.: Prentice-Hall, 1960 (78-79).

Page 366: Reprinted from A HISTORY OF NARRATIVE FILM by David A. Cook, by permission of W.W. Norton & Company, Inc. Copyright © 1981 by W.W. Norton & Company, Inc. (175).

Appendix

Pages 395-97: Reprinted by permission from "DAY FOR NIGHT: A Film Artist's Valentine," by Cindy Tierney.

Pages 401-3: Reprinted by permission from "Cinematic Techniques in CITIZEN KANE," by Thomas McGreevy.

Pages 407-9: Reprinted by permission from "That Sells Folks! Animation in Television Advertising," by Donna M. Weaver.

Photos

Part Openers

1: © 1946 Janus Films. Courtesy of The Museum of Modern Art/Film Stills Archive; 2: © 1982, Columbia Pictures Industries, Inc. All Rights Reserved. Courtesy of the Museum of Modern Art/Film Stills Archive; 3: © 1988 Touchstone Pictures and Amblin Entertainment. Courtesy of The Museum of Modern Art/Film Stills Archive; 4: The Museum of Modern Art/Film Stills Archive.

Chapter 1

Opener: © 1961 Janus Films. Courtesy of The Museum of Modern Art/ Film Stills Archive; 1.1a: © 1969 United Artists. Courtesy of The Museum of Modern Art/Film Stills Archive; 1.1b: © 1971 Columbia Pictures Industries, Inc. All Rights Reserved. Courtesy of The Museum of Modern Art/Film Stills Archive; 1.2: © 1964 Pathe Contemporary Films. Courtesy of The Museum of Modern Art/ Film Stills Archive; 1.3: © 1977 20th Century Fox Film Corporation. Courtesy of The Museum of Modern Art//Film Stills Archive; 1.4a,b: © 1938 Janus Films. Courtesy of The Museum of Modern Art/ Film Stills Archive; 1.5a-l: © 1941 RKO Radio Pictures Corp. Courtesy of National Film Archive/Film Stills Library; 1.6a-d: © 1970 Cinema Center Films. Courtesy of The Museum of Modern Art/Film Stills Archive; 1.7: © 1925 Janus Films. Courtesy of The Museum of Modern Art Film Stills Archive; 1.8: © 1941 RKO Radio Pictures Corp. Courtesy of The Museum of Modern Art/Film Stills Archive; 1.9a-d: Courtesy of Kratký Film, Prague, Czechoslovakia; 1.10: © 1948 Janus Films. Courtesy of The Museum of Modern Art Film Stills Archive.

Chapter 2

Opener: © 1951 United Artists Corp. Courtesy of The Museum of Modern Art/Film Stills Archive; 2.1, 2.2, 2.3: © 1952, United Artists Corporation. Courtesy of The Museum of Modern Art Film Stills Archive; 2.4: © 1941 RKO Radio Pictures Corp. Courtesy of The Museum of Modern Art/Film Stills Archive; 2.5: Courtesy of Professor Stewart McDugall, University of Michigan; 2.6: © 1973 by D.L.N. Ventures Partnership.

Chapter 3

Opener: © Warner Brothers, Inc. All Rights Reserved. Courtesy of The Museum of Modern Art/Film Stills Archive; 3.1-3.9: Anthony Giampaolo; 3.10: © 1962 Janus Films. Courtesy of National Film Archive/ Stills Library; 3.11: © 1982 Metro-Goldwyn-Mayer Film Co. and SLM Entertainment, Ltd. Courtesy of The Museum of Modern Art/Film Stills Archive; 3.12: A Janus Repertory Presentation. Courtesy of The Museum of Modern Art/Film Stills Archive; 3.13: © 1956 Janus Films. Courtesy of The Museum of Modern Art Film Stills Archive; 3.14, 3.15: © 1947 Universal Pictures. Courtesy of The Museum of Modern Art/Film Stills Library; 3.16: © 1941 Radio Pictures Corp. Courtesy of National Film Archive/Stills Library; 3.17: ABC Pictures Corp. Courtesy of The Museum of Modern Art/ Film Stills Archive; 3.18: © 1933 by Paramount Pictures, Inc. Courtesy of The Museum of Modern Art/Film Stills Archive.

Chapter 4

Opener: © by Lucas Film Ltd. All Rights Reserved. Courtesy of The Museum of Modern Art/Film Stills Archive; p. 86, 87, 88: Trademark and © Lucas Film Ltd. (LFL) 1981. All Rights Reserved. Courtesy of Lucas Film Ltd.; 4.3: © 1973 Paramount Pictures. Courtesy of National Film Archive/Film Library.; 4.4: © 1927 Janus Films. Courtesy of The Museum of Modern Art/Film Stills Archive.

Chapter 5

Opener: © 1984 The Saul Zaentz Company. All Rights Reserved. Courtesy of The Museum of Modern Art/Film Stills Archive; 5.1: "Audio-Visual Correspondence (A Sequence from *Alexander Nevsky*)" from *The Film Sense* by Sergei Eisenstein, translated and edited by Jay Leyda, copyright 1947 by Harcourt Brace Jovanovich, Inc. and renewed 1975 by Jay Leyda, reprinted by permission of the publisher; 5.2: © Walt Disney Productions. Courtesy of The Museum of Modern Art/Film Stills Archive; 5.3: © 1941 RKO Radio Pictures Corp. Courtesy of National Film Archive/Film Stills Archive; 5.4: © 1952 United Artists Corporation. Courtesy of Professor Stewart McDugall, University of Michigan; 5.5a,b: © 1941 RKO Radio Pictures Corp. Courtesy of National Film Archive/Stills Library; 5.7: © 1974 by Long Road Productions. Courtesy of The Museum of Modern Art/Film Stills Archive.

Chapter 6

Opener: © 1957 Toho Films. Courtesy of The Museum of Modern Art/ Film Stills Archive; 6.1a,b: © 1928, courtesy of The Museum of Modern Art/Film Stills Archive; 6.2a,b: © 1925 Janus Films. Courtesy of The Museum of Modern Art/Film Stills Archive; 6.3: © 1965 Columbia Pictures. Courtesy of The Museum of Modern Art/Film Stills Archive; 6.4: © 1941 RKO Radio Pictures Corp. Courtesy of National Archive/Stills Library; 6.5a,b: © 1957 Janus Films. Courtesy of The Museum of Modern Art/Film Stills Archive; 6.6: © 1957 Janus Films. Courtesy of The Museum of Modern Art/Film Stills Archive.

Chapter 7

Opener: © 1977, 20th Century-Fox Film Corp. All Rights Reserved. Courtesy of The Museum of Modern Art/Film Stills Archive; 7.1: © 1953 by Paramount Pictures Corp. Courtesy of The Museum of Modern Art/Film Stills Archive; 7.2: © 1982 by Warner Bros. Inc. Courtesy of The Museum of Modern Art/ Film Stills Archive; 7.3: © 1985 Tri-Star Pictures. Courtesy of The Museum of Modern Art/Film Stills Archive; 7.4: © 1986 20th Century-Fox Film Corp. Courtesy of The Museum of Modern Art/Film Stills Archive; 7.5: © 1977 20th Century-Fox Film Corp. Courtesy of The Museum of Modern Art/Film Stills Archive; 7.6a: © 1971 Warner Bros./ Pictures Distributing Corp. Courtesy of The Museum of Modern Art/Film Stills Archive; 7.6b: © 1987 Scotti Bros. Courtesy of The Museum of Modern Art/Film Stills Archive.

Chapter 8

Opener: © 1985 Universal City Studios, Inc. All Rights Reserved. Courtesy of The Museum of Modern Art/Film Stills Archive; 8.1a,b: © 1971 Columbia Pictures Industries, Inc. Courtesy of The Museum of Modern Art/ Film Stills Archive.; 8.2, 8.3: © 1987 by Paramount Pictures Corp. Courtesy of The Museum of Modern Art/Film Stills Archive, Photo by Andy Schwartz; 8.4a: National Screen Service Corp. Courtesy of The Museum of Modern Art/Film Stills Archive; 8.4b: © 1949 Warner Bros. Courtesy of The Museum of Modern Art/Film Stills Archive; 8.5: © 1975 Fantasy Films and United Artists Corp. Courtesy of The Museum of Modern Art/Film Stills Archive; 8.6a: © 1940 20th Century-Fox. Courtesy of The Museum of Modern Art/Film Stills Archive; 8.6b: © 1986 Warner Bros. Inc. Courtesy of The Museum of Modern Art/Film Stills Archive; 8.7: © Columbia Pictures Industries, Inc. Courtesy of The Museum of Modern Art/Film Stills Archive; 8.8a,b: © 1987 20th Century-Fox Film Corp. Courtesy of The Museum of Modern Art/Film Stills Archive, Photo by Andy Schwartz.

Chapter 9

Opener: © 1963, Embassy Pictures Corp. Courtesy of The Museum of Modern Art/Film Stills Archive; 9.1a,b: © 1895 Courtesy of The Museum of Modern Art/Film Archive; 9.2: © 1895 Courtesy of The Museum of Modern Art/Film Stills Archive; 9.3, 9.4, 9.5: © 1902 Courtesy of The Museum of Modern Art/Film Stills Archive; 9.6, 9.7a: © 1927 Janus Films. Courtesy of The Museum of Modern Art/Film Stills Archive; 9.7b: © 1970 by Warner Bros., Inc. Courtesy of The Museum of Modern Art/Film Stills Archive; 9.8a: © 1927 Janus Films. Courtesy of The Museum of Modern Art/Film Stills Archive; 9.8b, 9.9: © 1970 by Warner Bros., Inc. Courtesy of The Museum of Modern Art/Film Stills Archive; 9.10: © 1927 Janus Films. Courtesy of The Museum of Modern Art/Film Stills Archive.

Chapter 10

Opener: © 1948 Janus Films. Courtesy of The Museum of Modern Art/Film Stills Archive; 10.1: © 1915 Courtesy of The Museum of Modern Art/Film Stills Archive; 10.2a,b: © 1915 Courtesy of The Museum of Modern Art/Film Stills Archive; 10.3-10.6: © 1925 Metro Goldwyn Mayer/United Artists. Courtesy of The Museum of Modern Art/Film Stills Archive; 10.7, 10.8, 10.9: © 1941 RKO Radio Pictures Corp. Courtesy of The National Film Archives/Stills Library; 10.10, 10.11: © Janus Films. Courtesy of The Museum of Modern Art/Film Stills Archive.

Chapter 11

Opener: The Museum of Modern Art/Film Stills Archive; 11.1a,b: © 1920 Janus Films. Courtesy of The Museum of Modern Art/Film Stills Archive; 11.2a-f: © 1979 20th Century-Fox Film Corp. Courtesy of The Museum of Modern Art/Film Stills Archive; 11.3a,b,c: © 1943 Courtesy of the Museum of Modern Art/Film Stills Archive; 11.3d: © 1943 The Museum of Modern Art. Courtesy of Anthology Film Archive; 11.3e,f,g: Anthology Film Archive; 11.4 all: © 1963, Embassy Pictures Corp. Courtesy of The Museum of Modern Art/Film Stills Archive.

Chapter 12

Opener: © 1987 20th Century-Fox Film Corp. All Rights Reserved. Courtesy of The Museum of Modern Art/Film Stills Archive; 12.1: © 1960 Time-Life Films Inc. Courtesy of Anthology Film Archive; 12.2,12.3: © Warner Bros. Inc. Courtesy of the Museum of Modern Art/Film Stills Archive; 12.4a,b: © 1969 Paramount Pictures. Courtesy of The Museum of Modern Art/Film Stills Archive.

Chapter 13

Opener: © 1986 by Paramount Pictures Corp. All Rights Reserved. Courtesy of The Museum of Modern Art/Film Stills Archive; 13.1: © 1936 The Museum of Modern Art/Film Stills Archive; 13.2: © 1984 Warner Bros., Inc. Courtesy of The Museum of Modern Art/Film Stills Archive; 13.3 all: © 1929 The Museum of Modern Art/Film Stills Archive; 13.4a,b: Michael Snow; 13.5a,b: © by Warner Bros., Inc. 1973. Courtesy of The Museum of Modern Art/Film Stills Archive.

Chapter 14

Opener: © 1943 The Museum of Modern Art/Film Stills Archive; 14.3, pp. 371-77: Courtesy of The Museum of Modern Art/Film Stills Archive; 14.4a,b: © 1943 The Museum of Modern Art/Film Stills Archive.

Index